INSPIRING THIRST

Inspiring Thirst

Vintage Selections from the
✦ KERMIT LYNCH ✦
Wine Brochure

Photographs by Gail Skoff

TEN SPEED PRESS
Berkeley | Toronto

Ten Speed Press
Box 7123
Berkeley, California 94707
www.tenspeed.com

Distributed in Australia by Simon and Schuster Australia,
in Canada by Ten Speed Press Canada, in New Zealand by
Southern Publishers Group, in South Africa by Real Books, and in
the United Kingdom and Europe by Airlift Book Company.

The author and publisher wish to thank Wendell Berry for granting
permission to reprint "Confessions of a Water Drinker" (page 284);
Paul Bertolli for permission to reprint his recipes in "Paul Bertolli and the
Loire" (page 256); Jim Harrison for permission to reprint "Father-in-Law"
(page 271), "Reflexions" (page 344), "Wine Notes" (page 358), "My
Problems with White Wine" (page 365), and "Adventures on the Wine Route"
(page 382); Richard N. Olney Trust for permission to reprint "Domaine
Tempier" (page 118); André Ostertag for permission to reprint "The Words
and Wines of André Ostertag" (page 278); and Lulu Peyraud for
permission to reprint "Remembering Richard Olney" (page 351).

LIBRARY OF CONGRESS CATALOGING-IN-PUBLICATION DATA
Lynch, Kermit.
Inspiring thirst : vintage selections from the Kermit Lynch wine brochure /
by Kermit Lynch ; photographs by Gail Skoff.
p. cm.
Includes index.
ISBN 1-58008-636-5
1. Wine and wine making. I. Title.
TP548.L96 2004
641.2'2—dc22   2004018910

Printed in Canada
First printing 2004

1 2 3 4 5 6 7 8 9 10—08 07 06 05 04

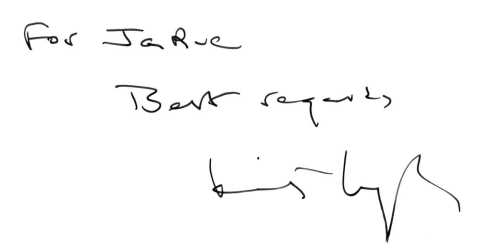

Dec. 2004

For JaRue

Best regards

I owe wine something for opening so many doors,

not only to underground cellars and grand châteaux,

but also to long-term relationships with

clients, staff, and winemakers.

WINE, LONG MAY IT SURVIVE.

CONTENTS

INSPIRING THIRST

BUSINESS HOURS
Wednesday–Saturday 1 to 6:30 P.M.

Yes, I opened a wine shop very much as a hobby,
as one sees by the original 1972 opening business hours.

INTRODUCTION

Before opening a wine shop in 1972, I was yet another starving rock 'n' roll musician, one who could barely afford to buy his own harmonica. The competition was pretty stiff back then, you know, people like Bob Dylan and Mick Jagger . . . Plus, I had a couple of handicaps: I couldn't remember the words to my own songs, and cocaine gave me nosebleeds. Still, I think to myself, if I'd had musicians like Keith Richards and Charlie Watts backing me up, I mighta been a contender.

Oh well, at least my sensitive nose came in handy later on.

Starving may be an exaggeration, because when my stomach growled too loudly to be ignored I would head for my little workroom and stitch together a purse made from Oriental rug scraps. The purses were easy to sell, but I hated the sewing and glue sniffing required to craft them. The business was called *The Berkeley Bag*, and in 1971 someone offered me money for it. How unforeseen. I took the money and ran . . . or flew, to Europe. Four months' worth.

In those days wine was my beverage at table, mostly from jugs, CK Barbarone, for example, whatever that was, although I did join a wine-tasting group. Then, when I returned from Europe, I decided to find a part-time job selling wine, trying to turn my hobby into some income.

At the time, Berkeley had four liquor stores with great wine selections. True, most of what they sold was from Bordeaux, along with a smattering from Burgundy, but you could find the great châteaux, including old vintages. In 1972, however, the wine trade fell into a terrible recession, so people weren't buying and stores were firing instead of hiring. No one would have me. Against all advice I borrowed $5000 from my girlfriend, Joan Connolly, and opened my own shop, all 800 square feet of it. By the time I had paid first and last month's rent, painted the walls, and done all the other little things you have to do, I had enough money left to stock my shop with 32 cases of wine for sale. I meant to form a new rock 'n' roll band, so my business hours were limited.

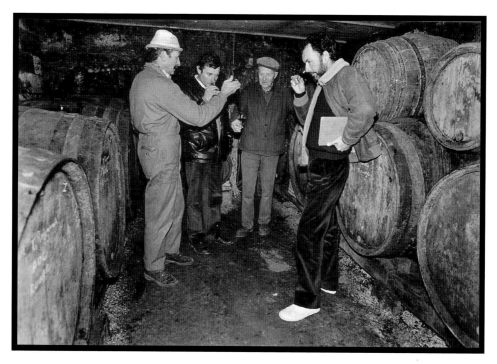

Raymond Trollat, Gérard Chave, Ernest Trollat, and Kermit "White Shoes" Lynch

I wish I could say that my business succeeded because of my foresight, but no, it just seemed to take off and drag me along with it. In fact, the wine recession may have allowed me to survive, even though I had no funds or collateral. Things were so moribund, importers and wholesalers were eager to advance me inventory. "Pay me when you sell it," I heard more than once. Before long the serious dumping of stocks began, and because all the other retailers were over-inventoried, I, with my empty store, was able to take advantage of the distressed pricing. Low prices on great wines began to attract customers to my hole-in-the-wall shop.

One day I received a telephone book–sized price list from Frank Schoon-maker Selections with huge price reductions. A Mazis-Chambertin, for example, might have ordinarily retailed at $40 or $50 per bottle. Buying it from Schoonmaker, I could retail it at $8.95. Most of the inventory was still in their growers' cellars in Europe. There weren't even bottles available to sample, and because I had promised my customers (in an opening "Statement of Principles") to offer only wines that I had tasted, I took several trips to Germany, France, and Italy to select from Schoonmaker's offerings. I traveled with their man, Karl Petrowsky, and learned so much about the wine world, especially in Germany, where Karl was received like nobility.

One afternoon at four o'clock, after tasting all day, we arrived at the famous Schwarzhofberger estate and were received by Egon Müller. We tasted and spit out endless cuvées of his new 1975s, then we moved into his ancient, dark, wood-paneled study where old bottles began to appear as quickly as the wine in them disappeared. There were three of us, no spittoon, and by the time Karl and I left at midnight, there were eight empty bottles on the table. One was the only Trockenbeerenauslese the estate had ever produced, which Müller had had to vinify in a crock in front of his fireplace in order to keep the fermentation going. Our final treat dated from the first decade of the 20th century, a 1906, maybe.

In all that time, however, we were never fed, from four to midnight, and as I walked carefully down the steps in the bright moonlight, I could hear Müller's rare Rieslings sloshing around in my otherwise empty belly. I suppose we could call such marathon events Basic Training for a future wine professional? I had my share.

From those early days, I also recall receiving in Berkeley three cases of assorted samples from a Southern California importer. Any and all were available to me at $12 per case. I looked through the junk until I pulled out a bottle of 1970 Château Grillet. Hmm, nice label, I said to myself, I wonder what this is, and went off to look it up in Hugh Johnson's book *Wine*. I also tasted the sample and proceeded to order 40 cases of Château Grillet at $12 each!

Every three or four months I would send my clients a cheaply made list of my inventory, but it began to dawn on me that business did not pick up afterwards. It occurred to me that my clientele might not know what a Château Grillet is, either. One month in 1974 I had an especially esoteric collection of wines arriving, so I decided to put a short explanation about each wine into my price list, to try and let my clients know what to expect when they uncorked a bottle. The day after I mailed that brochure, people showed up at the shop, and that is how these little propaganda pieces for fine wine were born.

✦ 1974 ✦

APRIL BURGUNDY SALE

WHAT WITH the atrocious price situation in Bordeaux, wine lovers might well look back to the great Burgundies for their luxury drinking. Certainly greater values are to be found today in Burgundy, even though Bordeaux produces roughly six times as much wine. *Grand cru* Burgundy in older vintages (excluding, of course, such items as Romanée Conti bottlings) is often half or even one-third the price of the classified growths from Bordeaux.

Our superb 1961 Clos de la Roche, a *grand cru* vineyard from Morey-Saint-Denis, bottled by Ponnelle, is regularly priced at $14.95 a bottle. A claret of equivalent quality, from the same vintage, would likely cost you $22.00 to $50.00 per bottle! These market conditions (along with my own personal love for the wines of Burgundy) have led (or allowed) me to focus upon Burgundies to a greater and greater degree when seeking wines that offer real excellence.

To encourage you to try these great wines, I'm reducing the price of all the older vintages of Pierre Ponnelle and Henri Duprey Burgundies while I am on my buying trip to Burgundy. The quality of these wines is very high. First, Dick Buck★ tasted and selected a large number of wines last April in Burgundy. I attended a series of tastings covering over 50 of his selections after these wines reached the Bay Area. I selected only the finest bottles for my own shop. Quality is guaranteed to the point that you may return any unopened bottle within 30 days of purchase.

★*When I opened my shop, I did not have an import permit. I was buying imported wines from Dick Buck of European Wine Selections in San Jose, California.*

1973 CHABLIS★

THESE WINES are from the cellars of Maurice Fèvre, an old-school wine-maker in his late 60s, who resides on the outskirts of the village of Chablis. I selected the wines from barrel at Monsieur Fèvre's estate in the spring of 1974.

The wines are very nearly *handmade* wines, and the quality of his few barrels of Chablis *grand cru* was amazing to me. His 1973s showed strength, depth, the superb fruit of the Chardonnay, and what can only be termed *breed*.

These are Chablis to age. They are uncharacteristically big, and if we are lucky they will still be improving 10 years after the vintage. Most Chablis fades after 5 or 6 years, but in an unusual vintage it is capable of much more. With Dick Buck I recently tasted a 1928 Chablis *grand cru* Moutonne that was remarkable. The bouquet that had developed over the years was a joy to breathe. The wine was still lively with acidity!

When sampling these 1973s, look upon them with an eye to the future. I predict they will be amongst the most prized bottles in your cellar—if you wait long enough!

★ *The Maurice Fèvre Chablis were the first wines I tasted and ordered in France.*

1973 CHABLIS *GRAND CRU* "LES PREUSES"

Perhaps more typical of Chablis than the Bougros, Les Preuses shows a fruity but undeveloped aroma, crisp acidity, and great length upon the palate. The balance is impeccable.

$7.20 PER BOTTLE $77.76 PER CASE

1973 CHABLIS *GRAND CRU* "BOUGROS"

A rounder, more viscous wine. From barrel its aroma was huge and full of depth, really stunning, though it is closed up right now.

$7.20 PER BOTTLE $77.76 PER CASE

1973 CHABLIS

There being a bit of overproduction in 1973, Monsieur Fèvre blended the overflow, most of which was from his Les Clos vineyard, and labeled it simply Chablis. Not quite as big as the *grand cru* wines above, it is also softer and has less aging potential. Still, superior Chablis and a bargain to boot!

$5.95 PER BOTTLE $64.26 PER CASE

❀ ❀ ❀ ❀ ❀ ❀ ❀ ❀

1971 CORBIÈRES · BELLICARD
NV SAINT-CHINIAN · CAVE COOPERATIVE

Never great but oftimes exceedingly good, the wines of the Midi taste much better at $1.99 per bottle than they do at $4.99 with a Bordeaux label. This Corbières is a full-scented, full-flavored wine, the bigger wine in every way, yet the Saint-Chinian has its virtues. This mild country wine is smoother, with a subtle bouquet of rose petals. Try one of each; both are dry wines, recommended as all-purpose reds, but absolutely perfect with cassoulet and rich country fare.

$1.99 PER BOTTLE $21.50 PER CASE

1969 BANDOL *ROUGE** "CUVÉE DE LA GRAVIÈRE"
DOMAINE DU VAL D'ARENC

A full-flavored, dark red wine from the Mediterranean coast between Marseille and Toulon. Tasting notes are from the prestigious French wine journal *Revue du Vin de France*:

> *Proves that 1969 was a good year in that region. Dominant fragrance of undergrowth, blackberries, and plums. Well-balanced flavor with a nice long aftertaste. In top shape.*

Try this wine. I think you'll be rewarded with a very enjoyable and unusual discovery.

$3.29 PER BOTTLE $35.54 PER CASE

**An early sign of my future passion for the wines of Bandol.*

❧ 1975 ❧

ALSACE

1973 GEWURZTRAMINER *RÉSERVE*
GUSTAVE LORENTZ

WALT DEICKE wrote from Alsace a few months back, enthusiastically recommending this wine to me, so I placed a rather large order. When it arrived in this country we tasted it together and his face fell. It smelled and tasted *nothing* like Gewurztraminer! Walt was sure he had been cheated, that the producer had shipped him a wine other than the one he had tasted there in Alsace. I returned the wine as highly unsatisfactory. Six months later Walt gave me a bottle with a smirk on his face and told me to try it again. The wine has turned around completely. Obviously when it came off the boat it was shook up from the trip— what we call "seasick." The wine now is marvelous, fully recovered! It is very clean and fruity, with such a beautiful spicy nose you might use it to show a novice what Gewurztraminer smells like. Highly recommended.

$3.49 PER BOTTLE $37.70 PER CASE

° ° ° ° ° ° ° °

1971 BOURGUEIL · JEAN CHAZAL

This is the Loire Valley's answer to Beaujolais, a light-bodied but firm red wine that can be drunk to best advantage three to four years after the vintage. It is a fragrant wine made of the Cabernet Franc grape, with a fresh raspberry character. Like Beaujolais, it is best served at cellar temperature. Blends harmoniously with spring fever and long sunny days.

$2.99 PER BOTTLE $32.30 PER CASE

1972 BURGUNDY

THE WINES listed in this mailer are part of Schoonmaker Selections' inventory still in France. I traveled to Burgundy in May to taste the wines and discover the finest of those offered for sale.

The Burgundy market is schizophrenic right now. In general, bargains are available only through American companies who are willing to sell at a loss. For example, had I purchased 1972 Clos de Bèze (Domaine Clair-Dau) directly from Clair-Dau, I would be offering the wine at $225 per case. By purchasing *the same wine* from Schoonmaker, I can offer it to you at $106 per case.

Needless to say, the Schoonmaker inventory is not inexhaustible. My advice is to take advantage of the situation while it exists, because the price of fine Burgundy purchased *at the source* remains sky-high.

Happily, while prices are low, the quality of the 1972 vintage is very high. I tasted a large quantity of 1972s from many shippers and estates, and it was difficult to pare the list down to these 14 wines. The vintage is much more dependable than 1971. Generally speaking, a wine from a reliable producer will be more than satisfactory. 1972 red Burgundies are of the same quality range as 1964 and 1969.★

They are *vins de garde*, or wines to lay down. They possess deep color and unusually full Pinot Noir aromas, and they are well-structured wines with strength and backbone. The fruit/tannin balance is absolutely exceptional and ensures not only long life, but a mouth-filling wine. The best combine depth of flavor, body, and finesse. In my opinion they are complete wines that lack only proper aging.

With the list of wines and their prices, I am including my tasting notes, jotted down quickly as I tasted the wines. It is impossible to be too specific when one is examining anywhere from 5 to 60 wines at a sitting, but I hope the notes will give some guidance as to the nature of the wine offered.

★*In fact, they turned out to be better than 1969 and not as good as 1964, generally speaking.*

1972 MAZIS-CHAMBERTIN · PIERRE GELIN

Beautiful dark garnet. The nose is very full and potent. A big hard wine that will be around for decades. All the makings of a great bottle. When it matures, a beautiful giant of a Chambertin. *(We tasted this Mazis next to Gelin's 1971 Chambertin Clos de Bèze, and the Mazis was the finer wine in all respects. At this price, quite a bargain.)*

$85.00 PER CASE

1972 FIXIN "CLOS NAPOLEON" · PIERRE GELIN

Closed in nose at present. Very tannic, very chewy. Will age long and well. Finish is full and sturdy.

$48.00 PER CASE

1972 CHAMBERTIN "CLOS DE BÈZE"
DOMAINE CLAIR-DAU

Monsieur Clair, the winemaker of the Domaine Clair-Dau, says this is his finest 1972. It is from vines 65 years old! The wine is ruby colored with a garnet depth to it. It is full of promise. Flavors are very intense, very concentrated, yet elegant. A perfectly made Burgundy from start to finish.

$106.00 PER CASE

Cellar in Burgundy

1972 BONNES MARES · DOMAINE CLAIR-DAU

A wine full of flavor! A long ager—much tannin. Flavors are very big, concentrated, and lasting on the palate.

$96.00 PER CASE

1972 MOREY-SAINT-DENIS "CLOS DE LA BUSSIÈRE" DOMAINE ROUMIER

(Roumier is the sole proprietor of this premier cru, *which borders Chambolle Musigny, below Bonnes Mares. After years of following the development of the 1959 and 1964 Clos de la Bussière from my own cellar, I can recommend the wine as an undiscovered, underpriced gem.)* The 1972 is a brilliant medium garnet. Nose is elegant, intense, very complex, and full of promise. A firm wine with ample flavor. One to age 6 to 12 years.

$53.00 PER CASE

1972 CHAMBOLLE-MUSIGNY · DOMAINE ROUMIER

Darker color; quite dark. More forward than the Bussière. Delicious! The finish is flavorful, long, and tannic. Good for drinking 3 to 10 years.

$53.00 PER CASE

1972 ÉCHEZEAUX · DOMAINE MONGEARD MUGNERET

Much quality here. Good deep garnet. The aroma leaps out of the glass. Very clean, very fruity. One of the best of the trip. Elegance, complexity, much length on the palate. Must buy! Drink 3 to 10 years. Better and cheaper than his Grands-Échezeaux.

$64.00 PER CASE

1972 NUITS-SAINT-GEORGES "LES BOUDOTS" DOMAINE MONGEARD MUGNERET

Perfect deep color. Nose a bit closed in, but there is depth there. An extremely full, tannic Nuits-Saint-Georges. Long, full finish. Quite a mouthful. Not as impressive as the Échezeaux right now because it lacks the finesse, but this Nuits is for longer aging and is not yet showing everything it has. *(Mugneret's 1972s are spectacular, one after another. Any of them are worth buying, but these three are his finest.)*

$64.00 PER CASE

1972 CLOS VOUGEOT DOMAINE MONGEARD MUGNERET

Absolutely lovely to look at. Like the Nuits-Saint-Georges, the nose is a bit closed in right now, but there is great depth here, waiting to emerge as it matures in cellar. On the palate, round, clean Pinot Noir flavors. A wine of elegance, finesse, and *breed*, with body and tannin for aging 6 to 12 years at least. *(We then tasted his 1962 Clos Vougeot. The '72 is a darker wine, with more stuffing, more backbone to it. But the '62 has developed such complexity of flavor, one can see what a wonderful future there is in store for the clearly superior 1972.)*

$96.00 PER CASE

1972 CHOREY CÔTE DE BEAUNE
DOMAINE TOLLOT-BEAUT

Good purplish color. Very clean Pinot Noir flavors. Full-bodied, clean, extremely enjoyable. Next to the 1971 Chorey, this is not as "fat," shows no chaptalization, and will live longer.

$42.00 PER CASE

1972 BOURGOGNE *ROUGE* · DOMAINE TOLLOT-BEAUT

An incredible bargain, even in the midst of all these bargains! Come into the shop and find out what this wine's true appellation is. It has the good color that typifies the vintage. The nose and flavor are intense with Pinot Noir fruit and with the new oak aging that Tollot-Beaut gave to all his 1972s. I urge my customers to try at least one case. Drink now and for the next five to six years. Delicious Burgundy at a Zinfandel price!

$32.00 PER CASE

1972 ALOXE CORTON · DOMAINE TOLLOT-BEAUT

Medium-deep garnet. Full, intense aroma. Very full, tannic, chewy. One to age. Will develop beautifully, but, as with all Tollot-Beaut's wines, it is gorgeous already.

$53.00 PER CASE

1972 BEAUNE "CLOS DU ROI" · DOMAINE TOLLOT-BEAUT

Very rich, ample bouquet. His finest 1972; better even than his Corton. Flavors are intense with fruit, beautiful new oak, and tannin. Again, the perfect balance of tannin gives the wine an incredibly long finish. So good already, it will be difficult to age it to proper maturity.

$64.00 PER CASE

1972 MEURSAULT · DOMAINE PONTINET-AMPEAU

Deep golden color. Nose has good Meursault character. Clean. Full on the palate with a fruity, long finish. Good wine. *(Though the 1972 white Burgundies are less successful than the reds, this Meursault from an excellent winemaker is a fine bottle.)*

$53.00 PER CASE

DOMAINE LEFLAIVE

WONDERFUL white Burgundies! And I am not alone in this opinion: our last shipment sold out within one week of its arrival.

Last May I visited Domaine Leflaive, and it is interesting to note that Monsieur Leflaive prefers his 1973 wines to those of 1972. The 1973 wines are fruitier, more elegant, better balanced for current drinking. I like the 1972 Leflaive wines because they have more stuffing to them and higher acidity for longer aging. My advice (not surprising): drink the 1973s; cellar the 1972s.

PER CASE

1972 *Bourgogne* Blanc $49.00
A blend of Leflaive's Puligny-Montrachet and his *premier cru* Clavaillon.

1972 *Bienvenue Bâtard-Montrachet* 125.00
Deep gold. Complex nose—beautiful balance of Chardonnay fruit and Limousin oak. A powerful, flavorful wine from the seven-acre *grand cru* vineyard.

1973 *Bourgogne* Blanc 57.00
Again, a declassified wine blended from various vineyards in Puligny-Montrachet. You can see Leflaive prefers this to the 1972 because he charges more for it.

1973 *Bienvenues Bâtard-Montrachet* 135.00
Already showing great complexity. Stunning fruity nose. It makes me thirsty just thinking about it!

✣ 1976 ✣

EITELSBACHER
KARTHÄUSERHOFBERGER

IT WAS LIKE a dream come true to unearth a few aged German Rieslings at the superb wine estate Eitelsbacher Karthäuserhofberger on the Ruwer. Their distinctive label above is really more neck band than label.

Usually I return from Germany raving to friends and clients about the old Rieslings I was fortunate enough to taste at the various wine estates. Now I have obtained a few cases of four different wines from the magnificent 1959 vintage.

I'm offering these old wines (more than fifteen years in bottle!) on a pre-arrival basis. You will receive them in mixed cases, three bottles of each wine:

1959 Burgberg Spätlese
1959 Kronenberg "Feine" Auslese
1959 Burgberg "Feine" Auslese
1959 Sang "Feinste" Auslese
$135.00 PER MIXED CASE

VILLAGE OF BOUZERON

Monsieur Aubert de Villaine is best known as coproprietor of the Domaine de la Romanée-Conti (that's his signature on the labels), but he resides in the tiny village of Bouzeron, where he makes his own Pinot Noir and Chardonnay. I found them to be well-made wines with structure, balance, and elegance. These introductory prices will be in effect until September 1.

1973 Bourgogne Rouge *(100% Pinot Noir)*
$3.99 PER BOTTLE $43.10 PER CASE

1973 Bourgogne Blanc *(100% Chardonnay)*
$3.89 PER BOTTLE $42.02 PER CASE

1972 ÉCHEZEAUX · DOMAINE DUJAC

Young brilliant garnet. One doesn't search for the aroma; it rises out of the glass with such force and density, you might wonder how the bottle held the cork. From a plot of soil peculiarly appropriate to Pinot Noir and a vintage I have long touted, Jacques Seysses of Domaine Dujac has created a wine of unique, intense flavors and impeccable structure. In ten years, a masterpiece. My advice: Sell the roadster, sell the stud *and* the mare, buy the Échezeaux!

$17.47 PER BOTTLE $188.68 PER CASE

1962 ROMANÉE-SAINT-VIVANT · H. AUDIFFRED

Cloudy, browning garnet. Nothing to the nose but oxidation. Flat and empty on the palate. No character or depth. Way past its prime.

$21.50 PER BOTTLE $232.00 PER CASE

1972 CHAMBERTIN CLOS DE BÈZE
"DOMAINE MARION" · BOUCHARD AÎNÉ

The price on this wine is a direct-import price. There is no middleman between Bouchard and me. You get, therefore, a good idea of actual current Burgundy pricing. I am buying the wine because, yet again, the Clos de Bèze Domaine Marion is at the top of the vintage. Brilliant garnet color. Aroma is typical of the domaine, peppery and complex. Big wine on the palate with loads of tannin. Not as rich, nor as immediately enjoyable as the 1971; however, its higher tannin and acidity will allow it to develop much longer. Clearly a wine for those who wish to have the best, regardless of cost.

$194.00 PER CASE

✢ 1977 ✢

1970 SASSICAIA

UNLIKELY, PERHAPS, but here we have a very impressive Cabernet Sauvignon made in Italy. It shows a pronounced varietal nose, while the effect upon the palate is akin to Bordeaux, explained by the fact that the winemaker is French and is using Bordeaux barrels. Regardless, the wine is extremely well made; to my taste it compares easily with over-$8 California Cabernets. Highly recommended!

$5.50 PER BOTTLE $59.40 PER CASE

1970 CHÂTEAUNEUF-DU-PAPE · DOMAINE LES CLEFS D'OR

In recent years, two producers stand out at Châteauneuf-du-Pape. Both, as one might predict, are small estates where the emphasis is on the craft of wine-making rather than the commercial considerations that dominate the larger firms.

The 1974 Châteauneuf-du-Pape from Paul Coulon (Domaine de Beaurenard) will arrive in May.

This 1970 from Jean Deydier is already in the shop at a very reasonable price. While it shows the sun-ripened richness and earthiness typical of the region, it also possesses a degree of subtlety and sophistication rarely encountered.

We're fortunate to stock and enjoy exceptional wines like this produced by small wine estates thousands of miles away. As yet, the French cannot enjoy California's limited-production counterparts, and if they could, imagine the enormous prices they would have to pay! Fine French wines are relatively well priced.

$5.99 PER BOTTLE $64.70 PER CASE

ARRIVING SOON

LAST NOVEMBER I toured France with Richard Olney, the justly renowned food and wine writer. He guided me to his favorite small wine estates, from Domaine Tempier in Bandol near the Mediterranean, "the only great wine produced in Provence," to the magnificent Pinot Noirs of Jean-Marie Ponsot in Morey-Saint-Denis, whose 1971 Clos de la Roche remains one of the spectacular Burgundies of my experience. These and other such selections will arrive during May.

Another shipment, arriving in a week, contains inexpensive white table wines from the Loire Valley, Mâcon, and Chablis, specially selected by Gerald Asher, wine writer extraordinaire for *Gourmet* magazine. Prices will range from $2.60 to $5.00 per bottle.

Included will be the outstanding Château Thivin from the 1976 vintage, a beautiful *grand cru* Beaujolais that you may have read about in the February *Gourmet*.

Many of these wines will be available exclusively in our Albany shop.

Because I will be in Europe buying new wines as these shipments finally reach us, there will no announcement in the mail for a while. However, the store will be open, and you will find these exciting wines in stock very soon and quite agreeably priced.

◦ ◦ ◦ ◦ ◦ ◦ ◦ ◦

1972 CLOS DE LA ROCHE · DOMAINE PONSOT

A classic-styled Clos de la Roche—robust, strong-flavored, with its distinctive undercurrent of stones (*les roches!*), but in no way heavy or coarse.

The aroma is youthful still, showing clean Pinot Noir fruit and a lovely deep cherry quality. On the palate, a surprising explosion of flavor after the tightly reined nose.

In a class with the top 1972 Côte de Nuits, the wine will mature in the manner of its 1964 predecessor, which is just now reaching maturity but has many splendid years remaining.

$127.50 PER CASE

1976 BEAUJOLAIS

I INTENDED TO SPEND one day of my spring buying trip in the Beaujolais, but the 1976 vintage is so spectacular another day was needed, and yet another . . .

They are wonderful wines, beautifully colored (deep purple with a bluish tint), abundantly scented (roses, berries, cherries, you name it!), and absolutely marvelous drinking (no sipping allowed).

Of supreme importance—do not drink these wines at room temperature. One memorable bottle of Chiroubles, downed at the Relais de Solutré with roast leg of lamb, was served in a lightly iced bucket (as was the second bottle!). In other words, it was served slightly cooler than cellar temperature. This method seems to intensify or bring into focus the fresh fruitiness of the wine and gives it a clean, lip-smacking crispness.

With this vintage of Beaujolais we are in for a rare treat; I've never tasted one like it.

LOUIS TÊTE (*NÉGOCIANT* AT SAINT-DIDIER-SUR-BEAUJEAU)

Richard Olney introduced me to Monsieur Tête, a very small *négociant* who has a tremendous reputation throughout the Beaujolais. Other *négociants* seek his advice before buying from growers. I wanted to buy everything I tasted at Tête's and finally settled on these *grands crus*:

		PER BOTTLE	PER CASE
1976	*Chénas* fifths	$4.50	$48.60
1976	*Fleurie* fifths	4.95	53.46
1976	*Moulin-à-Vent* fifths	5.25	56.70

1976 CÔTE DE BROUILLY · CHÂTEAU THIVIN

Another *grand cru* vineyard, estate bottled, but at a lower price than most Beaujolais-Villages. Again, it was through Richard Olney that I discovered Château Thivin's splendid wine. The February issue of *Gourmet* magazine contains Gerald Asher's beautiful, detailed article about the château, its wine, and its history. A rare bargain to my way of thinking, the wine offers the closest thing to "breed" you'll find in a Beaujolais.

$4.50 PER BOTTLE $48.60 PER CASE

TRÉNEL FILS (*NÉGOCIANT* AT CHARNAY-LÈS-MÂCON)

It was in Volnay, while visiting my favorite Burgundian winemaker, that I first heard of Trénel. When I told Hubert de Montille that I would next visit the Beaujolais, he grabbed pen and paper and wrote *Trénel*! Such an event sparks joy into the heart of the itinerant wine merchant. Tasting in Trénel's cellar, I found the best (and most expensive) Beaujolais of the trip. Yet, on direct import, they are no higher than the sugared, Côtes-du-Rhôned Beaujolais from the big factories. I regret I did not buy more from Trénel, because 1976 happens too rarely.

1976 Fleurie fifths

$5.50 PER BOTTLE $59.40 PER CASE

1976 Moulin-à-Vent fifths

$6.25 PER BOTTLE $67.50 PER CASE

◇ ◇

RED BURGUNDY AT CELLAR TEMPERATURE

AFTER SEVERAL trips to the Burgundy region, wining and dining with the people who make Burgundy, I have been convinced that we in California drink our French Burgundy at the wrong temperature.

It is no wonder, after such advice as Hugh Johnson's:

The ideal arrangement is to plan twenty-four, twelve, or even six hours ahead which bottle you are going to open, and stand it up in the dining-room or the kitchen, wherever it is warm.*

Not once have I seen a Burgundian winemaker serve a bottle at their room temperature, which I assure you is lower than ours.

The habit in Burgundy is to disappear to the cellar when the bottle is needed, bring it to table, pull the cork, and pour it. It is decanted only when the sediment is quite heavy, and even then never with great care.

I imitate that technique now, and I have found that when served at proper cellar temperature, the wines "taste like they did there." The wonderful fruit quality of the Pinot Noir is preserved when it is drunk cool. An extra attraction—you needn't decide which bottle to serve until you serve it.

I urge my clients, particularly those in the warmer sections of the state, and particularly during the summer months—do not bring your Burgundy up to room temperature (80° in Sacramento?), or you will be tasting quite a different beverage than you would taste in the Côte d'Or.

One last observation: Rarely do Burgundians chill their finest whites. More often than not, their Meursaults and Montrachets are drunk fresh out of the cellar.

*Emphasis mine.

1972 VOLNAY *PREMIER CRU* DOMAINE DE MONTILLE

A blend of three *premier cru* vineyards, each lot too miniscule to vinify separately.

Light to medium garnet. The aroma is very pronounced in the glass, yet refined and entirely seductive. A taste demonstrates why wine author Hugh Johnson calls Volnay his "special favourite" of Burgundy vineyards.

The basic constituents of the wine (Côte d'Or soil, Pinot Noir fruit, French oak) are present in a complex blend unmarred by doctoring, chaptalization, or poor vinification. The aftertaste truly lasts minutes (should you succeed in holding out that long before taking another swallow).

A Burgundy of unique quality and perfection.

$9.25 PER BOTTLE $99.90 PER CASE

CHÂTEAU GRILLET

NOW TAKING RESERVATIONS for the legendary Château Grillet, scheduled for arrival in November along with other great white Rhônes from Condrieu and Hermitage. The Grillet is coming directly from the château without the usual middleman costs. If the dollar/franc relationship holds, the wine will retail for about $12.50 per bottle. If Château Grillet doesn't mean anything to you, read Hugh Johnson's review in his lovely book *Wine*. The rarest of the great French wines!

↦ 1978 ↤

DOMAINE TEMPIER

It is impossible for me not to love the wines of Domaine Tempier. Once you have visited the Peyrauds in their 17th-century house surrounded by perfectly tended vines, eaten Lulu's garlicky food cooked over the coals, and drunk the wines with Lucien in his cellar, it is clear that they love wine and they love people drinking wine.

Their dedication and belief in the beauty of the ancient Mourvèdre grape is positively convincing. I believe they have made truly great wines and will continue to do so.

ALICE WATERS, Chez Panisse Restaurant

SITUATED NEAR the Bay of Bandol in the south of France, Domaine Tempier lies not far from overgrown, overcrowded Marseilles. The new autoroutes have brought Bandol close enough for the commuters, and there is too much new construction sprouting up, vying with the vines for earth.

One afternoon Lucien, Tempier's animated, 60-year-old *proprietaire*, pointed across his vines to a square, gray, concrete structure, a new apartment building nearing completion. "Rabbit hutches," he sneered. It will take a siege to displace the Peyrauds from their piece of earth.

But the wine itself! Because it is available only at Chez Panisse and KLWM, most American connoisseurs know nothing about it whatsoever. And Tempier is special—tasting any other Bandol tells you nothing.

From their red grapes—predominantly the Mourvèdre—they make a dry rosé and a dry red. When young the red is not exactly a delicate wine. It has the harshness and vigor and sunny ripeness of the south. With age it softens and develops nuances of flavor unimaginable in its youth.

However, it makes good drinking youthful—rough-edged, lively, a bit *sauvage*. Drunk mature, it has been compared by winemakers of renown to the great wines of the Côte de Nuits and Bordeaux. Like most small French wine estates, Tempier has no old wine to sell, so in order to know the wine old, one must cellar it oneself.

As versatile at the table as Zinfandel, Domaine Tempier blossoms and shows itself best when drunk with Provençal cuisine—any dish boasting olive oil, rosemary, garlic, fennel . . .

Harvest, Domaine Tempier

More specifically, try a bottle of the 1974 with this simple lamb dish: Prepare a marinade of finely chopped onion, parsley, dried herbs, crushed garlic, olive oil, salt, and pepper. Marinate chunks of tender lamb along with such things as whole mushrooms, squares of red and green peppers, etc. The secret to making this wonderful is to find a rosemary bush and fashion some of its branches into skewers. (If metal skewers must suffice, add rosemary to the marinade.) After two hours' marination, arrange the ingredients on the skewers. Grill over coals.

A bit of lamb, flavored with the smoke, garlic, and rosemary, a sip of Bandol wine—there you have it. Everything wonderful about each is intensified by the other.

(In March we will receive their 1974 Cuvée Spéciale, a wine more suited for cellar aging, and their surprising rosé.)

1974 Domaine Tempier
$4.95 PER BOTTLE

◦ ◦ ◦ ◦ ◦ ◦ ◦ ◦

1975 PINOT BLANC · GUSTAVE LORENTZ

At the very least one might say this wine's virtue is its lack of flaw (and its flaw its lack of virtue?). But there is flavor interest here too, from the Pinot Blanc grape, with a hint of Alsatian style to it. Dry, rounded, easy to drink, a bargain.

$2.79 PER BOTTLE $30.14 PER CASE

1973 VOSNE-ROMANÉE · DOMAINE MONGEARD MUGNERET

Pinot Noir grown in Vosne-Romanée exudes an indescribable, absolutely ravishing stink that some of us find irresistible. This perfume is sometimes, indeed often, more provocative in a lighter vintage like 1973. It teases when you breathe it in, then reappears and lasts on the palate long after you've swallowed. While this wine will keep, I like it now with its youthful acidity.

$6.95 PER BOTTLE $75.06 PER CASE

1976 MONTAGNY · DOMAINE VACHET

Introducing a new small estate, never before imported. The wine is a bit like its maker, Monsieur Vachet, a little cold and reticent on first meeting, but it grows on you.

Geographically Montagny lies between the Mâconnais and the Côte d'Or, and its wine is somewhat like a blend of the two—fresh, straightforward Chardonnay nose, but a more serious wine, with greater depth than a Mâcon, and bigger flavors. The splendid vintage 1976 introduces Vachet's wine at its best.

$4.50 PER BOTTLE $48.60 PER CASE

1974 CHÂTEAUNEUF-DU-PAPE · DOMAINE DE BEAURENARD

In Orange each year the winemakers themselves judge each other's efforts. Invariably Paul Coulon's Domaine de Beaurenard is in the top three (usually with Paul Avril's beautiful Clos des Papes).

Coulon's 1974 won the gold medal. It is not a heavy year like 1957. On the other hand, the flavors are not buried under an overabundance of tannin. And it is its *flavor* that makes this wine such a winner. One lingers over the wine rather than being knocked over the head. Strong, yes—but well-bred and elegant too. Paul Coulon is an extraordinary winemaker.

$5.75 PER BOTTLE $62.10 PER CASE

CHAMPAGNE BILLECART-SALMON

You can have too much champagne, but never enough.

E. RICE

CHAMPAGNE IS A MARVELOUS THING. It is wine, yet different. The more one learns to appreciate its distinctive qualities, the more one is appalled by the way the term *Champagne* has been abused—perhaps nowhere worse than here in California, where the word means nothing more than "bubbly."

The word has geographical significance (Champagne is a place, after all), denoting a specific mélange of environmental factors (soil, climate—even its air smells different!) that makes the wine it yields unique.

At least of equal importance is the centuries-old tradition of Champagne-making that exists there, the skillful marriage of noble grapes and noble *crus* to achieve harmony and finesse, and hopefully some moments of magic when the bottle is finally uncorked.

The short list of "Grande Marque" Champagnes is like a roll call of prestigious names: Bollinger, Krug, Roederer, and so on. Of the Grandes Marques, only a handful, including Champagne Billecart-Salmon, have remained unfamiliar to California palates.

Billecart-Salmon is an old house, founded in Mareuil-sur-Ay by Monsieur N. F. Billecart in 1818. Incredibly, the family has been in Champagne, in this same village, since the 16th century.

The director today is Jean Roland-Billecart, a man of impeccable taste who exudes an old-fashioned elegance. He manages to combine warmth and reserve in fine style. He is an enthusiastic, knowledgeable connoisseur of all the great French *crus*, which gives him a perspective shared by few French vintners.

My first taste of Champagne Billecart-Salmon was in the restaurant of a grand old hotel in Ay, before I had actually visited the firm. For the first time I thoroughly enjoyed drinking a Champagne throughout a meal.

It is difficult to describe a Champagne, more difficult than describing a wine. As I took notes on the taste of Billecart-Salmon it struck me that they were not usable because they seemed contradictory, or paradoxical.

It was distinguished and supple, fragrant (though not aggressively so), robust yet subtle, lively without excess, totally dry yet mouth-filling. No single quality leapt out at the expense of form. It possessed a definitive bead.

To celebrate the arrival of the Grande Marque Champagne Billecart-Salmon in California, Chez Panisse and BayWolf restaurants will prepare special Champagne dinners during which various cuvées of Billecart will be poured by the glass. You will discover a Champagne appropriate at any hour of the day or night, or as a perfect accompaniment to fine cuisine.

Telephone Chez Panisse (548-5525) or BayWolf (655-6004) for precise information and reservations.

The Champagne is available in the shop at the prices below. If they seem lower than the prices of other Grande Marque Champagnes, it is only because we buy directly from Billecart-Salmon. There are no middleman costs.

	PER BOTTLE	PER CASE
Non-Vintage Brut fifths	$9.75	$105.30
1973 *Cuvée N. F. Billecart-Salmon* fifths	11.65	125.82
1971 *Cuvée N. F. Billecart-Salmon* fifths	12.95	139.00

1976 CHASSAGNE-MONTRACHET
DOMAINE FRANÇOIS COLIN & FILS

There will be no scrambling to consume Colin's Chardonnays before they suddenly drop their acidity, or before their fruit turns to oxidation. They change ever so slowly, perfect for those who enjoy following a wine's development over a period of years.

It was at Jacques Seysses's table, at Domaine Dujac, and we all agreed that our 1969 Bâtard-Montrachet from Ramonet was tired. I admire Ramonet and I don't mean to malign him—his wines are a welcome addition to my cellar any day—but the next day I visited Monsieur Colin and tasted his 1969 Chassagne Les Vergers, which was still fresh in the half-bottle!

The 1976s are better than the '69s. Colin's are quite fruity, full, rich, and clean. My tasting notes on each vintage and *cru* stress their perfect structure and freshness.

			PER BOTTLE	PER CASE
1973	*Chassagne-Montrachet*	. . . .	$6.95	$75.06
1976	*Chassagne-Montrachet*	. . . .	7.50	81.00
1976	*Chassagne* Premier Cru *"Les Vergers"*	. . . .	7.95	85.86

SMILE WHEN YOU SAY
CROZES-HERMITAGE

ADDING A Crozes-Hermitage to your wine cellar may strike you as a bit unlikely. Crozes has been overshadowed by its big brother, Hermitage. ("An excellent substitute," declares Hugh Johnson, while under Crozes-Hermitage in Lichine's giant *Encyclopedia of Wine and Spirits*, "French red and white wines" is the total five-syllable expenditure of verbiage.)

But there is an exception to every rule (including this one?), goes the saying, and I assure you, you will find something exceptional in the Crozes of Monsieur Raymond Roure.

I discovered Roure thanks to Richard Olney. It was a wintry night two years ago. Roure's winery was up a winding dirt road that we missed time and time again. Roure scarcely said a word, but he dipped his thief into countless barrels and pulled cork after cork.

When I asked him why his Crozes is so different, he responded with his sole burst of animation, holding his thick hands to portray the rays of the sun slanting against the slopes of his hillside. "The others use bastard grapes," he said, "not Syrah. My vines are on the hill, with the same exposure as Hermitage."

But surely it is also that the grapes are turned into wine by Monsieur Roure.

It is a wine of Porthos-like dimensions, powerful and direct in flavor, marvelously heady. I imagine it warming up a cold night with perhaps a plate of roasted liver (since we can't obtain game) and some wonderful onion dish.

I did not buy the wine then, thinking Californians were accustomed to the Crozes that Schoonmaker imported, a simple, bargain-priced co-operative wine. Would my clients pay the higher price commanded by Monsieur Roure?

Since then I've been obsessed with the wine. Here certainly was a discovery of great talent, no matter the price. Obviously it will be ignored by the label buyer (but few of them find their way to my shop anyway!).

I returned last November to the little village of Gervans and secured Roure's Crozes. He got it to the boat on time, and it has just arrived for your tasting pleasure.

			PER BOTTLE	PER CASE
1974	Crozes-Hermitage Blanc "Les Grands Blancs"	. .	$5.85	$63.18
1973	Crozes-Hermitage Rouge "Les Picaudières"	. . .	6.50	70.20
1974	Crozes-Hermitage Rouge "Les Picaudières"	. . .	5.95	64.26

FOR THE JADED PALATE

1974 BANDOL "CUVÉE SPÉCIALE" · DOMAINE TEMPIER

This is the wine I promised a few months back. The tenths are drinking well, provided you give them a good rough decanting for the aeration. The fifths and magnums should wait. What a beautiful wine! It is a dark cherry color; it has a spicy, complex bouquet; its flavors are habit-forming; it is extremely versatile with cuisine; it ages superbly; there is no other wine like it in the world; *and* it's got soul!

$6.95 PER FIFTH $75.06 PER CASE

1976 BOURGOGNE ALIGOTÉ · A. & P. DE VILLAINE

A dry white for charcuterie lunches, light dinners, or as an aperitif before a special dinner. It is too good for Kir, be assured, and for two reasons: While most Aligoté is grown in the flatlands (Burgundy's least desirable vineyard area), this one is grown on the slopes near the village of Bouzeron, a site long recognized for Aligoté. In fact, last month Bouzeron received a new appellation specifically for its Aligoté. Secondly, this wine was vinified perfectly clean, balanced and elegant, by a winemaker seeking excellence.

$4.25 PER FIFTH $45.90 PER CASE

1976 CHINON "CUVÉE VIEILLES VIGNES" · CHARLES JOGUET

I recommend this perfectly made Cabernet Franc to those with cellars for aging wines. Those of you who have it already cellared might be interested in some comments from the winemaker, Charles Joguet.

The grapes, 100% Cabernet Franc, are from an old hillside vineyard. The summer of 1976 was unusually warm, resulting in perfectly ripe grapes at harvest. Monsieur Joguet says that Château Latour uses the finest cooperage available in France, but that when the barrels are new there is too much oak-flavor extraction for Cabernet Franc. Consequently, Joguet buys Château Latour's once-used barrels for aging his wine.

The 1976 is too young. He compares it to his 1959, which is, in 1978, absolutely ravishing.

It should be drunk at 58–60°. It should be opened six hours before serving *but*, he stressed, never decanted.

$6.95 PER BOTTLE $75.06 PER CASE

1977 CHINON ROSÉ "CUVÉE JEUNES VIGNES"
CHARLES JOGUET

Winner of the gold medal of all the rosés of the Loire, 1977. It is of the dry style, but soft and full of charm. It has traveled well, retaining its abundant fruit and delicacy. Drink chilled, with summer salads and light cuisine, or by itself. An uncommon treat.

$3.95 PER BOTTLE $42.66 PER CASE

1976 HERMITAGE *ROUGE* · BRUNO THIERRY

Possesses, like all successful '76 Rhônes, an aroma unique to its appellation. This is to say, it could be nothing but Hermitage. In California one speaks of "varietal intensity," but in selecting wines in France the notion of "typicality" has become increasingly important to me. I look for wines that have flavor characteristics distinctive to their appellation. It is easy to make a wine more "complex" by over-oaking it, or to make it "big" by over-chaptalization. I'm more respectful of the winemaker who works to preserve what is distinctive about his *cru*.

Thierry's Hermitage has good color and a nose strong but deep and still closed. It is full and round in the mouth, balanced, with a slightly rough, tannic finish that time will mellow.

Compare it side by side with our Côte Rôtie 1976 from Emile Champet for an intriguing example of "typicality."

$7.50 PER BOTTLE $81.00 PER CASE

1976 SAINT-AUBIN *BLANC* "MURGERS DES DENTS DE CHIEN"
THOMAS PÈRE & FILS

A superior wine from a lesser appellation is more satisfying than an inferior wine from a superior appellation. Or, it's the singer, not the song.

This Saint-Aubin *blanc* has a rich, buttery Chardonnay aroma but a long, lean finish more reminiscent of Chassagne than of Meursault.

$7.95 PER BOTTLE $86.86 PER CASE

1973 VOLNAY · DOMAINE DE MONTILLE

This wine brings to mind a forgotten author's guide to those who would become connoisseurs of wine. He advised buying a case of a single good wine, and to drink through the one case before moving on to another. After twelve bottles of one wine (opened over several days, I should think), one would be in a better position to form opinions about it—and about other wines.

I recommend this Volnay as the Burgundy wine with which to spend some such period of time. The Pinot Noir character is rendered with rare integrity and intelligence. It is a delicate, lovely thing, quite mature, definitely not for those who require the shock of excessive tannin to arouse their taste buds. It is also a wine that inspires aesthetic considerations.

$7.95 PER BOTTLE $85.86 PER CASE

1974 MOREY-SAINT-DENIS "MONTS LUISANTS"
DOMAINE PONSOT

A rarity for many reasons. It is a dry white *premier cru* Morey-Saint-Denis from a vineyard of Pinot Blanc situated just up the slope from Clos de la Roche. The wine makes impressive drinking already with its oak-tinged bouquet, its mouth-filling texture, and its long, lively aftertaste. The stony hillside is no doubt responsible for the wine's firm, perfect structure, allowing it to age slowly over many years. From Richard Olney's beautifully dank, moldy cellar, I have enjoyed bottles of Monts Luisants from the early '60s, still firm, still crisp and lively, turned by years in the bottle into something even more unique and extraordinary.

$7.95 PER BOTTLE $85.86 PER CASE

◊ ◊ ◊ ◊ ◊ ◊ ◊ ◊

1973 CÔTE RÔTIE · BRUNO THIERRY

I am convinced. Côte Rôtie is one of the world's great red wines. I'm also convinced that within a year or two its price will rise dramatically to reflect its quality. This is a reasonable prediction because there exist less than 200 acres of Côte Rôtie, and it makes as good a wine as clarets or Burgundies priced twice as high.

This 1973 is a perfect bottle of wine from start to finish. The aroma is opulent, exotic, almost textured—thoroughly typical of Côte Rôtie. In terms of structure, it stands between the voluptuousness of a great Burgundy and the tight-knit framework of great claret. The flavors and perfume persist long after one has swallowed. It is rich without heaviness, a good trick the French have mastered.

$7.95 PER FIFTH $85.86 PER CASE

MUSCAT DE BEAUMES-DE-VENISE
BRUNO THIERRY

I don't know that I've ever imported a wine that has been so universally loved. This is surprising because a year ago I don't think anybody had even heard of Muscat de Beaumes-de-Venise (henceforth MdBdV). And while the MdBdV craze is not exactly sweeping the nation, we can't keep the wine in stock. It is this simple: the stuff is absolutely delicious! The French like it as an aperitif; Wasserman's book *Wines of the Côtes du Rhône* recommends it be drunk with fruit, especially melon; I like it as light dessert. Or, boil it down to a thick paste and coat the one you love. Whichever you choose, our third shipment has just arrived.

$7.50 PER BOTTLE $81.00 PER CASE

1975 BANDOL *ROUGE*
DOMAINE TEMPIER

THIS IS a chance for enthusiasts of Domaine Tempier to save some money by ordering the new shipment in advance.

The 1975 is arguably the finest vintage I've been able to offer. On the other hand, 1976 produced a lighter wine than usual, the most delicious picnic wine imaginable, but a wine "for the thirst," not for one's cellar. There you have two rather persuasive reasons for laying in a good quantity of the 1975.

The price has increased over the last vintage, I daresay, because the French themselves have discovered the wine. Jean-Baptiste Chaudet ("the best wine merchant in Paris, therefore of the world" [!?], according to *Gault Millau*) wrote in his last brochure:

> *I have found a magnificent Bandol. A rosé, but above all a very strong red. A robust wine which can stand comparison with the greatest Bordeaux. This red Bandol is the very thing to accompany red meats, sauced meats, and confits. It is produced by Domaine Tempier.*

One thing I love about Domaine Tempier is the combination of—well, there is always something wild and unpredictable about it, spirited, shall we say, yet it is honest and impeccable, full of warmth and finesse.

$68.00 PER CASE FIFTHS

✧ 1979 ✧

PAUL COULON, "ARISTOCRAT DU VIN"

During November, I visited many small domaines in Châteauneuf-du-Pape and heard other winemakers refer to Paul Coulon as the *aristocrat du vin*.

They meant the man—handsome, stylish, mannered—but above all they meant his wine. From a soil and climate that too often produces heavy, sweetish wines, Paul Coulon's stand apart. They possess power, style, and finesse.

Finding his wine so different from other southern Rhônes, I pursued a correspondence with Coulon concerning his method of vinification. What follows are quotes from his letters, translated and rearranged.

> *My method of vinification, ancient and very special, permits obtaining wines very fruity and elegant in their youth, but does not impede their aging admirably.*
>
> *The vinification is always the same at Domaine de Beaurenard, employing two techniques:*
>
> 1. *Two-thirds of the grapes are crushed gently by an ancient crusher with slightly grooved, adjustable rollers. This system is very pliable. It crushes the grapes without grinding the strongly tannic stems that would give astringence and would mask the aroma of flowers and fruit that will form the bouquet. The aroma is engendered by alcoholic yeasts that transform the grape sugar into alcohol.*
>
> 2. *One-third of the grapes are added to the fermenter uncrushed, again without de-stemming. These will be the object of an intra-cellular "aromatic" fermentation, which is by nature enzymatic (which is to say, non-yeasty), and which brings a gain of aroma and very interesting flavors.*
>
> *The duration of the fermentation is about 15 days at a temperature of 83–85°, in a closed cuve.*
>
> *The utilization of these two methods of vinification brings us much closer to the old method of "crushing by foot" used with success by our ancestors.*

As one can see, this is entirely different from the "Beaujolais" technique of vinification, unsuitable for Châteauneuf-du-Pape, in which all the grapes are fermented whole, in an atmosphere of carbon dioxide. On the contrary, Coulon's method allows numerous components of the grape skin and stems (tannin, coloring matter, aromatic and flavoring elements) to be absorbed by the wine.

How does the wine age? Coulon gave me a demonstration to answer this important question. The bottles dated back to 1966. Each wine was enjoyable, even the youngest, the 1977. But with each year in bottle the aroma grew more profound, the color and body deeper, the flavors more astonishing and surprising.

Young, his wines have a flowery deliciousness that masks their depth and staying power. With age they acquire aromatic qualities rich and diverse, suggesting truffle, licorice, pit fruits, and leather, for example.★

His 1966 is entering middle age. 1969 and 1971 are still young.

The 1976 now in stock is a brilliant garnet, perfectly limpid with flashes of black and ruby. The aroma is dominated by flowers and spice. Harmonious, well structured, long on the palate. Already agreeable, but not yet showing the greatness we can safely forecast for this *aristocrat du vin*.

1976 Domaine de Beaurenard
$6.94 PER FIFTH $75.06 PER CASE

★ *Descriptive adjectives thanks to tasting notes of the 1964 Domaine de Beaurenard in the* Revue du Vin de France.

º º º º º º º º º

1976 BLAGNY *ROUGE* "LA PIÈCE SOUS LE BOIS"
DOMAINE FRANÇOIS JOBARD

"The parcel beneath the woods" is a small strip of Pinot Noir vines at the top of the hill between Meursault and Puligny-Montrachet. François Jobard is a talented young winemaker with the magic touch. The result is a fine 1976 red Burgundy with clean Pinot fruit, hints of cassis, a subtle oak impression, and an undertone of tobacco-box scent that reminds me of the first Blagny I tasted, a magnum of 1947 at the Troisgros Restaurant in Roanne. Good body; plenty of tannin to keep the wine; round and full of charm. This will be a ravishing wine when it blossoms and acquires aged character.

$9.95 PER BOTTLE $107.46 PER CASE

1976 DOMAINE
FRANÇOIS DE MONTILLE

Hubert de Montille was a youngster in the hot summer of 1947 when he made his first wine. It was a difficult year for Burgundy vignerons. . . . Those who were able to control the temperature in the vats made splendid wines; many failed. Hubert de Montille's '47s are still spectacular—big, deep-colored wines with the muscle of

youth and the complexity of age, the floral elegance of the Volnays and the struc-
ture of the Côte de Nuits.

Today Hubert de Montille is father figure and friendly counselor to the avant-
garde of young vignerons who have tasted the fruits of a quarter of a century's
experiments in vinification and have returned for the most part to traditional meth-
ods, eschewing abusive chaptalization, stemming, heating of the musts, and short
macerations, in the interest of producing healthy, natural wines, typical of their
specific climates—wines that develop unhurriedly and live long. Hubert's wines
are the symbolic yardstick against which the excellence of others is measured.

RICHARD OLNEY

His hallmark is elegance. De Montille's '76s are typically elegant, but fuller-
bodied than usual. Perfectly made wines! JOSEPH SWAN

In France, Monsieur de Montille is spoken of in the same breath as Aubert de
Villaine of Romanée-Conti or Jacques Seysses of Domaine Dujac. . . . Better
one bottle of this classic [de Montille's '71 Pommard Pezerolles] than two of a
forgettable commercial Burgundy at half the price! ROBERT FINIGAN

The wines of de Montille, while all individuals, do generally reflect the rigorous
style of winemaking and bear a familial resemblance to one another. The best have
a deep garnet color, with a youthful bluish cast. The aromas of the noses of the more
developed wines tend to be very spicy, rich and complex, redolent of the citrus, rasp-
berry components of Pinot Noir fruit. . . . The noses anticipate the texture and
flavors of the wine beautifully. The overall effect of these wines on the palate is
startling. Each is an elegant and finely wrought individual, in some ways more like
Bordeaux in structure than Burgundy. The Pinot Noir character is quite strong and
the flavors linger long on the palate. . . . On tasting the wines it becomes clear that
they are not chaptalized. They have none of the sweet, hot character that we have
come to associate with the nose and flavor of Burgundian Pinot Noir. . . .

JOEL PETERSON, International Wine Letter & Digest

THE RICHARD OLNEY reference to the '47s is appropriate here because conditions were much the same in 1976. A handful of vignerons made great wines
under difficult conditions, wines that will be drunk and discussed for decades;
the remainder are flawed, often by an overabundance of tannin and a charmless
harshness.

Hubert de Montille's '76s are the finest wines I've yet received from him—
classic Burgundies full of intensity, depth of flavor, and charm.

His demand cellaring. The Bourgogne will mature most rapidly—my guess
is three to five years from now. You can taste through the village of Volnay
searching in vain for *premiers crus* of this perfection.

The Volnay is darker, more intense, with a greater prominence of oak.

It is a waste to open the Volnay *premier cru* or the Champans at this stage; they
are mere infants.

The Pommard Pézerolles is deceptive because it can be enjoyed already. It offers itself with supple open arms. How did the man make such a ravishing, pretty wine in a hot year like 1976? It certainly will gain tremendously with five to six years' bottle age, but it has been irresistibly delicious since the first time I tasted it from cask in 1976.

		PER CASE
1976	*Bourgogne*	$96.00
1976	*Volnay*	138.00
1976	*Volnay* Premier Cru	178.00
1976	*Volnay "Champans"*	240.00
1976	*Volnay "Taillepieds"*	240.00
1976	*Pommard "Pézerolles"*.	240.00

WINES OF THE
SOUTHERN RHÔNE

1977 VACQUEYRAS · DOMAINE LE COUROULU

From a village west of Châteauneuf, three or four kilometers from Gigondas. The French would call this a *jolie vin*, or "pretty wine," because of its flowery bouquet and elegance. Le Couroulu is a small domaine, making red wine only. Should you visit Vacqueyras (it was extraordinarily beautiful last autumn with the change of season), ring the bell on the doors of the cellar and the Madame will come down to pour some tastes of the beautiful Couroulu for you. On the walls are the many gold medals winemaker Pierre Ricard has won in Paris. Very fine; highly recommended.

$4.95 PER BOTTLE $53.46 PER CASE

1972 AND 1976 CHÂTEAUNEUF-DU-PAPE
DOMAINE DU VIEUX TÉLÉGRAPHE

Châteauneuf concentrate! The Livingstone-Learmonth book *The Wines of the Rhône* describes it as "one of the finest of all Châteauneuf-du-Papes, a wine that is always splendidly full-bodied and well-balanced."

We have a small quantity of the 1972, which won first prize at the Concours de Saint Marc, a meaningful blind-tasting competition with the grower-producers themselves as judges.

Also, the rich, tannic 1976 vintage is available to those with cellars to age it. Both are intense, mouth-filling wines that reflect the sunny climate and stony terrain of Châteauneuf-du-Pape.

Winter at Vieux Télégraphe

1972 Domaine du Vieux Télégraphe
$9.75 PER BOTTLE $105.30 PER CASE

1976 Domaine du Vieux Télégraphe
$7.75 PER BOTTLE $83.70 PER CASE

WINE AND CUISINE
OF SOUTHERN FRANCE

YOU WILL HAVE more fun with the great Rhône and Provençal wines if you match them with appropriate cuisine. With spring about to fill markets and gardens with fresh herbs and vegetables, the time is right.

A SIMPLE SANDWICH LUNCH

With mortar and pestle make a paste of OLIVE OIL, GARLIC, NIÇOISE OLIVES, and ANCHOVY. Vary the quantity of each according to your taste preference.

Split a BAGUETTE down the center lengthways. Coat one-half liberally with the paste; sprinkle the other half with VINEGAR.

Fill with slices of fresh RED PEPPER, MUSHROOM, TOMATO—whatever you find in season.

Obviously this makes a casual luncheon, and the chilled wines taste great with the crunchy fresh vegetables.

Appropriate Wines:

1975 Domaine de la Bernarde

Either the red or the white from this highly regarded domaine near Aix-en-Provence would work. There is a suggestion of wild herbs in each, which adds interest. Or, start with the white, then at the right moment, switch to the red. ($3.99)

1977 Château du Trignon (Côtes du Rhone Blanc)

There is a spiciness; quite appropriate. ($3.50)

1977 Domaine Tempier Rosé

A connoisseur's rosé from the finest wine domaine in Provence. This rosé, incidentally, is the perfect bouillabaisse wine. ($6.50)

RATATOUILLE

I'm not sure why, but the ratatouille one concocts at home is infinitely superior to those offered by the delis and charcuteries. Make more than enough because it will be delicious cold the next day, and even better the day after that.

Slice two EGGPLANTS into ¼-inch rounds, or cubes, and sauté in OLIVE OIL until tender. Eggplant slurps up an unbelievable quantity of olive oil. If, God forbid, your system refuses to do the same, tenderize the eggplant in a steamer.

Meanwhile, in a stew pot (one that will not react rudely to tomato) sauté slowly in OLIVE OIL: sliced ONIONS, cubes of ZUCCHINI, chopped GARLIC, and sliced RED or GREEN PEPPERS (from which the seeds and core have been removed).

When tender combine everything in the stew pot and add peeled, sliced TOMATOES. Cook gently one hour.

Add freshly ground CORIANDER, whole GREEN OLIVES, and a handful of CURRANTS or RAISINS. Cook another half hour.

At the end, add fresh BASIL leaves and roughly ground BLACK PEPPER.

Serve hot or cold.

Appropriate Wines:

1977 Châteauneuf-du-Pape Blanc (Bruno Thierry)

I prefer a red here, but if you want white, it should be a rich, mouth-filling dry wine like this. ($7.95)

1977 Cairanne (Côtes du Rhône)

A flowery, elegant red Rhône with the right amount of astringency for the ratatouille. ($4.95)

1976 Châteauneuf-du-Pape Rouge *(Domaine de Beaurenard)*
My favorite ratatouille wine. The two are so good together you'll wish the wine were not quite so intoxicating so you could munch and sip endlessly. ($7.50) The 1977 Beaurenard just won the gold medal at the Concours de Paris. Watch for its arrival next fall.

PROVENÇAL-STYLE POT ROAST

You can employ your own techniques and refinements here, according to your knowledge and predilections.

The general idea is to braise in its fat a CHUCK ROAST that has been larded with cloves of GARLIC and sprigs of fresh ROSEMARY. Then add to the pot such things as sliced ONIONS, RED PEPPERS, thin strips of LEMON PEEL, BLACK OLIVES, ANCHOVY, whole CARROTS, a half-bottle Domaine Tempier—you get the idea.

Place it, covered, into a 300° oven all day. Everything will fall apart and meld together somewhat, but each bite will be different.

Appropriate Wines (this is the time to pull out the biggest, richest, most flavorful red Rhônes):

1972 Domaine du Vieux Télégraphe (Châteauneuf-du-Pape)
One of the great southern wine domaines, splendidly full-bodied, reflecting the sunny climate and stony terrain of Châteauneuf. ($9.75)

1976 Crozes-Hermitage Rouge *(R. Roure)*
Gerard Chave, the master vintner of Hermitage, told me that only Raymond Roure can make great Crozes-Hermitage. Here it is, showing all the color, depth, and body possible in 1976. ($7.80)

1975 Bandol Rouge *(Domaine Tempier)*
Should you use this wine in the cooking, as suggested, you must certainly serve it at table in order to create a perfect harmony of flavors. ($6.95)

GRILLED LAMB À LA LUCIEN

Last spring during a visit to Domaine Tempier, we enjoyed dinner prepared and served outdoors next to the vineyard, under a purple twilight sky. It gives me a fantastically warm, comfortable feeling to recall our simple menu.

Lucien Peyraud, patriarch of the great domaine, gathered a bundle of vine cuttings and set it afire. Into a double grill customarily used for fish he placed branches of thyme and plump lamb cutlets rubbed with olive oil. Then he laid the grill over the coals.

Obviously few of us can manage such perfect fuel, but the simplicity of the conception is inspiring.

You might marinate pieces of lamb in olive oil, herbs, and garlic and grill them on skewers fashioned from rosemary branches. You might throw rosemary branches onto the coals as you finish grilling lamb cutlets larded with garlic.

Whatever you come up with, hopefully you have cellared an older vintage of Domaine Tempier because now, as you might have guessed, with the garlic-herb-smoke-flavored lamb, is the time for it.

○ ○ ○ ○ ○ ○ ○ ○

SANCERRE · DOMAINE GITTON

One after another, each domaine I visited in Sancerre was using either glass-lined or stainless-steel tanks. Some were preparing to bottle their 1978s—a mere six weeks after the harvest!

At Domaine Gitton, my last stop, I found the '78s leisurely fermenting—in barrel!

Further indications of integrity and tradition at Domaine Gitton include their refusal to employ fertilizer in the vineyards, the use of wooden vinification implements, a natural gravity-flow winery, and the separate bottling of vineyard sites to preserve soil characteristics.

1976 Sancerre "Les Montachins"
$7.50 PER BOTTLE $81.00 PER CASE

1976 Sancerre "Les Romains"
$7.95 PER BOTTLE $8.86 PER CASE

1978 BEAUJOLAIS-VILLAGES · TRÉNEL FILS

The most delicious glug-glug imaginable. If mere deliciousness determined price, Trénel's Beaujolais would be the highest-priced wine in the shops. To enjoy while irresistibly fruity, full of sap, vigor, and dazzling flavors. A memorable (if transitory) wine, under $5.00 per bottle.

$4.75 PER BOTTLE $51.30 PER CASE

1977 SAVENNIÈRES · CHÂTEAU D'EPIRÉ

Why ignore Savennières? It is currently cheaper in France than Mâcon *blanc*, yet it is a noble *cru*. The answer must lie in our predilection for Chardonnay.

Savennières is Chenin Blanc, vinified dry. It is the best site (e.g., terrain and climate) for dry Chenin Blanc in France.

Château d'Epiré is barrel-fermented, barrel-aged; I think theirs tastes as it must always have tasted—the ripe peach-like per-

fume of the Chenin Blanc grape, the length and well-defined structure bestowed by Savennières' undernourished soil, the hint of oak throughout.

Savennières ages well.

$5.50 PER BOTTLE $59.40 PER CASE

CHARLES JOGUET AT CHINON

I**F** C**HARLES** Joguet had grown up in Burgundy or the Napa Valley, his name would be familiar to all wine lovers. This is not to disparage Chinon, where in fact Joguet was born and acquired his vineyards of Cabernet Franc. Wine is subject to fad—during the time of Rabelais, Chinon was the rage. Fads are by definition transitory. Don't follow fads! Seek the great wines.

The point is, Charles Joguet is one of the great vintners—he possesses an artist's aesthetic impulse and uncompromising integrity. At this point in his career he is driven. He will do anything, whatever the cost in money or time, to make his wine as perfect as it can be.

If your interest in wine exceeds the desultory, I urge you to check out what Charles Joguet is making in Chinon.

1978 Chinon Rosé

$4.50 PER BOTTLE $48.60 PER CASE

1978 Chinon Rouge *"Cuvée des Varennes du Grand Clos"*

$4.95 PER BOTTLE $53.46 PER CASE

° ° ° ° ° ° ° °

1976 SANCERRE *ROUGE* "LES ROMAINS" · DOMAINE GITTON

Dark garnet color. Strong Pinot aroma. On the palate, fat and round with a novel *goût de terroir*. Aren't you curious?

$6.50 PER BOTTLE $70.20 PER CASE

1976 SANCERRE *BLANC* · DOMAINE GITTON

The perfect example of Sancerre, yet which readers of my last propaganda bulletin have ignored. You might reply that the price is high—I counter that I had to pay a premium to obtain the few cartons remaining of the great 1976 vintage. Again, Sancerre is not versatile at table like Chardonnay. Plan a mussel or oyster feast, or smoked salmon, and serve well-chilled this elegant, steely, bone-dry Sancerre. (The difference between the vineyards offered: the Romains is stronger in the flint department; the Montachins is a bit more richly textured.)

"Montachins"

$6.95 PER BOTTLE $75.06 PER CASE

"Les Romains"

$7.95 PER BOTTLE $85.86 PER CASE

1977 FIXIN "LES HERVELETS"
DOMAINE CRUSSEREY

Introducing Monsieur Crusserey, whose only wine is Fixin. A small domaine, the winery is under his house. This man—well, I feel he is an important discovery. As with de Montille's Burgundies, the nose and flavors are not concealed under a deadly layer of sugar. The complexity and individuality inherent in Fixin's Pinot Noir grapes are allowed full expression.

The 1977 has a pretty nose—violets, black pepper, wild strawberry; strong, lean, well structured, more like a 1972 than any other recent vintage. You should cellar it at least three years.

$9.95 PER BOTTLE $107.46 PER CASE

1977 MONTAGNY · DOMAINE JEAN VACHET

Vachet consistently makes the finest Chardonnay in the village of Montagny. As evidence I can cite his repeated triumphs at the Concours de Paris, and this fine bottle, just arrived. Aubert de Villaine directed me to Vachet, saying the man is like his wine: the more you get to know him the more you warm up to him. Agreed!

$5.95 PER BOTTLE $64.25 PER CASE

1974 CÔTE RÔTIE · BRUNO THIERRY

First, I think it important to note that with our direct import capability we are able to offer Côte Rôtie at under $10 per bottle. It remains one of the few unquestionably outstanding red wines you can find from France *or* California under $10 today. The 1974 is unmistakably Côte Rôtie: voluptuously scented; combines power and delicacy; the product of the exotic flavor of the Syrah (80%) and Viognier (20%) grapes. For roast beef, lamb, roast chicken, cheeses.

$8.75 PER BOTTLE $94.50 PER CASE

DOMAINE PONSOT

1976 CLOS DE LA ROCHE

After we tasted his 1976 Clos de la Roche from bottle for the first time, Ponsot pulled out his 1961. Perhaps the '61 was the only wine to follow the 1976, not only because they have much in common, but because none of the vintages in between can match the 1976 for power and concentration.

Because of the size of the wine, Ponsot favored it with extra time in barrel, bottling it well after the other growers' '76 red Burgundies had been sold and shipped. Consequently it has a delicious vanilla quality, matched by enormous fruit.

Each time I've tasted the wine, from barrel or bottle, my tasting notes show a consistent enthusiasm: the wine is dark-colored; full-bodied; tannic but balanced for long aging; with unusual depth of flavor and unusual length on the palate.★

$275.00 PER CASE FIFTHS

★ *Not many 1976s aged well, but Ponsot's is still magnificent.*

1976 MOREY-SAINT-DENIS
PREMIER CRU "MONTS LUISANTS"

Ponsot's rare white Morey-Saint-Denis. The 1976 is a deep golden wine with more body and depth than any other vintage I've tasted. The characteristic stony flavor, a result of the vineyard's placement on the hill above Clos de la Roche, is pronounced in this vintage, underlying the strong fruit. Rich, supple, already approachable.

The wine earned the *Tastevinage* label awarded by the Chevaliers du Tastevin, but I asked Ponsot to use his own label. That *Tastevinage* label, prestigious though it may be, is certainly not the most charming label around; in fact, it has always struck me as rather a blight on some otherwise fine bottles of Burgundy.

$125.00 PER CASE FIFTHS

DOMAINE DU VIEUX TÉLÉGRAPHE

VIEUX TÉLÉGRAPHE is one of the few domaines to make a white Châteauneuf-du-Pape. The 1978 is round and full-bodied, with ample ripe fruit. Perhaps it is the style of cooking I do (unfussy, with a healthy dose of garlic and garden herbs), but very often a white Châteauneuf seems like the only wine appropriate. And it makes a beautiful prelude to the Domaine Tempier, or an older red Rhône. Only 20 cases available. ($8.95)

Remember the splendid 1972 Vieux Télégraphe, the red, with its big spicy nose and robust flavors? We just received our last 20 cases. ($14.95)

The 1972 won the coveted first prize at the Saint Marc's tasting competition in Châteauneuf-du-Pape. Now Vieux Télégraphe has triumphed with their 1977. First prize again! Needless to say, it's a beauty, splendidly full-bodied, loaded with flavor. It belongs in your cellar, though, being altogether too young for consumption at this time. ($8.75)

MONTEPULCIANO D'ABRUZZO

You are hiking alone over the Italian Alps. You've selected your freeze-dried food packets carefully. Your Côte Rôtie pellet is fantastically realistic dissolved in the icy spring water. Then the weather turns cold. First thing you know, you are freezing to death. You need shelter quick. A dim light in the distance. A small stone cottage. The peasants invite you to sit at their hearth. A bowl of hot pasta with tomato sauce and cheese is placed in your icy hands. And the wine, the wine is Montepulciano d'Abruzzo!! Dark, robustly flavored, a bit of roughness perhaps, but subtlety doesn't matter a whit in the presence of a rich tomato sauce.

$2.99 PER BOTTLE $32.30 PER CASE

Jean Gueritte, Cheverny

1978 CHEVERNY *BLANC* · JEAN GUERITTE

I have found a Sauvignon Blanc with the style and flavor of a first-rate Sancerre. I first tasted it in Paris, where it was the rage in the little wine shops and received glowing reviews in the press. Remembering its abundant fruit, impeccable balance, and perfectly crisp, lip-smacking finish, I've been anxious for it to arrive for use at my own table.

$3.95 PER BOTTLE $42.66 PER CASE

1978 BOURGOGNE PASSETOUTGRAIN
HUBERT DE MONTILLE

A superb Burgundy vintage; a winemaker head and shoulders above the rest; a wine that has no peer in terms of pure deliciousness. Last spring at dinner de Montille asked what I would like to drink from his cellar. Ordinarily I request his '59 or '61 Volnay Taillepieds, or his '66 Pommard Rugiens. I asked him instead to draw off a carafe of this 1978 Passetoutgrain from barrel. It is a one-of-a-kind marvel!

$8.95 PER BOTTLE $96.66 PER CASE

CHÂTEAU D'EPIRÉ

ACHÂTEAU D'EPIRÉ is two things. It is a wine grown in the best *climat* for dry Chenin Blanc in France: Savennières. And it is the 16th-century château in the village of Epiré, in which the *propriétaires*, Monsieur and Madame Bizard, reside.

The winery itself is located in the 12th-century village chapel. It is in this chapel that the wine is both fermented and aged in oak casks. No stainless steel, no centrifuge here—it is vinified as it was centuries ago. Perhaps it is the fermentation in cask that imparts to the wine a degree of complexity and depth unusual for Chenin Blanc.

There are photographs of the 16th-century château and the 12th-century chapel/winery on the wall of the shop; clever comments about the holy nature of the wine are invited.

The wine is startlingly good. It would be inexcusable to ignore it because you might have learned to avoid California Chenin Blanc. This is another story altogether, as you can see from Robert Finigan's description in his *Private Guide to Wines*:

> *1977 Savennières, Ch. d'Epiré ($5.50), is a startling and intriguing bottle. Its color, strikingly rich for a 1977, introduces aromas suggestive of ripe peaches and honey with perhaps a little spice thrown in. A dessert wine with sweetness concentrated by botrytis? No, a bone-dry but uncommonly flavorful Chenin Blanc suitable for elegant aperitif service or perhaps as accompaniment to fish or chicken dishes with inventive cream-based sauces.*

Now again, in his current issue, Finigan has seen fit to praise the same wine:

> *You would be hard pressed to find Chenin Blanc more skillfully rendered. The purity of varietal aromas and flavors is outstanding. . . .*

The 1976, just arrived, makes the 1977 look positively austere by comparison. The 1976 is more opulent, a riper-tasting wine, with even more flavor.

I ordered both the *sec* and the *demi-sec*. The *demi-sec* is dry enough; in my opinion it is at least as good as the *sec*.

In addition, we have received 10 cases of the 1971. I haven't tasted it; they're unloading the boat as I write this. The only old bottles of Château d'Epiré I have tasted were the 1970 and 1947. They tasted good.

		PER BOTTLE	PER CASE
1977	*Château d'Epiré*	$5.50	$59.40
1976	*Château d'Epiré*	5.95	64.26
1971	*Château d'Epiré*	12.50	135.00

❦ ❦ ❦ ❦ ❦ ❦ ❦ ❦

The winery at Château d'Epiré

1978 CHÂTEAU GRAVILLE-LACOSTE · GRAVES

A dry white Graves that I discovered at Chez Serge, my favorite Paris bistro. Their wine list is short, the wines impeccable, the prices fair, the food down-to-earth and superb. Château Graville-Lacoste makes wine to complement cuisine—the flavors are good, with a touch of vanilla in the aftertaste, but they will not dominate. The emphasis is on freshness, proportion, and *élan*.

$4.95 PER BOTTLE $53.46 PER CASE

1977 CÔTE RÔTIE · EMILE CHAMPET

I love this man's Côte Rôtie. I think his is the best these days. Even his 1975 (an "off" vintage that I bought only for my own cellar) shows tremendous aromas and flavors.

The man uses no fertilizers or chemicals in his vineyard; he vinifies as his father did and the father before him. Champet himself is refreshing—he refuses to take credit for the great quality of his Côte Rôtie. According to him, it is a simple matter of having his vines on the best part of the hill. "Monsieur Gentaz makes fine wine too," Champet told me. "His vines are on the same part of the hill." (The Côte Rôtie of Monsieur Gentaz arrives next month!) Champet acts as if his job is simply to avoid fouling up what his vines produce for him.

Guigal gets all the publicity around here. I think it is unwarranted. Taste Champet's Côte Rôtie and see for yourself.

$9.95 PER BOTTLE $107.46 PER CASE

❖ 1980 ❖

DOMAINE DE
LA CHARMOISE

1979 GAMAY

In November I went to France to select a Beaujolais Nouveau and rush it on board ship as early as possible so we could enjoy it at its freshest. I tasted many (indeed too many, bistro-hopping in Paris one day and long into the night), but sad to say not even Trénel's, the best I tasted, stirred up my interest.

The harvest in Beaujolais was too plentiful, and in order to compensate for the watery vacuity that resulted, growers beefed up the wines by pouring tons of sugar into the fermentation vats. A number of growers, including some prestigious names, have been formally charged with excessive sugaring.

What is wrong with sugaring, or chaptalization? Quite simply, it masks flavor. And it gives a false roundness or viscosity to the wine, obscuring the natural structure of tannin and acid. In a normal vintage, Beaujolais will reach around $11°$ natural alcohol. What I tasted in November was at $13°$ to $13.5°$, thanks to the sugaring. That is headache wine!

The Domaine de la Charmoise makes Gamay in the Loire Valley south of Blois. Their 1979 has all the fruit and freshness of a *vin nouveau*, but the winemaker did not sugar or filter the life out of it. It is as close to the grape as it can get and still be wine. At $11°$ alcohol, nothing is masked. Dry, crisp, marvelously ALIVE on the palate, it has a delicately distinct, almost steely *goût de terroir* underneath that holds one's interest.

Better than any Beaujolais Nouveau I tasted, and cheaper! I think this will surprise you.

$3.99 PER BOTTLE $43.09 PER CASE

1979 SAUVIGNON BLANC

Like the Gamay, their Sauvignon Blanc abounds with intense fresh fruit. Low in alcohol, but not in flavor or aroma. Impeccably vinified with a dry, lip-smacking finish, this is of the same school as the Cheverny from Jean Gueritte that we had last November.

$4.25 PER BOTTLE $45.90 PER CASE

CAVE RABASSE-CHARAVIN AT CAIRANNE

CAIRANNE IS a pretty little sun-drenched village that rises from the vast vine-covered plain known as Le Plan de Dieu, or God's Plain. Ancient picturesque villages interrupt the sea of vines, wearing comely names like Sainte-Cecile-les-Vignes, Violés, Sablet, and familiar wine names like Gigondas and Vacqueyras. These are drowsy, tree-lined Provençal villages with an occasional dog passed out in the shade, kids on motorbikes trying to get under your tires, men young and old single-mindedly rolling their iron *boules* in dirt squares, and wine. Above all, wine.

I time my trips to arrive in late spring when the air is warm and you can almost feel the vines growing. In my opinion the area deserves its name, Le Plan de Dieu.

But wait, I'm trying to sell wine, not a ticket to Provence. I wanted to make some point about the wine reflecting the temperament of the people and the region, its compatibility with Provençal cuisine, etc.

The wine is easy to enjoy. It does not demand or merit microscopic examination. This is wine to drink, and it is priced accordingly.

I heard of Abel Charavin, the winemaker, because his wines are listed in the Concours de Paris awards practically every year. Part of the credit must go to the placement of his vines on a rising slope east of Cairanne with a perfect southern exposure.

1978 VIN DE TABLE *ROUGE*

The result of his young vines.

$2.75 PER BOTTLE $29.70 PER CASE

1978 CÔTES DU RHÔNE *BLANC*

He makes a small amount of dry white. Medium-bodied, fruity, somewhat fleshy, with good dryness and balance.

$4.25 PER BOTTLE $45.90 PER CASE

1977 CÔTES DU RHÔNE *ROUGE*

A medium-bodied red from Grenache, Syrah, Mourvèdre, and Carignan. Intense nose and flavors, yet with a perfumed quality that is characteristic of his wines. A characteristic Charavin quality, I suppose. The Côtes du Rhône is a relatively vast area, and of the 1977s, this won the silver medal.

$4.25 PER BOTTLE $45.90 PER CASE

1978 CAIRANNE *ROUGE*

Flowery, long, delicious, his finest wine. Typifies the best qualities attainable from the appellation Cairanne.

$4.95 PER BOTTLE $53.46 PER CASE

1978 SANCERRE "LES ROMAINS" · DOMAINE GITTON

What is the most difficult wine to make? A wine whose components are evident, distinct, and harmonious without being fat or overblown and masking the flavors of the accompanying cuisine. The 1978 Domaine Gitton Sancerre (100% Sauvignon Blanc) is so fresh and unconstrained, so delicious to taste, and at the same time a model of refinement. The aftertaste is bone-dry, yet the scent returns like a sweet, elusive perfume.

$9.95 PER BOTTLE $107.46 PER CASE

1976 SAVENNIÈRES · CHÂTEAU D'EPIRÉ

There has been a great deal of interest in the Château d'Epiré *demi-sec* (barely off-dry in this case). It is delicious, but in what situation should one serve it? I gave a bottle to Jean-Pierre Moullé, chef at Chez Panisse Restaurant, and asked for his recommendations, which follow:

1. *It's the kind of wine, fruity, not too sweet, which is perfect alone, as apéritif, before lunch or dinner.*

2. *With a salad of thin-sliced prosciutto and fresh pear, doused lightly with olive oil.*

3. *The wine would be good with smoked charcuterie like sausages, ham, chicken or duck, trout, salmon, etc.* [That is how the *demi-sec* was served at the château.]

4. *Roll duck livers and blanched bacon strips in a cabbage leaf. Steam. Don't overcook. Add a little walnut oil, a pinch of coarse salt and black pepper. All the flavors are together in each bite.*

$5.95 PER BOTTLE $64.26 PER CASE

1978 CAHORS · COTEAUX DE LABOURIÈRE

The legendary black wine of Cahors! Rather a tantalizing description, but who has ever seen one poured? Hoping to corner the tannin-freak market, I hacked my way through the jungles of France to little-known Cahors. And indeed, finally, before my very eyes, I marveled to behold the black wine, black as ink, poured into the glass. Unfortunately, it tasted like ink, a primitive, unfriendly, bitter wine. The *proprietaire* clinked glasses with me, smiled proudly, and revealed the hoariest set of jagged, purplish black tooth remnants imaginable—then, introduced to the wife, I was horrified to see an identical set of rotten stubs unveiled by *her* friendly smile. Not wishing to be the first wine merchant to suffer a malpractice suit, I passed up the black wine of Cahors and decided to settle for something merely dark purple.

It can be served in the same gastronomic situations as Bordeaux wines, but it is better wine than similarly priced Bordeaux.

$4.95 PER BOTTLE $53.46 PER CASE

Entrance to Chave's cellar

1978 HERMITAGE
J. L. CHAVE

MY APRIL buying trip convinced me that in the string of four successful Rhône vintages (1976, 1977, 1978, and 1979) it is the 1978 that shines the brightest. There will be exceptions, of course—as always, one can point to the individual winemaker who succeeded more brilliantly in one vintage than another, but speaking generally 1978 looks like the finest Rhône vintage since 1971.

The best wines have everything. They are big, dark-colored, full-flavored wines, generous already but clearly destined for greater heights with proper cellaring. But they have more than size and weight—they do not lack, indeed they enjoy, immense flavor interest—not always the case in a big Rhône vintage.

It is well understood by now that Rhônes are smart buys today. But even putting value aside, the 1978s are great wines. I place Chave's Hermitage at the very pinnacle of the vintage, and if his wines had to sell at the same price as the great Bordeaux and Burgundies, I'd still be advising you to buy them because of their grand class.

The 1978 Hermitage *blanc* shows ripe fruit, yet it is dry and fine. It has a fullness and the solid structural framework to carry it for decades. It also has the elegance, form, and delicacy of flavor to complement great cuisine. I have an advantage over most readers because I've enjoyed several old vintages of Chave's Hermitage *blanc*—the '52 and '42 are particular favorites. I know how they develop over the years, gaining an incredibly deep golden color, an opulent honey-almond aroma, an awesome richness and viscosity on the palate. One thinks of the great Sauternes, but of course Chave's wine is perfectly dry. Highest possible recommendation!

The 1978 Hermitage *rouge* is quite tannic with big flavors to match. It is the quality of the flavor that amazes me. You will discover elements of cassis, black pepper, raspberry, wild herbs and flowers, ripe plum, etc. Chave says he hikes often because he likes to fish and hunt for food, and his 1978 reminds him of a walk through the local countryside with the different aromas of wildflowers and herbs filling the air. It is not a single flavor or aroma; it is an orchestration of flavors. Unbelievable! I'm not in the habit of finding exotic flavor associations in wines, but here it is striking. A remarkable wine!

$150.00 PER CASE (FIFTHS, TENTHS, OR MAGNUMS)

HENRI JAYER
VITICULTEUR À VOSNE-ROMANÉE
(CÔTE D'OR)

A CLIENT POINTED at the two or three stacks of red Burgundy in the shop and asked, "You used to specialize in Burgundy, didn't you?"

I've spent more time tasting in Burgundy than in all other wine regions put together. Burgundy remains the king of wines in my vinous aristocracy. If you ask me, I specialize in Burgundy.

However, I'm choosier than I used to be. Certainly this is a logical consequence of the formidable prices in Burgundy. The wine in the bottle must be worth its price no matter what it says on the label. But at the same time, discovering the wines of Hubert de Montille in Volnay changed my aesthetic approach to Burgundy. Sloppy vinification and dishonest wines *bug* me. I'd rather drink de Montille's simple, flawless Bourgogne *rouge* than a chaptalized, filtered (and often stretched) *grand cru*. Because, as a favorite California vintner from Forestville put it, "de Montille doesn't screw 'em up!"

All this to introduce a new hero, Henri Jayer of Vosne-Romanée, the most important discovery I've made in Burgundy since de Montille. Jayer shows a passion, intelligence, and integrity similar to de Montille's but works with *crus* from the Côte de Nuits such as Beaumonts and Richebourg.

Each *cru* tastes different. He doesn't manipulate them to impose a "house style." His Échezeaux has that thick, exquisite Échezeaux stink. The Nuits has a toasty, earthier complexity. He allows the character of the *cru* to express itself. When buying Burgundy, it is, after all, the character of the *cru*—the personality imparted by that specific piece of earth—that one is paying for. One hopes it has not been filtered out or sugared over.

Jayer's wines are not filtered; they are fined lightly with egg whites. They are raised in new oak. They show no chaptalization (sugaring to increase body and alcohol). Consequently the wines are alive; flavors are not masked; the structure of tannin and acid is not at all obscured. One luxuriates in the flavor of the Pinot Noir fruit, the nobility of the *terroir*, and the subtle, toasty quality imparted by the oak—the ingredients from which Burgundy *should* be made.

1978 will take its place among the great Burgundy vintages. *Gault Millau* says there hasn't been anything comparable since 1961. Its characteristics when vinified successfully—a perfect balance unmatched in the decade, an intensity of flavor in the class of 1961 and 1971, power and finesse together. They will provide enormous pleasure for many years.

PER CASE

1978 *Vosne-Romanée* $240.00
      The perfect Vosne-Romanée, full-bodied, generous, long.

1978 *Nuits-Saint-Georges "Murgers"* 336.00
      A *premier cru* on the Vosne-Romanée side of Nuits-Saint-Georges.
      On the same level of the hill with Malconsorts, La Tâche, and
      Richebourg . . . and it shows it.

1978 *Vosne-Romanée "Beaumonts"* 372.00
From 47-year-old vines. Powerful, tannic, endless aftertaste.

1978 *Échezeaux* 480.00
From 55-year-old vines. Six-bottle maximum per customer.

1978 *Richebourg* $70.00
All finesse, yet with enormous flavors. A classic "peacock's tail"
finish. Three-bottle maximum per customer.

1978 MEURSAULTS
DOMAINE FRANÇOIS JOBARD

To those familiar with François Jobard's past successes, with the 1978s you will find a vintage to match his enviable talent.

1978 MEURSAULT

Full-blown aroma. Mouth-filling, rich texture. Typical, classic, definitive Meursault. Full-bodied and full-flavored, but does not lack subtlety or delicacy. In my opinion, the finest Meursault *villages* he has produced.

$140.00 PER CASE

1978 MEURSAULT-BLAGNY

Blagny is a special favorite of those in the wine trade in Burgundy. The small rectangular vineyard, high on the hill between Puligny-Montrachet and Meursault, with stonier soil, is tilted toward the sun as if it had been designed by a vigneron. Blagny has some of the austerity and acidity of a Chablis and is always firmer, more reticent than other Meursaults when young. It must be aged four to five years before it reveals its qualities. The 1978 is of this style, but, typical of its vintage, it is fleshier than usual. Still, it is for those with cellars to await the blossoming.

$158.00 PER CASE

1978 MEURSAULT "PORUZOTS"

I was struck by the perfect marriage of fruit and oak here. The nose has that intriguing bread-in-the-oven aroma that starts the mouth watering. Perhaps the most opulent of the bunch, it will be good young, old, and in between.

$190.00 PER CASE

1978 MEURSAULT "GENEVRIÈRES"

Jobard, observing the blissful expression on my face as I tasted this wine, commented shyly that 1978 was especially kind to his Genevrières. Yes! Limit one case per customer.

$210.00 PER CASE

1978 BLAGNY *ROUGE* "LA-PIÈCE-SOUS-LE-BOIS"

His only Pinot Noir. I cannot imagine that it won't make a remarkable old wine. It is already remarkable: tannic, spicy, peppery, intensely aromatic and flavorful, easy to love.

$180.00 PER CASE

PUBLIC SERVICE ANNOUNCEMENT

OUR LAST SHIPMENT from France came in a refrigerated container as a safeguard against possible summer heat damage. But we got more than we hoped for. All the wines arrived tasting exactly as they did in the French cellars. No travel sickness whatever. Even the sensitive red Burgundies from de Montille, which in the past have required 6 to 12 months to recuperate from the voyage, taste perfect right off the boat. Believing it to be worth the extra 8 to 10¢ per bottle cost, from now on all our wines will be shipped in isotherm containers. Hopefully we need no longer say, "It's a great wine but you shouldn't taste it yet."

NEW ARRIVALS FROM BURGUNDY

1979 BOURGOGNE ALIGOTÉ · A. & P. DE VILLAINE

This Aligoté will be the finest you've tasted, and I can explain why. Before de Villaine blended his cuvées, I tasted through them and selected two barrels that were extraordinarily superb. Two barrels, the entire production of a tiny 70-year-old vineyard. The sappy juice was barrel-fermented and completely un-chaptalized. I requested that he bottle it unfiltered. Nothing added, nothing taken out. Depth, balance, a striking nose of fresh pear and pear skin, and a small price for perfection.★

$6.75 PER BOTTLE $72.90 PER CASE

★ *I still consider de Villaine's 1979 the finest Aligoté I have tasted.*

See Adventures on the Wine Route, *page 223.*

1977 CHÂTEAU DE MONTHÉLIE

Go ahead, believe the vintage charts and generalizers who warn against 1977 red Burgundies. Miss this lovely wine, the best dollar value in Pinot Noir I've found of late, with its nose of wild strawberry and undergrowth, its delicacy, balance, and just plain fineness. I don't know why, but de Suremain has a history of succeeding in questionable vintages, such as his 1973, still developing toward peak maturity. Combat Vintage Chart Mentality!

$9.95 PER BOTTLE $107.46 PER CASE

1978 BOURGOGNE PASSETOUTGRAIN
DOMAINE DE MONTILLE

Because de Montille produced only three barrels (around 70 cases) of Bourgogne *rouge* in 1978, he decided to blend it with a splendid batch of Gamay grown just below Meursault. Such a blend, one part Pinot Noir to two parts Gamay, is called Passetoutgrain. De Montille's is a vividly purplish wine; to see it splash into the glass is only the beginning of a great vinous experience. Powerful fruit aroma and flavors, with exactly the right balance of new Limousin oak. An intense wine with a strong, one-of-a-kind personality and an endless aftertaste.

$8.95 PER BOTTLE $96.66 PER CASE

1978 FIXIN "LES HERVELETS"
DOMAINE CRUSSEREY

French winemakers often use the word *baie* (berry) instead of grape. A look at the color of this undervalued *premier cru* shows why—it is such a brilliant bluish red you might think it had been pressed from boysenberries. And the winemakers like to use the word *joli* (pretty) to compliment certain wines. This Fixin is the sort of wine they'd call *très joli* because of its color and the abundant fruit from start to finish. Underneath the pretty surface one can see the perfect tannin/acid balance that will support its evolution into something grander and more profound with age.

$13.50 PER BOTTLE $145.80 PER CASE

◇　◇　◇　◇　◇　◇　◇

1978 SAINT-JOSEPH *ROUGE*
RAYMOND TROLLAT

You don't have to be rich to cellar a great wine. The appellation Saint-Joseph consists of 300 acres of vines across the Rhône from Hermitage. Like Hermitage, it is produced from Syrah. But there are Saint-Josephs and Saint-Josephs, Syrahs and Syrahs. It is indisputable that great wine can be made from Syrah only if it is grown on steep, granitic hillsides such as one finds at Hermitage and Côte Rôtie. I have tasted many Syrahs from farther south, grown on the plain, and they were without exception dumb, heavy, tannic wines. They lack the exquisite perfume, the strength *with* finesse that characterizes great Syrah. As you might have guessed, Trollat's Saint-Joseph vineyard is on a steep, terraced hillside with granitic soil overlooking the Rhône across from Hermitage. There are only three or four growers of Hermitage who produce better wine than Trollat's Saint-Joseph. Yet the price difference is dramatic. Imagine, then, a beautiful Hermitage-like red at $7.95.

$7.95 PER BOTTLE $85.86 PER CASE

1978 CÔTE RÔTIE "CÔTE BRUNE"
MARIUS GENTAZ

Old-style Côte Rôtie—in fact, the man's winemaking equipment belongs in a museum. Everything characteristic of Côte Rôtie is here in abundance. Dark-colored; a scent I will describe as thick; quite tannic but I believe admirably balanced. It is rather a hard one that, except for those who like to chew their wines, will take a decade to start coming around.

$150.00 PER CASE

THREE NEW
WINE DOMAINES

ROBERT CHEVILLON AT NUITS-SAINT-GEORGES

After Beaune, Nuits-Saint-Georges boasts the largest collection of *négociants* and large-scale wine firms in Burgundy. But this great wine town also has a warren of ancient cellars hidden beneath its old stone houses, small *caves* like that of Robert Chevillon, who produces only a few barrels each of five or six Nuits-Saint-Georges *premiers crus*. One could live in N.S.G. a year, I'm sure, and never find everyone who makes wine there. So, how to find something special with only a limited time to search? Luckily, two favorite winemakers (de Montille of Volnay and Roty of Gevrey-Chambertin)—and Becky Wasserman—told me independently of one another that Chevillon is one of the top vignerons in N.S.G. today.

The feeling of his *cave* and the taste of his wine turns one to thoughts about old-style Burgundian vinification. The wines have a somber aspect, a funky, earthy quality, a fruitiness not fresh and berry-like, but deeper, more complicated—I want to use words like herbaceous, *marc*-like, but without their negative connotations.

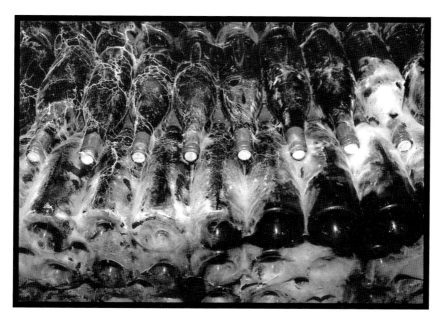

Chez Robert Chevillon

The wine recalls the cellar in which it was reared: the moist subterranean air; the raw wood smell of the new barrels; a pervasive vinosity.

Two *premiers crus* from 1977 have arrived: Nuits Les Cailles and Les Vaucrains.

$16.95 PER BOTTLE $183.00 PER CASE

RENÉ LOYAU AT VOUVRAY

Dry Vouvray, sweet Vouvray, and sparkling Vouvray, in an assortment of vintages from 1971 to 1978, made by a grand old personage in his 80s, who, when he speaks of wine, speaks poetry. One intriguing point—Loyau claims that Chardonnay and Chenin Blanc (*Pineau de la Loire*) were once identical. Over the cen-

turies, through a process of adaptation to their terrains and climates, quiddity evolved. Indeed, tasting his 1978 dry Vouvray I thought what an interesting prelude to a great Meursault it would make. His wines are a pristine expression of fruit and *terroir* with only one drawback—Loyau would part with no more than 60 bottles of any single wine.

ASSORTED PRICES

LAMÉ-DELILLE-BOUCARD AT BOURGUEIL

My favorite California Cabernet was home winemaker Norman Mini's blend of Cabernet Sauvignon and Cabernet Franc. Château Figeac, another favorite, is composed largely of the two types. Maybe the two varietals like each other. This 1975 Bourgueil is roughly a 50–50 blend of the two Cabernets. A dark, intense wine, lean, richly textured, briary. Flavors are still enveloped by tannin, but one perceives black currants and dead leaves. The wine is loaded, but don't pull that trigger yet—it will have a remarkable evolution in bottle. Instead of yet another Zinfandel or Cabernet Sauvignon, find a place in your cellar for this marvelous wine.

$7.95 PER BOTTLE $85.86 PER CASE

◊ ◊ ◊ ◊ ◊ ◊ ◊ ◊

1978 BANDOL *ROUGE* · DOMAINE TEMPIER

Were I asked by an Eskimo, "What is a Domaine Tempier?" this is the bottle I would uncork because the 1978 is so typical and so perfect an expression of Tempier's unique qualities. The color is deep and pretty, very much like the dark cherries that grow around Bandol. While certainly full-bodied and loaded with flavor (Provençal herbs, plum, black cherry), the wine is not fat, heavy, or overladen with tannin. It's like a lean, muscular dancer, handsomely attired. The Gene Kelly of wines? A cross between a black cherry and Gene Kelly? Were I tried and convicted (because of that last sentence) and condemned to live out my life with only one bottle of wine per week, I'd probably choose one of the great red Burgundies, but were I sentenced to the same wine each day, day after day, I'd choose this one.

$9.95 PER BOTTLE $107.46 PER CASE

1979 CHINON ROSÉ · CHARLES JOGUET

Joguet says this has a chance to be the finest rosé he's produced, but I cannot comment because it was still fermenting when I tasted it. Tasting notes: "stinky, gassy, succulent." I bought it because I've learned to heed Joguet's advice and in order to satisfy my abnormally sophisticated clientele, which, having quaffed down Joguet's 1977 and 1978, has been clamoring for more.

$4.75 PER BOTTLE $51.30 PER CASE

1978 BORDEAUX *ROUGE* · CHÂTEAU MAZEAU

There is a school of "substitute" wine propaganda: *"This Mâcon has the buttery, oaky blah-blah of a Meursault,"* or *"This Napa Chardonnay has the elegance and balance of a first-rate Chassagne."*

Speaking for myself, I want my Mâcon to taste like Mâcon, provided it is a good one. But in a propaganda piece like this, with a bargain-priced 1978 red Bordeaux to sell, the way to sell it would be: *Pitch-black color. Huge bouquet. Enor-*

mous body. You could eat this wine! Heaps of tannin. The overproduction of Château Latour.

Château Mazeau is actually a very pleasant red Bordeaux from a fine vintage. I wish it were a $3.99 Château Latour, but . . . it is cleanly vinified with the pretty fruit and impeccable balance that signals the 1978 vintage. What can one say? It drinks well, it's Bordeaux, and it's cheap. Recommended!

$3.99 PER BOTTLE $43.09 PER CASE

CHÂTEAU DU TRIGNON

RHÔNE WINE. It's badly said.
There are the northern Rhônes, where the Syrah makes the reds, and the Viognier, Marsanne, and Roussanne make the whites. The quantity produced is miniscule.

And there is the southern Rhône, a vast alluvial plain—vines as far as the eye can see.

Like a painter who chooses his surface, and who mixes the pigments on his palette to create different colors, the winemaker of the southern Rhône has a variety of soils and up to 22 permitted grape varieties with which to work. From this amalgam he can create anything from the noble to the ignoble.

The soils are complex. *Alluvial* refers to the soil deposit of a stream where it issues from a gorge onto an open plain. The Rhône River deposited mineral de-

The Dentelles de Montmirail

bris from the Alps ranging from sand to large round stones that soak up and throughout the night emit the warmth of the Provençal sun.

To find something special one must know innumerable wines and behind the wine the man who makes it. Is he serious? Honest? Are his methods intelligent? And how much does he respect his soil and his vines, because the first step toward making good wine is deciding which grape to grow in which soil. A wise choice will give the wine character; a poor choice and the wine will lack interest no matter which method of vinification is employed.

At Château du Trignon I discovered a vigneron with a deep commitment to quality. One day he guided me through the vineyards of Rasteau, near Gigondas, and pointed out the variety of soils within that single appellation. The changes from one type to another were vividly apparent, streaks of sand, riverbed stone, clay, etc. Most vignerons at Rasteau grow Grenache no matter what soil they have to work with. Monsieur Roux at Trignon yanked out the Grenache vines that had been growing in the stony parcels of land and replaced them with Mourvèdre, the ancient vine of Spanish origin that produces such marvels at Bandol's Domaine Tempier. Mourvèdre gives less quantity than Grenache, but the vine responds to the superior drainage and heat-retentive qualities of a stony soil and yields not glug-glug but wine to satisfy the most demanding palate.

Begin your acquaintance of Trignon's superior Rhône wines with these 1978s. All are estate-bottled. All are flawlessly vinified. They are wines of individuality, each with its pronounced style and personality. And, hardest to say, but most important, they possess a depth and diversity of flavors that are fascinating and remain fascinating bottle after bottle.

		PER BOTTLE	PER CASE
1978	Côtes du Rhône Blanc (Grand Prix Mâcon)	$4.50	$48.60
1978	Côtes du Rhône Rouge (Gold Medal Mâcon)	3.99	43.09
1978	Rasteau Rouge	4.95	53.46
1978	Gigondas	6.25	67.50

⋄ ⋄ ⋄ ⋄ ⋄ ⋄ ⋄ ⋄

1978 CHÂTEAUNEUF-DU-PAPE
DOMAINE DU VIEUX TÉLÉGRAPHE

In *Wines of the Rhône* by Livingstone-Learmonth and Master you will find this description of Domaine du Vieux Télégraphe:

> *This domaine draws its name from a site on the plateau near Bédarrides where in 1793 Chappe, the inventor of the optical telegraph system, built a tower to help him in his experiments. The 95-acre vineyard is now the property of Henri Brunier, who makes one of the finest of all Châteauneuf-du-Papes, a wine that is always splendidly full-bodied and well-balanced.*

I've had the fortune to taste the 1978 several times. It is a black, strong wine, with a firm structure of tannin and acid.

The soil at Vieux Télégraphe—well, you can't see the soil for the stones. The spectacular stony terrain gives the wine of Vieux Télégraphe complex aromatic and flavor components. It is not merely fruity like the wine from richer soils.

The 1978 is that rarity, an enormous wine yet a fine wine because of its balance and complexity. It should reach its summit in 10 to 20 years.*

$96.00 PER CASE

*Twenty-five years later, it is still at its peak.

1979 SANCERRE · DOMAINE GITTON

There are countless good Sancerres, but I always end up buying Gitton's, even though his are slightly more expensive than the others. There are three reasons.

First, his is from a slow fermentation in oak casks, and that is rare in Sancerre today. All his wine-making implements are of wood, and Gitton uses neither chemicals nor fertilizers in his vineyard. Everything combines to produce a very natural wine.

Second, Sancerre is a hilly little spot with a great variety of soils (flint, chalk, limestone, etc.). The *père* Gitton is foremost a man of the soil, who understands and makes a virtue of that variety; he keeps the wine from his different parcels separate in order to preserve, from each, its distinctive *goût de terroir*.

Third, his Sancerre tastes better than the others!

You might be surprised to hear that his 1979s are the finest we've imported, including his 1976 and 1978. The 1978s were perfect, easy, generous wines. The 1979s have more race, more breed. They are more intellectual wines because the personality imparted by each *terroir* has more clarity and depth.

Sancerre "Les Belles Dames"
$8.50 PER BOTTLE $91.80 PER CASE

Sancerre "Les Romains"
$8.95 PER BOTTLE $96.66 PER CASE

⊹1981⊹

1979 BORDEAUX *BLANC* · LAURENT MAZEAU

BELIEVE ME, we are not out to attract the cheap wine crowd. However, for some of us wine is a beverage drunk at mealtime. Those who know and love wine shouldn't have to fork over 10 bucks every time food appears on the table. Here's a pleasant, drinkable Sauvignon Blanc from Bordeaux at $2.89.

$2.89 PER BOTTLE $31.21 PER CASE

1978 MONTHÉLIE · COCHE-DURY

Fifteen cartons available from a young winemaker in Meursault from whom you will taste great things over the coming years. His Monthélie—well, sometimes one becomes depressed and imagines that wines like this no longer exist. Vivid deep color. Tannic, hard-edged. An intense, one might say "wild" (in the sense of untamed) Pinot Noir with great character and style. Peppery with wild currant . . . perhaps.

$14.95 PER BOTTLE $161.46 PER CASE

CHÂTEAUNEUF-DE-PAPE
DOMAINE DU HAUT
DES TERRES BLANCHES

WITH DOMAINE DE BEAURENARD and Vieux Télégraphe already on our list, why this third Châteauneuf domaine?

Well, its price, for one thing. When I saw his prices I had to keep my mouth from falling open in shock, lest he revise them upward on the spot.

And the wine is not like our other two domaines. To use a Beethoven analogy, if Vieux Télégraphe inspires comparison to the Fifth Symphony and Beaurenard to the Seventh, Haut des Terres Blanches is more like the Adagio from one of the late quartets. It is serious, dignified, less showy, and one must flatter it with a little more attention in order to penetrate its depths.

Diffonty himself, the winemaker, is extremely serious and meticulous. He possesses a critical attitude toward his wines that I find missing at some of the more famous domaines, where the winemakers have become spoiled by an abundance of accolades and think that anything they do is wonderful.

Accompanied by Jean-Marie Peyraud, winemaker at Domaine Tempier, we tasted through each vintage back to 1971, often sampling different cuvées from the same vintage. I selected the following three wines.

1978

A cuvée that includes 20% Mourvèdre (the grape of Domaine Tempier) from 50-year-old vines. Color deep, regal. Full of taste and richness but will need time in the bottle before the nose develops and blossoms. Recommended to those with facilities for aging.

$6.95 PER BOTTLE $75.06 PER CASE

1977

Many presume 1977 was weak because it was less than kind to the other wine regions of France. Connoisseurs in the southern Rhône are enthusiastic, however, because in their '77s all the components of the wines are distinctly in view—the aromatic and flavor qualities imparted by each varietal, the *goût de terroir*, the structure of acid and tannin, and the harmony of all the parts. Is there a word "typicity"?

It is a vintage for those who taste closely. Those with Vintage Chart Mentality will ignore the 1977 Rhônes, but in fact, in the south, it is a better vintage than 1976. I bought Diffonty's '77, even though his 1976 was available at the same price.

$6.75 PER BOTTLE $72.90 PER CASE

1974

Nose very complex. Old leather, apricot, earth. The structure and focus of hillside vines. Fine, mature, a look at the best qualities of Châteauneuf-du-Pape.

$9.95 PER BOTTLE $107.46 PER CASE

∘ ∘ ∘ ∘ ∘ ∘ ∘ ∘ ∘

1979 ENTRE-DEUX-MERS · CHÂTEAU PLESSIS

The price and appellation suggest the merely drinkable, at best a decent crisp, dry white. But hopefully you will agree that Château Plessis has more going for it. It is *not* bland, there's a lusty, *joie de vivre* quality to it—it would be good drunk from a tankard. It's what the peasants are drinking in that happy Breughel.

It is a firm, solid wine, fresh and nervy. It suggests springtime, fresh-mown grass, picnics, a bottle pulled from an icy stream . . .

$3.75 PER BOTTLE $40.50 PER CASE

DOMAINE SAINT-APOLLINAIRE
F. DAUMAS

IT MAKES GOOD sense to listen closely when a great winemaker recommends another. Both Chave at Hermitage and André Roux of Château du Trignon told me about Daumas. In fact, the three of them along with E. Guigal meet often to taste and offer constructive criticism for each other's wines.

Daumas has some strong ideas about winemaking that I don't yet fully understand. We've not had a chance to talk at length. But it's not far off the mark to call them "organic" wines—he opposes the use of pesticides and herbicides in his vineyard, and he disdains unnatural elements when vinifying. He sent me a laboratory analysis of each wine that included a new category, to my experience: *Résidus de Pesticides . . . Absence.*

But the wines themselves. In terms of style and character, these wines are set apart from anything else I have tasted. Not merely clean, they are pristine. They are Rhônes, yet almost delicate in terms of body. The flavors are strong and fine and they persist, and the reds have plenty of tannin.

By way of exaggeration to make the point, it is almost as if everything had been refined out of the wine except the most important part, the flavors and the character.

1979 BLANC DE BLANCS

Clean, ripe fruit. A delicate aroma that will drive Rhône lovers to drink. Very dry, fine, long. One could drink quantities of this without fatigue. Serve cool, not icy.

$4.95 PER BOTTLE $53.46 PER CASE

1978 RÉSERVE DU DOMAINE

A cuvée with a high percentage of Mourvèdre. Very fine, exquisite perfume. Mouth-filling but lean, muscular, no heaviness or fat. (Now how did he do that?) Beautifully flavored. Open two hours before serving, according to the winemaker.

$4.50 PER BOTTLE $48.60 PER CASE

1978 CUVÉE D'APOLLINE

Syrah-style nose. The finesse of the northern Rhône! One senses in these wines a new aesthetic, a glimpse into the future, perhaps.

$4.95 PER BOTTLE $53.46 PER CASE

◇ ◇

THE CASE OF THE CICERON ROUGE

MEXICO, WOMEN, don't tell me about it. I wear the scars, I don't need no lecture.

There was nothing to do but put the torch to the charcoal and run out to the meat man. I didn't know how I was going to do it, but I had to convince him I deserved his best cut.

Then to San Pablo for some vino. I slid a ten across the counter and said, "Wine me up, son."

"This one's got a great color," the counterman said, "really dark, really deep. And the complex aroma is dominated by Cabernet Sauvignon—it's sort of plummy, berry-like, with hints of freshly ground pepper like you get in a lot of these southern wines. It's a sensual, earthy wine. It shows good body . . ."

I didn't want to hear nothin' about no body. I grabbed the red, six in change, and cleared out with him yappin' about subsoil.

Nursed it past midnight. I was sorry to see it go.

Next day I counted coin. No sweat. I went back for a case of the scarlet water they call Ciceron. A class act.

$3.99 PER BOTTLE $43.09 PER CASE

MUSCAT DE BEAUMES-DE-VENISE
DOMAINE DE DURBAN

You may have noticed a good number of new Rhône domaines in this brochure. For those of you who don't keep up on these sorts of things, we have the finest list of estate-bottled Rhônes in Albany, California.

There are only five producers of the luscious Muscat in the village of Beaumes-de-Venise, and we import two of them.

Little known even in France, this is a wine that does take some arm-twisting in order to sell that first bottle. But the wine is so dramatically good, so unmistakably delicious, that only a real Scrooge could disdain it.

When I say delicious, I mean delicious like the best fresh peach you ever had, or the best strawberries, or that perfectly ripe watermelon on the hottest day of summer. Delicious!

When we mention that it is sweet we often hear the response, with nose scrunched up, "But I don't *like* sweet wines." Morgan and George then wrestle me into the straitjacket as I scream YQUEM, TROCKENBEERENAUSLESE, etc.

Two important facts about this ravishing wine:

1. *It has no relation to Muscadet, Muscatel, or Moscato Amabile.*

2. *It is about as sweet as a Sauternes, which makes it a good dessert wine, or try it as an interesting summer apéritif.*

$7.95 PER BOTTLE $85.86 PER CASE

TRIGNON'S RASTEAU

THERE WAS a lengthy piece on Château de Trignon in the November brochure. Since then their Rasteau 1978 has been our best-selling red Rhône. We've just received more of that 1978, a vintage to cellar, and 50 cartons of the 1974, a vintage at peak maturity, meaning that all the wine's components are in harmony and the aroma and flavors have developed to full potential.

Regular clients are aware of the work I've done in the little-known wine villages of the southern Rhône, villages like Cairanne, Lirac, Beaumes-de-Venise, etc. Châteauneuf-du-Pape and Gigondas have solidly established reputations—there's nothing to prove there, no arm-twisting to lead someone into the unknown. But in the nearby villages the grapes are the same, normally, and the prices are lower, normally, and one hopes there to find a wine with the interest and personality of the more famous growths.

The Château du Trignon's Rasteau is to me so far the culmination of that research. (And oh, what a jolly research it has been!)

It is best described as a cross between Paul Coulon's Domaine de Beaurenard Châteauneuf-du-Pape and Domaine Tempier's Bandol, but I realize that few have the tasting experience to conjure up such a blend in their mind.

The 1974 has lost its youthful fruit, though the color shows no sign of age. The aroma is opened up, it can be "read" and perceived like words on a page. There is a trace of old leather in the aroma, a characteristic of the 1974 Rhônes that one can detect in the 1967s too. On the palate it is a wine to savor, to notice.

1978 (to cellar)

$4.95 PER BOTTLE $53.46 PER CASE

1974 (to drink)

$5.95 PER BOTTLE $64.26 PER CASE

◇ ◇

THE 1979 VINTAGE IN BURGUNDY

THE WHITES are very good, sometimes excellent. Like the 1974 white Burgundies, they were attractive right from the start, and will conserve well.

For the reds it is more complicated. One sees one style in the Côte de Beaune and a completely different style in the Côte de Nuits. This is explained by the severe hailstorm in early June 1979 that literally stripped the growth from the vines in Nuits-Saint-Georges and Vosne-Romanée and, to a lesser extent, farther north. I arrived two days after the hailstorm and saw the awesome damage, which cannot be exaggerated.

The problem with the quality of the reds (and this is what the vintage chart manufacturers may glom onto) was the overproduction in the Côte de Beaune, and the resulting lack of concentration. There the vintage is reminiscent of 1973. However, some impressive reds were produced from old vines, as you will see later in the year.

In the Côte de Nuits the hailstorm rather drastically solved any problems of overproduction. There is very little wine, but what there is tends to be dark, intense, sometimes a little hard, but perfectly healthy, balanced, and desirable.

1978 RULLY *BLANC PREMIER CRU* · B. DE SUREMAIN

Don't enter this in your blind tasting because it will surely lose to the Arapajo Wild Cedar Blossom Canyon Creek Mountain Chardonnay (at 15° alcohol, tasters call it "Montrachet-like"). The Rully is not a showy wine. It is subtle, a wine of nuance that belongs on the table with cuisine. There is a hint (hints never win blind tastings) of vanilla bean in the Chardonnay fruit; a first impression of mouth-filling viscosity followed by a perfect chalky dryness. For those who prefer a tender caress to a punch in the nose.

$9.95 PER BOTTLE $107.46 PER CASE

DOMAINE FRANÇOIS JOBARD

FROM THE FIRST TASTE, in November 1979, Jobard's 1979 Meursaults have reminded me of his '74s. What wines those are now! And I underestimated them, cellared too few, and now, when they are at their peak, I must be miserly about pulling their corks.

Jobard's 1979s are flawless, lovely things, imbued with the succulence of perfectly ripe Chardonnay and the toasty impression imparted by vinification in oak.

One almost takes for granted the breed and finesse in Jobard's wines; it is overlooked because of the ravishing flavors. On closer look his wines seem fashioned, almost sculpted, by one who possesses a great aesthetic sensibility.

1979 MEURSAULT

A blend of Les Tillets and La Barre. Beat this price for great Meursault!

$120.00 PER CASE (FIFTHS AND TENTHS)

1979 MEURSAULT-BLAGNY

High up the slope between Puligny-Montrachet and Meursault. Especially generous and supple in 1979.

$145.00 PER CASE (FIFTHS AND MAGNUMS)

1979 MEURSAULT "PORUZOTS"

Will win the tastings because as usual it is the toastiest, the most showy and dramatic.

$180.00 PER CASE (FIFTHS AND TENTHS)

1979 MEURSAULT "CHARMES"

Along with the Genevrières, the best ager. Limit six bottles per customer.

$220.00 PER CASE (FIFTHS ONLY)

1979 MEURSAULT "GENEVRIÈRES"

A Meursault for the great occasions; complete, grand.

$190.00 PER CASE (FIFTHS AND MAGNUMS)

◦ ◦ ◦ ◦ ◦ ◦ ◦ ◦

1979 SAINT-JOSEPH *ROUGE* · TROLLAT

Gérard Chave, who makes *the* Hermitage, accompanied me to Trollat's rustic cellar. On that date there was no single cuvée of Trollat Saint-Joseph *rouge*—the casks had not been blended. So we tasted each cask, found a tremendous diversity, proceeded to taste each in various combination, and created our own mélange. No, not quite true. We disagreed at length as an amused Monsieur Trollat looked on in silent neutrality. I wanted a higher proportion of the most peppery, tannic barrel. Chave said, "*C'est votre goût Californien.*" As I was the one paying the bill, my view prevailed, for better or worse. The final cuvée is *very* fruity, fine, elegant, peppery, and tannic, much better than any of the separate cuvées. It exhibits the finest qualities of the noble Syrah.

$7.95 PER BOTTLE $85.86 PER CASE

VIN DE PAYS *ROUGE*

DOMAINE DE LA GAUTIÈRE–PAUL TARDIEU

Monsieur Tardieu loves his little piece of earth east of Vaison-la-Romaine in the southern Rhône. He possesses an amphitheatre-shaped hillside property and produces completely chemical-free products like lavender honey, olives, olive oil, a heavenly lavender fragrance, various nuts, fruits and their jams, and, thankfully, grapes. His grapes are transformed into red wine by Frederick Daumas, whose Domaine Saint-Apollinaire is nearby.

The wine possesses all the seductive, heady charm of Provence, the warmth and genuineness of Monsieur Tardieu, and the passionate intensity and attention to detail of Monsieur Daumas.

Its cheap price might tempt you to ignore it. Don't. This is wine you'll enjoy

Georgette and Paul Tardieu, Domaine de la Gautière

again and again and again, whether your budget is tight or unlimited. One of my associates in France told me she tasted the wine recently in Burgundy. "There was a bottle of Chambertin on the table," she confided, "but I drank Monsieur Tardieu's Vin de Pays."

$2.75 PER BOTTLE $29.70 PER CASE

° ° ° ° ° ° ° ° °

1980 CORBIÈRES "GRIS DE GRIS"
DOMAINE DE CICERON

It is a rosé (strike one!) from a little-known region (strike two!) . . . but wait, aren't you curious to know why I bothered? Life would be so much simpler if I stuck to well-known names. It is quite dry, absolutely fresh and delicious, especially during this time of year, and while I have no medical proof, I've noticed a gay, exhilarating effect. The world looks better through rose-colored Corbières? And while you're slurping down bottle after bottle you can laugh at your friends and say, "Hey, man, you're still drinking the same old stuff? Haven't you heard about the Domaine de Ciceron Gris de Gris from Corbières?"

Brave souls will discover an uncommon treat.

$3.75 PER BOTTLE $40.50 PER CASE

◇ ◇

DOMAINE COCHE-DURY

THE WINEMAKER is a young man whose father used to sell all his wine in cask to the Beaune *négociants*. Fortunately, the son has begun to estate-bottle the wines, and their brilliance is no longer dissipated in the *négociants'* blending vats. His wines burst upon the French wine scene with dramatic impact, literally dominating the gold medal awards for Meursault. An exciting collection of white Burgundies!

1979 BOURGOGNE *BLANC*

Perfumed, delicate, lovely nose, which is faintly reminiscent of the flower and fruit aroma of Viognier. Round and stylish.

$8.95 PER BOTTLE $96.66 PER CASE

1979 MEURSAULT

A blend of Narvaux and La Barre. Very fragrant. Strong personality. The French describe a full, viscous wine like this as "big-shouldered." Flavors continue to unfold in the long aftertaste.

$12.50 PER BOTTLE $135.00 PER CASE

Jean-François Coche, Meursault

1979 MEURSAULT "CHARMES"

In this case *Charmes*, or "charming," is an understatement. A showy, flashy Meursault rich with flavor. Three bottles per customer.

$19.95 PER BOTTLE

1979 MEURSAULT "PERRIÈRES"

Awarded the *Tastevinage* label, the Perrières is the serious, profound one: depth, infinite nuance, and a strong, complex, lingering finish. Six bottles per customer.

$19.95 PER BOTTLE

◇ ◇

1979 HERMITAGE · J. L. CHAVE

THE NECK LABEL reads, "winegrowers from father to son since 1481." That's 500 years at Hermitage.

500 YEARS.

I want bugles blasting, flowers strewn, pomp and circumstance, bacchic excess. Why not?

You might think it's grown a little stale after 500 years. Maybe it's time they sold their 18 acres, moved to Lyon, and put their money into condos.

But no, the current winemaker, Gérard Chave, is passionate, talented, honest, and has his eyes fixed on one goal: quality. You couldn't design a better Chave.

Bravo, Gérard! May this be just the beginning.

1979 HERMITAGE *BLANC*

It is delicious, irresistible, and it will improve, so figure this out carefully. You'll want at least a bottle per month, and this is a wine that will outlive most of us—that's a bottle a month for the rest of your life. I'll leave the exact calculation of your needs up to you.

Bright, vivid, golden color. Big bouquet, stuffed full of aromas. Loads of Hermitage/Marsanne character. On the palate, very strong, very fat, powerful, viscous. Tremendous aging potential. Less pretty at the outset, perhaps, than his '78, but more serious, deep, profound. In short, a classic white Hermitage.

1979 HERMITAGE *ROUGE*

Chave's red goes through drastic changes as it ages. When brand-new, his Syrah smells like a big fresh bouquet of wildflowers and wild berries. During my last trip I was surprised when Chave drew off a magnum from his most precocious cask of 1980 and plopped it on the dinner table for starters. What a wild, delicious treat it was.

After 12 to 24 months, ripe fruits dominate—the fruits of the region, logically enough—apricot, plum, cherry, with a noticeable smell and taste of the pit, or seed, of the fruit.

After a few years in bottle a spiciness begins to emerge, ofttimes with a truffly aspect. At all stages there is an impressive complex of smells and flavors.

The 1979 is very rich, with great possibilities for aging. Those without cellars should leave it alone. It is dark purple with an intense, deep nose. In July the pit-fruit stage had commenced.

There is a very intense core to the 1979 that will permit a slow evolution. In fact, Chave says that the distinguishing characteristic of the 1979 red is its perfect tannin. It has plenty of tannin, but it is not a hard, severe tannin. It does not mask the flavors. It permits the best Hermitage of all, one with great strength *and* elegance.

$125.00 PER CASE (FIFTHS, TENTHS, OR MAGNUMS)

◊ ◊ ◊ ◊ ◊ ◊ ◊ ◊

1980 MUSCADET DE SÈVRE-ET-MAINE · A. BRÉGEON

Some wines are to drink, not to ponder over. Muscadet offers enormous pleasures when:

1. *It is correctly vinified. Even a hint of SO_2 masks its charm.*

2. *It is drunk young. So sad to see restaurants serving the "great" 1976 vintage in 1981.*

3. *It accompanies oysters, mussels, crab, sole, practically any seafood that was* not *prepared Mediterranean style with tomato or heavy doses of olive oil.*

Everything was done to safeguard our Muscadet's freshness. Bottled *sur lie* and shipped immediately in an air-conditioned container, all its *nouveau* zest and charm has been preserved.

$3.99 PER BOTTLE $43.09 PER CASE

CHAMPAGNE JULES LASSALLE

I HAVE A FRIEND who believes so strongly in garlic that when she speaks I too become convinced that magical properties thrive within the clove.

That's just my imagination. I don't for a moment believe that objects possess magical powers, but if anything does, garlic does.

And CHAMPAGNE.

When I tasted Jules Lassalle's Champagne I realized that there had always been an ideal Champagne in the back of my mind: a vaguely steely, earthy, gunsmoke; exhilarating and inebriating, cold and full of warmth at the same time, at once luxurious and austere, almost severe, reflecting perhaps the severity of Champagne's northern climate and chalky earth.

As far as I know, this is the first Champagne from a single *propriétaire* available in California. That is to say, Lassalle buys no grapes; he controls his product from the planting and pruning of his vines through the harvest and vinification to putting the sparkling beauty into bottles.

The quality? See for yourself.

1973 CUVÉE ANGELINE

His vintage cuvée from red and white grapes.

$19.95 PER BOTTLE $215.46 PER CASE

1973 BLANC DE BLANCS

100% Chardonnay, gold medal at Epernay.

$24.95 PER BOTTLE $269.46 PER CASE

1975 CHIGNY *ROUGE*

His still red table wine produced from Pinot Noir.

$12.50 PER BOTTLE $135.00 PER CASE

1979 CÔTE RÔTIE · EMILE CHAMPET

Champet, after making a tannic blockbuster in 1978, has fashioned a charming, seductive beauty in 1979. In a face-to-face showdown, your money might at first seem safer on the 1978, but who would have chosen David against Goliath? Champet's 1979 is a dark beauty, just this side of opaque. It is a supple, velvety thing, tannic enough but in a softer, more tender style. Flavor, perfume, and that sensuous texture dominate the taste sensation, not tannin. The aftertaste recalls the initial aromatic impression, full of nuance, delicacy, and that exotic Côte Rôtie stink that drives men to drink.

$135.00 PER CASE

1979 CÔTE RÔTIE "CÔTE BRUNE" · MARIUS GENTAZ

Lovely blackish purple. Deep, thick Côte Rôtie nose with violets and apricot. Full-bodied, lots of warmth and richness. Perfectly balanced for long aging.

There is a tannic hardness at center, so wait a few years before you begin pulling the cork on this one. I love the way Gentaz described this 1979 to George Lang: "like a panther ready to spring."

Almost all the Côte Rôtie growers submit their wines to the judges of the Concours de Paris. Only this won the gold medal.

$150.00 PER CASE

NEW DISCOVERY IN VOLNAY
MICHEL LAFARGE

BECKY WASSERMAN has been telling me about Lafarge for years ("he won't export," she always said), but whenever I went to Volnay it was to see Hubert de Montille. Lafarge is a close neighbor of de Montille's. In fact, when I finally knocked on his door last spring I felt a little guilty standing there within view of de Montille's courtyard.

The two winemakers have very different personalities. True to norm, their wines reflect those differences. To generalize, de Montille has an aristocratic bearing, an almost haughty air of refinement, while Lafarge has dirty hands from toiling in his vineyard.

Lafarge's reds have more body; they're stronger, more intense. They are earthier, less stylized than de Montille's. Like de Montille's wines, however, they show an incredible amount of personality and class.

1979 BOURGOGNE ALIGOTÉ

Brilliant light straw color. Delicate aroma. Supple, delicious, with an unexpected richness for Aligoté.

$5.95 PER BOTTLE $64.26 PER CASE

1979 MEURSAULT

Those searching for blockbusters, please ignore this one. No, don't go away—this is lovely stuff. Our Coche-Dury '79 won the gold medal; this was runner-up with the silver.

It is from a parcel of Meursault named Les Vignes Blanches, which produces a wine with a subtle perfume—not overblown, more refined and delicate. On the palate, a marked *goût de terroir*, Chardonnay fruit, and a light touch of Burgundian oak. A fine wine, to serve when you have the time to savor it.

$12.50 PER BOTTLE $135.00 PER CASE

1979 VOLNAY "CLOS DES CHÊNES"

One of the finest growths in the Côte d'Or. Generous bouquet, full of Pinot Noir fruit and new oak. A sensation of opulence and aristocracy. Snap up one of our 20 cases before they're gone.

$19.95 PER BOTTLE $215.46 PER CASE

1979 BEAUNE "GRÈVES"

Leaner, more severe than the Volnay, less pretty, less seductive; very long, structured, with a marked personality that struck me as a little bizarre and very interesting.

$17.50 PER BOTTLE $189.00 PER CASE

∘ ∘ ∘ ∘ ∘ ∘ ∘ ∘

1979 BOURGOGNE *BLANC* "LES CLOUS" · A. & P. DE VILLAINE

Most wine buyers won't be interested in this because they like to pay a lot more for Chardonnay, but for those to whom price is no object . . . what a fine, delicious bottle of wine. The *Underground Wineletter* rated it a Best Buy, saying it possesses "the style and flavor of wines from the best properties."

$7.50 PER BOTTLE $81.00 PER CASE

DOMAINE TEMPIER'S BANDOL ROSÉ

Over the years I have drunk my share of rosés, domestic and imported. Since most domestic rosés are sweet I have wiped them off my list. There are good imported rosés but the one I love best is that of Domaine Tempier. It drinks like a red wine except for tannin, and has the fullness and richness associated with reds. The flavor of the mourvèdre *grape is there, and the fruit and the cleanness of a superbly made wine. For something that is more than a good summer rosé, Domaine Tempier rosé is my drink.* JOSEPH SWAN, California vintner

OUR BIGGEST single client for Tempier's rosé, barely outdoing Joe Swan, is Chez Panisse Restaurant because Alice Waters loves the wine and recommends it often with her cuisine. Her book, *The Chez Panisse Menu Cookbook*, should appear soon. It quite successfully communicates the spirit of Chez Panisse.

I asked Alice for a little something that would go well with Domaine Tempier's rosé. She responded with this Anchovy Toast recipe:

Cut a thin slice of good bread. Toast it. Rub it with raw garlic. Saturate it with your best olive oil.

Filet an anchovy (packed in salt). Rinse it well. Place the anchovy shiny side up on the bread and broil it under a hot flame until brown. Brush with olive oil. Serve with niçoise olives, basil leaves, dried tomatoes, whatever seems appropriate and handy.

$6.95 PER BOTTLE $75.06 PER CASE

VIETTI

1978 BARBARESCO "MASSERIA"

The ripe, enormously beautiful aroma tells you right away that it's a classic. You don't want to take your nose out of the glass. Dark color; great depth of flavor;

incredible complexity; everything in perfect harmony. And, the Vietti trademark—refined and virile at once.

Cellar a good supply of the 1978 Piedmont reds. As in France, however, quantities are not easy to obtain. The small producers like Vietti are downright stingy. On this Barbaresco we must enforce a six-bottle limit.

$14.95 PER BOTTLE

1978 BARBERA D'ALBA "CASTIGLIONE"

Barbera is usually rough country wine. Not Vietti's. His is fine, deep, round, delicious. It is a 1978 with lovely Barbera grapiness, and belongs in the top rank of Barberas (with, by the way, some lovely old Louis Martini vintages). I repeat, lay in some of these 1978 Piedmont reds. The best wines of the vintage will not be available for long, and it is a vintage people will be talking about more and more.

$5.50 PER BOTTLE $59.40 PER CASE

1979 DOLCETTO D'ALBA

A wine you'll love to drink often. Thank god it's back in stock.

Dolcetto is not sweet! It sounds sweet but it isn't. Yet how could anything so luscious and delicious be *dry*?

See the bee from the label? The artist drew it specifically for Vietti's Dolcetto. In fact, he swapped it for some Vietti Dolcetto. It appears that the bee is lapping up flower nectar, but there is no flower that will put an expression of such blitzed contentment on anyone's face. He's got his proboscis in the Dolcetto!

Vietti's Dolcetto is a robust dry red table wine, so lively and grapey and succulent that you want to drink it in big delicious mouthfuls.

Dolcetto is no good old; the 1979 is at its peak now. Serve cool.

$4.95 PER BOTTLE $53.46 PER CASE

° ° ° ° ° ° ° °

1978 CHIANTI CLASSICO · NITTARDI

The fastest-selling wine in our first shipment from Italy, now back in stock.

Remember the gorgeous label on it, from an ancient tapestry titled "The Effects of Good Government on the Countryside"? Our own benevolent government at first refused to allow us to import the wine, saying, "bared breasts cannot be shown on a wine unless it is a legitimate work of art." Look at the label. Imagine what sort of mentality came up with that statement.

$3.99 PER BOTTLE $43.09 PER CASE

THREE MATURE WHITE BURGUNDIES
ROBERT AMPEAU

WHILE THE French rave justifiably about the 1979 white Burgundies, Monsieur Ampeau shakes his head incredulously at the absurdity of selling them so young. We taste his '79s, then with a sly twinkle in his eye he tells me to wait. He trots off. Where to? To yet another *cave*, I'm certain, one full of treasures that the tax man can't find.

Out he comes, his large, thick hands holding several mold-covered bottles. He pours an opulent, viscous Chardonnay and waits while I sniff and taste.

"What is it?" he asks. He always tests me.

"It is so rich, so full-bodied, it must be the '71 Puligny Combettes."

As usual, I am wrong, which keeps Monsieur Ampeau continually delighted. He shakes his head no. "It is the Combettes . . . 1974."

He is selling the '74s now, the vintage that most reminds me of the '79s. They are at their peak, still guarding a healthy degree of freshness and fruit.

1974 MEURSAULT-BLAGNY

Abundant Meursault character. Good fruit and a vanillin oak quality. At its peak. No hurry.

$15.95 PER BOTTLE $172.26 PER CASE

1974 PULIGNY-MONTRACHET "COMBETTES"

Round, viscous, rich, mature. A textbook Puligny: elegant, silky, luxurious, complete. Highly recommended.

$19.95 PER BOTTLE $215.46 PER CASE

1970 MEURSAULT "PERRIÈRES"

Extremely fine; austere after the Combettes. Lean, long, and firm. Serve when you need an aged white as backdrop for the finest cuisine.

$17.50 PER BOTTLE $189.00 PER CASE

CHAMPAGNE LEGRAS
"BRUT INTÉGRALE"

LAST MONTH WE introduced a Champagne producer who owns and tends his own vines. This month again we have something different, and I think exciting, from the Champagne region.

At Champagne Legras I found a special bottling, their Brut Intégrale, which is made without adding the final *dosage*.

What is the final *dosage*? Best you check Lichine or some other wine book to get the whole story. Briefly, when Champagne referments in the bottle—creating the bubbles—all the sugar is used up. The completely dry Champagne is considered too dry for the average palate. And, of great importance, in a completely dry Champagne any flaw will show up vividly. Sweetness masks faults.

Thus the final *dosage* (the addition of sugar syrup to Champagne before the cork is inserted) is normal procedure in the vinification of sparkling wines.

As far as I know there are only four Champagnes made today without the final *dosage*. I tracked down three of them and selected Legras's Brut Intégrale. It has a clean, unique nose and a total absence of sweetness on the palate. Champagne cannot be drier. It is not at all cloying. One can drink glass after glass of the Brut Intégrale without fatigue. The palate remains fresh and alert to the nuance, the delicate fruit and *terroir* of true Champagne.

$17.50 PER BOTTLE $189.00 PER CASE

✦ 1982 ✦

FAUGÈRES
GILBERT ALQUIER

RESEARCH IN vain for information about the Languedoc (pronounced *long-dock*), the broad swath of southern France starting at the Spanish border that includes Carcassone, Narbonne, and Montpellier. In terms of sheer liquid volume, the largest wine-producing province of France! Where there's smoke there's fire—there had to be something worthwhile happening there.

Plus, the drive from Bordeaux to Provence is too long, so I had to stop somewhere. Why not Faugères, because *Gault Millau* had published an intriguing bit on its red wine, noting the granitic soil, which sets off this wine merchant's Syrah beeper, and its aroma of wildflowers, cassis, and *garrigue. Garrigue* I knew from Bandol. It is the organic forest-floor odor that makes walks in Provence such a charged experience (aromatically speaking), full of dead leaves, wild thyme, and rosemary.

The Languedoc is a rewarding, unspoiled place to tourist unless it's August. There is a savage beauty to it, stark and colorful at once, and the province abounds in medieval fortresses and cathedrals, impossible geological formations, sandy Mediterranean beaches, and great natural cooking.

The cooking is progressively more Provençal as one approaches Marseille, although the most famous dish—indeed, the most famous product of the Languedoc—remains the crusty cassoulet of Toulouse, white beans in a pot with an assortment of meats, hopefully including goose.

Our wine of Faugères is *the* wine to serve if you've been ambitious enough to concoct a cassoulet, but I vouch for it with a variety of hearty foods, including this simple egg dish that I was served for lunch, which turns out to be easy to copy. Preparation takes about twenty minutes.

To serve four:
1 medium-sized eggplant sliced into 8 rounds ¹/₂-inch thick
12 ripe tomatoes, peeled and chopped
16 cloves garlic, peeled and chopped
8 fresh eggs

Sauté the eggplant rounds in olive oil until lightly browned and tender.

Simmer the tomatoes and garlic in olive oil with crushed dried thyme or winter savory.

Fry the eggs in a bit of olive oil. Better undercooked than overcooked.

To serve, place an egg on a slice of eggplant and smother with the tomato sauce.

Far from the vile plonk and glug-glug for which the Midi is infamous, Alquier's Faugères has an unexpected finesse and perfume. It contains 30% Syrah and he's planting more. It is a beautifully vinified wine, and a perfect introduction to the other wines of the Languedoc that will be arriving in the future. As in any wine region, one has to find the talented winemaker.

$3.99 PER BOTTLE $43.09 PER CASE

MARSANNE

Tʜɪs ɪs getting out of hand! Our third Saint-Joseph producer! Although his name, Marsanne, is the name of the grape that produces white Saint Joseph, Monsieur Marsanne makes only red wine, 100% Syrah. Confusing? Monsieur Marsanne makes no Marsanne.

My first taste of his wine was in Burgundy when Aubert de Villaine served the 1977 at lunch in Bouzeron. It was strange to encounter the wine in the land of Pinot Noir and Chardonnay—it had such a strong Rhône personality, rustic enough and smelling of green olive and raspberry. It was as out of place as a penguin on the beach at Waikiki.

Then Gérard Chave, who has given me numerous superb leads on Rhône producers, took me to visit Marsanne's cellar, just down the road from Chave's house in Mauves. Old French wine books always mention Mauves as a favored site for Saint-Joseph.

As you can see, Monsieur Marsanne has some vines on the other side of the Rhône, too, appellation Crozes-Hermitage. His two reds share a similar style: rustic yet fine, honest, with plenty of Syrah fruit. The Crozes is a bit more tannic than his Saint-Josephs. His 1978 is a richer, bigger wine than his 1979, though not quite as pretty and aromatic.

		PER BOTTLE	PER CASE
1978	*Saint-Joseph* Rouge	$7.95	$85.86
1979	*Saint-Joseph* Rouge	6.50	70.20
1979	*Crozes-Hermitage* Rouge	6.95	75.06

° ° ° ° ° ° ° °

1980 CÉPAGE VIOGNIER
DOMAINE SAINT-APOLLINAIRE

Saint-Apollinaire makes the only 100% Viognier I know outside Condrieu and Château Grillet.★ The domaine prides itself on its natural, organic viticulture and vinification, but this wine is a little too natural. There is sediment. It could have used a light filtration. If you don't decant it, the wine will be cloudy in your glass. Plus, it needs an hour or two breathing time. If you do these two things, you will have an excellent, cheap Condrieu substitute because it has the nose and flavors.

$6.95 PER BOTTLE $75.06 PER CASE

How things have changed!

DOMAINE DE LA CHARMOISE
HENRY MARIONNET

EAST OF TOURS, toward Sancerre, scattered vineyards of Gamay and Sauvignon Blanc produce fresh, crisp wines, wonderfully alive with the taste of the grape, and wonderfully inexpensive. They are not profound wines for cellaring that will develop nuance and create a mood of reflection and wondrous murmurs from connoisseurs. Yet they marry well with the most refined cuisine. It was in this region, writes Waverly Root, "that the subtle, fine, expert cooking of modern France developed."

There are some, like Jon Winroth, the wine writer for the *International Herald Tribune*, who consider Marionnet's the finest wine within the appellation Touraine, and a profusion of gold medals supports that assessment. But you are in for a shock when you taste his 1981s. No little wine of the Loire, no matter how charming, has prepared you for these astonishing wines, so round, deep, and full of the taste of the grape.

Marionnet expressed satisfaction with his '81s but also fear that his regular clients in Paris wouldn't know what to make of them. It's like putting a record of Vivaldi on the phonograph and hearing the overture to *The Marriage of Figaro* leap out of the speakers.

Why are they so different? "*C'est la nature*," says Marionnet. He vinified them in his normal fashion. But it was a mixed blessing nature offered him—on one hand these grand, luscious wines, and on the other hand a catastrophic harvest one-third normal quantity.

1981 SAUVIGNON BLANC

Look at those legs! That's the first sign. To lovers of the "little" wines of the Touraine this may seem like a bit of a whore, and a rather well-built, garishly attired whore at that. On the palate a mixture of freshness, richness, and an intense taste of the grape. There is no raw grassiness—Marionnet attributes this to 100% destemming. It is rich, seductive, delicious.

$5.95 PER BOTTLE $64.26 PER CASE

1981 GAMAY

Deep bluish purple. A thick aroma in the glass, spicy with a touch of cocoa. The best of all possible worlds—intensity of flavor but only 11° alcohol. Relatively deep and tannic, but not heavy or coarse. This is fun to drink!

$4.95 PER BOTTLE $53.46 PER CASE

◇ ◇ ◇ ◇ ◇ ◇ ◇ ◇ ◇

Aldo Conterno, Monforte d'Alba

1978 BAROLO "BRICCO BUSSIA"
ALDO CONTERNO

Last spring I had the good fortune to accompany Burton Anderson through the Piedmont. Author of *Vino*, Anderson was touring the cellars to research an article on that picturesque hilly region, which gives us Barolo, Barbaresco, Dolcetto, and the finest Barbera of Italy.

Thanks to the esteem the vintners have for Anderson, I tasted countless beautiful wines, got a good look at the 1978 vintage, but saw nothing to shake my conviction that in Vietti and Aldo Conterno we have the two producers who are making the best Piedmont wines today.

Aldo Conterno wouldn't settle for less. He works from pride.

By coincidence, Aldo lived in the Bay Area for a few years and has relatives here.

He knows that they buy his wines in the shop.

Only wines of unquestioned excellence are offered on a pre-arrival basis, and in exchange for advance orders we offer a low price. Conterno's 1978 Barolo merits this special pre-arrival offer.

The 1978 vintage is finer than the 1971 and 1974. It produced big wines that will provide pleasure for decades. Oh, if I could sell you his '53 Barolo right now—that's the job I want!—but the way the wine market is now, you'll have to cellar this one and wait on it.

It's as dark as blackberry juice. Big, deep aroma; roasted coffee bean, violets, and heaps of berry-like fruit. A rich wine, almost 15° alcohol, but it is not at all raw or vulgar. Instead, the impression is one of tremendous depth of flavor, perfect ripeness, and great style. The harmony of tannin, acid, and fruit is reminiscent of the great Côte de Nuits Burgundies. The wine, in a good cellar, will endure and evolve indefinitely.

$120.00 PER CASE

1980 SAINT-JOSEPH *BLANC*
DOMAINE TROLLAT

Perhaps I was the first to import Trollat's Saint-Joseph because no other importer could find him. Five times now I've been to his place and each time lost my way and had to ask directions.

His home is perched atop a terraced crest way up in the hills above the Rhône, surrounded by Marsanne and Syrah vines. All seven acres of them. That's petite. His winery is in the cellar beneath his house. Trollat has no employees, even for working the vines. His are handmade wines from start to finish.

His 1980 *blanc* has a light straw color, lovely fruit, and a long, dry aftertaste with the flavor of hazelnut. It has the delicacy and finesse of a great white Burgundy or Bordeaux, so it can be served with the finest cuisine, but this is a Rhône wine, a wine of the sun, so it is equally appropriate with more rustic fare.

Served with ocean or river fish, or shellfish, the marvelous fruit of the Marsanne grape and the chalky *goût de terroir* from his steep hillside soil are thrown into proper relief.

$7.95 PER BOTTLE $85.86 PER CASE

BORDEAUX

1979 CHÂTEAU Y · BORDEAUX *BLANC*

What a wine, this dry white from Château d'Yquem! It's not all that dry, though, their 1979, and it has a ripe, botrytized bouquet that many Barsacs would envy. It is very warm, generous—reminiscent of a field of wildflowers on a hot spring day; there is a touch of honey and bitter almond, a faint suggestion of licorice in the finish.

The fruit and botrytis are so abundant and exquisite that you can serve it now, young as it is. Youth can be attractive too. Ideally one would watch it over a 10- to 15-year period, observing the evolution and the characteristics at each stage of maturation. That's interesting!

I say serve it as commencement to a meal that will be accompanied by great wines. It will sound the right note, preparing the mind, spirit, and palate for what is to follow. Certainly it needs a great red afterwards, demands a great red, is incomplete without a great red afterwards!

Or, consider if the pace of life were such that one could stop at around 4 P.M. to enjoy a glass of Château Y with a baguette and a wedge of Roquefort.

$17.50 PER BOTTLE $189.00 PER CASE

1978 CHÂTEAU RAMAGE LA BATISSE · HAUT-MÉDOC

For those who tasted the 1976, here is the 1978 we promised.

It's just down the road apiece from Château Mouton-Rothschild to Ramage-la-Bitisse. Ramage is the next château, about one kilometer away. And the wine-maker worked several years in Mouton's cellars, perfecting his craft. But the wine has about as much to do with Mouton as I have to do with Lynch-Bages, and if price is no object, buy Mouton.

However, if PG&E now takes your monthly Mouton allowance, Ramage la Batisse *is* quite Pauillac-like, as you may have seen in the 1976 before it was all snapped up in January. It is in the classic, old-fashioned style thanks to traditional vinification and lots of new oak each year. Maybe he *did* learn something from Mouton!

With its generous fruit and oak aroma, it can be enjoyed now, but this is a more backward wine than the 1976, and 1986 seems like a better time to commence drinking this lovely 1978.

$6.95 PER BOTTLE $75.06 PER CASE

LA RAITO (PROVENÇAL WINE SOUP)

THIS IS AN ancient Provençal recipe adapted from *Cuisine Provençale*, a cookbook I purchased at a village flea market. It is simple, delicious, and—with the garlic, olive oil, herbs, and red wine—basic Provençal.

olive oil	3 cloves garlic
flour	1 bottle Provence red
2 large onions	1½ cups boiling water
3 large tomatoes	1 spoonful capers soaked in milk
bouquet garni	5–6 walnuts
black olives	1 clove

Chop 1 onion and cook slowly in 4 tablespoons olive oil until golden. Stir in one spoonful flour until it turns color. Little by little stir in the red wine and the boiling water. Add the tomatoes, quartered, the garlic, a large onion speared with the clove, the crushed walnuts, and a bouquet garni composed of branches of fresh thyme, rosemary, fennel, and parsley.

Reduce at a slow boil by one-third, then strain.

Add the capers, a few pitted black olives, and garlic croutons.

Serve in white bowls to appreciate the soup's vivid color.

Variations: Cook an ocean fish like red snapper in your leftover soup. Or make a meurette provençale for serving poached eggs. Or transform it into a stew with chunks of vegetable like braised fennel and garlic.

❖ ❖

NEW ARRIVALS FROM SOUTHERN FRANCE

UNFAMILIAR, these wines are rarely seen beyond the provinces that produced them, but please, just for a while, forget your search for the greatest Chardonnay, Cabernet, Burgundy, or Bordeaux and spend two or three weeks exploring these new wines. You'll be regaled with great values and new flavor experiences, and you'll make the acquaintance of the cream of the crop of the wine domaines from one of the most wonderful spots on the face of the earth.

1981 VIN GRIS · DOMAINE DE CICERON

Produced from red grapes using white wine vinification. Ciceron has old Carignan and Cabernet vines (and a plot of Mourvèdre that flowers, has foliage, but, much to the bewilderment of the grower, produces no grapes). It is a crisp, dry, freshening sort of drink. Chill a bottle and watch the sun set, or serve with black olives and fennel or garlic sausages.

$3.99 PER BOTTLE $43.09 PER CASE

1978 TAVEL ROSÉ · RENÉ LOYAU

Tavel is purported to produce the best rosé of France. Yet it has been said that France's wines are white, red, rosé, *and* Tavel because Tavel is considered a serious wine, a wine of consequence, not simply a flowery little delight to quaff and forget. What in heaven's name is wrong with a flowery little delight to quaff and forget??

$8.50 PER BOTTLE $91.80 PER CASE

1979 CÔTES DU VENTOUX · DOMAINE DE LA VERRIÈRE

A dark, rustic red wine to serve with rich stews and charcoal-grilled red meats. It is robust and spicy.

It was produced on the southern face of the massive Mount Ventoux, east of Avignon, where 17 co-operative wineries produce almost all the plonk sold as Côtes du Ventoux. As usual, our selection is estate-bottled in limited quantities by a serious winemaker. He uses a Châteauneuf blend of grapes, slow fermentation, and oak-cask aging. The wine sells to locals who drive up the hill with their empty bottles. When I suggested that he export to me he acted like I had proposed some wildly deviant act. "How do you do it?" he asked suspiciously.

$3.99 PER BOTTLE $43.09 PER CASE

1979 RASTEAU · CHÂTEAU DU TRIGNON

Dark purplish garnet. Fine, deep bouquet; plummy with mushroom or undergrowth smells and a wild, charged spiciness. Tannic enough to permit 10 to 15 years' development. Marvelously complex.

$4.95 PER BOTTLE $53.46 PER CASE

1980 CASSIS · DOMAINE DU PATERNAL

Our interest here is the white wine of Cassis, not its celebrated Cap Canaille, the highest cliff in Europe, which rises ochre-colored out of the blue sea; not its fjord-like little inlets they call *calanques*; not its beaches; not eating its bouillabaisse while the sea crashes against the rocks below your restaurant . . . Its WINE (which rarely travels farther than the local restaurants) is golden-colored and dry, marries marvelously with Mediterranean-style pasta and seafood dishes, and has a distinct personality all its own.

The proprietor is an old fellow who nearly learned English in his youth by reading Shakespeare and used my presence to dust it off and gabble a bit.

He has a chalky hillside vineyard and puts a touch of Sauvignon Blanc into his blend.

His wine shows a sunny golden color, good clean nose with a touch of Marsanne honey, and a delicate floral impression on the palate. A wine of great class and deliciousness.

$6.95 PER BOTTLE $75.06 PER CASE

Noël Verset, ready to rock!

NOËL VERSET AT CORNAS

THE VILLAGE Cornas (like most French wine names, Cornas is not only a wine, it is a village) lies at the base of a steep, terraced mountain that was once covered with Syrah vines. The wine from this hillside is almost black, rather powerfully scented, and mouth-filling. Cornas is assuredly one of the world's four or five favored sites for the noble Syrah.

One must, however, fear for the future of the vine on this granitic slope. The acreage planted has decreased dramatically while more and more vines are planted on the flatland at the base of the mountain, where a more ordinary wine results.

There is no mystery to this. The problem is simple. There is not enough money in it and the work is backbreaking. Consequently, sons no longer follow their fathers into the vineyard. I buy from three growers at Cornas; none will be succeeded by family!★

Noël Verset has five acres of vine, all on the terraced slope, all *at least 70 years old*. Unless you can demand Romanée-Conti prices there is damned little luxury to be earned from five acres of old vines.

But what a wine he makes. It has a blackish raspberry color, a touch of vanilla atop the Syrah fruit, and a strong *goût de terroir*, a strong Cornas personality.

$7.95 PER BOTTLE $85.86 PER CASE

★ *The prodigal Clape son has since returned to work alongside his father.*

1979 HERMITAGE · J. L. CHAVE

1979 HERMITAGE *ROUGE*

Admittedly it is a grandiose claim and I'm risking what insignificant whit of credibility I have left to me, but I must state that this is the finest red Rhône I've imported. So far. I go out on a limb and state it so bluntly in order to communicate the enthusiasm I have for this grand, delicious, quintessential Hermitage.

It will endure, develop, and provide pleasure for decades and it can be served already, youthful though it may be, because it tastes so good. Fifty cases available.

$17.50 PER FIFTH $189.00 PER CASE

1979 HERMITAGE *BLANC*

If you're still reading you must be in the mood for grandiosities, so I might as well add that Chave's white Hermitage is the finest white wine produced in all the south of France today. Why?

1. *The incredible complexity of aromas and tastes*
2. *Its ability to evolve over decades if properly cellared*
3. *Its usefulness with both rustic and haute cuisine*
4. *Chave's brilliant, impeccable vinification, which is inspiring even to professionals who taste hundreds of wines per month*

The 1979 has various qualities but the bouquet deserves special attention. While generous enough already, there is still the sensation that it is only a child learning to speak. There is the fragrance of almond and linden (also present in his 1971 white) and there is a honeyed quality, honey from some craggy mountaintop wildflowers. There is apricot pit and anise. Have I gone too far? But it's all there!

To those who purchased from our previous shipment, uncork a bottle and consider if you'll require more. If you haven't cellared Chave's white, you're missing what Morgan Miller, glass in hand, called the Montrachet of the Rhône.

$14.95 PER BOTTLE $161.46 PER CASE

MONSIEUR LUIGI AT CAP CORSE

THIS IS A wine that I hope everyone will try at least once because for one thing it is so improbable—a great wine, a great *white* wine . . . from Corsica!

I went to the island looking for cheap reds, but none were cheap enough, if you ask me—what a horrid taste lingers in my memory of the tannic brawny plonk they make there. I didn't mind so much at the time because Corsica itself is something wild and memorable—the narrow road on cliffs that descend steeply into the Mediterranean. It is an island that makes you consider the nature of islands. You are atop a piece of earth that barely rises out of the sea. It can be a precarious feeling.

When I'd given up hope of finding any decent wine, *voilà*! Monsieur Luigi!

His is a dry white from the *malvoisie* grape.★ The nose is a flowery bouquet, exquisitely honeyed, very like

the bouquet of Château Grillet. On the palate, quite fresh with a rich sweetness of flavor that reminds one of a ripe Chenin or Sauvignon Blanc, yet the wine is dry. The aftertaste is good—dry, lean, a shaft of bitterness, endless.

Serve cool, not cold.

$7.95 PER BOTTLE $85.86 PER CASE

★*Monsieur Luigi called it* malvoisie, *but we call it Rolle or Vermentino.*

CÔTE CHALONNAISE

1981 BOURGOGNE *BLANC* "LES CLOUS"

A. & P. DE VILLAINE

Don't put this in your Chardonnay tasting because it will not register next to an oaky monster. It would be like a destruction derby between a Mack truck and an Alfa Romeo. For everyday driving, however, I recommend the Alfa.

This is lovely Chardonnay that shows its quality at table, where wine belongs. The nose has a delicate floral perfume and a hint of pear skin, like the 1979. On the palate, fresh and sleek, everything in proper balance. An aftertaste stony and quite dry.

This is Chardonnay you can serve often, and it will age well. It is priced right, you don't tire of it (on the contrary, it grows on you), and the alcohol level allows you to remember what you ate for dessert. Chardonnays this stylish are hard to find.

$6.95 PER BOTTLE $75.06 PER CASE

BEAUJOLAIS

I N THE SHOP when we recommend a Beaujolais there are two types of response: a smile of delight from those who have tasted good Beaujolais and can't wait to repeat the experience, or a grimace of disgust from those who have suffered from a badly shipped or badly vinified Beaujolais.

In my opinion 99% of the Beaujolais imported is undrinkable, with no resemblance to the real thing. There are two reasons. First, there is a huge demand for wines labeled Beaujolais, and the producers make an ocean of it, stretching their production to ludicrous levels. Even that is not enough for them, so plonk from Italy and the Midi is poured into the vats to stretch it even further. Bah!

But say an importer finds a good Beaujolais. That's not the end of it. It must be given special treatment if it is to arrive in California tasting like it does in France. It cannot sit on the dock in the sun at Marseille. It can't cook on a boat chugging through the Panama Canal. Our Beaujolais leaves in a refrigerated container and never rises above 55°. I taste it in the Beaujolais cellars and then here after its arrival. There is no change whatsoever.

And you must exercise the same caution. Don't leave your Beaujolais in a hot car. Keep it cool. And by all means serve it cool! Nothing worse than warm Beaujolais, while a healthy bottle served at around 55° is wine at its most delicious. That is why one drinks Beaujolais—not for its body, its complexity, or its aging potential—you drink it for its deliciousness!

Is anyone out there against deliciousness??

	PER FIFTH
Beaujolais-Villages · Trénel .	$5.75
Morgon · Domaine Thevenet	5.75
Saint-Amour · Trénel	5.95
Fleurie · Domaine Chignard	7.50
Moulin-à-Vent · Domaine Diochon	7.95

BORDEAUX

1979 CLOS TRIMOULET · SAINT-EMILION

As with anything handmade, this big wine expresses somewhat the personality of the man who made it. It's a bit closed at first but comes around after a while.

This guy wouldn't even look up from his work, cleaning a piece of winery equipment, to greet me. He looked unfriendly. He looked mean. And I myself was feeling a bit nasty, having spent the entire hot, muggy day tasting one dog after another . . .

He asked why I wanted to taste his wine, still not looking up at me. "To sell in California," I said. "No," he mumbled, "California does not interest me. *Pas de tout!*"

That was too much. My assistant had telephoned to set up the rendezvous; if export held no interest for him, why the hell did he agree to receive me in the first place? I turned and stomped off toward my car, without a word, jangling my car keys as loudly as possible.

"You can taste the wine," he called after me.

Well, in this business, who ever knows what one is going to find in the barrel? I have been received like a prince, with caviar and Champagne on ice, with servants serving and graciousness and hospitality abundant—only to find the wine for sale unpalatable. So I swallowed my anger and went back to his cellar to taste. That's my job. Soon he was uncorking old bottles and wondering if his wines might not be too tannic and full-bodied for Californians, and I was all aglow knowing that I'd discovered something exceptional.

It is a big wine, very dark in color, chewy, full of promise. As a matter of fact, the price is ridiculously low for a wine of this class.

One final thing. The winemaker suffers from a horribly persistent twitch in one eye, and that is why he kept his head lowered so long—the poor fellow was trying to hide something that embarrassed him.

$7.95 PER BOTTLE $85.86 PER CASE

RHÔNE

1980 CORNAS · AUGUSTE CLAPE

What Chave is to Hermitage, Clape is to Cornas. This is Syrah country and they are the masters.

Clape's 1980 is raspberry colored, vivid, lively, and brilliant. The Syrah grapes give black currants and the chestnut casks add vanilla to the aroma. Tannic, yes, but after all, this is Cornas, Cornas from 50-year-old vines!

Sitting there comfortably at home, you may think a case of the Clape is the last thing

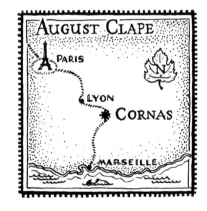

you need right now, but this will make good drinking for at least a dozen years, especially with grilled red meats and strong cheeses.

$8.75 PER BOTTLE $94.50 PER CASE

ALSATIAN DOMAINE ZIND-HUMBRECHT

RARELY DOES one encounter Alsatian wines from specific vineyard sites. Designations are usually by arbitrary quality level: Réserve, Cuvée Spéciale, Cuvée Incroyable, and so on. Wines from different vineyards are blended to create these quality designations. No harm in that, but for those of us fanatical about French wines, it is after all the character imparted by distinct soils and ex-positions that gives our palates a thrill.

Believe me, Alsace has soil variations just as distinct and important as those in Burgundy or Bordeaux, and at Domaine Zind-Humbrecht I found a winemaker whose passion is to preserve the personality of each *terroir*.

The policy of Domaine Zind-Humbrecht:

- *Proprietor of vineyards; traditional vinification in oak casks; the wines bottled at the domaine.*
- *Natural wines without excessive chaptalization, which means wines at 10° and 10.5° alcohol. That's refreshing!*
- *Wines fermented completely dry, without residual sugar.*
- *Preservation of the distinct personality imparted by each soil type.*

Property of an ancient Alsatian wine family, the domaine has passed from father to son without interruption since 1620!

1981 SYLVANER

A fresh, lively wine to quench the thirst. Light, supple, agreeable, very dry. The winemaker wisely leaves a touch of natural CO_2 in his wines, which gives them a hint of sparkle. A delight and a bargain.

$3.79 PER BOTTLE $40.93 PER CASE

1981 PINOT BLANC

Light body with plenty of aroma and freshness. Firm and long on the palate. Lovely dry, austere finish. A wine with lots of race and a pronounced Alsatian character. Altogether delicious with lots of finesse, this makes a great everyday dry white.

$3.99 PER BOTTLE $43.09 PER CASE

1981 RIESLING "BRAND"

The Brand vineyard is planted on a steep slope behind Turckheim in granitic soil that contains an abundance of potassium. Potassium intensifies aroma. (An aside: A brilliant French oenologue who has analyzed the soils of all the great vineyards of France told me that he found the highest percentage of potassium in . . . Chave's vineyard at Hermitage!!) The Brand Riesling is one of great finesse, very aromatic, very *primeur*, very Riesling. Light, seductive, dry, and lively on the palate. An absolutely stunning Riesling!

$6.95 PER BOTTLE $75.06 PER CASE

1981 GEWURZTRAMINER "HERRENWEG"

No one is going to taste this and say, "This is a BIG Gewurztraminer." No, this is something different, something lovely, very flowery and gay. Lead palates, stay home. The soil at Herrenweg is alluvial: sand, clay, and large pebbles. The Gewurztraminer ripens easily here and is always marked by its generous, expressive bouquet of rose and violet, spice and exotic fruits. You revel in the opulent aroma and flavors because there is no sugary body to stand in your way masking the complex taste components. A beautiful bottle of wine that can be drunk now or, judging by the perfect 1966 Herrenweg I tasted, it can be aged to develop the nuance of an old wine.

$6.95 PER BOTTLE $75.06 PER CASE

TRÉNEL FILS

WE SPECIALIZE in domaine- or estate-bottled wines, yet I remain loyal to two *négociants*—René Loyau in the Loire and Trénel Fils for Beaujolais and Maconnais wines. It may be no accident that both are men of advanced age and both have been in the business of wine long enough to know what it is about. A visit to Trénel is always a lesson for me because the man has 50 years' experience tasting, buying, and selling wine.

I trust him. Once a cuvée of Trénel Beaujolais went bad on us. I wrote to him explaining the problem. He replied that he *hates* to treat his wines in order to stabilize them. He *hates* using sulfur, filtration, or pasteurization. (Yes! Many imported wines on the market are pasteurized to ensure that they are too dead to do anything funny in the bottle.) However, in that particular vintage, he said, he had misjudged the strength and structure of the wine, that it had needed a little dose of SO_2 to keep it from falling to pieces. Enclosed in his letter I found a check for the total amount in question. That's honesty. That's proper. That's class!

A new shipment of 1981s has just arrived from Trénel. Highlights include an unchaptalized Mâcon of which Trénel was very proud.

Judging by past response, there is a growing number of you wine drinkers who don't want a mouthful of oak and butter each and every time you drink a Chardonnay. This unchaptalized Mâcon is so lovely, so fine, so honest an expression of the Chardonnay fruit and the chalky *terroir* of the region . . . I am going to continue to buy gems like this whenever I can find them. The big, rich wines are for special occasions, for particular cuisines. Otherwise, drinking them becomes fatiguing. This one is crisp, clean, and lively, with no false viscosity, and the alcohol is only 11°!

I know that even with our direct import price it is more expensive than other Mâcons, but try it and see if it isn't worth it. One hundred cases available.

Trénel's Côte de Brouilly is always among the finest of the *grand cru* Beaujolais. It is from old vines and shows the old-vine characteristics of solid, tight-knit structure and great finesse. The color is lively ruby with a touch of blue-purple. The nose is loaded with fresh new Gamay fruit and blackberry. No one is so talented at preserving the freshness of the fruit aroma and flavors as Trénel, and that's exactly what you want in a Beaujolais.

		PER BOTTLE	PER CASE
1981	*Mâcon-Villages*	$6.25	$67.50
1971	*Saint-Véran*	6.95	75.06
1981	*Côte de Brouilly*	5.95	64.26

THE DOMAINE DE FONTSAINTE

AFTER THE success of our Saint Jean de Bébian and Faugères from the Languedoc, I returned and did more work there and came up with this prize, the Domaine de Fontsainte.

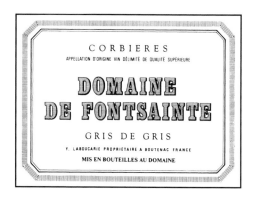

The vines of the domaine are in stony, chalky soil. Average production in the area is a mind-boggling 200 hectoliters to the hectare—Fontsainte produces only 55! The red spends a year in oak casks, also practically unknown in the region.

1981 GRIS DE GRIS

Gorgeous salmon color. Delicate floral nose. Plenty of richness for a rosé, but still quaffable, still thirst-quenching. The lovely flavors linger on and on and you wonder how a rosé can be so delicious and how a cheap wine can be so good.

$3.25 PER BOTTLE $35.10 PER CASE

1980 CORBIÈRES *ROUGE*

Good deep color. Fine, elegant, perfumed nose. There is black cherry, apricot pit, cinnamon, and vanilla. Round, full, with soft tannins and a touch of oak. The winemaker says people often find a flavor of venison in his red, but I've not had enough venison to know.

$3.75 PER BOTTLE $40.50 PER CASE

◦ ◦ ◦ ◦ ◦ ◦ ◦ ◦

1980 CHABLIS *GRAND CRU* "VALMUR" · RAVENEAU

Outside Chablis and Bandol, I've not claimed to have the *best* wine of any appellation. Ravaneau is the coldhearted fellow who for years rejected our efforts to import his great Chablis. The crusty old misanthrope now finds he likes selling to us because it's simpler than dealing with all those pests who came knocking at

François and Jean-Marie Raveneau, Chablis

his door buying a few bottles at a time. An added attraction, to his way of thinking: we are 6,000 miles distant.

At first he would grant us only his *premier cru*. Now we have his *grand cru* Valmur. It is the first opportunity in the U.S. to cellar this *grand cru* from the finest winemaker in Chablis.

$12.50 PER BOTTLE $135.00 PER CASE

THIS MONTH'S BEST VALUE

1971 MERLOT · LA BRAGHINA

In his book *Vino*, Burton Anderson says that wines from the small producer La Braghina are outstanding, but not easy to come by.

Here they are in Albany and at such a low price it is almost laughable.

Before the wine's arrival I was worried. Could it live up to my memory of first tasting it? Maybe anything would have seemed good, given the circumstances.

I am a music lover, and I had the pleasure to spend three days in the Veneto with Alan Curtis of Berkeley, the conductor and keyboard artist. His recording of C. P. E. Bach, the Couperins, and J. S. Bach's *Goldberg Variations* are among the most valued of my collection. He performs with uncommon intelligence, humor, and spontaneity.

But we spent all our time eating and drinking in the little hill-town inns north of Venice. Rarely would we be offered a wine list. "Red or white?" the waiters wanted to know. One night the red turned out to be this gorgeous Merlot. I had just arrived after ten days of Saint-Emilion and Pomerol and remember saying, "*This* is what Merlot should taste like!" No, it is not as rich as Pomerol; it doesn't have as much oak, but in its way it is as delicious—thus, a perfect everyday red.

The nose is berry-like Merlot with its barely perceptible herbaceousness; the flavors are fine and the wine has style—no coarseness or roughness. Just as impressive is the aftertaste—delicate, savory, long, nothing ponderous or vulgar, just the ravishing vinous perfume.

You'll want to drink it now, today, but hide some away. At this price one can afford to, and it should make good drinking for four or five years.

$2.99 PER BOTTLE $32.30 PER CASE

↣ 1983 ↢

BURGUNDY

1980 GEVREY-CHAMBERTIN "LES CHAMPEAUX" · MAUME

Very dark color. A briary, raw, young *premier cru* that reminded me of a Swan Zinfandel because of its tannin, full body, and intensity. There is black pepper, a licorice-like note from the marl in the Chambertin soil, and a tight, concentrated perfume that you find in an *eau-de-vie* or an old *marc*. It could only be from Gevrey-Chambertin. Long, long finish. I can't say yet when it will reach its peak, but I find it a rather amazing bottle of wine.

$17.50 PER BOTTLE $189.00 PER CASE

1980 NUITS-SAINT-GEORGES "LES CAILLES"
ROBERT CHEVILLON

Does color mean anything? Depth, great clarity, and brilliance—this wine is beautiful before you've even sniffed it. Not ruby, not garnet, not purple—this must be Nuits-Saint-Georges-colored, and it is a regal tone.

A wiry, muscular wine with sappy, intense Pinot fruit. *Cailles* means "quail," and these quail have been jogging. You feel the flavors all packed in, waiting to burst out—cassis and chalk above all. Tannic with a savory finish that lasts, that surprises until the next sip. Cellar it.

$17.50 PER BOTTLE $189.00 PER CASE

1979 BANDOL "LA MIGOUA" · DOMAINE TEMPIER

This is the first time you've seen a place-name or specific vineyard designation on a bottle of Domaine Tempier. La Migoua (*mee-gwah*) is the place up in the hills around Jean-Marie's house where I stay when I'm at Bandol. No one knows what the name *La Migoua* means—it's an old Provençal name, that's all they know.

With a good bit of courage (because the terrain is rugged) the Peyraud family planted little plots of vineyard here and there, many of them terraced, around Jean-Marie's house. 1979 produced enough juice to vinify for the first time a separate cuvée La Migoua.

What a wild, beautiful place it is! On walks I see and breathe in the fragrance of pine, wildflowers, wild rosemary, thyme, and anise. Provence! There are cherry, olive, and apricot trees growing untended, struggling leftovers from when the ancients covered the hills with orchards. And this aromatic feast has found its way into the wine.

Tasting notes on the 1979 Cuvée Spéciale La Migoua are from the people who make Domaine Tempier's wine, the Peyrauds themselves:

LUCIEN is the father. His passionate travail, a life's work, established the quality and reputation of Domaine Tempier: "*Color of very ripe black cherry. Very complex nose, plum and truffle. On the palate very full, round; tannin strong but supple.*"

FRANÇOIS has perhaps the most important job; he tends the vines: "*Robe of a beautiful intensity; nose strong, still very young with aromas of* sous-bois *(undergrowth or forest-floor smells) and fresh fruits—raspberry and black currant. A* vin de garde *with a great future.*"

JEAN-MARIE, the other son, occupies himself with the vinification at Domaine Tempier. La Migoua is his favorite child—he made the wine from grapes grown around his house: "*Beautiful deep color. Superb nose, intense but still closed. It still hides many beautiful things, like an unopened rose blossom. On the palate, rich, full-bodied, tannic; taste of fruit, ripe pomegranate. Still far too young. Great future in store.*"

This special cuvée is unusually generous and complex. You don't like it, you *love* it. A wine you'll want to drink often over the next 15 to 20 years.*

$98.00 PER CASE

Or 25 to 30 years, as it turns out. I have never cellared more of any one wine. I have about one case remaining to enjoy. How I love and hate to see it go.

CORNAS

I WISH SOMEONE like Hugh Johnson would write the story of a single wine village like Cornas. We have enough encyclopedias, guides to, and atlases. Cornas would make a great story—the long history of wine-growing there going back more than 1,000 years, disasters like the 1938 frost that killed many of the vines, the shrinking production as young people leave the hard work in the vineyards for union wages in the big industrial centers—well, it can't all be told here.

Cornas is a wine that I love. I buy from three Cornas growers—you might say we dominate the Cornas export market! It is one of the true values in great wine.

Its qualities are abundant, its flavors complex and mouth-filling, and it ages beautifully, yet it is priced well under $10 per bottle. To introduce you to this, the biggest wine of the northern Rhône, richer even than Hermitage or Côte Rôtie, there will be special prices in February only.

1980 CORNAS · MARCEL JUGE

Deep, ripe Syrah aroma—loaded with cassis-like fruit. The mouth-filling texture on the palate is gorgeous—deep, round, rich, tannic, of course, but the most supple, the most approachable of the three wines right now.

REGULAR PRICE $7.95   FEBRUARY PRICE $6.95

1980 CORNAS · NOËL VERSET

Darkest color—blackish purple. This has the strongest *goût de terroir* or mineral quality of the three because Verset's vines are 70 years old (!) and situated on the very steepest part of the terraced, granitic slope. That situation also explains the extraordinary sappy intensity and the powerful, long aftertaste with its fascinating hint of blueberry.

REGULAR PRICE $7.95   FEBRUARY PRICE $6.95

1980 CORNAS · AUGUSTE CLAPE

Clape was the first in Cornas to estate-bottle his wine and save it from the blending vats of the big *négociants*. Most writers say that Clape's is the best Cornas. In 1980 his is certainly the most complex with its *goût de terroir*, violets, black currants, raspberry, black pepper, a resiny rosemary-like fragrance, and a touch of *réglisse* at the end. It is a huge wine with flavors to match. Clape himself compares his 1980 to his superb 1972, which remains vigorous and youthful even today.

REGULAR PRICE $8.75   FEBRUARY PRICE $7.95

❖ ❖

NEW LOCATION

Beginning Tuesday, February 8
You will find us at
1605 San Pablo Ave., Berkeley
Corner of Cedar and San Pablo

❖ ❖

1980 MAS DE DAUMAS GASSAC

A Château Lafite of the Languedoc?" headlined *Gault Millau*. ". . . *Can hold its own against any French growth today*," declared the French *Revue Vinicole*.

What we have here is nothing less than astonishing—a great Cabernet comparable to the *cru classé* of Bordeaux and to any California Cabernet. It is the value of the month, of the year. Pour a glass. The quality, even with no regard to price, leaps out of the glass.

The domaine is in southern France, in the Languedoc. I have been working the Languedoc in depth my past four buying trips because it is an unexplored region of enormous possibility where prices remain reasonable. Ours is the finest selection of Languedoc wines in the United States and this is the jewel of the collection.*

The winemaker settled there ten years ago because he found the soil and climate perfect for growing Cabernet Sauvignon. It is what we call an organic wine—no chemical fertilizers or herbicides are employed in the vineyard. Production per acre is limited following the example of the great Bordeaux. The wine is aged in once-used oak barrels purchased from Château Margaux and Palmer. His oenologue is the celebrated Emile Peynaud, who also counsels Château Margaux and Lafite in matters of vinification.

As to the wine itself, the color is magnificent—a dark inky purple, one of the prettiest dark wines I've seen. The aroma evolves after breathing or decanting. It has a strong varietal character (Cabernet Sauvignon with a touch of Syrah); there is a cedary quality, deep cassis–like fruit, a hint of cherry and pine.

It is dense and tannic yet only 12.5° alcohol, so it is not mean or heavy. There is a superb richness of flavor and because of its great depth you have the impression that its youth hides many wonderful things. The flavors persist long after swallowing.

It is a beautifully vinified Cabernet Sauvignon. Flawless!

$4.95 PER BOTTLE $53.46 PER CASE

In this judgment, I no longer agree with myself. After aging and following the wines for years, my pick of the bunch from those early days of tasting in the Languedoc would be Alain Roux's Saint Jean de Bébian, Gilbert Alquier's Faugères, and the Corbières La Demoiselle from Domaine de Fontsainte. Alain Roux is gone now, Gilbert Alquier's sons have taken over, but at Fontsainte father and son continue in the tradition.

◦   ◦   ◦   ◦   ◦   ◦   ◦   ◦   ◦

1978 CHÂTEAU LA DOMINIQUE
SAINT-EMILION

You don't see us offer a wide selection of Bordeaux wines because the Bordeaux market is so label-oriented. I fancy myself a wine merchant, not a label merchant—what counts is what is poured into the glass. La Dominique represents the kind of Bordeaux business I like to do. I buy it directly from the château, avoiding the Bordeaux middlemen, assuring quality and best price.

The château was recently the subject of an article by Robert Parker in the *Washington Post.* "One of the top Saint-Emilion wines," he wrote, "considerably undervalued vis à vis its more publicized neighbors." At a tasting of 1955s Parker says La Dominique "eclipsed a number of more famous wines including the Cheval Blanc and Figeac." Parker concludes, "If you are not inclined to spend $40-plus for Cheval Blanc or Ausone, or have found Figeac and some of its neighbors overpriced and disappointing lately, a search for La Dominique is well worth the effort."

$12.50 PER BOTTLE $135.00 PER CASE

1981 CONDRIEU · CHÂTEAU ROZAY

The thesaurus has no superlatives superlative enough to do justice to the 1981 Château Rozay. It is a knockout!

Usually we recommend sipping Condrieu by itself to savor its exquisite perfumes. In this 1981 the Viognier fruit explodes out of the glass, and it cannot be served with just anything. We became intrigued by some old French cookbooks that suggest (to our amazement) serving Condrieu with lamb. George Lang has come up with this something special to accompany the 1981 Château Rozay:

Macerate dried linden blossoms [we sell them] and slivered segments of dried apricots and peaches in a glass of good white Rhône [we sell them]—include a clove or two.

Slip leftover lamb into the marinade and marinate overnight, refrigerated.

The next day, sieve the marinade. Use some of it in place of vinegar in a vinaigrette. Coat the salad greens of your choice with the vinaigrette, distribute the lamb thinly sliced and still cool on top of the leaves and then the softened slivers of the fruit. Pepper lightly.

Pour glasses of 1981 Château Rozay.

$14.95 PER BOTTLE $161.46 PER CASE

1981 CÔTES DU RHÔNE
CAVE RABASSE-CHARAVIN

I don't know whether Abel Charavin makes the best wine in Cairanne—once I tasted his I stopped looking. His house is outside the village up a vine-covered slope with a view of God's Plain, Mount Ventoux, and the Dentelles behind Gigondas. Charavin himself is a stocky rough-hewn sort, always dressed in shorts, his thighs as thick as my waist, muscled from working his slope.

His is a deep, hearty, purple wine, prettier than he is but with the same muscle. He was not ready to bottle his 1981 but I asked him to. I wanted it bottled immediately to preserve its fresh ripe fruit, fruit that might vanish if the wine rested too long in wood. It is not Beaujolais-style Rhône, not at all. It is traditionally vinified but early bottled at my request—there is pomegranate, black cherry, red plum, and peach in the aroma. Not bad at $3.59! On the palate a perfect balance with that point of tannin one expects in a Côtes du Rhône. It is supple, fine, delicious, with a beautiful impression of warmth and ripeness that does one's spirit good.

$3.59 PER BOTTLE $38.77 PER CASE

1982 SANCERRE
HIPPOLYTE REVERDY

1982 produced Sancerres that are going to please even those people who cannot abide the grassiness of Sauvignon Blanc. The grapes ripened fully and there is no sharp green edge to the wines. I tasted good Sancerres in several *caves* but selected Hippolyte Reverdy's because it was the prettiest, because it has none of the dread SO_2, because his price is far from painful, and because I liked his name. When you are named Kermit, there is a satisfaction to be gained by meeting an Hippolyte.

$5.99 PER BOTTLE $64.68 PER CASE

BORDEAUX

1979 CHÂTEAU SOCIANDO-MALLET
HAUT-MÉDOC

What a triumph! An absolutely magnificent claret from a château unknown in these parts. I wrote upon tasting it that everyone should snap it up quickly before the world discovers it and the price grows to match the quality. Now, already, the word is out. This month's *Revue du Vin de France* says Sociando exhibits "a character a bit lordly in the style of Latour, Montrose, or Léoville. One is face-to-face with a wine that merits to be classed at the level of a third growth."

The 1979 has a deep ruby color, a fine intense nose of red fruits like plum and cassis, a generous proportion of new oak, and a spicy Saint-Estèphe intensity. It is tannic and virile, powerfully flavored. Altogether superb! Highest recommendation!

$6.95 PER BOTTLE $75.06 PER CASE

1979 CHÂTEAU CERTAN-GIRAUD · POMEROL

I was guided to Certan-Giraud by the proprietor of La Conseillante. It is *very* Pomerol. It tastes like what you imagine when you think Pomerol. The color is brilliant blackish purple, the nose deep and young, black currant and black truffle. Lots of stuffing; long, intense finish.

One taste of the Sociando-Mallet or the Certan-Giraud and you'll know that one needn't pay big bucks or be a slave to big labels in order to drink great claret. For those who love old Bordeaux, these will evolve and improve for years, perhaps decades.

$7.95 PER BOTTLE $85.86 PER CASE

Vineyard in the Soave zone

SUMMER ROSÉ

I DON'T HAVE to buy rosé. That's not how I'll earn enough to buy a little stone house overlooking the Mediterranean. Nor do I have to put up with the incredulous expressions on my clients' faces when I recommend a rosé. "What do you take me for, a hick?" their expression demands. Or "Try that one on the next sucker, mister." Or, "Let's move on to something more serious."

In the course of my buying trips I run across excellent wines with a rosé color. I don't look for them. They appear.

What can I do? I'm in the cellar with a serious winemaker; there is a glass of something special in my hand that happens to be neither red nor white. I can't ignore it simply because the quality of California rosé has created a credibility problem for rosé in general. So I buy them anyway. In small quantities. No reason to lose money over it. But I have found some beauties for those of you with an open mind. And now, summertime, is their season.

1982 CHIARETTO CLASSICO · RIZZARDI

A blend of Corvina, Molinara, Rondinella, and Negrara grapes. Doesn't that make you thirsty? These red Bardolino grapes are vinified as if they were making a white wine. The wine is dry and refreshing, enormously fun to drink, but what is amazing is the fragrance. This rosé has lots of aroma, a pretty aroma that reminds me of *fraises des bois*, or wild strawberries. If this were a red or a white with such delicious flavors our 50 cases would be gone tomorrow, but because it is rosé-colored you probably won't have to rush in to score a bottle. However, you'll be delighted if you do.

$2.99 PER BOTTLE

1981 BANDOL ROSÉ · DOMAINE TEMPIER

Having imported and enjoyed this rosé for 10 years, I've come to the conclusion that year in and year out it is the finest rosé produced. In fact, I can no longer imagine a world without Bandol rosé.

$6.95 PER BOTTLE

1982 CHINON ROSÉ · CHARLES JOGUET

"A devil of a winemaker," according to Jon Winroth of the *International Herald Tribune*. "A heavenly rosé," according to our George Lang, here at KLWM. Devilish and heavenly together should not be missed.

$4.95 PER BOTTLE

1982 ROSÉ FRISANT · MAS DE DAUMAS GASSAC

A dark-colored rosé of Cabernet Sauvignon and Syrah. This rosé is *frizzante*— little bubbles. Particularly fun from an ice chest on a picnic. Or to focus concentration while you tend the grill.

$3.99 PER BOTTLE

1979 PALETTE ROSÉ · CHÂTEAU SIMONE

What's fun is serving Château Simone throughout a meal: start with their crisp, perfumed Blanc de Blancs, then serve this rosé with an appropriate dish, and conclude with their grand Bordeaux-like red. The vineyards grow just outside Aix-en-Provence, and Château Simone is one of the two truly great wine domaines of Provence.

$7.95 PER BOTTLE

o o o o o o o o

1982 PROSECCO · GIORGIO BUFFON

A cloudy, fizzy little white that is drunk like water in the vine-covered foothills north of Venice. Every bottle is a little different—some sparkle along quite mer-

Giorgio Buffon and his mother

rily, others have only a faint burble. There is a lot of gunk in the wine because it refermented in the bottle, so you have to stand it up a day or two before serving and decant it off into a water pitcher. A real decanter would be too serious. Or you can just drink it with the gunk. A wine glass, too, might be presumptuous—better use a water glass, as they often do in the Veneto. Or maybe you should stay away from this one entirely. I only hope it arrives without having blown all its corks because the bottles don't have wire on them like Champagne or any other self-respecting sparkling wine.

If you decide to try it, gunk and all, buy two bottles. One won't be enough.

$3.99 PER BOTTLE

OUR CHEAPEST WHITE

1982 BIANCO DI PITIGLIANO

For those of you with a palate for European wines, this dry white should come in handy when the wolf's at the door and you can't hack the California jugs. It does not lack subtlety; it is not clumsy; it doesn't smell like filter paper; it is not cloying or tiresome.

$3.75 PER MAGNUM $20.25 PER CASE

CÔTES DU RHÔNE

Either I'm a glutton for punishment or I'll do anything for a decent drink. In May I forced myself to endure 10 days in a 400-year-old stone house *centre ville* Sablet. Ten hard days—up at the crack of dawn, leaving the house bleary-eyed, barely noticing Sablet's Romanesque bell tower, its medieval ramparts (constructed, no doubt, to protect the town's precious wine cellars from thirsty barbarians), its stone fountain where a few of the village women still gather to do the wash, its winding narrow cobbled streets—no, it was off to the moldy cellars, slurping wine all day, palate aching, then home again after dark to dine on . . . all I can remember is basil, garlic, olive oil, and more garlic. Haven't these people ever heard of the taco?

The next thing I know, Morgan tells me that a freighter has just docked in Oakland loaded with god knows how many Côtes du Rhônes. Oh well, at least they're cheap.

Sablet is near Gigondas, which is near Avignon, and almost every village around there produces wine. Looking for one good wine I tasted hundreds and found several—each different, each valuable, each impossible to dismiss. You will be equally intrigued by the variety of wines produced in this rich viticultural region, the variety owing to different soil types, vinifications, and grape blends. You might decide upon a favorite, but each wine expresses something of beauty.

1980 SABLET · CHÂTEAU DU TRIGNON

See the village on the label? Returning home evenings I would search across the vine-covered plain for that bell tower to gauge the distance I still had to cover before I could eat dinner, enjoy a glass or two of Sablet, and fall asleep to the sound of the gurgling fountain outside my window.

The wine is equal parts Syrah and Grenache with a small proportion of Mourvèdre. The fruit flavors and aromas are quite intense here. The French say *plein de sève*, which translates as "sappy." But I have trouble calling one of my wines sappy. It means full of sap—not diluted—an impression of intensity and a concentration of flavors. The wine is mouth-filling, earthy, complex, tannic, long.

$4.95 PER BOTTLE $53.46 PER CASE

MÂCON

1982 MÂCON-VILLAGES

This is as near to the wine-making process as I've been, as close as I ever *want* to be, in fact. It is a cuvée of Mâcon that I blended or constructed myself in order to have a wine in bottle that fit my image of how a Mâcon should smell, taste, and feel.

Normally when I buy I specify the barrels I prefer. It sounds crazy but even the same wine, once it is put into separate barrels or vats, develops differently. To receive the best, each must be tasted and evaluated. As for blending, for years I have, with the help of Gérard Chave, blended my own cuvée of Trollat's Saint-Joseph.

The Mâcon cellars at Viré are more extensive than Trollat's so the project was more complicated and time-consuming. First I tasted each cuvée separately, noting the distinguishing characteristics. For example:

#56—fine, fruity, très primeur
#57—heavier, bitter finish
#64—closed nose, good structure
#81—aromatic, flat, short

And so on. Then I returned to the most promising cuvées and began putting them together in various proportions. Strangely, the results were not always predictable. Combining a light and fruity cuvée with a closed and rich one was just as likely to produce a wine light and closed as one fruity and rich. The addition of 5% of a certain cuvée was enough to add or subtract a certain quality from the final blend.

To say I'm happy with the result is an understatement. It tastes exactly like I think Mâcon should taste. I did not set out to produce a minor Meursault. I wanted a wine typical of the best Mâcon qualities—untiring to drink, seductively fresh and lively, the accent on fruit and finesse rather than alcohol or oak; a wine appealing for its gaiety, not its seriousness, but aesthetically complete and satisfying all the same. A Haydn, not a Liszt.

Lively fragrance with a clean, uninhibited expression of Chardonnay fruit. Medium-bodied, freshening to the palate, a textural quality that holds the flavors well without heaviness or high acidity. Dry but succulent, long and fine.

$4.95 PER BOTTLE $2.75 PER TENTH

⋄   ⋄   ⋄   ⋄   ⋄   ⋄   ⋄   ⋄

1981 DOMAINE DU VIEUX TÉLÉGRAPHE

The Concours de Saint Marc is a yearly tasting competition held in the village of Châteauneuf-du-Pape. Wines of the new vintage are tasted and compared, and a prize is awarded to the three best wines. Most growers submit samples from several different casks. When the three finest cuvées of 1981 were unveiled the judges were shocked to find all three labeled Vieux Télégraphe!

After a hasty conference Monsieur Brunier of Vieux Télégraphe withdrew his second and third cuvées to permit other growers' names to appear on the awards announcement. He's like that, a frank, big-hearted Provençal-type who enjoys immense personal popularity among neighboring winemakers.

The jury also reviews three-year-old wines. In 1981 the 1978s were reconsidered. First place: guess who?

I repeat all this to support my conviction that Vieux Télégraphe is the top domaine at Châteauneuf today.

The *Wine Advocate* claims that the 1981 is the best Vieux Télégraphe since 1978. Even in the long list of great Vieux Télégraphes the 1981 would stand out by virtue of its intensity, balance, and finesse. But ultimately it is the aroma and flavors that make the 1981 so special. It is so complex you would laugh if I named all the flavor associations it suggests to me.

Brunier gave me a carton of 1981 to sustain me this June while I vacationed in Provence. In this manner I got to know the wine rather well and I recommend it highly.

$88.00 PER CASE FIFTHS $90.00 PER CASE MAGNUMS

1981 BORDEAUX

LET US SETTLE this outrageous vintage dispute once and for all. Let's forget all the hype, the rankings, and the raves that we've read and let us simply Tell It Like It Is! I've been there; I've tasted the wines; I've followed their evolution, and I can assure you that 1982 is incontestably the finest Bordeaux vintage since 1981.

1981 CHÂTEAU SOCIANDO-MALLET
HAUT-MÉDOC

You have just begun to hear of this estate, which borders Calon-Ségur, but someday it will be as famous as, say, Lynch-Bages. The *French Wine Review* says it deserves to be elevated to "at least a third growth." (Lynch-Bages and Calon-Ségur are only fifth growths.)

The 1981 is a fabulous success, so powerful and intense—this is not *petit château* wine, this is classic Médoc in the style of Latour and Léoville. A *vin de garde*, this is great claret you will be enjoying, showing off, and talking about for years to come.

I predict Sociando will be reclassified upward into the *cru classé* one day and that you will be asked to pay twice this price and even at that it will still be a good buy.

$75.00 PER CASE

1981 CHÂTEAU HAUT-MARBUZET
SAINT-ESTÈPHE

Situated between Montrose and Cos d'Estournel, Haut-Marbuzet is one of the best discoveries I've made on my trips to France. I happened upon it in my favorite Bordeaux bistro. I remember the waiter pouring it (I'd never heard of Haut-Marbuzet) while I sat speechless gazing at the truly regal color as it splashed into my glass. "What the hell is this?" I thought. I've seen plenty of handsome-looking wines, but the color of the 1979 was incredible—dark, brilliant, blackish purple like crushed blackberries. I was hesitant to sniff it and break the spell, but my steak had arrived and it was time for a sip of red wine. The next day I hurried to the château only to find the 1979 already sold out. That's all right; the '81, once again, is superior to the 1979. It is a bold, gloriously full-bodied Saint-Estèphe tasting of mint, vanilla from 100% new oak, and heaps of black currant, as Harry Waugh would say. It reminds me of some of the classic Heitz and BV Cabernets.

$120.00 PER CASE

VALUE OF THE MONTH

O N VACATION. One month in Provence with no work, no tastings—drinking wine from a water glass, in fact, so I wouldn't automatically swirl and sniff and analyze. Drinking because wine tastes good! My cellar consisted of Chave's white Hermitage, Bandol rosé, and Vieux Télégraphe for the red.

One night at dinner my host was Jean-Marie Peyraud, Domaine Tempier's winemaker. He served me a glass of red wine. "I won't tell you what this is, Kermit," he said. "What do you think of it?"

I grabbed the glass, slugged down a mouthful, and said it tasted fine to me.

"No, seriously, Kermit. I think this might be interesting for you. What do you think it is?"

Inside I was cussing, fuming, trying to guard my precious vacation against any intrusion. When quitting cigarettes, let's say you smoke one—you haven't really quit, have you? So, one serious look at a glass of wine and I felt my vacation violated.

But so it was, alas, back to the grind. It was purple wine that Jean-Marie served me, rather a dark purple at that, and the nose was like a generous bouquet of violets. It suddenly occurred to me that Jean-Marie had recently traveled into Italy to the Piedmont with a wine-tasting group. A clue!

"It is a young, 1981 or 1982, Nebbiolo from the Piedmont," I proclaimed.

Jean-Marie's face dropped like he'd swallowed a bad oyster. "An Italian wine?" he asked.

"Er, uh, well, uh . . ." The master taster at work. I took another sniff. Violets! Fresh violets with black currant. It smelled great. What fun it would be to cut another slice from the *gigot* and slurp down another big, lazy swallow of this delicious wine.

Violets and black currant? Aha! Northern Rhône! It reminded me a little of Clape's Cornas, though it wasn't quite such a powerhouse as that. "It's a Syrah! A Cornas. A Saint-Joseph?" I kept plopping out names as Jean-Marie sadly shook his head no, no, no.

"Kermit, what would be a good price for a wine like this?"

I said it seemed a good $7 to $8 bottle.

Jean-Marie looked at me like Conners looks at Lendl after acing him at match point. "It's a Bergerac 1982. Not expensive. You could sell it for $4 or $5."

The next morning I once again broke my vacation vows by telephoning the Château de Combrillac to order 200 cases of their 1982.

Bergerac? That's east of Bordeaux. And the wine definitely tasted sort of east of Bordeaux too.

$4.25 PER BOTTLE $45.90 PER CASE

NEW RHÔNES

1981 CHÂTEAU GRILLET

Our allotment of the 1981 is 120 bottles. That leaves 108 for sale.

$29.95 PER BOTTLE

1979 CHÂTEAUNEUF-DU-PAPE · DIFFONTY

This was almost our value of the month—a 1979 Châteauneuf-du-Pape at only $5.95.

Ninety-nine percent of the wine drinkers don't care whether their red wine says Châteauneuf, Bordeaux, or Edna as long as they like the taste. It must be due to the traveling I do through the different wine regions, but I do care that my Volnay tastes like Volnay. If I open a bottle of Volnay and it tastes like Châteauneuf-du-Pape, I'm bugged even if it tastes like good Châteauneuf-du-Pape. It's a purist streak. I like to hear the *Goldberg Variations* on a harpsichord, not played to a polka beat in an accordion transcription. Here we can all rejoice; it's damned good wine and it really tastes like Châteauneuf-du-Pape. The warmth, the strength, the ripe fruit bouquet, the marked stony aspect . . . and it costs little more than a simple Côtes du Rhône in other wine shops.

$5.95 PER BOTTLE $64.26 PER CASE

❖ 1984 ❖

LATEST ENTRIES IN THE GUNK, FUNK, AND FIZZ SWEEPSTAKES

1982 PROSECCO · GIORGIO BUFFON

A FEW HARDY souls overlooked my previous tongue-in-cheek send-up of this lovely sparkling wine, so we succeeded in selling our 50 cases. *Thank you!* But I am pretty sure that my staff and I, along with just a handful of you, accounted for all those 600 bottles. One thing is certain: those brave enough to try a bottle returned again and again for more. The vast quivering multitudes wouldn't risk $3.99 to try it.

This time around I ordered 75 cases, hoping to pick up a few stragglers.

One thing I neglected to say in my previous write-up: Prosecco, the most popular drink in the hills north of Venice, tastes great. It sparkles; it is white, dry, and crisp; it is like a light, quaffable Champagne, an irresistibly fresh, simple charmer that livens the spirit.

$3.99 PER BOTTLE $43.10 PER CASE

1982 FREISA · ALDO CONTERNO

Your mate is in the mood for Champagne; you want something red and robust. No problem. Serve Aldo's Freisa.

These wines sparkle, the Prosecco and Freisa, and they have a substantial deposit because they ferment naturally in the bottle and they are not disgorged. You have to decant them—that, or stand up the bottle an hour before serving. Big deal.

Freisa sparkles, but it is not a light little sparkler; nor is it soda pop glop. It is actually rather a deep-colored red wine, vibrant and grapey with a raspberry-like edge to the flavor and a healthy lashing of tannin. The bubbles in Aldo's Freisa are natural—no carbon dioxide or bulk-process for him—thus the gunk, or deposit; thus the quality.

There is something elemental about this nearly still-fermenting grape juice. Aldo's Freisa is especially recommended for sausage, pasta, and for observing Dionysian rites and orgiastic frenzies. It might have been the favorite wine of Bacchus himself. I've seen statues of Bacchus; he was not critically swirling, sniffing, and scribbling down tasting notes. He was having a good time, and that is what Freisa is all about.

Aldo says serve it at room temperature. If so, I suggest that your room be pretty cool.

$4.95 PER BOTTLE $53.46 PER CASE

MORE FROM
ALDO CONTERNO . . .

1979 BAROLO "COLONELLO"

When I say that Aldo's 1979 Barolo is approachable I don't mean that it is light-bodied or ready to drink. It is not light. It is full-bodied—even though your gums don't bleed after you've chiseled out a swallow.

Barolo doesn't have to be a woody, dried-out, astringent monster. I think I'll win this argument someday and the palate-benders are going to be recognized as gross and vulgar. The search will be for harmony, flavor, and balance in Barolo wines.

I import Aldo Conterno's, who for decades has been making Barolo that tastes good without endangering its capacity for aging. You can age a rock, but even after 100 years it still tastes rocky. A 50-year-old Conterno tasted this fall was absolutely exquisite.

$12.50 PER BOTTLE $135.00 PER CASE

SOME DEPOSIT, NO RETURN

EUROPEAN WINEMAKERS are scared to death that their wines will be returned to them because of sediment, and many of them go to ridiculous extremes to make sure that their wine won't throw any deposit. Many would rob their wines of life and flavor rather than see a speck of sediment in the bottled wine.

The actions of a few idiot importers and restaurateurs and the negligence of the wine press toward the problem has created a situation in which the wine-makers' fear is real and legitimate.

For those of us who like real wine, honest wine, natural wine, it is becoming a problem of frightening proportions.

As I am reminded time after time by French winemakers, the problem origi-nated here in the States. A perfectly honest, correct wine would be shipped to America and its importer would refuse to pay for it because of some sediment. As you might suspect, the unpaid winemaker was disturbed. He reacted by search-ing out a method to prevent a deposit in his next vintage and by warning all his winemaker friends to do the same.

But today the winemakers are having trouble in France too, where wine drinkers should know better. French restaurateurs routinely send back wines

with sediment because they have encountered enough lame-brained clients who consider flawed a wine that is not absolutely brilliant and crystal clear. Bah!

This year I ordered a wine from a producer and instructed him to take nothing out of the wine, to bottle it unfiltered. He made me sign a statement swearing that I would not refuse payment if his wine threw a deposit!

How does a vintner ensure that there will be no sediment in his wine? He filters, he centrifuges, he pasteurizes, or he does something called "cold treatment," where the temperature of the wine is lowered to $-7°$ so that any solid matter freezes and falls out.

But these specks of solid matter, these teensy harmless particles, come from the grape itself. They have flavor; they have texture; they have nutrients that help the wine develop over the years. This solid matter is part of the wine, and except in certain rare circumstances it is blasphemous to take it out.

If you think a deposit is something unclean, a sign of a troubled wine, don't worry; the marketplace is full of sterile wines and you have a big selection from which to choose. Of honest, natural wines there are damned few and each year they are more difficult to find.

For the wines that I buy I insist that the winemaker leave them whole, intact. I go into the cellars now and select specific barrels or cuvées, and I request that they be bottled without stripping them with filters or other devices. This means that many of our wines will arrive with a smudge of sediment and will throw a more important deposit as time goes by. It also means the wine will taste better. Sediment is a sign of a natural wine.

I have compared samples of wines bottled with and without filtration. They were, at the start, before filtration, the same wine, but you would never guess it. The character and flavor lost to the filter pads is enormous. Filtered wine is curiously very much like a diluted wine—add 20% water to one of our reds and you will have an idea of what filtration would have done to the wine—filtration or pasteurization or who knows what they'll think of next.

When you buy wine and you see some sediment, don't return it as if it has some malady. Be glad.

◇ ◇

1981 CÔTE RÔTIE MARIUS GENTAZ

A SPECIAL CUVÉE. A rarity. One barrel, 25 cases of Côte Rôtie of a quality rarely seen outside the cellars.

The old-timers have barrels like this, but they are either blended with their other barrels at bottling or hidden away for family birthdays and anniversaries. Marius Gentaz agreed to bottle one barrel for me at a special price.

The juice comes from vines over *70 years old* from the steepest part of the Côte Brune, from a parcel called La Landonne. I imagine this is what well-made Côte Rôtie used to be like before the surface area of the appellation was officially expanded and before financial considerations led growers to pull out their old vines to replant new higher-yielding clones of Syrah.

It needs *at least* 10 years, better 20. It is a waste of money (and great wine) to open bottles now.

$22.50 PER BOTTLE $243.00 PER CASE

◇ ◇

1980 BARBERA "ROCCHE" · VIETTI

Vietti asked, "Why don't you buy my Barbera? In Italy it's my most popular wine."

"Because there is what I call The California Palate," I explained, "formed by the huge, fat, local wines. I'm afraid they'll find your Barbera sharp and acid in comparison."

"But that's what we want in Barbera," Vietti countered. "It's a wine to drink with food. With certain plates like *bagna caôda* you need that little bite. It's perfect with our local food."

Judge for yourself. I told Vietti to send me his best Barbera and we'll keep him informed of customer response.

$4.75 PER BOTTLE $51.30 PER CASE

◇ ◇ ◇ ◇ ◇ ◇ ◇ ◇

Alfredo Currado, Cantina Vietti

1982 SAINT-JOSEPH *ROUGE*
RAYMOND TROLLAT

Hugh Johnson cites Bernard Gripa as "perhaps the best grower in Saint-Joseph." I feel entitled to an opinion because I've imported so many Saint-Josephs over the years, including Gripa's. The finest Saint-Joseph—indeed, one of the most splendid wines of France—is Trollat's. Those of you with his '78 or '79 in your cellar, uncork a bottle and take a whiff—you'll be in for three or four cases of his magnificent 1982. The '79 is now breathtakingly aromatic, one of the most striking wines I've imported. Trollat is to Saint-Joseph what Chave is to Hermitage, Clape to Cornas, and Gentaz to Côte Rôtie: the master.

Each year I wind up the steep hillside to Trollat's cellar accompanied by Gérard Chave. We taste all the barrels; we discuss each; then we begin retasting and blending in order to produce the finest cuvée possible, a demanding tasting experience because each barrel is different, and quite rewarding because Chave is a great taster, and our blend of Saint-Joseph is as dear to me as any wine I import.

1982 is a superb vintage here. It may prove better than 1978. It is incredibly aromatic, a big wine with perfect tannic/acid balance, and the aftertaste is endless as the Syrah perfume comes back to haunt the olfactory senses.

This is great wine and you'll want to drink it often over many years, so go after this one in quantity.

$7.95 PER BOTTLE $85.86 PER CASE

BURGUNDY

RED BURGUNDY vintages. I buy wine by the barrel, not by the vintage, and in Burgundy especially I believe Vintage Chart Mentality does more harm to the consumer than good. The chartists award high marks to vintages that are dark and tannic. However, red Burgundy need not be dark and tannic to be special (or to age well). Because of the vintage charts many cellars are filled with 1976 red Burgundies, which with a few notable exceptions are dark, dumb, charmless wines. Too much sun means too much ripeness, which destroys the Pinot Noir's fabulous, expressive perfume.

The finest red Burgundy I tasted last year was the 1954 La Tâche, a nearly rosé-colored wine. But the aroma of that wine was simply magical. Up to now I wouldn't have imported a wine as light in color and body as that 1954 because of the California palate for chunky reds. That 1954 proved that a wine can be light-bodied and still be aromatic and generously flavored.

It was only recently that I felt I could use words like elegance and finesse in these brochures. Americans think *elegant* means *light*, which is absurd. Both full- and light-bodied wines can be elegant. Thankfully, taste has evolved and *elegance* is a word one can now employ without killing sales. I hope.

And hopefully I can import some of those exquisite lighter-bodied red Burgundies that I was turning down a few years back. Light-*bodied*, not light-flavored. After all, *light* and *full* have nothing to do with quality. Body determines the use of the wine, not its quality. The '80 Pommard below is light, the '79 is huge; they're both extraordinary. One might serve the '80 with roast chicken, for example, and the '79 with leg of lamb. Or start your dinner with the '80 and proceed to the weightier '79.

1980 Pommard · *Coste-Caumartin*

$9.95 PER BOTTLE $107.46 PER CASE

1979 Pommard "Argillières" · *Domaine Lejeune*

$18.75 PER BOTTLE $202.50 PER CASE

1981 NUITS-SAINT-GEORGES
ROBERT CHEVILLON

Over the years I've run into some amusing tidbits on Nuits-Saint-Georges in the French wine literature.

One source decided that geographically Nuits-Saint-Georges is the *rognon* (kidney) of Burgundy. That would make Chambertin the brain, Santenay the toe, and Beaune not admirably placed at all.

Still, I think the author's idea interesting because there is a subtle flavor in a true Nuits that corresponds to the particular flavor of good grilled kidney. Another writer uses the aromatic analogy of hung game birds. Many writers note the brambly, cassis-like flavor of a Nuits, but this other quality, a bit wild, carnal, renal perhaps, is harder to define and can presumably be ascribed to some component of the soil at Nuits, just as the suggestion of licorice in a Chambertin can be attributed to the marl in the soil there.

A good doctor prescribed the wine of Nuits-Saint-Georges to the Sun King, Louis XIV, when he suffered an unknown *maladie*. When the king's health was restored the tasty remedy enjoyed a vogue at court. Lord, send me a doctor like that!

One book concludes its report with the words "*Un verre de Nuits prepare la vôtre.*"

Chevillon's 1981 Nuits-Saint-Georges is quite a bargain for two reasons. First, his '81s stand with Jayer's as the finest wines of the vintage. Second, because the crop was so small, Chevillon was forced to vinify his great *premier cru* wines Les Saint Georges, Perrières, and Roncières together with his village wine. Thus you have an outstanding Nuits of *premier cru* quality at the price of a simple village wine.

It is well structured, a bit tannic, and needs three to four years' aging.

$14.95 PER BOTTLE $161.46 PER CASE

DOMAINE TEMPIER

By Richard Olney

I FIRST TASTED Domaine Tempier at the Salon des Arts Ménagers in Paris. The wine was the newly bottled 1953, so it must have been in 1955. It was a great discovery—but, at that time in my life, great discoveries abounded. I did not know that a new star was rising in the viticultural firmament, that 1953 was only the second vintage that had been bottled at the domaine (the wine having been sold in barrels for the preceding century and a half), and that the distinctive and lovely label (designed by Madame Peyraud's artist father, Alphonse Tempier) with its little line drawing of an antique frigate was a recent creation (I have always imagined that the frigate was a tribute to the Phocaean Greeks who landed in Marseille 2,500 years ago and are thought to have planted the first vineyards in Provence with cuttings from their native Ionia—but, examining the drawing now, with its sails and *fleurs-de-lis*, I think that it must be a memory of much more recent times, when barrels of Bandol were given a long sea voyage so that the changing temperatures and the movement of the ship would hasten the wine's evolution). And how could I know that, a few years hence, I would settle on a hillside only a few kilometers distant from Domaine Tempier and that the mad and wonderful Peyraud family would become lifelong friends?

Domaine Tempier is a wine—it is also a family; exuberance and finesse are the traits common to both. The Peyrauds are Lucien (who pretends to be retired), Lulu (*née* Lucie Tempier), the two sons, François (who cares for the vines) and Jean-Marie (whose eagle eye controls the vinification, the cellars, and the paperwork), four married daughters, none of whom live far away, and Laurence, the Parisian of the family, who often acts as Tempier's ambassadress to the capital—and, of course, the wives, the husbands, and a gaggle of grandchildren. The house, in which the family was raised—comfortably crumbling but solid, faded rose and ochre souvenirs reflected in the façade—was Lulu's grandparents' house, as were the original Tempier vines. The offices and the cellars are here and the comings and goings are constant. Thoughtful friends have posted a sign, borrowed from a railway crossing, at the entrance to the property—the word "train" in the legend "Un Train Peut En Cacher Un Autre," has been replaced by "Peyraud." François and Jean-Marie and their families have houses on separate sections of the property but, when the family receives, either Paule, François's wife, or Catherine, Jean-Marie's wife, is in the kitchen helping Lulu prepare the meal.

The Tempier-Peyraud theatre is a theatre of hard work which, from the outside, seems to be an ongoing celebration of the table and Bacchus. Typical is the ritual bouillabaisse, served on special occasions throughout the summer (and always for the *repas de vendangeurs*, the last day of grape-picking) on the terrace in front of the house, a ballet of dappled light playing through the grape arbor to the background accompaniment of the cicadas' chant:

Jean-Marie Peyraud, Lucien Peyraud, and François Peyraud

Soupe de poissons, an alliaceous broth made from an abundance of little Mediterranean rockfish in which wild fennel is the dominant herb, is prepared in the kitchen. To the side of the terrace, a bonfire is built of the stumps and roots of old vines, the great copper cauldron is filled with the dense fish broth and put to heat . . . A kettle of mussels and scuttling little Mediterranean crabs (*favouilles*) and a vast platter of fish with a few quartered potatoes mixed in, rubbed with saffron and anointed with the domaine's olive oil, are brought to table—their beauty must be admired before they are plunged into the boiling essence (and, as often as not, there are several cameras clicking away). The fish are mostly larger versions of those used to make the soup—*rascasses, girelles, rouquiers, galinettes, vives, Saint-Pierres*—plus a few *cigales de mer* ("sea cicadas"—blunt-nosed Mediterranean rock lobsters) and sections of conger eel and anglerfish. The crabs, the potatoes, and the firmer-fleshed fish are thrown into the pot; eight or ten minutes later the remainder goes in, and five minutes later we are at table.

For the preceding half hour, after having tasted the new wines in the cellar, we have all been mulling around with glasses of the domaine's Bandol rosé in hand, nibbling at sea urchins and *vioulets*, if they are in season, or at *crudités*; some will opt to stick with the rosé throughout the bouillabaisse, but most of us will begin drinking the cool young red wine of the year, brought up from the cellar in pitchers, a joyous explosion of fresh fruit with a suggestion of effervescence (for it still has at least a year in the wood ahead of it before growing up into a serious and dignified wine, ready for bottling). Jean-Marie will have chosen and de-canted older wines for the cheeses, and he delights in making us guess the vin-tages; Lucien may suddenly exclaim, "What's going on here? I thought there was none of this left!" and Jean-Marie will say, "Of course, Papa, I hid it," adding, for our benefit, "If I didn't hide the old vintages from Papa, there would be none left."

Those of a scientific bent claim that it is impossible that the air of a country-side—the resinous scents of the pine forests, the wild thyme, savory, rosemary, oregano, fennel, and mints of the *garrigue*—can be reflected in the bouquet of a wine, that it is merely a poetical notion, the conceit of an illogical mind . . . Never mind, at the Peyrauds' table, we find them there; wild berries, licorice, truffles, spices, violets, and cherries turn up also.

The entire Bandol appellation is contained within a huge natural basin facing the sea, defined by a belt of surrounding mountains and providing an especially privileged microclimate, of which the village of Bandol (in the past an impor-tant wine-shipping port, today a fishing port where tourism vies with the more ancient trade) marks the center—or, if one thinks of the natural formation as an amphitheatre, Bandol is the stage. The vines, planted on terraced hillsides, are exposed to the southeast, the south, and the southwest, receiving a maximum of sun, and are, at the same time, protected both from spring frosts and from the in-tense summer heat by the proximity of the sea. The earth from which the vines must eke their nourishment is so poor as to be useless for any other crop. Here, in varying proportions, it is composed of yellow and red clays, chalky rubble, and limestone; it is gravelly, stony, sometimes sandy. An arid soil is one of the prereq-uisites for all fine wines; it forces the vines to send their roots deep into the earth's mineral-rich substructures for nourishment and curtails excessive vitality, con-centrating strength in a few bunches of grapes (this must go hand in hand with radical winter pruning, of course, and it means also that a vine in its first few years cannot produce wine of the same quality as a mature vine with a deep root system).

During the 18th and 19th centuries, the wines of the Bandol were celebrated for their firmness and long-keeping qualities, due largely to a preponderance of the Mourvèdre grape in their makeup. After the devastation of the vineyard by phylloxera in 1870–1872, little Mourvèdre was replanted on grafted stock, for it produces less than the other regional varieties and is a late ripener. By 1941, when the right to its *appellation contrôlée* was conferred upon Bandol, so little Mourvè-dre was grown that the Bandol growers were granted a five-year period of grace in which to tear up inferior vines and replant Mourvèdre to raise its production to 10% of the total for the red wines. Largely through Lucien Peyraud's continu-ing struggle over the last 30 years (a struggle that has produced opposition as well as many friends), the legal minimum was later raised to 30%, and today it stands at 50%. The other principal grape varieties are Grenache and Cinsault. The max-imum legal production is 40 hectolitres to the hectare. The rosé wines must be raised in wood for 8 months before being bottled and a minimum of 18 months in wood is required of the red wines.

At Domaine Tempier, 25 hectares (approximately 60 acres) are planted to vines, of which over 70% are Mourvèdre, the remainder mostly Grenache and Cinsault, plus a couple of rows of Syrah and a handful of centenary Carignan vines (about 4%). The average age of the vines is 22 years (grapes from the young vines do not enter into the Bandol vats, but are used to make a delicious little *vin de table* that is drunk as a daily wine by family and friends); the average production is 31 hectolitres to the hectare (about 330 gallons to the acre).

For the rosé wines, the grapes are pressed as they arrive from the picking, teasing a blush of colour from the skins—in certain years, a *saignée* of must—a "bleeding"—is drawn off after a few hours of maceration from the vatted grapes destined to make the red wine, which both deepens the colour and the tannic structure of the red wine and firms up the colour and the muscle of the rosé. The grapes are stemmed for the red wine, fermentation and maceration on the skins lasts from 7 to 14 days, depending on the year, before the new wine is drawn off to finish its secondary fermentation, known as "malolactic" (a breaking down of the malic acids into lactic acid and CO_2, which results in a natural deacidification), and to slowly ferment out any residual sugars during its prolonged sojourn in the vast 5,000-litre oak tuns in which it will be pampered for the next 18 months to 3 years before being bottled.

The wine is natural: The soil is rarely and discreetly fertilized with manure, the yeasts are those that have settled into the vineyard and the cellars over generations of Tempiers and Peyrauds in a process of self-selection without the aid of laboratory cultures, the grapes are picked when their natural sugar content registers, in a normal year, from 13° to 13.5° potential alcohol (a light year may produce only 12.5° or an exceptionally rich year over 14°, the latter being the most troublesome of the two when it comes to raising the wine), the wine is neither stabilized with SO_2 nor in any other way (centrifuging, freezing, heating, etc.), nor is it fined. Before being bottled it is lightly filtered (a practice that Kermit Lynch is determinedly trying to discourage). The ancient precepts are respected: the wine is put into bottles only *à la vieille lune*—when the full moon has begun to decline—and only when the barometer is high.

The force and the tannins of the Mourvèdre grape permit the wines of Domaine Tempier to live long and to age with grace. The piercing notes of wild berries, green leafy things, fresh almonds and cherries, typical of the young wines, melt into the ensemble with the passage of time, and an old Tempier, tasted blindly and out of context by professionals not intimately familiar with the wines of Bandol, is often tentatively guessed to be a Médoc. Although wine literature stubbornly and randomly imposes the decade as the maximum drinking limit for a red Bandol, not a single vintage have I tasted since the first bottling of Domaine Tempier in 1952—and most have been tasted as recently as within the last couple of years—that is nearing the decline.

DOMAINE TEMPIER AT CHEZ PANISSE

Dᴜʀɪɴɢ ᴛʜᴇ sᴇᴄᴏɴᴅ week of May, Chez Panisse will produce nightly menus composed by Richard Olney to accompany the wine of Domaine Tempier. Telephone 548-5525 to reserve your place at table for this special gastronomic event. See Domaine Tempier at its best, with the cuisine of Provence. Olney, Panisse, and Tempier should be a magical combination.

1981 NUITS-SAINT-GEORGES "LES CAILLES"
DOMAINE ROBERT CHEVILLON

Les Cailles means "the quails." I wonder why the vineyard was so named. The bird is colored in variegated shades. Is the name a comment on the variegated taste impression of the wine?

The quail does not like to fly. A curious bird, it prefers jogging. Chevillon's Cailles has the physique of a jogger; it is lean-bodied, tight, muscular.

Waverly Root wrote, "The flesh of the quail is more lightly colored than that of strong flyers, and its taste less overpowering and more subtle—at the optimum point, in many opinions, between the blandness of barnyard fowl and the pungency of more athletic wild birds."

Brillat-Savarin called them "the daintiest and most charming" of the wild birds, but the wine in question is far from dainty.

Or did a winegrower, once upon a time in Nuits-Saint-Georges, take leave of his wife to go prune that section of his vineyard where a family of quail had taken up residence? "I'll be pruning there where the quail are." *Les Cailles.*

Tasting Chevillon's 1981 Cailles you really see the effects of the year's meager production. One drop on the palate makes quite an impression because of the concentration of flavor. The sap that normally went into two grapes went into one.

Which is not to say that it is a big, fat wine. His Cailles is never thus. It is tight and lean with a tannic edge to it. When I taste a drop I want to drink all there is of it. Each taste is so intriguing, so Burgundian, so marvelous, and I don't want the marvel to cease. This is going to make a great bottle of Burgundy.

$16.95 ᴘᴇʀ ʙᴏᴛᴛʟᴇ $183.06 ᴘᴇʀ ᴄᴀsᴇ

1982 DOMAINE DU VIEUX TÉLÉGRAPHE

Fʀᴏᴍ ᴛɪᴍᴇ to time this job doesn't seem so bad after all. I write these notes to you from sunny Provence after a visit to Henri Brunier's Vieux Télégraphe at Châteauneuf-du-Pape.

The visit began around 10 A.M. with a tasting of the various cuvées of 1983. Then we got down to work on the 1982. I was permitted the opportunity to taste all the casks and select my favorite for California. Two stood out, and the bottling you receive will be a blend of those two.

1982 is marvelous at Vieux Télégraphe, very forward and generous, tasting great right out of the casks. The nose is complex with Mourvèdre accents, black cherry, and plums. The texture is soft and supple and the flavors coat the palate. It is firm and long, with the characteristic stony finish.

It tasted so good we put the two selected cuvées together into a bottle and carried it upstairs to accompany Madame Brunier's roast leg of spring lamb. Lunch faded gently into the afternoon with ripe cheeses and older bottles of Vieux Télégraphe, but it is that vibrant, flavorful 1982 that rests in my memory.

$78.00 PER CASE

1982 BOURGOGNE *BLANC* · FRANÇOIS JOBARD

In all the world of wine with its mind-boggling array of fine Chardonnays, François Jobard stands alone; no one has successfully imitated his style. While other wines dazzle with power and oak, butter and butterscotch, they can seem garish once your palate has adapted to the Apollonian restraint François Jobard's wines exhibit.

His are never overblown, even in years like 1971 and 1976. His seem fresher than others from the start, and they retain that youthful freshness long after the blind-tasting champions are faded and flat. And there is always that perfect whisper of new oak, never overdone for easy effect. Impeccably vinified models of finesse and breed, Jobard's wines show a master's touch.

$7.95 PER BOTTLE $85.86 PER CASE

THE 1983 BEAUJOLAIS FROM TRÉNEL FILS

With Notes Written by Monsieur Trénel

TRÉNEL HAS BEEN in the Beaujolais business for fifty years. He is a *négociant*, along with Loyau at Vouvray the only *négociant* from whom I buy.

In the Beaujolais region Trénel is respected for his seriousness and his palate. I have visited domaines from whom Trénel selects his cuvées and found Trénel's bottling superior to the domaine's own estate-bottling. I reorder wine from him (Pouilly-Fuissé, for example), and receive a negative response when I *know* that there is a lake of it available to him—it is just that there is none available that he deems worthy of his name. Such virtue is rare when the bucks are there for the taking. That's why I have confidence in him, that and because he knows more about Beaujolais than I do.

The 1983 Beaujolais are so impressive that I bought a large variety in order to provide you with an in-depth look at what the different Beaujolais *crus* have to offer. And I asked Trénel to write tasting notes on each of his wines.

SOME GENERAL REMARKS ON THE WINES OF OUR REGION: BEAUJOLAIS-MÂCONNAIS

By Monsieur Trénel

THE WINES FROM our region are not specifically wines to lay down, wines that improve with age.

Like everything alive there is a period of ascendance, then they reach a plateau for a period more or less long, then descend more or less quickly. This is, moreover, true for all wines, but it is difficult enough to predict ahead of time.

One recommendation: drink our wines from the moment they please you and don't keep the simple Beaujolais and Beaujolais-Villages for more than one year, and two or three years for the *grands crus* and the white wines.

1983 Beaujolais-Villages "Cuvée Spéciale"

This wine is fine, elegant, and above all light-bodied, typically Gamay with its grapey aroma. Don't expect more than it can give, which is to say: the pleasure of a fresh, quaffable drink that won't spoil your digestive system.

$5.50 PER BOTTLE $59.40 PER CASE

1983 Chiroubles

As always, the Chiroubles is the most "Beaujolais" of the great growths. Chiroubles is a *grand cru* thanks to the pride and the care of its wine producers and the relatively low yield of its hillside slopes, but it remains very "Beaujolais" because of its fresh grapey taste, the simplicity of its aromas, and its drinkability. It is easy to drink!

$5.95 PER BOTTLE $64.26 PER CASE

1983 Morgon "Le Py"

Le Py is one of the best vineyards within the appellation Morgon and one of the most typical. Aroma of pit fruits (cherry, kirsch). Morgon is one of the Beaujolais growths that ages the best, along with the Juliénas and certain Moulin-à-Vents.

$5.95 PER BOTTLE $64.26 PER CASE

1983 Juliénas

A wine rich, supple, full-bodied, almost severe—it doesn't give everything yet, but it will blossom soon enough in the next few months; it is therefore a wine with a future. For the moment, aroma of peach and reseda. (KL: *From old vines, the Juliénas is a powerful grand cru, mouth-filling, tannic, the extreme opposite of the fresh, gay Chiroubles.*)

$5.75 PER BOTTLE $62.10 PER CASE

1983 Moulin-à-Vent "La Rochelle"

La Rochelle is the top vineyard of the appellation Moulin-à-Vent. The wine from this beautiful cuvée attains a rare approach to perfection in the actual tasting. Aroma of strawberry and violet; the wine is round and long on the palate. Its charm is all in its delicacy, but that won't stop us from hoping for a long conservation, perhaps three years, perhaps four . . . But why take risks? It would be better to profit from it immediately.

$7.50 PER BOTTLE $81.00 PER CASE

◇ ◇ ◇ ◇ ◇ ◇ ◇ ◇

1983 POUILLY-FUMÉ · ROBERT DAGUENEAU

Nowadays I often taste through a cellar and select my barrels. It is not as simple as taking the good and giving the boot to the bad because in a good cellar most of the barrels taste good, the mistakes having already been sold off in bulk to a *négociant.*

In Dagueneau's cellar the barrels were unmarked, so in order to keep them straight we began christening each barrel as we tasted and tried to comprehend its wine. One was baptized Annie Girardet. Another barrel (which will arrive this fall) could only be honored with the name Simone Signoret.

This current arrival was christened Catherine Deneuve for reasons we all perfectly understood as the wine swirled in our glasses.

$7.50 PER BOTTLE $81.00 PER CASE

Robert Dagueneau, Pouilly-Fumé

François Jullien de Pommerol, Domaine Lejeune, Pommard

POMMARD

WHILE SEARCHING for kind words about Pommard I find that English authors exhibit a restraint toward the wine that is puzzling if not downright suspicious:

Anthony Hanson: "I avoid Pommard like the plague . . . "

Hugh Johnson: ". . . the least wonderful and the best known of the villages of Burgundy."

H. W. Yoxall: ". . . pleasant drinks without much authority . . . light in body . . . not very exciting . . . "

The English may be celebrated for their reserve, but this time they've gone too far.

Don't they realize that Roman artifacts have been unearthed at Pommard? The Romans, of course, were the original Masters of Wine, having seemingly cultivated the vine at every noteworthy viticultural site in the Old World, including such task-worthy geological configurations as Hermitage and Côte Rôtie. You're going to disagree with a Roman about wine? Plus, no one has ever heard of a Roman drinking Port with Dover sole.

If the Romans were at Pommard there was passably good drink there.

I've tasted great bottles from the village of Pommard. Why haven't the English?

Of course, the French themselves are not always polite toward Pommard. Pierre Ponnelle said to me 10 years ago, "You could piss in a bottle, label it Pommard, and the English would buy it."

I've not tasted that one, but in Pierre Ponnelle's joke I find a clue to explain the English critics' attitude toward Pommard. England (and the rest of the world, for that matter) did not know domaine-bottled Pommard, which is rather a recent happenstance in the wine world. Yes, there *were* domaine-bottled Pommards, but they were quite few. The Brits knew shipper-bottled Pommard, and there is much evidence to support a view that what they were tasting had little to do with real, live Pommard.

Camille Rodier in *Le Vin de Bourgogne* wrote that "there is no wine more subject to fraud and one can figure that more Pommard is consumed across the world in a week than is harvested in ten years at Pommard itself." Hmmm.

Many gave up buying bottles labeled *Chablis* until they tasted one from François Raveneau. And a bottle labeled *Nuits-Saint-Georges* can contain anything from orange-colored plonk to the regal, purplish-colored brew brimming with earthy berry-like fruit that we buy from Robert Chevillon.

Let's be reasonable. Bad wine is not contagious. One rotten Pommard does not act like a rotten apple.

And wine sold in England as *Pommard* because a shipper decided it could pass as *Pommard-like* should not be allowed to bias our . . . Do you see what I mean? Pour a glass of one of my Pommards. Regard its color. Take a sniff. Taste it. Slurp it around a bit. Then decide whether or not you like Pommard.

True Pommard is grown at Pommard. It is to the Côte de Beaune what Gevrey-Chambertin is to the Côte de Nuits. It never shows the elegance of Volnay, just as Gevrey never has the elegance of a Chambolle or a Vosne-Romanée. Like Gevrey-Chambertin, it is an expressive wine, hard and a bit unruly in its youth, but a phenomenon nonetheless. The youthful berry and awkwardness disappear quickly, but the firmness and virility remain. As an old wine Pommard is earthy, more animal, more toward spice, dead leaves, and black truffle. There is a dark side to its character that I like.

MARZEMINO CONTEST

1982 MARZEMINO · GIORGIO BUFFON

Marzemino is dry red table wine. Like most of the wines with the "Buffon" touch, it sparkles. It tastes good served slightly cool.

Marzemino plays a role in Mozart's *Don Giovanni*. It is the wine the great seducer drinks with his last supper. Musical references are flying; Leporello is whispering insults while he swipes bites of pheasant from his master's plate; the Don himself feels reckless. There is danger and abandon in the air. The end is at hand.

"Hurray for good wine, the support and glory of mankind," sings Don Giovanni.

The Don was no pauper. To compile a list of conquests like his, you can't waste energy worrying about money. He could have chosen an expensive Barolo or Brunello to celebrate his forthcoming descent into hell. Or the Italian wine named *Inferno* would have been an obvious choice.

But no, the Don drinks Marzemino, and he even takes time from his headlong descent into the flames to declare it *"Eccellente!"*

Learned texts have been written about nearly every aspect of the opera. Was Donna Anna raped? Seduced? Rejected? Unfulfilled? But no one so far has seriously confronted the Don's wine selection.

The best typewritten answer to the question "Why did Marzemino accompany the Don's Last Supper?" will win a recording of the opera. If we receive more than one entry, decision of the judge will be final.

But how can you intelligently answer the question if you haven't tasted the stuff?

$3.29 PER BOTTLE $35.53 PER CASE

A RHÔNE DISCOVERY

1981 SAINT-JOSEPH *ROUGE* · CLOS DE L'ARBALESTRIER

Arriving near Tain l'Hermitage on the Rhône River at sunset, I was too late, too cold, and too tired to do any work.

My innkeeper placed before me a platter of tender raw ham, sausages, cornichons, and black olives. There was a pot of mustard, a pot of sweet butter, crusty bread, and a bottle of Saint-Joseph.

The wine tasted so old-fashioned, so anachronistic, that it transported me back in time and I sat alone enjoying a daydream in which I was in the company of that great traveler and teller of tales, Alexandre Dumas. He would have ordered the innkeeper to see that a barrel of the wine be sent back to his Paris estate.

What a prize to find something like this in 1984. Old-fashioned, rustic—but *not* obsolete.

All the ingredients are present for a great Syrah: an amphitheatre-shaped vineyard of 40- to 60-year-old vines that receives sunlight from dawn to dusk; small production; fermented and aged in old oak casks; unfiltered.

The vineyard is full of apricot, peach, cherry, and plum trees, and the scent of pit fruits is pronounced. In this age of Star Wars technology there is something about this ungarbled product of the earth that is good for the soul.

$6.50 PER BOTTLE $70.20 PER CASE

❖ 1985 ❖

ITALIAN REDS

1982 CHIANTI CLASSICO · NITTARDI

I AM BORED by all this hoopla over the "new" Chianti, in which you will find no juice from white grapes (Trebbiano), no prickle, no bitterness, no fun.

They are trying to turn Chianti into one of those faceless international wines: pick it ripe, let's add some Cabernet Sauvignon, let's smother it with new oak . . . you can't tell if it is from Italy, France, California, South Africa, or Australia.

Here is the old-fashioned Chianti, the kind that raised your spirits in your favorite *trattoria* in Florence, that went so well with the cuisine, that was next to free. Classic Chianti Classico!

$2.99 PER BOTTLE $32.29 PER CASE

1983 FREISA · VIETTI

David turned up his nose and said it smelled like lees. Morgan turned on to it with his second glass. George was in Mexico. Ted asked, "Is this another one of your funk, gunk, and fizz wines?" I quaffed it with visions of sausage and pasta. I love Freisa.

It is dark purple, bubbly and snappy, raspberry-scented, and I serve it cool and I serve it often.

$4.95 PER BOTTLE $53.46 PER CASE

◦ ◦ ◦ ◦ ◦ ◦ ◦ ◦

1983 RAVENEAU CHABLIS

Raveneau is a man of few words. When he mumbled that I would do well to set aside a good quantity of his '83s in my own cellar it was not as if Lee Iacocca had

advised me to buy Chrysler stock. An optimistic or positive word from Raveneau sits in the stone-cold Chablis air as if chiseled there. He didn't even gaze earnestly into my eyes when he said it.

His '83s are rich, powerful Chablis with plenty of acidity underneath, wines to drink over two decades. They are reminiscent of his

'59 vintage. The Hotel l'Etoile in *centre ville* Chablis still has Raveneau's 1959 Montée de Tonnerre on their wine list. That makes it worth a detour despite the cuisine. On my first buying trip to France in 1974 I ordered Raveneau's 1929 from the same hotel's list.

		PER CASE
1983	*Vaillons*	$135.00
1983	*Butteaux*	120.00
1983	*Chapelot*	135.00
1983	*Montée de Tonnerre*	186.00
1983	*Blanchot (six-bottle limit)*	210.00
1983	*Valmur (six-bottle limit)*	210.00

1984 CORBIÈRES *BLANC*
JEAN BERAIL

Muscadet has long been considered the perfect all-around inexpensive dry white. It is the café white of Paris. However, there is one drawback: Muscadet does not work with Mediterranean cuisine. Once you introduce olive oil, garlic, and tomato, Muscadet will detract from your cuisine and such cuisine will cancel the virtues of your Muscadet.

It is difficult, however, to locate an inexpensive southern French white that has the freshness and zip of a good Muscadet. Berail's white Corbières solves our dilemma. It is perfect with Provençal cuisine, the balance is impeccable, it is fresh and clean, and its verdant crispness excites the palate and the appetite.

$2.99 PER BOTTLE $32.30 PER CASE

1983 SAINT-JOSEPH *BLANC*
TROLLAT

The Trollats are a father-and-son team, aged 80 and 50, respectively. The father did not filter his white; the son now does. Almost everyone filters whites today.

I objected to the nose of a sample bottling of this 1983 because I detected a smell of cardboard, a smell wine often picks up as it passes through the filter pads. "What if you don't filter my barrels?" I asked.

The father, Ernest, pulled out a moldy old bottle. "This was not filtered. Let's see if it's okay." It turned out to be a 1972 (white!) Saint-Joseph. It was fabulous!

So, this '83 is unfiltered and may throw some deposit if you age it. Believe me, it is worth a little lack of brilliancy in order to keep all the flavors intact. This is a big vintage for their white. Show me an Hermitage *Blanc* with this much personality and it will probably be Chave's.

$7.95 PER BOTTLE $85.86 PER CASE

Lundi   Saucisson Vigneronne
Mardi   Lapin aux Pruneaux
Mercredi   Andouillette au Vouvray
Jeudi   Jarret du Porc
Vendredi   Barbare au Four

SPECIAL SAMPLER CASE
WINES OF THE LOIRE

Aᴸᴸ ᴛʜᴇ ʀᴀɢᴇ in Paris this spring seemed to be the little wine bars featuring wines and cuisine from the Loire Valley. They are popping up all over Paris. They are inexpensive, and if you fall into a good one you won't at all envy those tourists who had to strap themselves into suit and tie to spend hundreds of dollars at one of the multi-starred gastronomic Disneylands which to a greater and greater extent rely on Americans for their continued existence. In the little bistros you won't be surrounded by English speakers because these joints are frequented by locals. You'll know that you are in Paris, France.

One of the oldest and most conveniently located is Au Sauvignon in the 7th arrondissement (80, rue des Saints-Pères). There is no cooking; there is wine, charcuterie, and cheese from the Loire, plus a few sidewalk tables that permit you to observe the action on the street in this old quarter of the city.

Just around the corner from the Panthéon (19, rue des Fosses-Saint-Jacques) in the 5th there is a real scene going on at the Café de la Nouvelle Marie. The service is slow and surly—you've got to earn your glass of Anjou whether you're known there or not—and the platters of sausage and ham are the best I've tasted. You can order Chinon, Bourgueil, and various Loire whites by the glass. Patricia Wells's *Food Lover's Guide to Paris* calls it "Paris' quintessential wine bar." A wild accordionist who appears from time to time is actually worth a listen.

Aux Négociants (27, rue Lambert in the 18th) is funky and good. I don't understand the name because they don't serve *négociant* wines. Here you'll find delicious farm cheeses, homemade *rillettes*, and a good selection of Loire wines, including the rare Jasnières. The *plat du jour* is listed on the chalkboard.

Off in the 11th arrondissement (70, rue Alexandre Dumas) I found a young wine fanatic who merits attention at his new Bistrot La Davinière. I tasted some unusual discoveries there—a *demi-sec* from Azay-le-Rideau ($1 per glass) made a lovely apéritif, round yet steely firm underneath. He pours Reverdy's Sancerre and a delicious Chinon from old vines that was clean and expansively flavored and served at the proper temperature. You can cap off lunch with a glass of 1970

Vouvray *demi-sec*. Prices are low: a generous helping of the day's special, *Boeuf en Daube d'Orléans*, worked out to $3.50. My bill rose to unlikely heights because I had to research his exemplary collection of Loire wines.

I left Paris and headed for the Loire Valley, where I succeeded in gathering together a good variety of the region's fruity, mineral wines. You owe yourself the pleasure of knowing these wines better. In the sampler case you'll start with a sparkling Vouvray that might make you forget Champagne; there is a good range of whites, a fantastic rosé, and three reds.

SPECIAL SAMPLER CASE $52.00

TOCAI FRIULANO
ABBAZIA DI ROSAZZO

EVERY SO OFTEN I fall in love with a little-known wine and it bugs me that everyone else isn't enjoying it too. The next thing you know I'm preaching the virtues of the wine to my staff, to my friends, to winemakers, to whoever enters the shop. Perhaps it is not so bad after all, if that evangelical streak helps keep me enthusiastic about my work. Domaine Tempier's soulful red inspired a lengthy crusade. A couple of years ago I chastised the wine world for ignoring the big reds from Cornas, and lately I have certainly done more than my share to turn the Western Hemisphere on to the charms of Dolcetto d'Alba. Now along comes northern Italy's dry white Tocai. Try one. I love the stuff, but I've noticed that my customers' eyes tend to glaze over whenever I recommend it.

Meanwhile, of course, Italian whites labeled Chardonnay (usually utter bores) sell by the truckload over here, while the Tocai, a wine that is the opposite of boring, a wine of unmistakable character, goes begging. It gives me fits; something original and fine is ignored while something vulgar and blatant is valued.

For one thing, the taste of Tocai is hard to define. The normal catchwords don't apply. One would be hard-pressed to come up with a Tocai jingle. Then there is the problem of Tocai's name. We encountered a similar problem with Dolcetto at first because Dolcetto sounds sweet. *Dolce*, right? But Dolcetto is not sweet. Tocai is not sweet, it is dry . . . which brings up the confusion with the sweet Tokays from California (*plonk*) and Hungary (*wow*), and with the Tokay from Alsace (*dry, usually*).

- *Tocai is not Tokay.*
- *Tocai is native to northern Italy, and as far as I know it is not to be found elsewhere.*
- *Tocai makes a wine of noble pretensions only in Italy's Friuli, where it is planted on the evergreen slopes up against the Yugoslavian border.*

Tocai is a wine difficult to describe. Victor Hazan finds "fruity, floral, and herbal aromas," then seeking precision he goes for broke with "almonds and, more faintly, of fennel," a valiant effort, in fact. I would never have noticed the green almond or the nearly indiscernible anise note had it not been for Hazan's suggestion. He's right, but it is subtle; Tocai's aroma is seductively elusive, which is one of its virtues.

I suggest trying one all by itself to start, because you'll see it more clearly by itself and because it serves as a stimulating aperitif. It goes with a variety of dishes but has a special affinity for smoky-tasting food, charcoal-grilled vegetables, fish, birds, pork . . . Those restaurants that specialize in charcoal-grilled meats should feature a good Tocai, but then of course their customers would never order a bottle because *no one over here knows anything about Tocai Friulano!*

How about a special price to encourage you to try Tocai?

For example:

$4.95 PER BOTTLE $53.46 PER CASE

FINE RHÔNE WINES FROM CHÂTEAU DU TRIGNON

BECAUSE GRAPES possess the talent to express *terroir*, the first step toward making fine wine is deciding which grape variety to grow in which soil. Sometimes one has no choice; for red Hermitage only Syrah is legally permitted. However, like a painter who chooses his surface and who blends the pigments on his palette to create different color tones, a winemaker in the southern Rhône has a variety of soil types and up to 22 permitted grape varieties with which to work. Thus the enormous variety of styles available to the consumer.

There is no "best" producer of Côtes du Rhône. I have imported several, but I keep going back to Trignon because there is always something different, interesting, and exciting for me to taste. The winemaker belongs to a small group that meets several times per year in each other's cellars to taste and talk wine: Chave of Hermitage, Peyraud of Domaine Tempier, Guigal of Ampuis, Perrin of Beaucastel, Roux of Trignon.

The Château du Trignon lies between Sablet and Gigondas with a perfect view of the splendid Dentelles de Montmirail, one of the Rhône Valley's magical sites. Here the Romans settled (smart fellows) and grew wine grapes in the first century A.D.

Our sampler case of ten bottles will keep you up to date on this fine domaine. It contains three different vintages, including three examples from the 1981 vintage.

SAMPLER PRICE $39.00

1983 BORDEAUX

THE 1983 BORDEAUX are imposing, boldly flavored wines, very often showing enormous concentration and extravagant personalities. In the years to come I predict that it will be quite a special event to pull a 1983 claret out of one's cellar.

It is a desirable vintage. Again. The third fine vintage in a row. An extremely questionable musical analogy can be made here: 1981, the most classic of the three vintages, recalls Haydn's music. 1982 is something divine. Mozart springs to mind because there is a deceptive impression of facility—anyone can appreciate the quality of the '82s, and truth be told it took no great talent to vinify them. They possess a god-given perfection, and if the angels drink wine (what else?) they'll be drinking '82s. It follows that 1983 is our Ludwig van Beethoven vintage, a bit too wild and tempestuous for angelic circles. Fist shaking is not permitted in heaven. These '83s are far from tame or timid. As a new piano was developed to withstand Beethoven's most thunderous passages, so a wineglass seems barely able to contain these audacious 1983 clarets.

		PER CASE FIFTHS
1983	*Château Sociando-Mallet* · *Haut-Médoc*	$104.00
1983	*Château Moulin de la Rose* · *Saint-Julien*	98.00
1983	*Château de L'Hospital* · *Graves*	128.00
1983	*Château Haut-Marbuzet* · *Saint-Estèphe*	135.00
1983	*Clos Trimoulet* · *Saint-Emilion* Grand Cru	78.00
1983	*Château la Dominique* · *Saint-Emilion* Grand Cru Classé	145.00
1983	*Château L'Arrosée* · *Saint-Emilion* Grand Cru Classé	160.00
1983	*Château Bon Pasteur* · *Pomerol*	138.00
1983	*Château la Conseillante* · *Pomerol*	306.00
1983	*Château Doisy-Daëne* · *Barsac*	112.00

◊ ◊ ◊ ◊ ◊ ◊ ◊

1983 CORNAS · A. CLAPE

In a way it is crazy to return once and often twice a year to taste with winemakers like Clape. It is a long haul from Berkeley to Cornas. Since I have purchased each and every vintage from Clape since his 1976, why not simply mail in my order?

Madame de Lacaussade, Château de L'Hospital

Auguste Clape's cellar at Cornas

After all these years can't Clape and his great Cornas vineyard be trusted to produce good wine? Yes, but by being there in person I might stumble upon something like this cuvée. No one else in the world (except possibly Madame Clape) will receive this particular cuvée of Clape 1983 Cornas: 100% old vines. Old vines, which is to say, 80 years old!!

In any cellar, there are differences from cask to cask. Tasting through Clape's '83s, this one was staggering: purplish black color; huge blackberry aroma; enormous body; voluptuous tannic texture—easily the finest young Cornas in my experience.

$128.00 PER CASE

1981 GIGONDAS
GEORGES FARAUD

This is what I mean by ultra-traditional. A visit to Faraud's cellar at the entrance to Gigondas is like a visit to the 19th century. If you wonder what Gigondas tasted like back then, uncork this beauty.

As usual, the story starts with the soil. There are three terrains at Gigondas:

1. *The sandy, stony riverbed around the River Ouvèze*

2. *The mid-slopes near the village*

3. *The steeper vineyard sites, which at Gigondas, while they contribute certain qualities, will not alone yield the generously flavored, heady wine we expect from a bottle bearing the name Gigondas*

Georges Faraud, Gigondas

Faraud has the ideal combination; he is one of the few who owns plots of vines upon all three soils. His production averages 25 hectoliters to the hectare, a pitifully small production, about one-third the production at Meursault in a bountiful year. Thus, the power, the sap, the concentration of flavors in his wine. Thus, Faraud's Spartan lifestyle. He drives a tractor, not a Mercedes.

You will see releases from 1983 and even 1984 Gigondas already, while Faraud is just releasing his 1981. It spent these years in his large oak *foudres*. That is how Gigondas used to be done.

1981: Deep purple with glints of black. Fruity, sappy nose. Very pretty, deep, ripe flavors. The enormous tannins have been tamed during the wine's sojourn in cask. The 1981 is a great vintage here, and it will continue to please into the next century.

$7.95 PER BOTTLE $85.86 PER CASE

1984 PINOT BIANCO
ABBAZIA DI ROSAZZO

THERE IS THE lovely story that Gouges at Nuits-Saint-Georges noticed a branch of his Pinot Noir bearing white grapes. He grafted and reared it and there was born a new variety, Pinot Blanc. Perhaps that is how Gouges acquired his Pinot Blanc, but there is evidence of its cultivation in the Roman era.

Jean-Marie Ponsot's Monts Luisants at Morey-Saint-Denis is Pinot Blanc, and he believes that Pinot Blanc was planted there centuries ago, that the plant was in fact the source of the name *Monts Luisants*, which translates as "glowing hillsides." "Pinot Noir leaves turn red in the fall," says Ponsot, "the leaves of the Blanc turn golden yellow, never red. When the sun sets you can see light glowing from the leaves. It is poetry, and true."

It seems that Pinot Blanc, or Pinot Bianco, was first introduced to Italy's Friuli by the Count Latour of Capriva. The plantings began to spread with the reconstruction of the Friuli vineyards after the phylloxera. It has adapted well because the Friuli possesses soils and microclimates similar to Burgundy. Old-timers in the Friuli still refer to Pinot Bianco as white Burgundy.

In the Friuli (whose wines, as one writer said, "are more exquisite than renowned") the Pinot Blanc gives a racier, livelier wine than found in Burgundy. It is not chaptalized, for one thing, and it sees little or no oak in the vinification.

Even without oak there is a natural toasty quality to Pinot Bianco's aroma, an aroma that can be extremely delicate and fine in the hands of a talented wine-maker. There is an intensity to the wine; the vine's production is small and the clusters are compact. Intense, yes, but not heavy or ponderous. You find nerve and roundness in the same mouthful of wine, which I would call an ideal combination.

The Abbazia's Pinot Bianco is a gorgeous wine that will provide lots of drinking pleasure. From a small vineyard with a centuries-old tradition, we have 100 cases.

$5.95 PER BOTTLE

⊰ 1986 ⊱

1984 FAUGÈRES · GILBERT ALQUIER

FAUGÈRES is a lazy-looking village in the Languedoc north of Béziers. It consists of a few stone-walled, tile-roofed houses shaded by the ever-present plane trees, which diminish the swelter of the Mediterranean sun. I have noticed no café, no bar, no *tabac*. The streets are always empty. The activity takes place in the cellars or in the vineyards that surround the village. I cannot remember what prompted me to visit Faugères that first fruitful visit to the Languedoc, but I left having placed an order for Gilbert Alquier's superb red wine and have repeated ordering from him ever since, except in 1983 when I arrived too late and Alquier had already filtered the soul out of his entire vintage.

"The French are crazy," he moaned. "If they see a single little speck in the wine, they think something's wrong."

I got to this 1984 early and selected the finest cask, unfiltered. It is a beautiful wine and tastes like it should cost more.

Alquier's vineyard is planted in Syrah, Grenache, and Mourvèdre. If you recall his 1982, the character of the Mourvèdre dominated with its wild herb and black cherry aroma. In 1984 it is the Syrah that dominates with its finesse, wild berry, and violets. Deep purple color, complex aroma, good chewy quality. A wine at once fine and rustic.

Serve this hearty red with pizza, Provençal dishes, *coq au vin* and other stews, or grilled meats. It can also stand up to strong cheeses.

$4.95 PER BOTTLE $53.46 PER CASE

1982 DOMAINE TEMPIER

WE HAVE OFFERED how many excellent Domaine Tempier vintages? I began with their 1971. 1976 is the only vintage I did not import; 1976 when a harvest deluge turned the grapes into water balloons. Normally the sun shines bright at Bandol, but even amidst the long list of successes 1982 stands out at Domaine Tempier. The winemaker says that since they began making Bandol in 1951 the greatest years have been 1964, 1970, 1971, and 1982.

Presented below are Tempier's two finest cuvées, the single vineyard wines La Migoua and La Tourtine. The distinct personality of each is amply displayed in 1982, believe me. It is best to take some of each. How much? You'll want to drink it now, 20 years from now, and at all points in between.

"LA MIGOUA"

Last year I explained the difference between the two vineyard sites, but it bears repeating. La Migoua is a wild site with vines planted irregularly here and there upon rugged, mountainous terrain. The air is scented with pine, wildflower, rosemary, thyme, and anise. Amidst the rows of vines you still see cherry, olive, and apricot trees, struggling leftovers from when the ancients covered the mountainside with orchards. This aromatic feast gives the cuvée La Migoua its special character. The 1982 is uncommonly rich and loaded with flavor. It will last 20 to 30 years if you want it to.

"LA TOURTINE"

A vineyard must have been in Mother Nature's mind when she designed this steep amphitheatre-shaped hillside with its perfect south-facing exposure to the path of the sun. No one knows when man thought to tame it by unearthing the largest stones and arranging them into a series of walls up the hillside that would hold enough soil in place to permit cultivation. Nowadays terraces are repaired, but the task of constructing new ones, stone by stone, is rarely undertaken, even at Côte Rôtie. La Tourtine is also special because here one finds some of the oldest Mourvèdre vines at Bandol. The 1982 is a powerful wine, sinewy, with nerve and backbone.

$135.00 PER CASE (TENTHS, FIFTHS, OR MAGNUMS)

A PROVENÇAL DINNER

Apéritif	CASSIS *BLANC*
Tapenade Lulu	CHÂTEAU SIMONE *BLANC*
Artichoke and Garlic Stew	BANDOL ROSÉ
Grilled Lamb Chops	BANDOL *ROUGE*
Cheese	CHÂTEAU SIMONE *ROUGE*

TAPENADE

Purée ½ cup pitted black olives, 1 clove garlic, ¼ cup capers, 4 anchovy filets, and 1 tablespoon Provençal herbs. Slowly incorporate about ⅓ cup olive oil in a slow stream until you have a runny paste. Spread onto toasted rounds of baguette and serve.

ARTICHOKE AND GARLIC STEW

Trim small artichokes of the stalks and top portion of leaves, pull off the tough outer leaves, then pare down to the tenderest part of the leaves and hearts. Sauté for a few minutes in olive oil, then add an unbelievably generous amount

of fresh thyme. Add the unpeeled cloves of several heads of garlic. Pour in a glass of water or white wine and lower the heat to a gentle simmer. Stew for an hour or so until the garlic cloves are meltingly tender and can be squeezed out of the skin onto bread or toast.

GRILLED LAMB CHOPS

Marinate thick chops with olive oil and finely chopped garlic. Cover with fresh rosemary branches for an hour. Grill over hot coals, throwing rosemary sprigs onto the coals during the grilling to flavor the meat with aromatic smoke.

Serve with potatoes roasted in the coals and grilled zucchini. Season the potatoes and wrap them twice in foil. Nestle them into moderately hot coals and cook until tender. Slice the zucchini lengthwise, brush with olive oil, and grill until a fork slides through effortlessly.

1984 CONDRIEU
PIERRE DUMAZET

Dumazet stood gazing at me rather somberly, I thought, given the praise I had just heaped upon his 1984 Condrieu.

"I have heard from other producers that you take their red wines unfiltered, but what about whites?" he asked.

"It may be more dangerous with white wine," I said, "because people expect a white to be absolutely brilliant. But I do buy unfiltered whites. I ship them in a refrigerated container to protect them, and they are amongst the most-sought-after whites that I import."

"I want my wine in bottle to taste exactly like this," Dumazet said, lifting up his glass of '84 drawn directly from barrel. "If you want to gamble with me, I won't filter it this year."

We are gambling on you, the buyer, not on the wine. The wine is sound. Will you accept it if it throws a deposit? Must Dumazet emasculate the aroma and flavor in order to avoid some harmless sediment? His wine has always tasted best right out of the barrel. Unfiltered, the aroma is incredible, so splendid and fragrant that it leaps out of the glass to meet you. There is tension and nerve and texture to it. Unfiltered, the aftertaste is almost endless, and I am convinced that it will age well.

$24.95 PER BOTTLE $269.46 PER CASE

TUSCAN SAMPLER

THE BIG TO-DO in Tuscan wine today is Cabernet. Cabernet and new oak in Chianti-land! I taste them and think *nice wine, but* WHY BOTHER?

Cabernet seems to make decent wine wherever it ripens, from Spain to South Africa, from Chile to Australia. *All right, yet another*, is my response when I taste the latest rehash of the Cabernet recipe.

A good traditional Chianti goes for four to ten bucks, while a Cabernet from the same soil—aged in new oak, of course—apparently finds eager buyers at two to three times the price. Thus, there will be more and more of those faceless international Cabernets until the public's thirst for them is quenched.

I like Chianti and I don't want it to disappear.

Upon Tuscany's sunbaked landscape silvery green olive trees color the hillsides. Cypress shape the horizon. The third component of this enchanted trilogy is the vine. Uprooting traditional varieties in order to plant those from Bordeaux seems a sacrilege. Purists unite! Enjoy the traditional-style Tuscan reds in this month's nine-bottle sampler of wines from Castello di Cacchiano, Casavecchia di Nittardi, and Fossi.

SAMPLER PRICE $44.00

DOMAINE ZIND-HUMBRECHT
GOÛT DE TERROIR

SOME ARGUE that the mineral components that nourish a vine contribute little to a wine's taste. David Bruce says, "I'm not inclined to think soil types are as important as many people think." Ridge's Paul Draper and Chalone's Dick Graff, on the other hand, make a direct correlation between soil and a wine's character and quality.

Léonard Humbrecht, a giant of a man whom Hugh Johnson describes as "a fanatic for the individuality of each vineyard's soil and microclimate," laughs deeply and incredulously at the possibility of harboring any doubts. Then he pours tastes of his wine to prove his point.

Is there such a thing as *goût de terroir*? Or is it a French wine *über alles* publicity gimmick? The proof is in the glass. Get to work and judge for yourself. Here are two wines from the same grower, same grape, same vintage, same vinification, same cellar, same shipping and storage conditions . . . Only the soil is different.

Hengst. Quite stony. Limestone.

Herrenweg. Sand and gravel, rich in clay.

My own impression is that the *Hengst* shows depth and body, the *Herrenweg* finesse and delicacy. The *Hengst* aroma is more exotic with floral, spicy tones, while the *Herrenweg* seems livelier, fresher, more typical. *Hengst* is muscular, solid, the *Herrenweg* lighter, more graceful. Gene Kelly and Fred Astaire. The *Hengst* (which means "stallion") seems more a *vin de garde*. According to Léonard Humbrecht, the difference in personality is attributable to the difference in soil.

1984 Gewurztraminer "Hengst"

$8.95 PER BOTTLE

1984 Gewurztraminer "Herrenweg"

$9.95 PER BOTTLE

HOW TO EAT WELL?

WHAT DOES it take to eat well? So well that you make sounds of satisfaction. Toast slices of good bread. (Acme Bread Co. next door has a *levain* bread that is perfect, but any good bread will do.) Scrape the toast's rough surface with a clove of raw garlic. Use as little or as much of the clove as desired. Dribble a bit of olive oil over it. Lay an anchovy filet on it. Then it is ready to eat. One, two, three. Minutes have elapsed. The only thing lacking is a glass of Bandol rosé. You will wonder at how easy and how happy a marriage it creates.

One's knowledge of the anchovy may be limited to those stinky, salty, briny beasts, packed into tins, that must be soaked and rinsed and deboned before use. Most Americans can't deal with it.

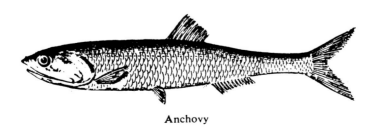

Anchovy

Unless you live where anchovies are fished, you have never tasted anchovies like ours from Pic in Saint Hilaire d'Ozilhan. For those who love Mediterranean food, our anchovy filets are a godsend. Conserved in reusable jars. In oil. No salt. NO SALT. They need not be deboned. Such anchovies! And the flavor is delicate and delicious. The anchovy toast recipe can be a starting point. Add fresh sliced tomato if you will, or chopped parsley leaves, roasted peppers, raw chopped shallots or red onion, sliced hard-boiled eggs, ground black pepper, or all of the above. Or use the anchovies in salads or stews, on pizza or pasta.

In a wonderful book, *An Omelette and a Glass of Wine*, Elizabeth David notes that anchovies are reputed to be lust-provoking, then she suggests a provocation that is more in keeping with the subject at hand: anchovies are thirst-provoking. However, I believe salty anchovies were her subject. Ours are not thirst-provoking. Ours are Domaine Tempier rosé–*inspiring*.

Robert Parker, Jr., has called Domaine Tempier's rosé the best in France. Master vintner Joseph Swan has called it the best rosé in the world. I have called it the best wine in the world. This is a wine you love instead of like, and now we have the best weather for it.

Pic prepared the anchovy; you prepare its bed. Domaine Tempier prepared the rosé.

Anchovy Filets
$17.50 PER JAR

Domaine Tempier Bandol Rosé
$4.25 PER TENTH $7.95 PER FIFTH

DOLCETTO SAMPLER

DOLCETTO IS a delicious dry red from the Piedmont, Barolo country. I drink about two dozen Dolcetto to one bottle of Barolo. I am a Dolcetto enthusiast. I will not be satisfied until it is so popular that we must put it on allocation. Thus far, my failure to communicate the joy of drinking great Dolcetto looms large within my wine merchant's purple-stained soul. We sell hundreds of cases; we should be selling thousands, given the abundant deliciousness and low price of Dolcetto. In a desperate attempt to convert you I shall appeal to your basest instinct:

DISCOUNT!

Not a discount to move unsold stock. No, these are newly arrived wines from the 1985 vintage. And for this Dolcetto crusade I enlist not just any brand X producers: these '85s are from Vietti and Aldo Conterno.

All the books say Dolcetto is light. Bull. Those you uncork from this sampler are all big, juicy, mouth-filling wines. Barolo is hard, but Dolcetto is soft and smooth and rolls down easy. There is a little corner of it almost hidden in the velvet texture that seems tart and reminds me of eating wild berries.

I like to drink Dolcetto at 55–60°, but Conterno and Vietti serve it at room temperature. It goes with anything that can support a lusty, luscious dry red, but for starters serve a cool bottle outdoors tonight with grilled meat. Drinking it, there is a Dionysian gaiety. Allow yourself to be seduced. It is that kind of wine, that kind of pleasure.

NORMALLY $44.00

SEPTEMBER ONLY $36.00

◦ ◦ ◦ ◦ ◦ ◦ ◦ ◦ ◦

1985 FLEURIE *"LES MORIERS"* · CHIGNARD

Fleurie has been called "the most feminine of the Beaujolais great growths." That is from an old book, so leave behind if you can the question of sexual stereotype. Still, one has to wonder about the validity of that statement when you sniff and taste Chignard's Fleurie. You hold a sip, you suck in some air so the wine ripples over your tongue, releasing its heady perfume. Picture Les Moriers in your mind, a hillside parcel that thrusts downward right into the Moulin-à-Vent zone—Moulin-à-Vent, which another French text calls the most masculine of the Beaujolais growths. Masculine, feminine? One observes the classic symptoms of *Vinum hermaphroditus*.

1985. Deep color, purple, black, and blue. Aromatic, ripe, complex. The average age of Chignard's vines: 60 years. It has the old-vine potency and finesse endowed with the opulence of a big year. A magnificent Fleurie with Moulin-à-Vent tendencies.

$8.95 PER BOTTLE $96.66 PER CASE

1978 VOUVRAY *MOUSSEUX*
RENÉ LOYAU

AVAILABLE FOR current consumption: 90-year-old René Loyau's ravishing, mature, 8-year-old sparkling dry Vouvray. *Méthode champenoise.*

"Imagine," says Loyau, "the others have sold five or six vintages before I sell mine. Nowadays no one makes it like I do, even in Champagne. They've all collected their money, but if all you look at is money you end up with nothing of value. My 1978 rested four years on its lees. *Four years it nourished itself!* And look, look what you have in your glass. Your clients should understand all this."

Produced exclusively from the noble *pineau de la Loire*, Loyau's 1978 has an

Kermit Lynch and René Loyau

aroma more wine-like than Champagne's. The stony hillside vines gave it its sap and gunflint aspect. It is deliciously flavored, with a lively Champagne-like bead.

It not only works as a festive holiday wine that will set those who serve it apart from the pack; it also has the flavor authority, the dryness, and the vinosity to make it appropriate with cuisine.

Highest recommendation! For something different this holiday season, ask for the *sparkling* Vouvray.

$9.95 PER BOTTLE $107.46 PER CASE

◊   ◊   ◊   ◊   ◊   ◊   ◊   ◊

1985 GRIGNOLINO · ALDO CONTERNO

Ripe, wild boysenberry and effervescence!

Unlikely to be appreciated except by those who have voyaged and dined in Italy, this fizzy dry red is a typically Italian pleasure. We import a few cases primarily for ourselves. *Serious* wine drinkers don't understand a gay little quaffer like this. *Triste!*

$4.95 PER BOTTLE $53.46 PER CASE

☆ 1987 ☆

1985 MOULIN-À-VENT "VIEILLES VIGNES"
BERNARD DIOCHON

A MAGNUM IMPLIES size and grandeur and this Beaujolais *grand cru* does not seem misplaced in a magnum. If you liked our other 1985 Beaujolais, here is the king of the vintage.

It is remarkable for the following reasons:

• *Old Vines*

Over 70 years old. Old vines are not cost-efficient. The roots go deeper into the earth. They nourish the vine from a variety of mineral constituents. They lack the abundant productiveness of younger vines, but the juice eked out is fabulous.

Bernard Diochon, Moulin-à-Vent

· *Vinified in Oak*

Today the Beaujolais is a land of stainless steel. In stainless it is easier to preserve fruitiness. Almost everyone in the Beaujolais claims there is no loss of quality, but that is not what my palate tells me. Diochon's oak fermenter and oak casks give a depth and weight and complexity that make the wines from stainless steel seem superficial in comparison.

· *Bottled Unfiltered*

This meaty, savory wine went directly from cask into bottle without being stripped of any color, aroma, flavor, or body. Sniff it; that immense aroma would have been diminished had Diochon crammed it through a filter. Unless you have tasted other vintages from Diochon, I don't think you have seen what is possible at Moulin-à-Vent.

· *Shipped in a Reefer*

A *reefer* here means refrigerated container. Heat kills a wine's fruit. Refrigeration is expensive, but to those who buy wines without knowing how they were shipped, good luck. You will need it.

$9.95 PER BOTTLE $107.46 PER CASE

TWO UNDERRATED CLARETS

OUR BORDEAUX selection is distinguished from others for two reasons. We emphasize undiscovered masterpieces, searching out the best quality/price ratio, and we ship all of them in refrigerated containers to keep the quality intact for you. I do not change my buying policy when I arrive at Bordeaux. I look for old-fashioned clarets with individual personalities, and I buy direct from the winemakers. Label-conscious buyers may seem puzzled by the château names, but when Robert Parker listed the ten finest "undiscovered" wines of Bordeaux I was proud to see that we import five of them: La Dominique, Sociando-Mallet, Bon Pasteur, Haut-Marbuzet, and L'Arrosée.

1984 CHÂTEAU LE BON PASTEUR · POMEROL

The proprietor is Michel Rolland, an oenologist who provides consultation to several *châteaux*, including La Dominique and La Conseillante. He knows the science of wine, yet his vinification remains traditional. He makes a thinking man's claret.

Standing outside his *chai*, he pointed to the nearby vineyards of Château Pétrus, just a few feet and a bunch of bucks away. Yes, his expression was wistful. Lovers of the wines of Pomerol will want to get to know his brilliant wines.

$12.50 PER BOTTLE $135.00 PER CASE

Château Simone, Palette

1983 CHÂTEAU SOCIANDO-MALLET · HAUT-MÉDOC

A brilliant ruby rim circles the deep, opaque, purplish heart of this wine in the glass. The aroma is ripe and briary with cassis fruit, violets, and vanilla bean. Its unctuous body is girthed for the moment by significant tannin. It is loaded with concentrated black currant flavors that you want to chew in order to eke out the taste from each wonderful drop. Don't miss it. The winery is already sold out.

$12.50 PER BOTTLE $135.00 PER CASE

◦ ◦ ◦ ◦ ◦ ◦ ◦ ◦

1985 CHÂTEAU SIMONE *BLANC*

To find another southern French white that offers the class and aging potential of Château Simone's, one must go as far north as Hermitage, to Monsieur Chave's cellar. In Domaine Tempier we have the finest red, in Château Simone the finest white, of Provence. It is time you discovered this stunning, delicious dry white before the incomparable 1985 is all sold out.

Alexis Lichine's *Encyclopédie des Vins et des Alcools* (1980) contains the following outrageous statement:

> *Very agreeable when one drinks them* [Simone] *in the old city of Aix-en-Provence, they lose their charming vivacity and their gaiety if one exports them.*

Has Lichine not heard of a refrigerated container? I guarantee Château Si-mone's white tastes here exactly as it does at the splendid château. It is bursting with freshness.

The 1985 is utterly delicious, magnificent, a knockout: honey, acacia blos-som, linden blossom, pear, pine, mint . . . *Wow!* How can a grape do it?

In a decent cellar this will make good drinking over the next two decades. How many whites will do that for you?

$12.50 PER BOTTLE $135.00 PER CASE

DO THE CONDRIEU

FROM THE MEMOIRS
OF MADAME DE VIOGNIER

AT VERSAILLES an overcast sky veiled even the rising of Louis XIV, the Sun King. Throughout the morning and into the afternoon the gloom grew even darker and the king was in one of his moods. Everything he said, which was little enough, had a sinister bite. Even when Mademoiselle de Blois leaned over before him almost touching the carpet in order to present him with a good view of her magnificent décolletage, hoping perhaps to brighten the royal demeanor, Louis seemed not to notice those two luminescent white moons that had been the talk of the court. Instead, he seemed to draw even further into himself until everyone began to fear for their position and place in his majesty's presence.

Monsieur Couperin entered the chamber, seated himself at his harpsichord, announced a new composition, *Le Tombeau de Lully*, and began a mournful trib-ute to the deceased, which, beautiful as it was, seemed to turn the clouds a shade or two darker.

Louis called for wine, strong wine. A young girl new to the court appeared at his side and begged his permission to serve the wine of her province.

"Better one of the Cardinal's Bordeaux wines," the King muttered, "or any-thing with a venomous sting."

But the girl defied the king. Her wine was not venomous, nor did it sting, nor was it red. Louis raised the glass to his nose, sniffed it, and his eyes widened in disbelief. "Is this wine at all?" he asked. "Or is it some sweet nectar of the gods?"

"Oh, it is wine, sire," the pretty little thing responded with a deep curtsy, "a wine that has captured the rays of the sun."

Louis beckoned to Couperin to come taste, and the musician said that the wine must have been vinified by Bacchus himself expressly for the Sun King.

Louis allowed his glass to be refilled. "Regard how it fills the room with light despite the clouds outside." He took another swallow. "Oh, and it fairly dances upon one's tongue. What is this divine potion that has brightened my day?"

"It is from Condrieu, sire."

At which point Couperin seated himself at his instrument and played the gayest, most joyful dance piece imaginable. The opening notes emerged with the radiance of a rising sun. The king rose and began to dance with the young girl, and soon everyone was dancing with joy.

Afterward, gasping for air and drinking to quench his thirst, the king asked Couperin the name of that lovely dance.

"Why, sire," said Couperin, "it is a new piece, if one can call it a piece at all because it just came to me this moment. I call this dance *Le Condrieu*."

1985 CONDRIEU · CHÂTEAU ROZAY

Normally I recommend Condrieu as an aperitif because its exotic aroma and its opulence make it too difficult to match with food. If you must match it with something, match it with a recording of Lully, Rameau, or Couperin. But this 1985 is so balanced, dry, and fine, I think you should work it into your menu and find plates with which it will marry well. It is fun tasting it and imagining what to serve alongside it.

George Lang created a cold lamb and dried fruit salad that would work. I tried this 1985 with grilled salmon and it was marvelous.

As to the wine itself, I think the 1985 will generate a high level of excitement. It seems a perfect example of one of the most delicious white wines of the world, the Condrieu.

$29.95 PER BOTTLE $323.46 PER CASE

1985 CORNAS

TWO MAGNIFICENT wines here, two of the most dramatically flavored Syrahs I have had the pleasure to taste. In my opinion, although it is too early to say for certain, these 1985s surpass even the 1978s.

Asking which is best, Clape or Verset, is like choosing between Beethoven and Bach. Question without answer. In 1985, one must have the two, and even then you will wish you owned more.

Tasting notes on the two are identical: deep purplish black color. Explosive aroma, thick with a heavenly scent of blackberries. Giant wines, loaded with tannin and body and flavor. Perfect balance; nothing is missing or out of proportion.

Do you like Syrah? Don't miss these.

1985 Cornas · Auguste Clape
$192.00 PER CASE FIFTHS $198.00 PER CASE MAGNUMS

1985 Cornas · Noël Verset
$186.00 PER CASE

With which plate do you serve a "big year" Cornas?
If you have a large group over for dinner, you might consider this recipe:

SQUIRREL MUDDLE

This makes a one-dish meal for the entire neighborhood.

About 70 squirrels, cut up
2 large stewing chickens, cut up
6 gallons water
2½ pounds salt pork, chopped
2½ gallons butter beans (lima beans)
3½ gallons cubed peeled potatoes
4 gallons chopped peeled tomatoes
1 gallon cubed peeled carrots
2½ gallons freshly cut corn
1 gallon shredded cabbage (optional)
1 pod red pepper, chopped
1¾ cups salt

¾ cup black pepper
2½ cups sugar

Clean, dress, and cut up squirrels and chickens. If your folks are not ardent squirrel hunters, increase the number of chickens. If you use all chickens, this recipe will take 24 stewing chickens.

Bring 4 gallons water to boil in a 30-gallon iron kettle. Add squirrel and chicken pieces. Cook, stirring often, until meat comes off the bone. (Take out pieces of bone before serving to small children.) Add remainder of water, as needed.

Chop salt pork, fry out, and add pork and drippings to boiling mixture. Add beans, potatoes, tomatoes, carrots, and corn in order as each is prepared. Continue cooking and stirring until vegetables are tender.

Add cabbage and seasonings, and cook, stirring, 1 hour, until stew is thick and flavors well blended. Remove kettle from the coals to serving area by hooking the handle over a heavy pole, several helpers carrying each end. Makes 15 gallons.

From the Farm Journal's Country Cookbook, *Revised, Enlarged Edition (Doubleday, 1959). ("All recipes in the book, old and new, have been carefully adapted to today's ingredients and style of living.")*

1985 BOURGUEIL

"DOMAINE DU GRAND CLOS" · AUDEBERT

When I have free time in France I like to look for wine books. One of my favorites is *Les Vins de Loire* by Pierre Bréjoux, which has yet to be translated into an English edition. Too bad, because Bréjoux's enthusiasm and talent could awaken

Americans who overlook the charms of the Loire Valley wines. Published four decades ago, Bréjoux's little book cites Le Grand Clos as one of Bourgueil's three finest hillside vineyards and Audebert as one of the best winemakers. When I buy a wine from what was considered a favored site four decades or even four centuries ago, it is a confirmation. That particular soil in which the vines nourish themselves has proven itself. This is no Andy Warhol fifteen-minute sensation, you see; there is tradition here, a track record.

It cannot be substantiated, but it is likely that wine from Le Grand Clos was enjoyed by the following inhabitants of the region: Richard the Lion-Hearted (an unwilling guest at the nearby Château de Chinon); Rabelais, the satirist, whose father had a farm nearby; Descartes, the philosopher; the novelist Balzac; and Louis XIV's sinister, Bordeaux-loving minister, the Cardinal Richelieu . . . not to mention the Romans, who, as usual, left ruins. And now you too, in the privacy of your own home, can join this select list of personages who have lowered their illustrious beaks into a glass of Bourgueil's Le Grand Clos. Act now!

Audebert's 1985 is easy to like. Ph.D. not required. Its aroma is typical of Le Grand Clos: cassis and raspberry with a stony, briary edge. It makes pleasurable drinking now, if the bottle is cool to the touch, or you can age it until that outspoken fruit disappears to be replaced by something more subtle and complex. Ideally, put down a case and uncork a bottle a year, enjoying each stage of its evolution.

$6.95 PER BOTTLE $75.06 PER CASE

◊   ◊   ◊   ◊   ◊   ◊   ◊   ◊

1984 BOURGOGNE PASSETOUTGRAINS
DOMAINE LEJEUNE

A wine that suffers the curse of an unwieldy name, *Pass-too-grawn* is the Burgundian blend of at least one-third Pinot Noir with Gamay.

Why drink Passetoutgrains? Well, for starters, Domaine Lejeune's 1984 is an extraordinarily good bottle. I bought it because I thought you would like it despite its name. The color is pretty and vibrant. The wine has a fabulous aroma and taste. The aroma is complex with a touch of oak, yet easy and seductive. It was bottled directly from barrel by gravity flow, unfiltered, so everything in barrel is rendered intact.

Passetoutgrains never reaches the heights of Burgundy's noble growths, nor does it aspire to. This is Burgundy from another angle, with the accent on the region's earthy, rustic soul.

Waverly Root defined Burgundian cuisine as "peasant cooking elevated to its greatest possible heights." We are talking substantial, rib-sticking cuisine straight from the farm, baptized in full-bodied sauces: *coq au vin, boeuf bourguignon*, that is where your Passetoutgrains will shine. Here is a red wine those who love Burgundy can savor often, a wine to enjoy with home cooking like pot roasts and stews, a wine that provides the taste and smell of Burgundy without demanding too much of your concentration or your pocketbook. Nor does it require long aging. You can pour it tonight.

By the way, if you know how to make a red wine sauce (that savory sauce made with mushrooms, pearl onions, and bacon that makes *coq au vin* such a treat), it can also be served to advantage with eggs. Place two poached eggs on a piece of toast scraped with fresh garlic and smother them in the sauce. This is not breakfast! And with a glass of Lejeune's Passetoutgrains alongside, you have a memorable wine and food marriage.

$6.95 PER BOTTLE $75.06 PER CASE

1985 CÔTES DU RHÔNE *ROUGE*
CUVÉE SÉLECTIONÉE PAR KERMIT LYNCH

In my favorite stomping grounds, in the shadow of the Dentelles near Gigondas, I found this delicious red Rhône from the 1985 vintage. It is a well-structured, flavorful cuvée that can be uncorked now, but I hope some buyers will hide some away for a few years. Remember, it is not only pricy wines that benefit from aging.

It has a vivid purple color. The aroma is so pretty and assertive that it is a bit of a shock in a simple Côtes du Rhône. Fruit aromas like plum and blackberry dominate, with suggestions of black pepper. It is full-bodied, but perhaps not in the usual sense of the term: there is no hard, vulgar tannin, nor does its gut hang out over its belt buckle. *Intense* might be a more appropriate word than *full-bodied.* The real thrill is the fresh quality of the fruit, both in the aroma and on the palate—none of that heavy, baked fruitiness that is the sign of careless vinification in southern France.

Highly recommended, and those who put down a case will have a good chuckle in four or five years because of their foresight.★

$5.75 PER FIFTH $62.10 PER CASE

★*A client, Martin Belles, showed up with a bottle of the 1985 in 1995, and the wine had aged beautifully and still had a future. After 10 years it seemed handsomely middle-aged.*

1986 BIANCO DI CUSTOZA

Perhaps the less said about this scrumptious little quaffer the better, because if expectations were raised too high, one would surely be underwhelmed upon tasting it. This is the sort of wine that is best when it comes as a delightful surprise, a "farmer's daughter" sort of wine.

Imagine that you are on a business trip. The freeway is clogged with traffic; the sun fills half the sky and is scorching hot; there is no breeze to clear the exhaust fumes; your brain feels like a baked tomato. Finally you get to your hotel, clean up, sit down to table, and ask the waiter for the wine list.

"White or red," he answers, "you got your choice."

Being a cultured, logically minded person, you decide to commence with the white. When you raise the glass to your nose it reminds you of the smell of slicing open the first melon of the summer. It is as elusive and freshening as a cool breeze. There is a joyful touch of sparkle on the tongue. Served nice and cold, it is enough to freshen your point of view.

Wine can be carefree fun and this one is.

$4.95 PER BOTTLE $53.46 PER CASE

1986 CHARDONNAY · PECORARI

Looking over the selection of Chardonnays I have recommended over the past 15 years, one could accuse me of being a Burgundy chauvinist. And I am. To me Chardonnay means white Burgundy, and the rest are, for better or worse, pretenders to the throne. Still, I cannot resist the charms of this Italian Chardonnay from the Friuli, a Chardonnay that imitates no other wines. It has a pale color with little sparkles of CO_2 when it is poured into the glass. The aroma reminds me of white peaches, acacia blossom, and clove, but all so subtly rendered that I feel silly even mentioning it. It has a plump feel in the mouth and a strong finish. As long as you don't enter it into a Chardonnay contest, you are in for an unusual and delicious treat.

$7.95 PER BOTTLE $85.86 PER CASE

1986 CHIARETTO · CORTE GARDONI

Defined by the *World Atlas of Wine* as a "very light red," Chiaretto looks like rosé to almost everyone else. It is produced along the shores of Lake Garda near Verona, where human nature demanded something beautiful in the glass to accompany the surrounding landscape. There is the serene blue-gray surface of the lake, there are the mountains striving to attain Alp-hood, and there is a soil so fertile you can almost hear the vegetation grow. Fruit trees, cypresses, olive trees. And the grape vines are trained upon trellises so that the leaves cascade back down to the ground, permitting the harvesters to work in the shade.

Chiaretto has a bright red cherry color, a subtle, lovely aroma, and it finishes with a touch of bitterness—that welcome sort of bitterness like bitter almond. Serve Chiaretto by itself as the sun sets beyond the bay, or enjoy a glass while grilling dinner outdoors. And it is the ultimate picnic wine.

Tasting notes: *Slurp!*

$4.95 PER BOTTLE $53.46 PER CASE

1984 BANDOL *ROUGE* · DOMAINE TEMPIER

Is there anything more pathetic than wine propagandists who think they can sell you a bottle of wine by relating some envy-provoking experience they allegedly

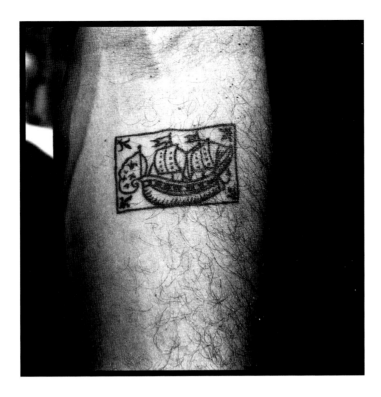

experienced? You know the sort: *I was in a gondola on Lake Garda under a trellis of rosebuds attended by vestal virgins who poured me a chalice of ruby nectar, which just happened to be this Chianti I'm trying to sell . . .* As if what happened to them has anything to do with your life or mine. Here is mine:

The Peyrauds at Domaine Tempier had carved an entire barbecued lamb outdoors under a radiant Provençal skyscape. There was an open magnum of 1984 red keeping its cool in an ice bucket. I was calmly admiring the color of that 1984 in my glass when Lucien Peyraud came back from the orchard and plopped down a big straw basket full of black cherries in front of me. The cherries were exactly the same color as the wine! And that may be as close as I will ever be to an awareness of cosmic unity and harmony.

Summertime wine? Certain reds work and others don't. When it turns hot, some of the reds we import reveal unexpected virtues if served at a cool temperature. Either uncork one right up from a cool cellar, or, particularly if you are dining outdoors, place the bottle in a lightly iced bucket. Or put the red in the fridge until it's cool, not cold. We have red wines that shine under such conditions. Domaine Tempier's 1984 is one. Ask us about the others.

$5.25 PER FIFTH $113.40 PER CASE

DOMAINE PIERRE BERTHEAU

HOW DOES AN importer find a great winemaker? Sometimes from the lips of another great winemaker. Monsieur Ponsot of Morey-Saint-Denis told me I should look up Bertheau. At first, Bertheau was reluctant to sell because a neighbor in Chambolle (you would recognize the name) told him that for America it is necessary to filter a wine twice. I told him that was bull something-or-other, and Bertheau said, "But his importer told him it is the law in America."

Not yet, Pierre, but we are getting there!

Apart from all that, Bertheau makes some of the biggest, richest wines in Burgundy. His 1978, 1983, and 1985s are some of the darkest, most tannic Burgundies I have tasted. Time bombs. If you need a Burgundy for tomorrow night, your money is ill-spent here.

		PER CASE
1985	Chambolle-Musigny	$240.00
1985	Chambolle-Musigny "Les Charmes"	324.00
1985	Chambolle-Musigny "Les Amoureuses"	522.00
1985	Bonnes-Mares	720.00

Pierre Bertheau, Chambolle-Musigny

DOMAINE ZIND-HUMBRECHT

1985 RIESLING "BRAND"

Without a doubt the star of the 1985 vintage for Alsace is the gifted Léonard Humbrecht. Few winemakers anywhere in the world could claim such a splendid line-up.   THE WINE ADVOCATE

And what about his 1984s, now sold out? And his 1986s, which are going to knock your socks off. Humbrecht is not a one-vintage phenomenon. But he is at the top of his craft, and his 1985 Riesling from the *grand cru* vineyard Brand shows why his wines drive wine lovers to their version of *Bliss Consciousness*.

You will not taste another Riesling like it, anywhere. It is an individual, one of a kind. How can there be, rising from a glass of fermented grape juice, such an unexpected and altogether ravishing aroma of rose petal? You know, the perfume that melts your face into a rapturous smile when you lower your nose into a densely fragrant rose blossom?

But do not think that this is a fragile piece of work. At Richard Olney's, first a Tempier Bandol and then a Chave Hermitage were obliterated by his rich cabbage, pheasant, pig's feet, and red wine stew, so out of desperation for something to drink we returned to our apéritif wine, this Riesling, which not only stood up to the stew, it seemed to amplify everything that was wonderful about the dish.

Lovely stuff!

$14.95 PER BOTTLE $161.46 PER CASE

MAS DE CADENET

CÔTES DE PROVENCE

Before I talk about the wine, I've got to tell you about the place. What an amazing location for a vineyard. Mont Sainte Victoire (celebrated by a series of Cézanne paintings) rises, towers, looms, *inhabits* the northern horizon. The vines are on softly rolling hillocks covered with round, Châteauneuf-like stones. The scene is vast and arid and timeless, the endless pattern of stones, the regimental rows of grapevines, an occasional tattered cypress . . . The Provençal sun beats down with incomparable luminosity, and a dry *mistral* roars past with a fierceness that erodes any feelings of self-consequence one might possess. It is grandiose, and somehow, even though it is only a few kilometers from the Aix-Nice autoroute, there is a feeling of isolation, brought on perhaps by an awareness of Mother Nature's crushing indifference.

The vine gives good juice here. The white is Clairette *blanc* and Rolle (30% each) and Ugni *blanc*. It smells a little like the green almonds they eat in Provence, along with a thick, ripe fruitiness that seems to characterize the '86 whites around there, including nearby Château Simone's. Full-bodied, round, lots of flavor.

Their red has suggestions of Châteauneuf-du-Pape and Bandol. Spice combined with berry and black cherry. Fleshy and well built, it should be drunk cool for the first year or two, then afterwards, treat it as you would any fine red. Syrah, Grenache, Carignan, and Cabernet Sauvignon, blended and aged in oak.

$4.95 PER BOTTLE $53.46 PER CASE

◊ ◊ ◊ ◊ ◊ ◊ ◊ ◊

1986 FLEURIE "LES MORIERS" · M. CHIGNARD

According to Henri Jayer, without risk there is no great wine. I cannot guarantee to you that this 1986 Fleurie will not eventually go off in the bottle. The risk will be yours. If risk free is your bag, or if you cannot keep this wine at a cool temperature, leave it alone.

It is a bit of an experiment on Michel Chignard's part because it was

1. NOT *de-gassed to remove its natural CO_2.*
2. NOT *gassed with SO_2.*
3. NOT *filtered.*

It is the same wine that tasted so good from the barrel. This will be interesting . . . and the wine is a knockout! Gamay fruit, *fleurie* flowery, steep, stony hill . . . what we have been working toward in the Beaujolais.

$12.50 PER BOTTLE $135.00 PER CASE

DOMAINE TEMPIER

1980 BANDOL *ROUGE*

A seven-year-old wine.

I wandered into the cellars unannounced one day last spring to find Jean-Marie Peyraud, the winemaker, pouring a bottle of wine *into* a barrel. (Usually it works the other way around.) Why? Because French wine *connaissance* has gone so haywire that the public will not accept a natural deposit, which is what the 1980, after six years in bottle, has thrown.

Jean-Marie was going to uncork each bottle, filter and rebottle it, rendering it (limpid but fatigued) acceptable to modern-day French restaurateurs. I tasted it and bought it on the spot, as is, as the good Lord meant it to be, deposit and all. Decanteth it and ye shall have a perfectly mature bottle of Domaine Tempier, cheap.

$9.95 PER BOTTLE $107.46 PER CASE

1984 CUVÉE SPÉCIALE "LA TOURTINE"

Their first 100% Mourvèdre (*moor-ved-ruh*). The grapes are from the La Tourtine slope, where they have their oldest (46 years old) Mourvèdre vines. For the first time we can begin to define the qualities of the Mourvèdre, the noblest meridional grape variety. It will not be Tempier's last pure Mourvèdre, although there will be none from 1985 or 1986. I have already tasted the 1987: zing went my strings.

$12.50 PER BOTTLE $135.00 PER CASE

✥ 1988 ✥

NEW ARRIVALS
FROM NORTHERN ITALY

A RECENT WINE tour of northern Italy turned up some new talents whose exciting wines will appeal to those who possess a healthy sense of wonder and enthusiasm for the endlessly complex world born of the simple fruit of the vine. Got that?

Northern Italy is hard work, resisting eating and drinking too much lest one's digestive system clunk to a halt. It is also a wine enthusiast's paradise. From the castles of the Piemonte to the steep Alpine slopes to the lush hillsides along the Yugoslavian border, no one knows or ever will know everything there is to know about this little universe where travelers can be astonished by the rustic deliciousness of a carafe wine in a country inn or by the grandiose aspirations of a dense young Barolo.

Included in our extensive new selection from northern Italy:

1986 TOCAI FRIULANO · PAOLO CACCESE

Here is the new-style Italian white—fruity and dry, crisp and refreshing. It captures the exotic tendency of Friuli's most original contribution to fine wine, the Tocai, but it is also rendered with superb finesse. With nose to glass, green weeds and white peach might come to mind, or might not.

$7.95 PER BOTTLE $85.86 PER CASE

1985 MERLOT · RADIKON

A winemaker named Radikon? It may sound as if he arrived from the planet Krypton, but Italian he is, even if he looks more Slav than anything else. This is a super wine, the finest red I have tasted from the Friuli, and a challenger to the best from France and California. Ironically, Radikon complained that his neighbors do not understand this kind of Merlot. To them it is abnormally enormous. It has a deep black, purplish color and a complex aroma of great purity. A big, handsome, thick wine at 14.2° alcohol. In a rush of enthusiasm I described it as "Pétrus without the oak."

$12.50 PER BOTTLE $135.00 PER CASE

MANGIA-MACCHERONI

1983 BAROLO "ROCCHE"
CANTINA VIETTI

Lulu Peyraud explained once that her father, Alphonse Tempier, was a shrewd businessman. He always put his money wherever no one else was looking. With attention focused on Rhône, Burgundies, and Cabernets, this is a good time to buy Barolo. Here is a great one, and it is only $14.95.

It satisfies on every level. It gives immediate satisfaction and it has aging potential. It is not one of those hard-as-a-rock Barolos. The aroma is complex with mushroom, almond, tobacco, and cherry. It has an expansive, mouth-filling texture and a haunting aftertaste.

$14.95 PER BOTTLE $161.46 PER CASE

º º º º º º º º

1986 RIESLING "CUVÉE SPÉCIALE"
DOMAINE ZIND-HUMBRECHT

From his different casks of 1986 Rieslings this one leapt out from the others so dramatically that Humbrecht decided to label it *cuvée spéciale*. Even those of you who think you do not like Alsatian wines or do not like Riesling, take a chance, splurge, be reckless. If this doesn't do it, you may need a palate transplant. Powerful, viscous, noble, endless, incredible!

$9.95 PER BOTTLE $107.46 PER CASE

HENRI JAYER RETROSPECTIVE

1983 ÉCHEZEAUX

Brilliant medium ruby. Exquisite perfume that has layers of aroma beneath it waiting to emerge. Rich, unusually large-scaled and tannic for Jayer. An infant, cellar it at least another 8 to 10 years.

1982 VOSNE-ROMANÉE "CROS PARANTOUX"

Light color. Classic Vosne-Romanée aroma, pristine fruit and *terroir*. Round, no rough edges, superb finesse. A delicate jewel that can be enjoyed now or held another four to five years to develop the special bouquet that comes with bottle age.

1982 ÉCHEZEAUX

Light color. Less developed aroma. Velvety at first, then the tannin emerges. A magnificent bottle with perfect balance and intense flavors. Chewier, fleshier than the preceding wine. If you have a few bottles, leave them four to five years before you even begin to pull a cork.

1981 RICHEBOURG

Complex bouquet in which the *terroir* is more pronounced than the fruit. It reminds me of being underground in Burgundy, those wine-soaked earthen cellars. Typical of Richebourg, there is a majestic blossoming of flavor on the palate. Not for long aging, but it remains too tight and tannic for the moment. Another three to four years should suffice.

1980 RICHEBOURG

The prettiest color, a medium ruby that glints and flashes like a ruby. It has the aroma of new wine. Amazing how slowly the 1980s are developing. Young, piercing Pinot fruit. Perfect acid and tannin balance. An endless, surging finish. Hold.

1979 VOSNE-ROMANÉE "AUX BRÛLÉES"

Medium ruby with orange edges. Broad, rich perfume. Mouth-filling texture. A powerful, muscular wine with great breed. Can be enjoyed now but will develop further.

1978 VOSNE-ROMANÉE "LES BEAUMONTS"

A perfect bottle, especially for those who love a ripe fruit aroma. Everything is there except maturity. Medium–dark color. Ripe, opulent aroma. A big wine that leaves an impression on the palate for a long time.

1977 NUITS-SAINT-GEORGES "AUX MURGERS"

Pale, mature color. Fabulous, earthy, Burgundian stink. The aroma is worth the price of admission, thank goodness, because the palate impression is light and short, typical of its vintage. Mature.

(Each of us named a favorite, though no one wanted to. Morgan Miller and Craig Jones finally selected the 1980 Richebourg, Fran Kysela the 1978 Beaumonts, David Stewart the 1982 Échezeaux. Although I cannot say it was the grandest wine, my nose kept returning to the 1982 Cros Parantoux.)

◊　◊　◊　◊　◊　◊　◊　◊

1982 BRUT CHAMPAGNE
PAUL BARA

Champagne can be visually intoxicating, and Bara's 1982 is worth watching. The bead rises in a swirling, swaying, sensuously elegant ballet. However, beyond its festive froth there is a wine-tasting experience to enjoy. The aroma makes me think of fresh cream, toast, and ground pepper. Not the pepper one finds in Rhône wines, this is like a hint of the finest hand-ground powder. There is a mouth-filling taste, a luxurious richness, and an exquisite subtlety.

An added attraction: Paul Bara Champagne is shipped from France at cellar temperature. It is unusual to taste a Champagne in the United States that has not suffered from heat in transit no matter what you pay for it.

A remarkable cuvée. 100% *grand cru*.

$22.50 PER FIFTH　　　$243.00 PER CASE

1986 CASSIS *BLANC*
CLOS SAINTE MAGDELEINE

Back in 1969 before Bacchus waved his magic wand and turned me into a wine importer, I was banging about Europe on a penny-pinching holiday. Needing a rest en route from Barcelona to Salzburg, I pulled off the highway to find a hotel. The nearest village was Cassis, proving that accidents are not always tragic. I did not know that the beauty of the place had attracted painters such as Vlaminck, Matisse, and Dufy, or that there were literary connections with Marcel Pagnol and M. F. K. Fisher. I simply needed a bed.

And stayed a week. I ate in the cheap backstreet restaurants: fish soup, fish stew, grilled fish, *fruits de mer*, always with a bottle of the local sun-drenched white wine. All the vintners produce red and rosé, but those don't matter. It is its unique dry white that puts Cassis on the wine map.

The 1986 will convert cynics who say the incomparable beauty of the site makes the wine taste good. The vintage plays a role; conditions were perfect. The aroma is ripe and grapey, and all the flavors are intact because the Clos Sainte Magdeleine has agreed to forgo a filtration at the *mise en bouteille*. A blend of Ugni *blanc*, Clairette, Marsanne, and Sauvignon *blanc*, here is the wine to enhance seafood and shellfish. On a warm evening it serves as an appropriate apéritif. It goes particularly well with Roquefort and goat cheese. And you sailors, here is the wine for your boat's ice chest. It tastes as good on the Pacific as it does on the Mediterranean.

$8.95 PER BOTTLE $96.66 PER CASE

1987 CHIARETTO
CORTE GARDONI

The sun is setting. The garden is watered. The baby is googling. The chops are on the grill. And you are looking at life through a rosé-colored glass of cool Chiaretto that just arrived from northern Italy. Great color, great perfume, delicate flavors, bone-dry.

$4.95 PER BOTTLE $53.46 PER CASE

DOMAINE TEMPIER

1985 BANDOL "CUVÉE SPÉCIALE"

I nicknamed this *Cuvée Lulu* because, like Lulu Peyraud, Lucien's wife, it has such a lively, free spirit that it seems to be bursting at the seams. A vigorous wine that has an irresistible unruliness, if you can picture that, and a finesse that is waiting to emerge. Not a bad combination.

Eighty-four percent Mourvèdre, from a blend of their best vineyards, the nose is packed with Tempier character, and it seems to leap out of the glass. After all, no one has ever accused Lulu of being shy.

$14.95 PER BOTTLE $161.46 PER CASE

❧ 1989 ❧

1987 GAVI · STEFANO BELLOTTI

ONE OF THE simplest and most fabulous gourmet treats is to pull the cork on this Gavi and serve the wine with smoked salmon on toast.

This is a complex wine with mineral, honey, chestnut, and wildflower aspects, a blossoming richness of flavor, and an unusual touch afforded by aging in acacia barrels. It is the result of organic farming and vinification. A very special and beautiful wine. I urge you to try it.

One more observation: When our new employee, John "Little Richard" Olney tasted it, he exclaimed *Good Gavi, Miss Molly!* Since then, we keep him hidden in the stockroom.

$8.95 PER BOTTLE $96.66 PER CASE

FINAL PRE-ARRIVAL OFFER

MY LAST VISIT to Chave's was in the company of John and his uncle, Richard Olney. As is Chave's delight, he led us through a remarkable array of his separate cuvées, vintage 1986, then he drew a taste from a large *foudre* of what we presumed to be his final blend of the separate vineyards. We oohed and aahed, said *mon Dieu* and congratulated him.

"Oh no," he said, "this is the blend of the rejects, which will be sold off to a *négociant*. Here's the blend *I* will bottle."

The deep purplish Hermitage that he splashed into our glasses is what we are offering at a special pre-arrival price until April 1. You would be happy with the rejects; the cuvée bottled by Chave is a brilliant wine.

He kept on pulling corks, notably the 1935 red, the 1929 white, the 1929 red. They were vinified by his father. Why not save a few bottles of 1986 for your own kids?

1986 Hermitage Blanc

$276.00 PER CASE

1986 Hermitage Rouge

$330.00 PER CASE

NEW BOOKS

JEFFERSON AND WINE

Edited by R. de Treville Lawrence III

"GOOD WINE IS a necessity of life for me," wrote a president of our United States. It was no bush-league president; it was Thomas Jefferson. This welcome volume of almost 400 pages is full of Jefferson's pronouncements on, and experiences with, French wine. Readers will enjoy his skeptical opinion of *négociants*, his arguments against wine tariffs and taxes, and his firm belief that wine encourages good health. What an intelligent antidote to today's anti-wine barracudas.

Reading it, you will see that I am not the first to be a fanatic about proper shipping conditions for imported wines. Jefferson addressed the problem almost 200 years ago. Then there is a copy of his letter (in French) to Lur-Saluces ordering 30 dozen bottles of Château d'Yquem for George Washington and 10 dozen for himself. There is his account of his travels through Burgundy, the Rhône, Provence, the Languedoc, and Bordeaux. During his first year in the White House, Jefferson spent one-third of his $25,000 salary on food and wine!

Fascinating stuff about this endlessly fascinating American.

$22.00

ADVENTURES ON THE WINE ROUTE

By Kermit Lynch

MY OWN BOOK has been well received by the critics, but of course the praise is not unanimous. One critic remarked, "Lynch is no Cervantes." It stings, but his criticism is absolutely right on the mark. I am no Cervantes. The masquerade is over.

A critic from Texas called me "the wine lover's color man, an entertaining combination of John Madden and Howard Cosell."

Seriously, however, one criticism has cropped up three or four times, so I want to respond. They object that I write about the wines I import and exclude other worthy domaines. Obviously I wrote about the people and places I know best, but that is not my only explanation. I believe wine must be shipped at proper temperature. If not, it loses some of its stuff before it reaches our shores.

I wanted to include, in the book's Châteauneuf-du-Pape section, Vieux Télégraphe plus one other domaine that I admire, but whose wine I do not import. In my experience, bottles from that domaine tasted here can be cooked and prematurely old. Readers know that I am totally, passionately convinced that wine must be shipped in refrigerated containers. Had I praised a wine that I know is improperly shipped, and so inspired someone to search out a bottle of it, what would they think of my palate and judgment when they uncorked the wine and poured out such a miserable example? Given my commitment to proper shipping conditions, it would have been dishonest to recommend wines that over here can be mere shadows of their former selves. The decision to leave out such wines was a conscious one.

Published by Farrar, Straus and Giroux.

$19.95

PART III

THE 1982 BORDEAUX phenomenon. Remember the consumer stampede? Buy any and all! Greatest vintage since 1961! Most of us in the wine trade agree that the single most important market factor in the wine rush for 1982s was the unbridled enthusiasm of writer Robert Parker, who is an indefatigable, talented, honest wine taster.

Six weeks ago in the *New York Times*, Frank Prial put into print the rumblings and doubts of many wine buyers who have cellars stuffed with 1982 Bordeaux, and worry that the wines are not aging well, or aging too rapidly. Maybe 1982 is not all it was cracked up to be, people are saying.

But how many vintages could live up to the almost universal hype accorded those 1982s? A genie would have to pop out of each bottle to satisfy one's expectations.

The 1985 red Burgundies received a similar star treatment. And what a coincidence, they have a style *exactly* like the 1982 Bordeaux. Will they be criticized later on if they fail to taste as good as they did when they were first released?

If you follow the journalists when you buy red Burgundy, you've probably got an ulcer by now. You were supposed to avoid 1980, then suddenly you were supposed to scramble to snap up what bottles remained for sale. 1981 and 1982 (a personal favorite) were, and continue to be, ignored. 1983 went from Vintage of the Century to the garbage dump in a few short months, and who knows, maybe it will turn to gold again someday. 1984? Hold your nose! Trash. A disaster. If a wine merchant tries to sell you one, report him to the fraud detail.

But wait a second. Recently, leaving Burgundy for the Rhône, I wanted some good bottles to uncork for my Rhône producers, who are unanimously, chauvinistically, jealously critical of Burgundy. To show them how good red Burgundy can be, I took along bottles of a Pommard Boucherottes from Coste-Caumartin, 1984. 1984! Why did I take a lowly 1984 when I could have poured them a 1983 or 1985? Because the wine in the bottle was so dramatically good, that's why. By the way, I did not buy, import, or sell the 1985 Pommard Boucherottes, although it would have been a cinch to sell it amidst the 1985 vintage hysteria. It was not worthy. I did buy the 1986. It is worthy.

And I remember the 1971s and 1972s that I tasted during my initial buying trips to Burgundy. According to the press, 1971 was another Vintage of the Century, and 1972 an acidic flop. The vintage charts continue to treat 1972 as a loser. Luckily, my cellar is well stocked with 1972s; they took their time and they age beautifully, much more gracefully than the 1971s, *in my opinion*. Some 1986s remind me of 1972.

I want you to realize once and for all: Even the winemaker does not know what aging is going to do to a new vintage; Robert Parker does not know; I do not know. We all make educated (hopefully) guesses about what the future will bring, but guesses they are. And one of the pleasures of a wine cellar is the opportunity it provides for you to witness the evolution of your various selections. Living wines have ups and downs just as people do, periods of glory and dog days, too. If wine did not remind me of real life, I would not care about it so much. Some wines start out clumsy and tight and then blossom. Some sparkle like a comet and fade. The 1982 red Burgundies seem to remain as fresh as the day they were bottled.

My experience, seventeen years in the wine trade, has taught me never to reject a vintage out of hand, and never to go overboard with enthusiasm. I cellar my favorite wines in all vintages. That is what I consider fun.

Frank Prial's article may be an opening, politely stated salvo against Parker's unrestrained enthusiasm for the 1982 vintage. He may become a target now, as other critics call into question his judgment. The fact is, there are some glorious 1982 red Bordeaux, but I would hate to drink one every night. I am glad I have some 1980, 1981, 1983, 1984, 1985, and 1986 down there, too. Which is the best vintage? I don't think there is one. It depends on YOUR palate, the cuisine you are matching, the maturity of the wine when you uncork it, and the particular domaine or château.

Another issue here is the incredible power the wine journalists have gained in the marketplace. When I come back from a buying trip with a wine that has really excited me, if it wears the wrong vintage strip I have trouble getting anybody to even try a bottle, much less cellar a case. You consumers, for the most part, are ready to let journalists decide what goes into your cellar and glass before you are ready to trust a professional wine merchant, or even your own palate. I think I understand why. You don't yet trust your own palate as much as you trust a rating or numerical score. And you might think a merchant is biased because he is selling the wine, while a journalist is not. If so, you are forgetting something important. The journalist *is* trying to sell his article, his paper, or his review. And what sells papers? Sensationalism over truth any day. Parker became an oracle following his oft-quoted zeal for the 1982 Bordeaux. *The Wine Spectator* became the talk of the wine world after their famous article calling the 1983s from Romanée-Conti trash. I call both episodes sensationalism, and I pity those who have endless 1982 Bordeaux in their cellars, as well as those who missed the stunning 1983s from Romanée-Conti. I wish I had been their importer.

Trust the great winemakers, trust the great vineyards. Your wine merchant might even be trustworthy. In the long run, that vintage strip may be the least important guide to quality on your bottle of wine.

The Kermit Lynch Vintage Chart

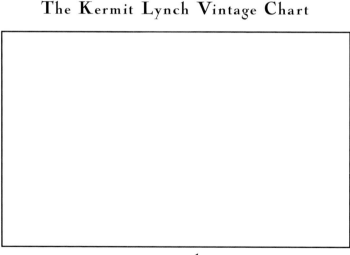

cut out and save

Another problem: The Bordeaux vintners enjoyed the 1982 vintage madness. The Burgundians took note of the stampede for their 1985s. All ripe, forward wines. No mystery. Big, soft, easy. So a lot of winemakers are masking the originality of their wine and the vintage in order to receive early critical approval by fashioning something that is easy and will earn high points. No mystery. Let's have every vintage taste the same! Why not have all wines taste exactly the same? Then you won't even need a score! But I'll tell you, it is already difficult enough finding wines with distinctive personalities. If you consumers follow the herd, then wines with originality, wines that taste different, wines that provide real interest, are going to become even more difficult to find.

What is the most common critique I hear about the American consumer from the French winemakers? "They are like sheep!"

I tell them that my customers are different.

FINO SHERRY

A VISIT TO Jerez shattered my prejudices about the wine known as Sherry. I had an image in my mind—an icy English winter, a huge stone castle, a gray-haired man or woman in front of a room-sized fireplace sipping heart-warming sweet amber Sherry because the doctor had forbidden Port.

In Jerez, where Sherry is made, I was never served anything sweet. Mostly, people drank Fino, and not only with *tapas*. Chilled, light, dry Fino accompanied the wonderful cuisine of Jerez, which consisted primarily of charcoal-grilled seafood from the Gulf of Cádiz.

Try it with our local catch, fish or shellfish. Mussels grilled on the half-shell are delicious. Before grilling, splash on a drop of olive oil, a drop of Fino, and a sprinkling of minced garlic or shallots.

One curious custom: Fino was invariably served from half-bottles. Even if four or five bottles were uncorked for a large group, they were always poured from tenths. It is because freshness is highly valued in Fino, as opposed to Amontillado or Oloroso. No one wanted to uncork a bottle that might not be emptied. If some Fino remained in the bottle, it was poured down the drain, not saved for later. Consequently, I ordered a big proportion in the traditional half-bottles.

$3.25 PER TENTH $5.95 PER FIFTH

 ◦ ◦ ◦ ◦ ◦ ◦ ◦ ◦

1987 MÂCON *BLANC*
PERRUSSET

When working the Beaujolais, I eat at Au Bon Cru in the Fleurie vineyards. It is frequented by truck drivers, traveling salesmen, and winemakers. I go there for its rib-sticking family-style cuisine. You sit at long tables wherever you can find a seat, no reservations, gravy (sauce) on the mashed (pureed) potatoes. Last year I ended up across from a mud-stained young man; we struck up a conversation and discovered that our philosophies about wine were very much in accord. He was about to begin making wine using grapes his family had been selling off to a *cave cooperative*. Last fall I visited his tiny cellar and sampled his first effort. It is fine and fruity, typical of the refreshing, unheavy Chardonnay Mâcon is capable of providing us. I ordered the maximum he had to sell, 100 cases. I think you are going to enjoy it.

$8.95 PER BOTTLE $96.66 PER CASE

END NOTES

THANK YOU FOR the many responses to my remarks in last month's brochure, but in that tirade against Vintage Chart Maniacs, I forgot a couple of things.

Recently I served Pommard Rugiens from three vintages: 1973, 1971, and 1969.

Folks, I kid you not, the best bottle was the 1973! Now, I recall it well when the journalists of the day were touting 1969 as the Vintage of the Century. Like all vintages of the century, the 1969s were dark, big wines. Ungenerous, maybe, but BIG. That's all it takes, right? Our 1969 remained big and ungenerous. It is growing old without revealing its charms. Then, two years later, 1971, another Vintage of the Century! Again, BIG wine, but this time generous, fat, and ripe. 1973 was lambasted: weak, watery, zero aging potential. I imported a few cases of the 1973 Rugiens, but no one wanted them. They weren't BIG. Today that 1973 has the most gorgeous aroma, the finest balance, and the loveliest flavors. Alongside it, the 1971 seems thick and flat, as if it had spent too many hours in front of the tube guzzling beer.

The journalists were wrong; I was wrong; so were the vintage charts and most of the winemakers. Wine is not as predictable as some would have you believe.

A couple of years ago, I asked Jean-Marie Ponsot which vintage during the 1970s produced his favorite Clos de la Roche. 1973, he said. (I didn't even buy his 1973!) It has the purest expression of the Clos de la Roche character, he explained.

When buying red Burgundy, I think we should remember:

1. *Big wines do not age better than light wines.*

2. *A so-called great vintage at the outset does not guarantee a great vintage for the duration.*

3. *A so-called off vintage at the outset does not mean the wines do not have a brilliant future ahead of them.*

4. *Red Burgundy should not taste like Guigal Côte Rôtie, even if most wine writers wish it would.*

5. *Don't follow leaders; watch yer parking meters.*

DOMAINE DE FONTSAINTE
1988 GRIS DE GRIS

LET US SIMPLIFY things and call this *gris de gris* rosé.
For months we have been sold out of the great Domaine Tempier rosé.
Crisis! So of course they ran out at Chez Panisse Café too, and replaced the
Tempier with Bonny Doon's California Mourvèdre rosé. That is how I discov-
ered the Bonny Doon. Wonderful stuff! These three rosé wines—Fontsainte,
Tempier, and Bonny Doon—have the same spirit. They are incredibly FUN TO
DRINK, and DELICIOUS, and abnormally VERSATILE. What would summer be
without them? Or winter, for that matter.

The Fontsainte has only one virtue over the other two: it is considerably
cheaper.

$5.95 PER BOTTLE $64.26 PER CASE

CASTELLO DI CACCHIANO

WHEN I ASKED Elisabetta Ricosoli the date her family acquired Cacchiano,
she replied, "Our family has always owned it, as long as records have been
kept. I don't know exactly when we first planted vines. Somewhere in the early
Middle Ages."

Cacchiano is the ultimate in traditional Chianti. Our cuvée is bottled unfiltered. While their 1986 differs from the 1985 in style, it is just as good. Comparing the two is like comparing Joguet's 1985 and 1986 Chinons, the 1986 brighter,
with more nerve.

Cacchiano also produces a Vin Santo, a dessert wine that rivals all but the top
two or three Sauternes. The grapes are picked quite ripe, then left on wooden
trays to dry out. One hundred kilos of grapes produced 17 kilos of Vin Santo! IT
IS INTENSE! The grapes are crushed and the juice is sealed in barrel for five years.
If you have stopped buying today's technological Sauternes, turn your attention
here. Try a bottle. The wine in your glass is my strongest argument.

Finally, the olive oil. Here is a noteworthy story. *Traveler* magazine exposed an
olive oil fraud. A few years ago, in 1985, production in Tuscany was nearly zero
because of a serious freeze. Nonetheless, almost every property released an olive
oil. The reporter did his detective work and discovered that Spanish and other
oils were sold under the original Tuscan labels, some at $25.00 and $30.00 per
bottle, with no mention that the olive oil was not Tuscan. Lots of famous names!
Not Cacchiano. Cacchiano was singled out as the only great domaine the reporter
found that sold no olive oil from that disastrous year.

1986 Chianti Classico fifths
Vin Santo fifths
Olive Oil 6-pack 500 ml

It still works.

1987 BERNARD MAUME

Maume's 1987s remind me of one of those mighty organ toccatas by Bach. However, whereas Bach fathered twenty children, Maume has only seven. His 1987 Gevrey-Chambertin is so magnificent a bottle (richly textured, an aroma of great depth brimming with cassis, Gevrey *goût de terroir*, smoke and oak nuances), it would make many other contemporary Burgundies shrink to half-bottle size in comparison.

The Lavaux is typically the most tender and velvety, the Pallud masculine, tannic, backwards.

These remind me of Maume's 1979s, which are now so remarkable I find myself saving bottles for the most special occasions, when I want to pull out a showstopper.

		PER CASE
1987	*Gevrey-Chambertin*	$288.00
1987	*Gevrey "En Pallud"*	$390.00
1987	*Gevrey Lavaux Saint-Jacques*	$480.00
1987	*Mazis-Chambertin*	$600.00

EXPLORING CAHORS
SPECIAL SAMPLER CASE

WHERE DOES the smart money look when purchasing wine? They look where no one else is looking. So I would advise you, look now to Cahors. That is what I did, and after exploring it, I left in love with the region, enthusiastic about two domaines, and amazed by the low prices.

I found a growing tendency to make wine for immediate consumption, which seems strange when you consider that they are working with Malbec, Tannat, and Merlot. The other unfortunate tendency is to filter the poor things to death. I tasted many good wines in barrel, but headed for the door when I tasted them in bottle. The two domaines I am offering make weighty wines that can age well, and that were bottled intact, unfiltered.

The Pineraie is aged in a good proportion of new barrels, and the results are sensational. The winemaker uses new oak like a special seasoning to enhance his dark, rich wine.

The Clos la Coutale ages its Cahors in large oak *foudres*, similar to those at Tempier or Vieux Télégraphe. The wine has a clearer expression of spice and fruit, but each method has its virtues, so I bought both.

The aromas are gorgeous, broad and deep and ripe. They are round, expansive wines (they seem less astringent than Bordeaux) with their own distinctive flavors, which you are going to find utterly delicious.

The landscape along the banks of the river Lot is dramatically beautiful, and at every turn you spot another old stone farmhouse in which you wish you could settle down. You can, however, stay in one, an ancient stone mill transformed into a hotel called La Source Bleu (The Blue Spring) after the astonishing color of the water from a spring that gurgles like a lullaby outside your window. Lovely grounds to explore, swimming pool, river, great cuisine, excellent local wines. It is in Touzac, near Puy-l'Évêque, telephone 65.36.52.01.

To introduce the best wines of Cahors, our sampler case consists of eight bottles, two domaines, two vintages.

3 1987   *Domaine de la Pineraie* $6.95
3 1987   *Clos la Coutale* 7.95
2 1986   *Clos la Coutale* 8.95

NORMALLY $62.60

SPECIAL SAMPLER PRICE $50.00

DISCOVER VOUVRAY
SPECIAL SAMPLER CASE

PERHAPS RANTING and raving produces results. I notice a growing interest in the great and overlooked wines of Vouvray, which must be due to my periodic temper tantrums, because no one else in the wine world is talking about them. No, their eyes are on yet-the-latest oaky Chardonnay.

In order to rev this interest up to a higher level, I spent a week researching Vouvray. The sampler showcases the results of my research.

Vouvray is overlooked here for two reasons. First, it is not Chardonnay. Second, a lot of sweet, sulfury Vouvray was shipped to the U.S. by *négociants* after WW II. It is similar to our distrust of rosé wines. Once bitten, forever shy. However, as you have learned, in the hands of a talented winemaker (Joguet, Bonny Doon, Tempier, etc.) rosé can be a delight. In our sampler, you can taste the mixed palette of wines Vouvray has to offer, from some of its best *terroirs* and most talented vignerons.

I meant to move around and report on various hotels, too, but once installed in the Hôtel La Choiseul in Amboise, I stayed. They have a swimming pool and a lovely outdoor patio where you can enjoy an unusually fine *petit déjeuner* in the bright morning sun, or a glass of Vouvray *pétillant* at sundown before dining. All the rooms offer spectacular views, either of the broad, graceful Loire, of the chalky inhabited cliffs behind the hotel, or of the Château d'Amboise.

A tour of the château is a must. I hope you fall upon the same tour guide I had, a dyed-in-the-wool monarchist who does not attempt to hide it. He is still fuming because the king and his court no longer reside there. With sinister joy he pointed out the iron grill balcony where the Huguenots were lynched and left hanging for days as a lesson to troublemakers. And alas, there was the day King Charles VIII bonked his noggin on a doorway and breathed his last royal breath. The guide reported with gnashing-of-teeth how 80% of the château was demolished after the revolution, when the villagers tore it to pieces and used the stones to rebuild their own houses down the hill. What is this world coming to? The 20% that remains of the original château is grand enough, but imagine what it must have been like whole, when Leonardo da Vinci spent his final days there. His crypt is in the chapel.

Back to the business at hand: Vouvray's wines are versatile at table, but there are limits. They won't work at all with Mediterranean cuisine. Chop suey, yes; aioli, no. I find that all the various types of Vouvray complement charcuterie, above all *rillettes* or *rillons*. The *sec* is excellent with fried fish or shellfish. *Sec* and *demi-sec* work well with salmon however it is cooked, and with sauced fish and chicken dishes (you see a lot of *beurre blanc* in the region). The *pétillant* is as fine an apéritif as you can find, as it straddles the fence between Champagne and dry white. It can therefore serve at table in place of a dry, still Vouvray, and I once enjoyed a glass at a winemaker's table with cake, as dessert. A great *moelleux*, such as offered in this sampler, requires nothing more than a corkscrew, glasses, and friends.

The Vouvray sampler includes:

1988 Vouvray Sec · *Domaine Champalou*

$6.95 PER BOTTLE $75.06 PER CASE

1984 Vouvray Sec · *Domaine Courson*

$6.25 PER BOTTLE $67.50 PER CASE

1988 Vouvray Pétillant · *Domaine Champalou*

$8.95 PER BOTTLE $96.66 PER CASE

1985 Vouvray Pétillant · *Domaine Courson*

$9.95 PER BOTTLE $107.46 PER CASE

1982 Vouvray Demi-sec · *Domaine Courson*

$7.95 PER BOTTLE $85.86 PER CASE

1986 Vouvray Moelleux · *Domaine Allias*

$14.95 PER BOTTLE $161.46 PER CASE

SPECIAL SAMPLER PRICE $75.00

1987 HERMITAGE
J. L. CHAVE

Chave's white Hermitage, like his red, is the French wine that ages the longest . . . and the best. GÉRARD ASTIER, *Les Vins de la Vallée du Rhône*

MOST CHAVE BUYERS are repeat buyers who cellar every vintage, as I do, and pull out whichever seems most appropriate to a given occasion. Is it the moment for a young or an old bottle, light or powerful, tannic or supple?

I asked Chave to describe his 1987 in comparison to 1985 and 1986.

"The 1987 has a more floral quality," he said, "and it will open up more quickly. I'm not saying the 1987 won't live as long, not at all, it is too soon to say, but it does have the advantage of earlier accessibility."

1987 HERMITAGE *BLANC*

Even the color is complex: golden with glints of green and a touch of maroon, which comes from the skin of a ripe Marsanne grape. The nose is honeyed, floral, with a dash of new oak and a lemony note that goes nicely with the honey. On the palate, very elegant and subtle, and it is a wine that blossoms and grows in richness as the aftertaste persists.

$276.00 PER CASE

You must open one as soon as it arrives in order to appreciate Chave's success in 1987. The aroma is unlike any other vintage I have tasted: quite thick, generous, spicy, minty, smoky, with wild berry, violets, and ravishing new oak. Tasting it is like touring a large house; you walk through one room and look it over, then into another, admiring a painting on the wall in one room, the fireplace in another, a sofa, a carpet. The wine is a taste tour, ever changing.

Both red and white are wines that seduce you, grab your attention, and make you want to spend time exploring them, getting to know each room more intimately.

$330.00 PER CASE

LULU'S AIOLI SECRET

L ULU IS LULU Peyraud of Domaine Tempier. Aioli is the garlicky mayonnaise of Provence, but the word *aioli* can also refer to the mayonnaise and all the assorted goodies onto which the people of Provence traditionally heap it: sweet potato, carrots, artichokes, hard-boiled egg, sea snails, salt cod, octopus stew, garden tomatoes, beets, and so on. For grand occasions when guests are numerous (the end-of-harvest celebration, for example), Lulu always serves bouillabaisse or a grand aioli.

For some reason bouillabaisse and aioli have taken on some sort of spiritual significance to me. When I eat them, I satisfy more than one kind of hunger.

Why then did the aioli gods turn on me? For years my aiolis fell apart no matter how careful I was! Drop by excruciating drop I would add the olive oil, turning all the while until my arm wanted to fall off, 15, 20 minutes, and then in a matter of seconds my precious aioli would separate into an unappetizing glop of olive oil and raw egg. In frustration I finally tried to make it in a blender. *Even that fell apart!*

So I sat down with Lulu, mortar and pestle, garlic, egg yolk, and olive oil, and asked her to show me how it is done.

"You add a little salt first to help grind the garlic to a paste, then the egg yolk, then you stir in the olive oil. It's easy." She said.

Folks, that is exactly how I always did it, so I insisted she demonstrate.

Well, first, there was no drip-drip-drip. Lulu splashed in a healthy glug of oil and turned it with the pestle until it firmed up, then glug-glug, another pour. I couldn't believe my eyes. Surely it was bound to unbind.

But, to hurry along . . . Lulu did have a step she hadn't mentioned. When her aioli began to thicken too much, she added a spoonful of tepid water. Since learning the tepid-water trick I haven't lost a single aioli and my life is more meaningful. But why had no one ever explained that you don't want your aioli to get *too* thick? I always thought that was the goal.

Surprisingly, Lulu serves not rosé, but red wine with aioli. Soul food, soul wine. A young, *cool* red. The 1986 works; the 1985 is already too evolved for an aioli. Save it or an older Tempier for the cheese platter, when the aioli is finito.

OUR NEW GIFT CERTIFICATE

THERE ARE AT LEAST three great virtues about our newly designed Gift Certificate. One, it is quick and easy to purchase. Two, it is a gift you give, but the recipient can come in and select whatever he or she fancies. Three, you are free to decide the amount of the certificate yourself.

You might decide that your father had such important input into the fact of your existence that he merits a $500 certificate. Besides, it would be nice if there were something decent to uncork when you visit him.

Your worst enemy? $2. Let him try to find an imported wine at two dollars. It will drive him crazy. You will have the pleasure of giving a gift that is going to cost him money.

Your husband's lover? $20. She deserves a bottle of French Champagne for keeping him out of your hair so often.

The perfect gift! Liberty and justice for all!

❧ 1990 ❧

1988 GAVI "MONTEMARINO"
STEFANO BELLOTTI

STEFANO BELLOTTI has the sort of winery you like even before he pulls a cork. The entrance is lined with olive trees; there are plum, cherry, apricot, and other fruit trees all around the house and vineyard; his huge, fluffy dog wears a happy smile; his entire work crew, strangely enough, is lovely and female; he is advocating organic farming for wine grapes as you head to his cellar to taste the new vintage.

Who cares what his wine tastes like, right? But, of course, it tastes great. Other Gavi tastes like water next to Bellotti's. His is what I call *true* wine; it doesn't follow the latest fad or formula for success; its taste reflects the place and the person from which it comes. With such a beautiful Italian white, you sit up and notice what is in your glass.

$12.50 PER BOTTLE $135.00 PER CASE

1987 PETIT CHABLIS · LAVANTUREUX

I am opposed to numbered scores for wines (as well as symphonies, paintings, lovers, etc.), but if you must use points, I propose that perfection be the measure. I see too many perfect bottles scored in the 80s because they are not from hip appellations. Better a perfect Petit Chablis, I say, than an imperfect Montrachet. When a type of wine realizes its potential, it deserves 100 points.

What is a perfect Petit Chablis? It is crisp, lively, its fruitiness enhanced by that stony Chablis *goût de terroir*. It has class but does not aspire to overwhelm you or your cuisine. On the contrary! It satisfies all the Chablis requirements except aging potential.

$8.95 PER BOTTLE $96.66 PER CASE

AN INTRODUCTION TO
RED BURGUNDY
· SPECIAL SAMPLER OFFER ·

Some of us who love wine love good red Burgundy most of all. Beaune, Nuits, Gevrey . . . the passion can rise to extremes: the buying of it, the aging of it, the tasting and appreciation of it. No wine is more fun to critique.

Others are hesitant to get involved because Burgundy can be a confusing and expensive proposition. *How do I orient myself without wasting time and money?* seems to be the issue. Red Burgundy is not easy. It *is* complicated. But it *is* worth the effort to get to know it.

To help you get your bearings straight, I reviewed every wine in stock and organized this special sampler that consists of three different groups to taste. You may:

1. Taste the three groups one after another the same night.

2. Taste each group separately over three different nights.

3. Taste them one bottle per night using your memory to make the contrasts and comparisons.

Yes, experimenting with red Burgundy is expensive. The prices keep many from ever appreciating these great wines. However, A BIG PRICE DOES NOT GUARANTEE A GREAT BOTTLE and A LOW PRICE DOES NOT MEAN A LOUSY WINE. Gambling that these sampler wines will tempt you to further explorations along the Burgundian wine route, normal prices are *cut in half* for this sampler, which is broken down into these three categories of estate-bottled red Burgundy:

THE VILLAGES OF BURGUNDY

According to the literature, each village is supposed to have a distinct character. Here are three *premiers crus* from three of the Côte de Beaune's finest villages. Compare them. What sets them apart? Volnay and Pommard are side-by-side on the map, yet their wines are reputedly quite different. Is it true or is it not? Why is Volnay Champans always costlier than a *premier cru* Savigny-lès-Beaune? Does it deserve to be? Which of the three is best from the quality/price point of view? Which would you bet on for long aging?

1987 *Savigny-lès-Beaune "Les Jarrons"* · *Guillemot* $17.50
1986 *Pommard "Les Croix Noires"* · *Boillot* 19.95
1983 *Volnay "En Champans"* · *Monceau-Boch* 19.95

THE HIERARCHY

Each village has its own character, yes, but *within* each village there is a precisely defined classification, a sort of aristocracy of dukes, princes, kings, and un-American things like that. In this flight it is essential to begin with the generic Côte de Nuits-Villages, then on to the specific village wine, the Nuits-Saint-Georges, and conclude with the great *premier cru* from the same village, the Nuits Les Pruliers. What if you prefer the Côte de Nuits-Villages? Are you wrong? A commoner? No, but you will have found a bargain. Or is tasting them in succession like climbing up the quality ladder? Is the hierarchy, the Burgundian aristocracy, valid?

PER BOTTLE

1986 *Côte de Nuits-Villages* · *Rossignol* $14.95
1986 *Nuits-Saint-Georges* · *Chevillon* 29.95
1983 *Nuits-Saint-Georges "Les Pruliers"* · *Boillot* 24.95

THE WINEMAKER

Which is more important in Burgundy, the vineyard site or the winemaker? The soil or the vinification? Here you can compare three mature red Burgundies from a vintage whose wines show their typical *goût de terroir.* The '83s were dominated by the *goût de l'année,* the '85s by the *goût du cépage* (grape variety), but the successful '84s show what makes Burgundy the best spot for Pinot Noir: its soil. Same vintage, same grape variety, same village, only the vinification is different, so you can really see and taste how important the winemaker's role is. Comparing them, ask yourself how the three differ, but also, what do they have in common? What do they share that we can call Gevrey-Chambertin character? Once you have trained your palate and your intellect to pose questions like these, you are on your way to appreciating red Burgundy.

Pierre Guillemot, Savigny-lès-Beaune

ORGANIC WINE?

ALICE WATERS asked me to put together a tasting of our organically produced wines for the Chez Panisse staff. What a good idea! Actually, I had never quite in my own mind lumped such wines together into a definitive group entitled *Organic Wines*, and I certainly did not import them because of their . . . organicity? Organiqueness? . . . but the idea of tasting them all together interested me, and then it amazed me to see what a number of them we have to offer.

Apparently the idea intrigues others, too, because Alice said there has never been such a large turnout for a Panisse tasting.

Most people who search out organic products are motivated by a desire to avoid poisoning themselves, the earth, and its atmosphere. If drinking organic wine prolongs my life and the life of the planet, so much the better, I volunteer, but frankly I bought them because they taste good. I buy organic tomatoes for the same reason. Don't call it a crusade; it is only my weakness for flavorful wine.

What is wine? Why do we care about it so? I am convinced that there is something almost spiritual about natural wine, about partaking in its combination of earth, sun, and the fruit of the vine. Wine can put your head in the clouds while your feet remain deeply rooted in the soil. So I want the most expressive, least emasculated, least mucked-up, most alive, natural wine possible. And organic winemakers tend to be the ultimate purists: if they don't like chemical fertilizers or herbicides in their soil or chemical pesticides on their vines, they are not likely to overchaptalize or oversulfur or sterilize or acidify or artificially color or flavor their wine.

So I go out of my way to taste in the cellars of organic winegrowers. More often than not, organic wines are not good enough to buy because of some flaw in the vinification. So don't think I am telling you that organic wine means good wine. But the successful ones can be spectacular. I have never tasted a Gavi with the flavor authority of Stefano Bellotti's, never had a *vin de pays* with the class of Gautière's, and then there are the two world-famous wines from the south of France, Mas de Daumas Gassac and Domaine de Trévallon.

Organically produced wines can be great wines.

As diverse as the wines were, the tasting of them as a group succeeded because there does seem to be some charismatic quality they share. They are extremely expressive, vigorous, full-flavored wines, far from bland, far from dull, loaded with appeal and personality. You might enjoy putting together a similar tasting to see what conclusions you draw from it.

These are the wines we tasted:

PER BOTTLE

1988	*Sauvignon* · *Due Terre*		$12.50
1988	*Tocai Friulano* · *Due Terre*		9.95
1987	*Côtes du Rhône* · *Domaine de la Jasse*		6.95
1987	*Mas de Daumas Gassac*		$19.95
1982	*Domaine de Trévallon*		sold out
1988	*Gavi "Cascina Ulivi"* · *Bellotti*		9.95
1988	*Gavi "Montemarino"* · *Bellotti*		12.50
1988	*Nibio* · *Bellotti*		12.50
1985	*Domaine du Bas Deffens*		5.95
1989	*Beaujolais* · *Ducroux*		7.95
1988	*Domaine de la Gautière*		sold out

WORDS OF THOM. JEFFERSON
THREATEN AMERICA

GOV'T. ACTS TO PROTECT NATIONAL HEALTH

Thomas Jefferson, author of our Bill of Rights (freedom of speech, press, and all the nuisances), was recently censored by the U.S. government because he said something that can no longer be said about wine: *that it is healthy.* Jefferson wrote,

Wine from long habit has become an indispensable for my health.

The Bureau of Alcohol, Tobacco, and Firearms refused to allow Jefferson's quote on my import strips. But don't worry, I'm sure they censored Thomas Jefferson for your own good. That is usually the rationale for government suppression of individual rights. But come on, Uncle Sam. Thomas Jefferson???

EDITORIAL OPINION
MORE ON JEFFERSON

Last month I quoted the words of a hero of mine, Thomas Jefferson:

Wine from long habit has become an indispensable for my health.

Our current government will not permit Jefferson's quote on the wines I import. However, the words "may cause health problems" are now mandatory on wine bottles. Not that wine causes health problems, no, it doesn't say that, but I must put on each bottle that it *may* cause health problems. What convincing legislation!

Scissors *may* cause bleeding.

Water *may* cause drowning.

Life *may* cause death.

Music *may* cause Muzak.

There are endless maybes, but the one about wine is obligatory while Thomas Jefferson's contrary opinion is censored. They also refused quotes from the Bible (is nothing holy?) and Louis Pasteur, quotes that said bluntly that wine is healthy. What a revolting development it is, all this.

If you think a bottle of fermented grape juice is dangerous to your health, you need a heart, soul, and brain transplant. Well, I suppose if you filled a pool with it, and fell in, and couldn't swim, and there was no lifeguard on duty . . .

Thomas Jefferson was the author of our Bill of Rights, which is the envy of so much of humanity. He was our third president, and wine importer to our first! Here are a few other quotes from Jefferson that the Behavior Control lobby would not want you to see. Read at your own risk:

I have lived temperately . . . I double the doctor's recommendation of a glass and a half of wine a day and even treble it with a friend.

By making this wine vine known to the public, I have rendered my country as great a service as if I had enabled it to pay back the national debt.

I think it is a great error to consider a heavy tax on wines as a tax on luxury. On the contrary, it is a tax on the health of our citizens.

Good wine is a necessity of life for me.

I rejoice as a moralist at the prospect of a reduction of the duties on wine by our national legislature. . . . Its extended use will carry health and comfort to a much enlarged circle.

Wine . . . the true old man's milk and restorative cordial.

Yes, Jefferson *is* dangerous, but to whom? He is no threat to you or me, but he has always posed a threat to the people who approve censorship if *they* decide it is for *your* own good. And isn't it delicious that these people, waving their flag of health, resort to censoring the Bible and the author of our Bill of Rights? The whole thing has been a very telling experience. Beware.

Let us begin to counter the anti-wine attacks of the Behavior Control lobby. Let us get some waves flowing in the other direction. Plato was right—wine is a beautiful gift of nature. I don't want it uglified. If, in your reading, you run across some useful quotes about wine, send them to me and I'll publish them here each month. For example:

I have enjoyed great health at a great age because every day since I can remember I have consumed a bottle of wine except when I have not felt well. Then I have consumed two bottles. A Bishop of Seville

Do not think I am trying to tell you that wine is healthy. I wouldn't do that. That would be illegal! But I do wish the current batch in Washington would stay out of my life and leave their misleading health warnings off my lovely bottles. Vague, misleading health warnings may lead to behavior control.

◇ ◇

1989 harvest, Domaine Tempier. Our man John Olney worked the 1989 Bandol harvest at Domaine Tempier. He knows the vintage inside and out! And my successor, Marley Lynch, was there, too. I explained to her that good wine starts in the vineyard, and it seemed the best place to begin training her palate. Here she analyzes Tempier's Mourvèdre grapes. Across the road she tasted the grapes of a neighboring domaine but spit them out with an expression of thorough disgust. She's on her way!

1987 BANDOL *ROUGE* "CABASSAOU" · DOMAINE TEMPIER

What to call this? A special *cuvée spéciale*? A *cuvée* super-*spéciale*? It is from the heart of La Tourtine, the steepest section where the oldest Mourvèdre grows. That parcel has always been called Cabassaou. This is the first time that the Peyrauds have, out of curiosity, vinified it separately. The 50-year-old Mourvèdre vineyard gave this incredibly intense, juicy wine that has the finesse and class of a great Bordeaux. Abundant quality; limited supply.

$22.95 PER FIFTH $247.86 PER CASE

1989 CORBIÈRES *BLANC* · JEAN BERAIL

This is our best dry white wine value except for the others because:

1. *The presentation is classy. Bottle, label, cork, capsule, etc. It* looks *expensive.*

2. *The wine is delicious. In France it is what I stock for everyday guzzling. So do most of my friends. It is hard to beat.*

In fact, I polled our staff and their parents, and the wine scored an average 99.17 (statistical errorability factor: $12^2 \div 13/14$).

Under future California tax and health laws, a wine this good and this cheap will be illegal.

$5.95 PER BOTTLE $64.26 PER CASE

NUITS-SAINT-GEORGES "LES PRULIERS"

A RE THERE STILL bargains in great red Burgundy? None are cheap, but what if you could purchase *grand cru* quality at a *premier cru* price?

These two *premiers crus* from the great vineyard Les Pruliers are "smart money" wines. Put me to the test. Place a stack of cash and a pile of twelve bottles of Les Pruliers in a cool humid cellar and see which ages better, which makes your life more pleasurable in 10 years' time. You know I'm right!

Les Pruliers has long been a magical name to me, and I dreamed of one day finding a worthy one. What is the character of a perfect Pruliers? It is more dense and mouth-filling than other Nuits-Saint-Georges. If it were a string quartet the cello would dominate. No gay little charmer, it would be in the spirit of a Beethoven late quartet, the opus 131 or 132. And it is a wine that requires age before it shows its full potential.

We have about one barrel, or 300 bottles, of each Pruliers. Those who follow my advice and cellar six of each will be awarded a 20% discount off the normal bottle price.

1987 NUITS-SAINT-GEORGES "LES PRULIERS"
DOMAINE ROBERT CHEVILLON

Denis had the fortune to apprentice with his father, Robert, and they work side by side.

Deep, generous nose, classic Pinot Noir. Quite a luscious feel on the palate with ravishing flavors.

$34.00 PER BOTTLE $367.20 PER CASE

1987 NUITS-SAINT-GEORGES "LES PRULIERS"
DOMAINE BOILLOT

Just as full-bodied, but old vines give it a tighter, more muscular structure. Dense, tannic, earthy, a touch of the sinister . . . sinister? . . . well, folks, flavors are hard to describe, but you will want to be present when this one matures.

$28.00 PER BOTTLE $302.40 PER CASE

SPECIAL MIXED–CASE PRICE: $297.60

HOW TO EAT WELL

IT'S EASY. These eggs take no more than five minutes to prepare, and you need not be a culinary genius to succeed.

THIS IS NOT BREAKFAST!

First you pour yourself a glass of cool Beaujolais (see below).

Then you fry fresh eggs slowly in butter, covered, until the whites are firm but the yolks remain runny. Salt and pepper, then slide them out onto a warm plate.

Deglaze the pan with two tablespoons red wine vinegar. Reduce by half. Thicken with a slice of butter and pour it over your eggs. You will want bread or toast for sopping up the sauce.

You will also want another glass of Beaujolais! The only other wine that comes close to working is Joguet's young-vine Chinon. But these Vinegar Eggs with Beaujolais create one of my favorite combinations. The following Beaujolais are currently available:

		PER BOTTLE	PER CASE
1989 *Beaujolais-Villages* · *Château Gaillard*	. . . .	$8.95	$96.66
1989 *Beaujolais Régnié* · *Christian Ducroux*	. . . .	9.95	107.46
1989 *Fleurie "Les Moriers"* · *Chignard*	. . . . .	13.95	150.66
1989 *Morgon* · *Château Gaillard*	. . . .	10.95	118.26
1988 *Moulin-à-Vent "Vieilles Vignes"* · *B. Diochon*	. .	12.95	139.86

1989 CLOS NICROSI · TOUSSAINT LUIGI

Has anyone ever told you that this Corsican beauty is, with the exception of Chave's, their favorite dry white from southern France? I expect not. You might ridicule the thought unless you age a bottle three or four years and see what it delivers: Incredible complexity! Towering deliciousness! Aromas bouncing all over the inside of your nose! Honey, flower blossoms, Corsican wild herbs (*le maqui*), mineral, apricot, grilled almonds, lemon peel, and so on and on. It is an amazing, overlooked treasure from the hillsides of Cap Corse.

$16.50 PER BOTTLE $178.20 PER CASE

INTRODUCING
GEVREY-CHAMBERTIN

Some of the greatest red Burgundy; it is the biggest, and fullest of bouquet.

H. W. YOXALL

Color, power, and baroque splendor.   HUBERT DUIJKEN

An admirable mélange of grace, vigor, power, and finesse.   LAROUSSE DE VINS

I forgot the name of the place; I forgot the name of the girl; but the wine . . . was Chambertin.   HILAIRE BELLOC

Frankness, solidity, bouquet, and body.   DANGUY ET AUBERTIN

Firm and well-colored, fleshy and flavorful, of a robust constitution but equally of a great elegance and a grand bouquet.   PIERRE BRÉJOUX

IT OCCURRED TO ME that I import more Gevrey-Chambertin than any other red Burgundy. Here is an attempt to begin to explain why, and then a special offer to introduce you to the splendors of great Gevrey-Chambertin:

An unfiltered Gevrey's color, whether light or deep, always has a flickering suggestion of shadow to it.

The nose rises up to meet you with a thick smoke-like texture and gives you a preview of the depth the wine will have on the palate.

A Gevrey must not be overly sophisticated. It must always have a touch of rusticity to it to seem real.

Some men seem more feminine than others but remain men. Some Gevreys seem more feminine than others but remain masculine (Charmes, Lavaux Saint-Jacques, and Corbeaux, for example).

There is a firm backbone, and this backbone seems to have a slightly bitter edge to its flavor.

Even when tight and closed up in youth, Gevreys are easy to appreciate, yet they do not reveal how grandly aromatic, complex, and noble they will become when mature.

Serve your Gevreys with game, fowl, red meats, or cheeses.

Never drink one during the warm months. Gevrey-Chambertin is winter wine, soul-warming red wine, comforting like a blazing fire.

SPECIAL OFFER

Gevrey-Chambertin Sampler

Three vintages; four producers; two village wines, two *premiers crus* and two *grands crus*. Here is a broad, valuable look at one of the world's greatest wine villages. And it is like getting four bottles free.

		PER BOTTLE
1988 *Gevrey-Chambertin · Domaine Rossignol*	. . . . .	$24.95
1987 *Gevrey-Chambertin · Domaine Boillot.*	. . . . .	. 22.50
1987 *Gevrey "Les Corbeaux"* 1er Cru *· Domaine Boillot.*	. . .	. 24.95
1986 *Gevrey "Lavaux Saint-Jacques"* 1er Cru *· Domaine Maume*	.	. 35.00
1986 *Griottes-Chambertin* Grand Cru *· Domaine Ponsot*	. . .	. 59.95
1986 *Mazis-Chambertin* Grand Cru *· Domaine Maume*	. . .	. 49.95

NORMALLY $217.30

SIX-BOTTLE SAMPLER PRICE $110.00

THANKSGIVING

Throughout eighteen years of business I have withstood the temptation to tell you what to serve with turkey. To demonstrate that middle age has not fixed my brain in concrete, that I am still full of fire and rebellion, I'm going to shatter tradition and tell you what to drink with the traditional Thanksgiving feast: California Chardonnay.

Oops, no, just kidding.

Let us look at the problem more closely. You are sitting around the bird with your uncle who annually proclaims, "I'm no wine con-oh-sewer, but I know what I like," and your grandmother who says, "Red wine gives me a headache and white wine gives me heartburn," or your father-in-law who wants to know, "What, now you're too good for Mogen David?" For turkey I would descend into my cellar and stay there. No, I mean I would pull out all the mistakes I cellared and will never drink. This is their shining moment! Turkeys deserve turkeys.

No, seriously, I would never do that. I am too selfish. I like Thanksgiving fare, so I serve what I want to drink. With a large group at table here is the occasion to orchestrate a series of wines. Usually I decide to go with red Burgundies, once the apéritif is out of the way. I might start with an '88 or '89 Fleurie or Moulin-à-Vent, then to a Pommard or Volnay from the early 1980s, then to an older *grand cru*, a Mazis or Bonnes-Mares, 1971 or 1972, for example.

If you have enough guests, this month's Gevrey-Chambertin sampler would go beautifully with the roast bird and dressing, and it would give you the chance to taste through an assortment of great red Burgundies at one sitting. Serve them in the order listed, not all at once.

By all means, finish off the meal with our Moscato d'Asti. It is light (7° alcohol), it is sparkling, it has a sweet touch, it is delicious, everyone will love it, you *and* your uncle, your grandmother *and* father-in-law, plus it is only $8.95. Finish the feast with a sparkle.

✦ 1991 ✦

DRUET SAMPLER

A number of people in the trade are promoting the red Loire Valley wines as a wonderful alternative to over-priced Cabernets from Bordeaux and Burgundy. However, I recently tasted through the 1988s and 1989s from top producers such as Charles Joguet, Pierre-Jacques Druet, Olga Raffault, and Couly-Dutheil. No matter how hard I tried, even in a super-ripe year such as 1989, these wines still come across as vegetal and unattractive. Sorry!

ROBERT PARKER, *The Wine Advocate*

These are a combination of the way we hear wines used to taste in the "good old days," with the best elements of the new wine-making. Fans of Druet's friend Charles Joguet, as well as anyone who appreciates real wine-making, will want these wines in the cellar and will want to follow Druet closely in the future; based on these few wines, this is another summit of the appellation, such as Gérard Chave, Michael Lafarge, or Joguet.   CLAUDE KOLM, *The Fine Wine Review*

Wow! WHAT A DRAMATIC difference of opinion. So, Druet and I assembled a special sampler case to tempt you to taste and JUDGE FOR YOURSELF!

I cannot imagine who would be promoting Chinon and Bourgueil as *alternatives* to Bordeaux. They don't taste like Bordeaux, thank goodness. Except for a few exceptions like Sociando-Mallet, I find that today's Bordeaux have a lackluster sameness to them. Greedy overproduction, I'd say, plus the fact that the châteaux all seem to follow the same wine-making recipe. Bored-*eaux*, if you ask me. I guarantee that the Cabernets of Joguet and Druet are *never* boring.

I also think it is too bad (especially for talents like Joguet and Druet) that someone with Parker's tremendous influence rejects an entire region's wines. Here at Chinon and Bourgueil people have been making wine for at least 10 centuries, wine praised by the likes of Rabelais and Kermit Lynch, and all of a sudden we learn that it was all in vain. Too bad *The Wine Advocate* wasn't around back then; Parker could have saved those hopeless devils centuries of time and effort.

All right, I'm having my own facetious brand of fun. It is certainly Robert Parker's right to dislike these wines, and some of you are going to agree with his judgment. Others will agree with Rabelais and Claude Kolm. These are thrilling wines! It is exciting to discover them. With an open mind you might fall in love with them like I did. It is fun to fall in love.

What we have are six bottles from four different vineyards and four different vintages. You will notice the absence of a 1985. Druet suggested including one, but, believe it or not, I preferred the 1984, a perfectly mature bottle from a light year.

The 1986 Grand Mont: old vines; a serious wine with a captivating *goût de terroir*.

1987 Beauvais: deep, rich, fine; a perfection that is still three to four years from peak.

The 1988 Chinon has a smoky, new oak aroma and an incredibly ample feel on the palate. *Try not to like it!*

1988 Bourgueil Les Cent Boissellées: black pepper and black currant aroma; loaded with flavor.

The 1989 from the same vineyard will age, but uncork it now for a gorgeous, purplish blast of room-filling Cabernet Franc. You can almost dance to it.

Discover this great young winemaker, Pierre-Jacques Druet. According to the *Revue du Vin de France*, "His racy, fleshy, concentrated Bourgueils are the new reference point."

		PER BOTTLE
1989	*Bourgueil "Les Cent Boissellées"*	$12.50
1988	*Bourgueil "Les Cent Boissellées"*	11.25
1988	*Chinon "Clos Danzay"*	16.50
1987	*Bourgueil "Beauvais"*	12.50
1986	*Bourgueil "Grand Mont"*	16.50
1984	*Bourgueil "Grand Mont"*	13.50

NORMALLY $82.75

SPECIAL SAMPLER PRICE $60.00

◦ ◦ ◦ ◦ ◦ ◦ ◦ ◦

1989 VOUVRAY "MOELLEUX" · CHAMPALOU

I have seen claims that 1989 is the vintage of the century in the Loire. How can anyone call it the vintage of the century if they have not extensively toured the 1947s, the 1929s, the 1921s? Or the upcoming 1990s?

However, never one to miss a bandwagon, I will go even further: *1989 is the vintage of the past 14 centuries!*

Back to reality: This is Champalou's sweet, botrytized honey-dripper, the kind you cellar and pull out in 10, 20, 30, or 40 years to great applause.

Good going, Dad!
Hey, good thinking, Pop.
Father, you might have done magnums.

Golden-colored, enveloping richness, perfect structure, and the complexity of the noble rot.

$14.95 PER BOTTLE $161.46 PER CASE

1988 DOMAINE TEMPIER

BLESSED BANDOL experienced three dry, hot years in a row: 1988, 1989, and 1990. So, coming up from Domaine Tempier: three solid, truly exceptional, incredible, brilliant vintages. No, I am not exaggerating. Winemaker Jean-Marie Peyraud is on cloud nine, ecstatic about all three. It is as if he woke up in heaven without having died first. Three perfect vintages!!! Unheard of. When I taste with him, I can tell that his personal favorite is 1988. To give you an idea of his personal taste, Jean-Marie also rates 1982, 1971, 1970, and 1964 as favorite Tempier vintages. He likes them big and he likes them ripe. But me, well, I have been happily sloshing down an extraordinary amount of 1987 Tempier, and I would feel unfaithful if I now came out and claimed that 1988 is better. And what of the 1989s? Black and intense, leaner than 1988 but just as powerful. Sugar Ray Robinson, for those of you who recall his wicked flash and style. My tasting notes include the word "class" often enough, whatever that tastes like. I did have a chance to taste through Tempier's 1990s before I left France. Incredible. Bursting with flavor. Again!

The original Domaine Tempier label, before Bandol became an official appelation in 1941

Can there be too much of a good thing? I will be the guinea pig for the experiment. Stop when we have had enough, Jean-Marie. No, not yet.

1988 BANDOL "LA TOURTINE"

Deep purplish black. There is a large proportion of Mourvèdre and 1988 is a big year, so this is about as dark as Tempier gets. For gorgeously deep-colored wines, Tempier is hard to beat.

Complex, thick aroma, more ample than usual in a young Tourtine. Chewy, explosive fruit. Take the personalities of Athos, Porthos, and Aramis, put them all together, and you've got a 1988 Tourtine—a big, handsome, swashbuckling wine, seductive with spirit and breed.

$198.00 PER CASE

1988 BANDOL "LA MIGOUA"

I have used the word before for La Migoua's bouquet: *cornucopian*. That is what I think of when I put my nose into the glass, a horn of plenty out of which cascade peach, apricot, black cherry, and other fresh, ripe fruits. This is one of the most amazing Tempiers I have tasted. Be sure to open a bottle when it arrives. You must experience it to believe it.

$198.00 PER CASE

∘ ∘ ∘ ∘ ∘ ∘ ∘ ∘

1989 UVAGGIO · DUE TERRE

This, on the other hand, this one might inspire you to say *Wow, wait a minute, Holy cow,* or *Right on!* Due Terre makes what I call soul wine, because it satisfies the soul, that dark cavernous interior where few wines dare descend. So, naturally the attractive couple who make the wine are quite special. I told him that if only I spoke Italian better, he and I would surely become bosom buddies. I told his wife that if she were not already with him, we would too.

This is exotically flavored, and no other wine, Friuli or otherwise, resembles it. Moreover, it is a Jaded Palate *Pick to Click.*

$12.50 PER BOTTLE $135.00 PER CASE

1990 LENTISCO ROSSO

A big, staggeringly concentrated red of guigalian extract with truckloads of jammy fruit, lumberyards of new oak, a bomb shelter–like structure, a mind-boggling crossword puzzle–like complexity, and a novocaine-like finish. This is a block, buster. The 100-point scoring system barely contains it. (Tasted triple blind in a one-man submarine having foregone conjugal relations for 100 hours.)

Just kidding, folks. Would I inflict something like that on your tender palates? This is actually another fresh, bright, ultra-lively red that you can enjoy without getting splinters in your nose or alcohol burns on your tongue. It is barely over 11°. It is 100% Sangiovese. I serve it cool.

$6.95 PER BOTTLE $75.06 PER CASE

VENETO

PROSECCO BRUT · NINO FRANCO

Stop reading. Come to the shop. Buy a bottle of this Prosecco. Continue reading while you sniff a chilled glass of this dry, white, low-alcohol sparkler. Thus will you see my prose change from bungling to revelatory.

I am a longtime Prosecco seeker, and this is the finest I have found. The aroma seems to dance (hurry, take another sip) upon the star-burst surface (quick, another) of the wine.

What I am trying to communicate here is that you will like the nose and bead. It sparkles more gently than Champagne; it is less manic. Plus, you don't worry about snob appeal or getting ripped off. I, for one, drink it more often than I drink Champagne.

In the Veneto it was dazzling with a platter of San Daniele prosciutto and an assortment of the best sliced salami I have ever eaten.

$9.95 PER BOTTLE $107.46 PER CASE

FREE SPEECH FOR WINE

THE NOSE

WHAT IS A NOSE? When I was a college student in the early 1960s, I wrote a short story called "The Nose." In my story the nose was a thinly (for such was my talent) disguised phallic symbol. Oh, well. What can I say? I was young, naïve. I was Freshman. And back in those days *everyone* believed in Freud. Freud this, Freud that.

Thanks to various twists of fate, I turned into a wine importer, and nowadays I have a different appreciation of the nose and its functions.

What does this have to do with new medical evidence which suggests that, unless you guzzle recklessly,

1. *wine drinking reduces the risk of heart disease significantly (Lancet, August 1991) and*

2. *enjoying wine while you are pregnant will not endanger your fetus (British Medical Journal, July 6, 1991)?*

Well, the other day I was driving along with my three-year-old daughter when, all of a sudden, alarms went off in my head and I rolled up the windows as fast as I could. Why? Because my trusty nose had sniffed something foul emanating from a factory up ahead. It told me, "Danger! Do not breathe those fumes."

Later that same day I sniffed a glass of Bandol rosé and my nose told me, "Mmm, smells good. Ingestion okay."

What is a nose for? It is not only for breathing. Your mouth can handle that. Isn't a nose there to sniff out danger?

Stick your nose into a glass of wine and listen to its judgment. For centuries mankind has judged that *of course* wine is good for you. Two new studies confirm the nose's advice.

"We found a dose response, with the more alcohol consumed, the more reduced the risk for heart disease," said Dr. Eric Rimm of the Harvard School of Public Health. (Note that hardly any of the participants exceeded five drinks per day.)

"Pregnant women probably need not abstain from alcohol altogether," concluded Prof. Charles Florey in the *British Medical Journal*, adding, "The children of mothers who had reduced their intake did not differ from those of abstainers."

Now read that health warning on your wine label. Come on, Uncle Sam. That has got to go! Don't bug citizens needlessly.

◦　◦　◦　◦　◦　◦　◦　◦

1990 POUILLY-FUMÉ "EN CHAILLOUX"
DIDIER DAGUENEAU

You take a look at Henry Jayer and Didier Dagueneau, and it is hard to imagine the two of them together.

There is something of the small-town farmer to Jayer, even with those bright, intelligent, wholesome eyes and that expression of complete directness and openness. He seems perfectly groomed, even in coveralls. He is in his 60s, semi-retired, and there is not much hair left. Dress him up in a black tux and he could pass for the cellist in a Russian string quartet.

Didier Dagueneau is young. Bushy hair. Bushy beard. Rides a black motorcycle. Asked me if I could find him a copy of Dylan's *Blonde on Blonde*. He would fit right into some raunch-and-roll band from the 1960s.

Yet these two opposites attract. Jayer and Dagueneau are buddies. Their attitudes about wine brought them together, and they often head out on wine-tasting excursions. (No, not on Didier's Harley-Davidson. I asked.)

Robert Parker said that Didier Dagueneau made the finest Sauvignon Blanc he's

DIDIER DAGUENEAU
EN CHAILLOUX

ever tasted. And I would say, what Jayer is to Pinot Noir, Didier is to Sauvignon Blanc. A master. You will ask yourself if you have ever tasted a better one. 1990? Perfection.

$19.95 PER BOTTLE　　$215.46 PER CASE

◇ ◇

OYSTER BLISS

LOOK AT ONE fresh on the half shell. The mouthwatering beauty of it. The colors. How it glistens. Slide your finger upon its surface. What an incredibly sexy texture. Some consider it an aphrodisiac. Others remark upon the rush of energy and well-being it provokes. The French attack a platter with gusto. Americans mostly say yucko. *But not here!* "Dare not serve me one, serve me a dozen" is the KLWM staff motto.

The best oysters this side of the continent will be shucked and presented *in our very own parking lot* by our friends at Monterey Fish Market, and, naturally, our best oyster wines will be available, too. Muscadet, Chablis, Graves *blanc*, things like that. Champagne, anyone?

Live it up! Improve thine outlook!

Wine and oysters for sale!

Saturday, December 7 · Noon to Four

Be there or be square!

◇ ◇

GEVREY-CHAMBERTIN'S
PHILIPPE ROSSIGNOL

IF PHILIPPE Rossignol had a *grand cru* . . .

That is a big if. *IF* Rossignol had a *grand cru*, a Charmes, Mazis, Clos de Bèze, if he owned one of those giants, his life would be quite different. Given his talent, his *grand cru* would be one of Burgundy's most-sought-after wines, and he would be driving a new Mercedes to three-star restaurants to entertain his American importer instead of complaining bitterly about the money it now takes to fill the tank of his Renault Cinq.

This is not one of those glitzy domaines you read about, owned by some insurance company. Rossignol struggles to get by, he, his wife, and three kids.

He is a winemaker, but he owns no vines, so he must rent them, and the price is steeper than the hillsides of Gevrey-Chambertin. What is left to live on is skimpy. I think his story is interesting, especially today when some people act as if a Burgundian is born greedy.

Rossignol is a winemaker owing to guts and determination. He inherited no vines, but he fell in love with the métier by way of his sister, who married winemaker Joseph Roty. He worked in Roty's cellar from 1976 to 1981.

At the same time, he was helping an old-timer from the village tend his vines. When the fellow retired in 1978, Rossignol rented his parcel of Gevrey-Chambertin and his well-placed Côte de Nuits-Villages. His first bottling, the 1979 vintage, made quite an impression here because of its power, structure, and perfume. It was easily the match for anyone's 1978s.

Rossignol would love to buy some *grand* or *premier cru*. Of course! But, he says, "You have to be rich. And even then any profit would be for the next generation."

In 1989 he added another vineyard to his list, but again he is not the owner. The local *notaire* introduced him to someone from Monaco who wanted to invest in the Côte d'Or. Rossignol selected the parcel because of its superb old vines. Two-thirds of his Fixin En Tabeillion (The Scrivener) go to the owner, only one-third to Rossignol.

When I asked Rossignol what he seeks in a wine, he answered, "First, I want my wine to give pleasure to whoever tastes it. And I think Burgundy is a wine that should age well. I like a wine that opens up slowly, that is not facile, not the *primeur* style. I like a structured wine that will develop elegance with time."

He makes a natural wine, true to its *terroir*, with no herbicides or pesticides. "I am against doctored wines, wines that have been transformed to achieve some notion of ideal balance by adding acidity or by over-chaptalization or by taking out tannin by filtering." He says he would rather drink a slightly unbalanced wine than a doctored wine.

For a decade now I have been importing and enjoying Rossignol's deep, dark red Burgundies. That first selection, his 1979 Gevrey-Chambertin, is stunning today. Another thing I admire, another reason I think you should try his wines, is his realistic pricing. You get much more than you pay for when you buy a Rossignol. His are Burgundy's best values, especially when you consider that his Bourgogne puts most Gevreys to shame, and his Gevrey puts most Chambertins to shame.

I want to support Rossignol and spread the word. Here in the shop this month, we will often have a bottle of his open for tasting, so you can judge for yourself.

WINES AVAILABLE

		PER BOTTLE
1989	*Bourgogne* Rouge	$11.95
1989	*Côte de Nuits-Villages*	13.75
1989	*Fixin "En Tabeillion"*	22.50
1989	*Gevrey-Chambertin*	22.50
1988	*Bourgogne* Rouge	12.50
1988	*Côte de Nuits-Villages*	14.95
1988	*Gevrey-Chambertin*	22.50

DECEMBER SPECIAL

12 bottles Rossignol receives 15% discount
24 bottles Rossignol receives 25% discount

✦ 1992 ✦

1990 *VIN DE PAYS*
DOMAINE DE LA GAUTIÈRE

Origin: Provence.

Color: Yes.

This is one of those freaky things that happen too rarely, like when the one you love turns out to love you, too, when everything comes together and it all seems too good to be true. This wine of humble appellation, nondescript label, and modest price achieves the impossible, because it does just about any trick you can ask a red wine to do.

It effortlessly satisfies the following:

· *A cheap, robust, everyday red.*

· *A Syrah perfume that turns your thoughts to the northern Rhône.*

· *A Cornas-like color.*

· *An irresistible drinkability like the best Beaujolais Nouveau you ever imagined but never found.*

· *A Châteauneuf-like spice.*

· *It seems complex, yet it is unpretentious.*

· *It is full-bodied and does not lack punch, yet it goes down so easily, one's glass always seems empty.*

· *Everyone will down it right away, yet it could age for years.*

In 1990 everything came together and the Domaine de la Gautière has surpassed itself. Don't ignore it because it is cheap.

$6.95 PER BOTTLE $75.06 PER CASE

CORNAS 1990

Clape and Verset, the twin peaks of Cornas, live almost across the street from each other. A one-minute walk. What memories I have of each cellar! The young black wines, the marvelous bouquets when older bottles are uncorked, the shocking deaths in rapid succession of sweet Madame Verset and Noël's hardworking 94-year-old father, then the recent return of Auguste Clape's son to work alongside him.

Clape garners more media attention because he is more lucid than Verset. However, with his ancient vines and his traditional vinification, Verset is to Cornas what Gentaz is to Côte Rôtie. Neither has a son to follow, so each bottle is a treasure that will serve us in years to come as witness to the way Syrah used to be.

Do not ask me which is better, Clape or Verset, because I cellar both of them. How could you reject one?

Do not ask me to choose between 1988, 1989, and 1990 because I cellar every vintage of each Syrah master. What an occasion it is to pull out a Clape 1979 or 1980, and just the other day I uncorked my first Verset 1982. Wow!

As large as the wine world has become, with liquor store shelves crammed with bottles from Chile and New Zealand and who knows where next, these thick, deep Syrahs from the terraced Cornas slopes remain extraordinary prizes and, even though the price has doubled since 1979, extraordinary bargains that you will enjoy for a large part of the rest of your life.

1990 Cornas · *Auguste Clape*

$258.00 PER CASE FIFTHS

1990 Cornas · *Noël Verset*

$228.00 PER CASE FIFTHS

◦ ◦ ◦ ◦ ◦ ◦ ◦ ◦

1988 DOMAINE TEMPIER "CABASSAOU"

The Mourvèdre's quality is appreciated after 50 years of tireless devotion and promotion by the inimitable Lucien Peyraud of Domaine Tempier. Today, certain California versions are hard-to-find collectors' items and priced accordingly; famous Châteauneuf-du-Papes like Beaucastel make news when they announce planting larger percentages of Mourvèdre.

But let us go back to the beginning of the grape variety's renaissance, when Lucien rescued it from oblivion. Lucien was the friend and associate of the Baron Le Roy, at that time the most important figure in French wine because of his creation of the *appellations contrôlées*, and also proprietor of the great Château Fortia at Châteauneuf-du-Pape. Lucien dared to predict to the baron that with his Mourvèdre at Domaine Tempier, the day would come when a bottle of his Bandol would sell for more than a bottle of Châteauneuf-du-Pape, the king of the southern reds. The baron had a good laugh. But who laughs last? Bravo, Lucien. Hats off to you, you wonderful man. Your dream has come true.

It was 1941. A steep vineyard beneath the medieval village of Le Castellet (where Pagnol's *La Femme du Boulanger* was filmed) was uprooted and replanted, not with Grenache, Cinsault, or Carignan, but with Mourvèdre! Those vines are now 50 years old. The 1988 crop was vinified separately and labeled with the old Provençal name for the vineyard, Cabassaou.

In France it sold out in a day after *Cuisine et Vins de France* called it the greatest Bandol ever made. And why not?

Pure Mourvèdre.

The perfect *terroir*.

Old vines.

Great vintage.

That Peyraud soul.

1990 DOMAINE DU VIEUX TÉLÉGRAPHE

DOMAINE DU VIEUX TÉLÉGRAPHE PRODUCES
THE FINEST CHÂTEAUNEUF-DU-PAPE OF OUR TIME

Other domaines do rise to an occasional occasion, but none comes close to Vieux Télégraphe's record in terms of consistency, typicity, and aging potential.

Consistency

To those who question my claim, let's see what your favorite did in a vintage like 1984 or 1977. Vieux Télégraphe not only made "a good wine for the vintage," as they say, it made beautiful, classic Châteauneuf-du-Papes that require no apology whatsoever and even outperform most competitors' efforts in the so-called great vintages.

At our staff tasting of several vintages of Vieux Télégraphe going back to 1971, I threw in bottles of other domaines in order to show my staff that they are selling the finest Châteauneuf-du-Pape money can buy. I wish you could enjoy the same experience. You would order two cases of 1990 instead of one.

At our tasting, we enjoyed the company of Jean-Louis Chave. He seemed bowled over by Vieux Télégraphe's consistent personality and consistent level of perfection from vintage to vintage. As he puts it, "It is in the difficult years that one learns whether or not a vintner really knows how to make wine."

And now, in *Wine and Spirits International*, there is a review of Châteauneuf domaines. The highest praise is reserved for Vieux Télégraphe: "Since the seventies this estate has consistently made one of the best Châteauneuf-du-Papes in every vintage." *In every vintage!*

Quality at Vieux Télégraphe is not intermittent or accidental. It is the result of untiring effort and perfectionism.

Typicity

If the word *typicity* does not exist, it should. Imagine, you want a baguette with dinner so you buy one, carry it home, and when you tear into it you find it full of cinnamon and dried apricots. Tasty or not, you are stuck with a baguette that lacks *typicity*. When I want a Châteauneuf-du-Pape, that means something; when I uncork it, I want it to taste like Châteauneuf-du-Pape, to express Châteauneuf-du-Papeness. Or Châteauneuf-du-Papicity?

It's the stones!

The wine world's grandest achievement (which will never be matched by the upcoming "United Nations of Oaky Cabernets and Chardonnays") remains France's system of *appellation contrôllée*, which was constructed to define and preserve the work of centuries of trial and error that resulted in the right grape varieties and vinification for each region's soil and climate. In my cellar you will not find any Pinot Noir from Bandol or Cabernet from Tuscany.

Châteauneuf-du-Pape boasts a very special *terroir*. You have now seen photos of those amazing stones, called *galets*, those rounded, colorful stones that you can smell and taste in a Vieux Télégraphe. There is also that blessed climate. The summer air is warm, fecund, and intoxicating, and there is the *mistral,* Provence's supernatural grape dryer, which prevents mildew and rot.

Traditional vinification also contributes to the typicity of Vieux Télégraphe. No Châteauneuf-du-Pape tastes as much like Châteauneuf-du-Pape as Vieux Télégraphe, and that is its reputation *in Châteauneuf-du-Pape itself!* You can make a good wine by departing from traditional vinification, by carbonic maceration, by heating this or cooling that, by buying Bordeaux barrels or whatever your little heart desires, but your Châteauneuf-du-Pape will lack typicity.

Aging Potential

I have tasted a few 1988, 1989, and 1990 Châteauneuf-du-Papes that really show their stuff already. They can mambo, polka, fox-trot, and jitterbug too. They can even shake their booty. But I assure you, they will be wilted and gone by the time your Vieux Télégraphe takes the floor.

I have seen the 1989 Vieux Télégraphe criticized because it seemed closed and ungenerous. *In 1991!* God forbid that Vieux Télégraphe should change their recipe in order to seduce the critics on release day. This reminds me of the winemaker who told me, "You Americans want to be told that a wine will age 50 years, but you want to be able to drink it tonight."

In our tasting, we learned that the wines from the big vintages (well, even their incredible 1977) really blossom only after 10 or 12 years. Then the wine turns into something else, something so much more refined, generous, and multidimensional, and so much more of a treasure. If you can wait at least a decade before attacking your 1988, 1989, or 1990 Vieux Télégraphes, you will receive much more than you bargained for. To me, of the vintages of the 1980s, only 1987, 1984, and 1982 have really arrived, fully opened up. As for the others, you still have to search with your nose the relatively reticent bouquets. But once you hit that ravishing 1979, the bouquets surge up out of the glass to meet you, the aromas are thick and complex, and instead of a good wine, you have a great one.

HOW ARE THEY DOING?

1986

While *class* is an unusual word to apply to a Châteauneuf-du-Pape, this vintage shows a lot of it. The aroma displays the famous Vieux Télégraphe gunflint. There is perfect balance from start to finish. The finesse is striking. The 1979 was like this a few years ago. While still youthful, this is a wine that I would enjoy drinking now or in 20 years!

1985

Brooding depth to nose. Totally backward and undeveloped. A sweet perfume that is seductive. Round, deep, long. Broad and richly textured with ripe fruit in the finish. Nowhere near ready.

1984

As was the case from the very beginning, when it was in *foudre*, this is aromatic and delicious. Each time I taste it I derive enormous pleasure from the fact that vintage chart maniacs never get to enjoy it. It is being swallowed and loved only by dyed-in-the-wool V. T. fans. To drink now. *Santé*.

1983

Still closed in. You sniff and search for the nose and once you find it, mmm, yes, spice and cinnamon and all sorts of promising perfumes. This one is reserving itself for future glory. Certain glory. It will be a great Vieux Télégraphe. Rich, youthful, with an enormous body, it feels like it is one day going to explode with flavor and perfume. To treasure and to hold.

You might be interested to know that alongside our bottling, I uncorked the filtered version that was sold to all of Vieux Télégraphe's other clients. Jean-Louis Chave found it excellent, but lacking the intensity that a 1983 should have. The filtered is certainly much more forward a wine than our unfiltered, with less of a future, however, and less weight. Less, less, less. Good, yes, but less of everything except maturity.

1982

The Bruniers tell me their filtered 1982 is over the hill. Our unfiltered is at its peak. It is a lighter vintage than usual, but impeccably balanced, and it has a lovely fading rose blossom perfume, and that stony, gunflint aspect is super-present here. To drink.

1981

Where did my 1981 go? In my cellar I could not find a single bottle, much less a case!

1980

Before lunch recently the Bruniers served this to me blind, after having spent the morning assembling their 1990. With great confidence I declared it to be the 1978. Oh, well. My palate must have been fatigued after the strenuous task of tasting and blending and retasting all morning. No, not really, I'm afraid to say. I made exactly the same goof three years ago when they also had Robert Parker to lunch. So much for my palate. And in front of Mr. Parker! But this is a big, complete, vigorous V. T., and it tasted perfect, so it had to be the 1978. See? If you own some 1980, you have an unexpected jewel, but I would leave it to age another four to five years.

1979

Right now, this is my favorite of the bunch. Why? Because it is so subtle and fine and it is just entering maturity. Would that I might mature so admirably. The longer you hold your nose in the glass, the more astonished you become. This is no flash in the pan, no one-night stand. This is the kind of wine you want to marry.

(What language! I swear I was spitting throughout the tasting.)

But this is extraordinary stuff. It is to drink, and I hope you have a good bunch of it in reserve because it is going to last and, who knows, maybe even get better. Open one soon!

1978

The other day I was reading the new wine magazine *Rarities*, in which John Tilson opined that Vieux Télégraphe has not equaled the quality of their 1978. That is not my opinion, *not at all*. This is a wine that is very much alive, still almost adolescent and unformed. It is very tannic still, with an aroma dominated by a controversial anise-like quality. It did not inspire the enthusiasm of the 1979 or 1980. It was ever-changing in the glass. I hope it is going through a difficult stage, because it has tasted better, and it is certainly not going old on us. To watch, hoping for a beneficial evolution. My daughter is going through a difficult stage, too, and I have not given up on her!

1977

A mature bouquet that comes right out at you. It seems austere on the palate, but only because it follows the voluptuous 1978. It does not otherwise suffer, really, after the 1978, which is surprising. You do not think "off vintage." Lots of *goût de terroir*, with an almost claret-like balance and structure. Drink without feeling hurried.

1972

Here we finally arrive at old-wine flavors. You see a wrinkle or two, a few flecks of gray hair, but it is still handsome, brimming with confidence and vitality. This is completely opened up, the glass is full of aroma, and this one comes up to greet you. Everyone at the tasting found different aromas. In other words, it is complex. I thought of tobacco box, spices, dried fruits. Above all, it impresses by virtue of its complexity, elegance, and generosity.

1971

Meaty, smoky nose. Turning tender on the palate. Still intense, full-bodied, but *tender*. Incredible length. Rich yet fine. So rich in flavor, yet you don't consider it fat or super-concentrated. Age works its magic; Vieux Télégraphe turns tender!

Conclusion

The V. T. style was amazingly consistent through the different vintages. There is real personality and lucidity here. There are so many flashes in the pan in today's wine world, but Vieux Télégraphe is solid, consistent, trustworthy, and it has the potential for evolving into something grandiose if you can keep your hot little corkscrew out of it for a decade or two.

Vineyard in the Languedoc

LANGUEDOC/ROUSSILLON

Don't follow leaders,
Watch yer parking meter.

BOB DYLAN, *Subterranean Homesick Blues*

I BLOW UP into a bloody rage, for all the good it does, when advertisers exploit the likes of Mozart or Beethoven in order to sell a product. (Thank God they have not yet discovered Haydn.) Or when something like John Lennon's music is used to sell tennis shoes. Dead artists cannot decline jobs. Nor can they cash royalty checks. What ghoulish exploitation.

Yet here I stand, quoting Bob Dylan. What a hypocrite! But no, no, this is different, I swear it. First, in the words of our immortal ex-president, "I am not a crook"; Bob Dylan is not dead, and anyway, this is wine of which we speak, the fruit of the vine, not tennis shoes.

Throughout many a century artists have expressed their love and devotion to wine. Even Nathaniel Hawthorne penned a thinly disguised anti-filtration allegory in his short story "The Birthmark." And there is Thomas Mann's internationally acclaimed opus about the health benefits of drinking Côte Rôtie, *The Magic Mountain*. Bob Dylan's love for wine is evidenced above all in his ode to the noble Riesling grape, *Visions of Johanna*. His oblique reference to the wines of the Languedoc should be interpreted as an attempt to discourage paying unnecessarily high prices ("watch your parking meter") for famous labels ("don't follow leaders").

IF YOU ARE LOOKING FOR VALUE,
LOOK WHERE NO ONE ELSE IS LOOKING

Last year I devoted four separate trips to exploring the Languedoc/Roussillon in southern France. This is the wine world's greatest Land of Opportunity, reminiscent of California in the early 1970s when everything was exploding and new wines were popping up with astonishing frequency. I tasted hundreds of wines and came up with some discoveries that are going to blow your mind and save you money, if you are in the mood.

Like California, the Languedoc has a warm climate that makes grape growing easy. They ripen! And fortunately the Creator was generous when it came to dispensing stony hillsides. There are fabulous *terroirs* there. Fabulous! Daumas Gassac ("the Château Latour of the Languedoc," according to Hugh Johnson) was the first to prove it, and others are waiting in line for similar success and recognition.

There were problems to overcome in the region, and they are rapidly being overcome:

1. *High-yielding, low-quality grape varieties were traditionally planted because buyers went there looking for quantity and high alcohol. The why of it is a long story.*

2. *The hot, dry climate and cellars of the Languedoc can and still do ruin most wines before their first birthday.*

3. *Crude vinification produced overly astringent wines lacking length and finesse.*

These problems are so easy to overcome, you have to wonder why they waited until the 1980s to begin doing it. A pioneer was necessary, someone like Aimé Guibert at Daumas Gassac, someone to prove that there would be a clientele for a high-quality Languedoc wine, to prove that such an endeavor would be profitable. I encountered several young winemakers who have ripped out the ordinary grape varieties and replanted with noble varieties, especially Syrah, Mourvèdre, Cabernet, Chardonnay, Marsanne, and Viognier. And that mouth-puckering, dried-out astringence can be avoided by:

1. *De-stemming the grapes*

2. *Air-conditioning and humidifying the cellars*

You cannot make fine wine in a hot, dry cellar, but now they can re-create cellars as perfect as a Burgundian cellar. The technology is available. I assure you, make a Chambertin in a typical Languedoc cellar and it would be cooked and dead before one summer is past.

The gems I found are BIG wines, big enough for anybody, but they have none of that painful, dry astringence. I wouldn't do that to you. I promise you full-bodied, balanced, elegant wines. After all, finesse, length, and balance, three of wine's most desirable qualities, are all impossible if astringence leaves your palate puckered.

THE SAMPLER SELECTIONS

To tempt you to try the unknown, I have organized 12 of our new discoveries into a sampler case, enabling you to taste a range of the most exciting bargains in the wine world at even lower than normal prices. Here then is the cream of the crop from four recent tours of the Languedoc/Roussillon.

DOMAINE CLAVEL

The domaine is 3 kilometers from the Mediterranean near Montpellier. Wine grapes have been grown here since at least 1123! That is a good sign. It shows that the soil has something special. In fact, it resembles the terrain at Châteauneuf-du-Pape, with those smooth, rounded stones. Proximity to the ocean (as at Bandol) provides perfect warmth and humidity for the Mourvèdre grape. The winemaker is against the use of herbicides and pesticides.

CHÂTEAU LA ROQUE

Here the vineyard dates from 1259. It is 18 kilometers north of Montpellier, in a rather dramatic landscape. The vines are on the side of an amphitheatre-shaped hill facing southeast. It is quite a place. I wish you could see it. And the owner is a fanatic for quality and justly proud of his wine's distinctive personality. He harvests manually, the temperature is controlled during the fermentation, and the red is aged in new barrels. It was, however, the 13th-century monks who provided the perfectly icy, perfectly beautiful vaulted stone cellar.

MAS CHAMPART

A young couple here, toughing out their first difficult years, trying to make a go of their petite domaine. We will aid them if they keep coming up with such winners.

CHÂTEAU SALITIS

Located near fantastic Carcassonne is the unknown appellation Cabardès. It is an unusual site with fascinating soils. They have the stones, similar to Châteauneuf-du-Pape. They have gravelly sections, similar to Bordeaux, and they have some chalky parcels. The grape varieties come from Bordeaux and the Rhône: Cabernet, Merlot, Syrah, and Grenache. Some of the vines are over 60 years old.

DOMAINE GAUBY

I await an extravagantly enthusiastic response from you on this domaine. Here are a couple of reds of mind-boggling intensity and deliciousness. The vineyard is near Perpignan in the Vallée de l'Agly. Everything here is on super-steep hillsides. It is a rugged, impressive landscape. The soil is varied: chalk, granite, and schist. The cellar is air-conditioned and humidified, and the wine is unfiltered. You are in for a treat! We will see more marvels in the future because all the ingredients for great wine are there, and the winemaker knows what to do with them.

ARNAUD DE VILLENEUVE

What a playground for someone like me. De Villeneuve has endless fascinating cuvées, and he allowed me to blend this with that and that with this; plus, he agreed to bottle unfiltered following my instructions, so blame me if you don't like the results. In other words, no one else in the world as we know it is drinking these wines except those who shop at KLWM.

TRAVEL TIPS

To those of you planning to vacation in France, why not consider the Languedoc/Roussillon, especially if you have a spirit of adventure? It is not easy to find decent accommodations. Most hotels are closed during the winter (except in the big cities), and during the summer, near the ocean, tourist madness takes over. So, best to visit in May/June or September/October.

Before leaving, read the appropriate sections of Waverly Root's *The Food of France*. Even if you don't go, why not read it just for fun?

I am now going to give you some haphazard advice that might help you should you follow the route from Montpellier toward Spain.

Try to avoid going into Montpellier *centre ville* by car. It is a nightmare of one-way streets and inappropriate signposts. I have been lost in the Montpellier maze more than once. No street seems to take you where you wish to go. No matter which sign I followed, I kept ending up at the same unwanted intersection again and again until I was well past the ranting and raving stage. Like that general during the Vietnam War, I wanted to nuke the whole town back into a Stone Age parking lot, or whatever it was our fearless general said.

Around Montpellier, I say leave the coastal autoroute and take the N109 to Gignac, then north a few gorgeous kilometers for a visit to the Mas du Daumas Gassac, still the Languedoc's finest wine as well as a wondrous sight to see and one of the wine world's most compelling stories. Nearby is a memorable, cozy restaurant, Le Mimosa, in Saint Guiraud (telephone 04.67.96.67.96). Good cooking, and the English sommelier (a retired cellist, I believe) has a wonderful palate and an astonishing collection of great bottles.

Then stay on the unlikely roads and explore small villages like Faugères, Saint-Chinian, Pézenas, etc. Explore. There are beautiful winding mountain roads to the north with parcels of scrub and vines here and there, lots of cypress and plane trees, and occasionally you round a curve and find a grand vista opening up all the way to the sea. It looks a lot like Provence used to look in the Pagnol days, before it became overpopulated and overconstructed.

Just an aside: In the village graveyards of both Provence and the Languedoc, cypress trees were planted to rise from the ground and reach into the blue sky. This lively growth in a cemetery is a comforting concept, given the reality of the human situation. Therefore, cypress trees can take on a sort of special significance.

Plane trees line the roads. They were planted by people who traveled by foot or by horse, people who figured out that it is better during the summer to travel in the shade. This remains true in the era of the automobile. And now, today, their plane trees are old and thick, beautiful creatures to behold.

The medieval city of Carcassonne is worth seeing. Then set off on the back roads through the Corbières to Perpignan. This is all unspoiled France, with spectacular scenery.

Perpignan has a nifty location. Spain is only a few kilometers away, and you feel its proximity. The Pyrénées are right there, and you are not far from the beautiful Mediterranean ports of Collioure, Port-Vendres, and Banyuls-sur-Mer. However, stay in Perpignan. Perpignan seems to be happening. There is excitement there. People are creative, lively, and enthusiastic.

By now you deserve some good food, a tasty wine, and a spacious room with a comfy bed.

I found two exciting hotel/restaurants in Perpignan, the Park Hotel and the Villa Duflot, which has luxurious rooms and a swimming pool. Both have superb Mediterranean cuisine with a Catalan accent. The wine lists abound with inexpensive local discoveries.

Or, if you prefer a quiet village in the foothills of the Pyrénées, drive the 25 or 30 kilometers to Céret. Les Feuillants is a hotel/restaurant with only three rooms! The cooking is creative but not cutesy or weird. The wine list is too full of great bottles, making it difficult to decide upon one. Ask the sommelier. She knows her stuff.* The local museum, by the way, has pieces by Picasso and Matisse.

And do not forget to go to the village of Calce in order to see the incredible *terroir* of the Domaine Gauby. It is like seeing Côte Rôtie for the first time, and you will see with your own eyes why the Domaine Gauby is going to provide us with great wines.

Sorry, but the chef and the sommelier both left and opened a place in the Médoc at Château Smith-Haut-Lafitte called La Caudalie.

STAFF SELECTIONS

I AM PROUD of my wine selections. I am on the road almost six months a year in Italy and France to ensure the highest possible quality and value, and, thank goodness, my wine selections have received national recognition. But what about my staff? They are top quality, too, and they are here to serve you. Make use of them, of their knowledge and helpfulness.

As people walk through my shop, I see them gliding by, gazing at the unknown labels, wondering what to buy, passing up the unusual, unknown wines. I find myself saying, "Oh no, they just passed up that beauty." But after all, how can they know what is inside the bottle simply by looking at it?

Ask my staff. They have traveled to Europe to visit the cellars. And whenever a container arrives, my staff assembles to taste and discuss every new wine, every new vintage.

You could have a lot of fun and make a lot of new discoveries by asking one of the staff to assemble a collection of wines for you.

Don't tell them what you like. Discover wines you did not know you liked.

I suggest you just tell us how much you would like to spend on a mixed case and let us do the work. Venture into the unknown. My people are professionals. You will receive a collection of bottles that will represent several French and Italian wine regions. One bottle might be from the Languedoc, the next from the Rhône, from the Loire, Tuscany, Friuli, Provence, etc. It is quite an expense to provide wines for my staff tastings. Why not profit from their firsthand knowledge and have a lot of fun with your case of surprises at the same time?

I take this opportunity to announce the appointment of Bruce Neyers as national sales director for Kermit Lynch Wine Merchant. He will work only with national accounts, so you will not see him in the shop, but Bruce is a great addition to the team. As you may know, he spent the last several years with Joseph Phelps Vineyards, as well as overseeing the small Napa Valley winery that bears his own name. Bruce spent several years in the imported wine trade and a year in Europe making wine before he joined Phelps. He has been a private client, buying my selections for his own cellar since I began 20 years ago. Yes, he can pull out the old Vieux Télégraphes, the aged Versets and Jobards and so on. He knows wine and he knows the wine business. I am thrilled to be working with him.

And Chantal Wirth is our foreign *légionnaire*. She is another staff member you won't see in Berkeley because she runs our European office in Beaune, France. Five years ago I hired her away from Faiveley, the wine house in Nuits-Saint-Georges. Chantal is French, but she also speaks flawless English and Italian. She maintains contact with all our growers and makes sure our wines are shipped properly. Chantal also possesses a remarkable palate (meaning she always agrees with me) and is ever on the lookout for new, exciting wines to add to our list so you will be tempted to return again and again.

⸰ ⸰ ⸰ ⸰ ⸰ ⸰ ⸰ ⸰

OLIVE OIL · LAURA MARVALDI

At Vinitaly, the Italian wine fair in Verona, I was speaking with Gianni Piccoli, producer of our Bianco di Custoza. All of a sudden he pointed across the hall and said, "See that lady with the basket? She makes the finest olive oil in Italy."

"Well, don't let her get away," I said.

He brought her over. She pulled a bottle from her basket and poured a taste of

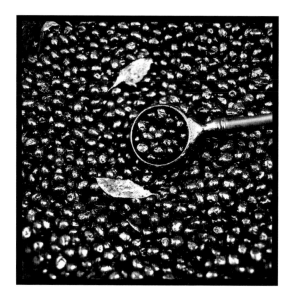

Black olives

her oil into a wineglass. What an aroma! Complex, spicy, generous. It smelled better than any of the hundreds of wines I tasted there. For salads, I don't even mix it with vinegar. A dash of lemon, maybe.

When she left, Piccoli said, "Pour it on grilled fish. I guarantee you, there is no better sauce."

$39.95 PER BOTTLE

1990 DOMAINE BOILLOT

HOW DOES THE refrain go? "You're gonna lose your good thing now." The blues song is about love, as usual, but I think I will apply the line to the Boillot brothers' great red Burgundies. They are shipping us unforgettable wines. They do everything right. But the U.S.A. is in danger of losing these red Burgundy treasures unless I succeed in getting out the word.

Tasting their wines in barrel was always one of the highlights of my trips to the Côte de Nuits. Not just good wines. Exciting wines. A wine-tasting high. Finally I convinced them to put their wine into bottle for me just as it was in barrel. Unfined, unfiltered. For the rest of the world, they are stripped of their magnificence. Still, my clientele has been slow to catch on, for three reasons:

1. *There are enough Boillots in Burgundy to confuse even themselves.*

2. *Their label is less than eye-catching.*

3. *They have small holdings in 16 different Burgundy appellations, Côtes de Beaune and Nuits, which further adds to the confusion.*

More examples of how they do everything right: Already this year, before mid-June, they had removed half the grapes from their vines in order to increase flavor and concentration. Imagine the quantity of liquid assets they sacrifice! And when they must re-plant in their 70-year-old Nuits Pruliers vineyards, it is one vine at a time, as necessary. Hardly anyone does that, because it is so costly and time-consuming, but it is the only way to maintain that stunning old-vine quality, so the Boillots do it.

Grandfather Boillot, 92 years old now, started the domaine by buying vineyards in Volnay and Pommard. His son, Lucien, moved to Gevrey-Chambertin, worked with Clair-Dau, and began purchasing vines in Gevrey-Chambertin, including the great *premier cru* Cherbaudes. The vineyard name is intriguing, by the way. It comes from the same source as charnel, or *carnale*, leading some to suppose that there was in antiquity a cemetery there. I think it relates more to the character of Cherbaudes's wine, which is strikingly gamy, fleshy, *charnu*. I've never tasted another Pinot Noir like it, and I adore it.

Another Gevrey *premier cru* was added, Les Corbeaux, which means "ravens." It is as pretty, sleek, and high-toned as Cherbaudes is deep and meaty.

In 1978, Lucien Jr. joined his father in the winery. He bought small plots of Fixin and Gevrey-Chambertin.

In 1982, two *premiers crus* were added, Volnay Les Angles and Pommard Croix Noires.

In 1983, brother Pierre joined in, and in 1984 he and Lucien heard from their sister that an old fellow in Nuits-Saint-George was retiring, had no sons, and might be convinced to sell his 70-year-old vines in Les Pruliers. The deal was done, and we can cellar what is one of the greatest Nuits-Saint-Georges produced today.

Then, in 1988, the brothers inherited four of the Côte de Beaune's finest *premiers crus*: Beaune Epenottes, Volnay Brouillards and Caillerets, and Pommard Fremiers.

I asked the brothers, what is the compliment they most like to hear? They agreed that it is when they are told they have preserved the unique personality of each piece of earth.

And for me, whether tasting out of barrel or bottle, one of the great pleasures is comparing Les Angles with Caillerets, for example, or Cherbaudes with Corbeaux. That is why I urge you to cellar their wines as I do, with bottles from more than one vineyard. I rarely serve one Boillot. Serving and comparing two magnifies and helps define the unique vineyard character expressed by each, a Burgundy lover's passion.

Do not miss these glorious 1990s from Boillot. I've been buying in Burgundy for 20 years. Boillot's 1990s are classics that will give you decades of pleasure and excitement.

SOUTHWEST SAMPLER

WHILE WINES from the southwest are quite the vogue in France, our wine writers have not showered us with information. My curiosity was aroused, so for the past three years I have devoted time to exploring the region, and now you can sample the best it has to offer.

The average wines are not worth your attention, but the best are dazzling. *Gault Millau*, for example, compared Domaine Cauhapé's Vendanges Tardives Jurançon to Château d'Yquem and named it one of the 10 best bottles of the decade. A Jurançon! Have you ever even had the opportunity to taste one?

You are in for some big surprises, and even with our Bush-league dollar, exploring the southwest won't cost you much. Be adventurous. You'll be glad.

CAHORS

Is the best known of the wines of the southwest. I buy two of them because I like them both.

1989 Clos La Coutale

Coutale is aged in *foudre*, the big oak casks that are also used, for example, at Vieux Télégraphe and Tempier. There is a beneficial evolution in wood, but no oak taste. The ripe 1989 fruit is, therefore, unobscured. Round, mouth-filling, and complete, it is only 12.2° alcohol. Serve it like you would a good Bordeaux, keeping in mind that you cannot find a Bordeaux this good at the price.

$9.25 PER BOTTLE $99.90 PER CASE

1990 Château Pineraie

At Pineraie, the wine from his old vines is aged in new Bordeaux barrels. It is 85% Côte Noir and 15% Merlot. In 1990 he allowed me to blend his two best cuvées, and he bottled it unfiltered. Unavailable in France, this luxury cuvée has a deep color, lots of ripe, juicy fruit (cassis and blackberry), great depth and structure. Impressive!

$9.95 PER BOTTLE $107.46 PER CASE

TURSAN

Is a tiny appellation of almost all white wine. There is the *cave cooperative* and then there is the fabulous wine domaine of three-star chef Michel Guérard. What a wine! And the grape varieties are:

50% Baroque
25% Gros and Petit Manseng
17% Sauvignon Blanc
8% Sémillon

There is no other wine like this. It is loaded with personality. Guérard is quite a chef and quite a taster. I found his notes more interesting than mine, so here they are:

1990 Château de Bachen

Pale golden color tinged with green. All freshness and vivacity. Good intensity, slightly lemony, mineral, and floral with a faint touch of honey. Supple, with a good balance between the taste of sun-ripened fruit, citrus fruits, and a refreshing acidity. Here is the harmony the Baroque grape can give if grown on its favorite *terroir*.

$16.95 PER BOTTLE $91.53 PER SIX-PACK CASE

JURANÇON

Is a white wine appellation south of Pau. The steep hills are covered with green vines and luxurious forest foliage. A rare wine even to the French, most of it is consumed in the region of production. Dry or sweet, the local grape varieties—Gros and Petit Manseng—give an utterly fascinating, exotic perfume found nowhere else.

1991 Jurançon Sec · Clos Guirouilh

The nose is striking with fresh flowers, honey, and a touch of vanilla from partial vinification in new oak. There is a wonderful balance of richness and acidity in this perfectly dry white.

$11.50 PER BOTTLE $124.20 PER CASE

1990 Jurançon Sec · Domaine Cauhapé

This is the greatest example I have tasted. It is 100% old vines, 100% Petit Manseng, vinified in 100% new oak. The wine is of such intensity, the new oak is harmonious. Deep, exotic nose. Round, supple, rich, and incredibly long on the palate. An experimental cuvée, here you will see dry Jurançon at its best, and it is a match for the greatest white wines anywhere. This you must taste to believe.

$19.95 PER BOTTLE $215.46 PER CASE

1990 Jurançon Vendanges Tardives
Domaine Cauhapé

In 1985 Cauhapé's winemaker, Henri Ramonteu, was chosen "Winemaker of the Year" by *Gault Millau*, largely because of his awesome late-harvest wines. His efforts are compared to Yquem and Zind-Humbrecht. His 1990 lives up to the vintage hype. It is extremely rich, sweet, and lively. Honeyed with a touch of green leaf and new oak, the class and finesse are remarkable. I would taste the onebottle from the sampler, for the experience, and cellar a few more because age is only going to make it more of a treasure.

$24.95 PER BOTTLE $269.46 PER CASE

MADIRAN

Used to be shipped to Bordeaux to add color and muscle, much like the Châteauneuf-to-Burgundy story. Today there are around 20 estate-bottled wines available. I've tasted almost all of them and rejected them. Why? Madiran's most famous, most expensive domaine I judged to be more a monument to oak than to Madiran. The others, because of the way they vinify the tough Tannat grape, I found to be painfully tannic and astringent. After three visits to the area, when I had all but given up the idea of presenting you with a wine from Madiran, I made one last visit, to Château Laffitte-Teston. Here is our best red wine discovery of the year. The pity is, the availability is limited. Laffitte-Teston is going to be a hit.

1990 Madiran · Château Laffitte-Teston

Power and elegance! Usually you have to pay a bundle to find them combined in one bottle. The nose is complex with black currant, raspberry, black pepper, and a perfect touch of new oak. Touch? Jean-Marc Laffitte, a giant of a man, has it. His Madiran, supple and velvety, has none of the astringence that mars his neighbors' efforts.

$9.50 PER BOTTLE $102.60 PER CASE

1990 Madiran "Vieilles Vignes"
Château Laffitte-Teston

A cuvée of 100% Tannat. Seventy-year-old vines! Deep color, almost black. Incredibly luscious aroma, loaded with blackberry and vanilla. Concentrated, meaty, generous, long on the palate. A rare opportunity to taste a wine of pure Tannat. You are in for a treat.

$13.50 PER BOTTLE $145.80 PER CASE

CÔTES DU FRONTONNAIS

Heading east from Madiran toward Toulouse and the Languedoc, I stopped to visit the Ribes family at Château Le Roc, whose efforts with the little-known Négrette grape have been highly touted by the *Revue du Vin de France*. The grape was thought to produce pale, light, inconsequential wines. There is nothing light about their 1990! They gave it a long skin maceration and blended in some Cabernet and Syrah.

1990 Château Le Roc Rouge

Good, deep nose, reminiscent of a "little" Trévallon. Expansive, pretty fruit in the bouquet and on the palate. It is as if Trévallon tried to make a "pretty" style, a wine with interest, but for immediate, easy pleasure.

$6.95 PER BOTTLE $75.06 PER CASE

NORMALLY $122.50

SPECIAL SAMPLER PRICE $88.00

❖ 1993 ❖

Olive tree

OLIVE OIL

Mᴛ ᴊᴏʙ ɪs ɴᴏᴛ all bad. Sometimes it takes me to the magical countryside near Arles, Les Baux, and Saint-Rémy, where this Provençal olive oil is produced. I like the landscape even more than the plentiful Roman ruins. Van Gogh liked this place, too. I remember seeing a painting of his, an olive orchard under a large moonlit sky with a figure of a man (obviously him, his reddish hair?) chasing through the grove after a woman. He captures the stark, rustic majesty and romantic spirit of the place. I do not know if he captured the woman.

If you go, I found a beauty of a hotel in Arles called the Nord Pinus, located on the Place du Forum. And you must go to the nearby Restaurant Vaccarès for its Provençal cuisine and unbelievable wine list full of several vintages of Tempier, Trévallon, Chave, Clape, and even a 1976 Chinon from Joguet, all well priced. Be sure and reserve a table on the terrace because the street scene below is a treat.

Visit Fontvieille on the way to Saint-Rémy, and lunch at the Bistro du Paradou in Le Paradou, a favorite of both Patricia Wells and Lulu Peyraud.

Avoid the three-star Beaumanière in Les Baux. Oof! Ouch!

The local olive oil we offer has been praised by Provençal poets such as Mistral and Giono, so it must be good. It is produced in Maussane in its still-functioning, ancient (early 16th-century) olive mill. Here the prized olives are crushed by giant granite grindstones, museum pieces anywhere else, then cold-pressed and bottled unfiltered.

This is the most exciting olive oil I have encountered in France, and I urge you to compare it to what you have been using.

$26.00 PER LITER

∘ ∘ ∘ ∘ ∘ ∘ ∘ ∘

1991 COTEAUX DU LANGUEDOC *ROUGE*
CHÂTEAU DE LASCAUX

This domaine is in Vacquières, a village that could serve as location for a medieval movie set.

Last year I visited, but the winemaker and I could not agree on price. We were both a little too stubborn. This year we both gave in a bit, and I am happy to introduce this unusual, complex red to you at last. There is a consistent *goût de terroir* here from vintage to vintage that is quite appealing. It shows the aromatic herbs of the *garrigue*, Syrah fruit, and a floral or wildflower aspect, all rendered with a touch, or a finesse, rare in the south. I mean, it is terribly drinkable, not heavy, not tough. That lovely perfume persists quite generously on the palate, too. Eighty percent Syrah.

$7.95 PER BOTTLE $85.86 PER CASE

1990 CORBIÈRES *ROUGE* "RÉSERVE LA DEMOISELLE"
DOMAINE DE FONTSAINTE

I wish you could have tasted the 1982 Demoiselle I pulled from my cellar recently. Ten years old, at its peak, incredibly delicious, with a complexity of aromas the youthful vintages don't hint at, including a ravishing cinnamon note that had all of us smiling and shaking our heads in disbelief.

Cellar an inexpensive wine? I know, not many collectors do. Too bad. If you like, though, we will charge you more for it so you won't feel weird. Anything to please the customer.

The 1990 should outperform that 1982! It shows the typical Demoiselle aromas with a suspicion of oak. Everything is discreet, restrained, fine. It is rich but not heavy, tannic but not astringent.

Fonsainte's old-vines La Demoiselle is the thoroughbred of the Corbières.

$8.95 PER BOTTLE $96.66 PER CASE

Vineyard in the Languedoc

TRAVEL TIPS WITH RECIPE

WARNING. You may have to be a little weird to enjoy a tour of the Languedoc. It does not fit the average American's idea of touristic France. There are no three-star restaurants. The hotels are usually the kind I had to stay in on my first trip to France when I was a hippie with a guitar. There is no nightlife unless you create your own. Villages often have one or no restaurants, so I found myself eating the *plat du jour* in village bars with the laborers, drinking plonk from a carafe.

However, if you have a nostalgia for the old France, France before the TGV, the Concorde, the autoroutes, the ticky-tacky modern architecture, then the Languedoc can be appealing. There remains something primitive about it.

I had hoped to collect a lot more hotel and restaurant tips, but even after five visits in 1992, I came up fairly empty-handed. Maybe I should be asking you for recommendations.

Near Montpellier, in Sommières, I can recommend the Auberge du Pont Romain. The rooms are spacious. There is a park, a pool, and a view upon a 2,000-year-old Roman bridge. The food is unremarkable.

Heading west from there, in the foothills where the finest wines are produced and the landscape the loveliest, it is a wasteland in terms of lodging.

There is a restaurant that for me is like an oasis on these trips, Le Mimosa (04.67.96.67.96), in Saint Guiraud near Aniane and Daumas Gassac. The cuisine and wine list are remarkable.

One of my favorite stops is in Roquebrun, north of Béziers, although neither the hotel rooms nor the cuisine explains it. I love the scenery and the old village, built upon the cliffs overlooking the river Orb. The barely adequate hotel is called Le Petit Nice.

For memorable accommodations and cooking, I urge you to continue on to Perpignan, where the Park Hotel has comfortable rooms and great regional food and wine.

Also in Perpignan I found an unpretentious restaurant in the old section called Casa Senza. It has everything: ambiance, authentic Catalan cuisine, and local wine selections. The chef presented one dish right up my alley, so simple you wonder how it can be so delicious. The recipe reads like a stuck record. All you do is take a gratin dish, sprinkle in some olive oil, put in a layer of big, flat pieces of red pepper, olive oil, salt, and pepper, then eggplant slices on top of that with olive oil, salt, and pepper, then sliced onions, olive oil, salt, and pepper, topped with tomato halves, olive oil, salt, and pepper. Put it in a hot oven for about an hour. Wow! Serve it with meats, or as a main course with rice, and, of course, a Languedoc red.

Have fun. And don't forget to drop in on any of our winemakers. They will be excited to receive you and show off their stuff.

FREE SPEECH VICTORY

W E WON, we won!
No, not the lottery. We won the right to quote Thomas Jefferson on our import strips, and I feel good.

Good wine is a necessity of life for me.   THOMAS JEFFERSON

At first the Bureau of Alcohol, Firearms, and Tobacco, which must approve all wine labels, would not permit the quote. Censored, because, they explained:

1. *"Good wine" might be understood to mean that Jefferson is endorsing the product. I differed, reminding them that Jefferson has been dead for about 200 years, so only a lamebrain would think he had tasted a wine currently for sale. Besides, when he said "good wine," he was only making the point that bad wine was* not *a necessity of life for him. Amen.*

2. *"Necessity of life" is a health claim, therefore not permissible. Although Jefferson often claimed that wine is good for one's health, you really have to mangle and distort the English language in order to make "necessity of life" a health claim.*

Finally, I wondered in my appeal to the BATF if it isn't dangerous for a government agency to get into the business of censoring the words of our third president, one whose writing formulated a lot of the values we Americans cherish dearly, like the various freedoms we must constantly struggle to preserve.

We won our appeal, and soon our wines will begin appearing with Jefferson's lovely quote.

Raise your glass to free speech for wine.

◊   ◊   ◊   ◊   ◊   ◊   ◊   ◊

1991 BOURGOGNE *ROUGE* "LA DIGOINE"
A. & P. DE VILLAINE

In Pommard this fall, I took a wine writer to Domaine Coste-Caumartin. Tasting the 1991s, he said, "This can't be a 1991." I asked why not. "The 1991s aren't supposed to be good," he said.

Since then Clive Coates has given the 1991 Burgundies a ringing endorsement ("The vintage is not to be missed"), but there still seems to be consumer confusion about them, maybe because 1991 was poor at Bordeaux. If you feel confused or doubtful about my recommending 1991s, for heaven's sake spend $15 and *taste for yourself*. If you can resist or criticize Aubert de Villaine's 1991 red Burgundy La Digoine, I will wear a tie to work. It is nothing short of beautiful. Moreover, it is stunningly delicious. What an aroma! It has everything you could possibly desire from a Pinot Noir except the majesty of one of Aubert's other vineyards (Romanée-Conti, for example).

A lot of people are spending a lot more money on fancier labels and drinking wines much less satisfying. Taste this beauty and judge for yourself.

$14.95 PER FIFTH $161.46 PER CASE

BARGAIN OF THE YEAR?
1990 VACQUEYRAS
LE SANG DES CAILLOUX

ATTENTION: Lovers of old-fashioned Rhônes such as Faraud's Gigondas, I have a surprise for you. Here is a great 1990 from a superb domaine called Sang des Cailloux (Blood of the Stones) and it is only $9.95.

Wait until you see the color. This wine lives up to its name. It is the darkest, prettiest blood you will ever see.

And the aroma! Loaded with spice and black pepper, the magical scent of the Provençal *garrigue*, and all so expansive you can breathe it in.

And the palate? Provence so thick you can chew it before swallowing. And it has an intriguing stony finish that calls to mind a great Vieux Télégraphe, the impression that the wine was filtered over stones. Don't worry. It was not filtered. So where does that stony, gunflint finish come from? Easy to explain. The rain water *is* filtered by Sang des Cailloux's stony soil, then sucked up by the 30-year-old vine roots, eked out into the grapes, which are then vinified and put into bottles. Of course it tastes like stones!

After striking out for years in search of a worthy Vacqueyras, Patricia Wells (who has a property nearby) advised me to visit Sang des Cailloux. I bought their excellent 1989, then along came 1990, which is the finest Vacqueyras I have ever tasted. I'll go further. I think it is one of the most impressive southern Rhônes I have ever tasted, and it reeks of my beloved Provence.

The 17-hectare domaine is run by Monsieur Ferigoule (pronounced *fairy ghoul*). He has 20% Syrah, 5% Cinsault, 10% Mourvèdre, and 65% Grenache.

It will age beautifully. At the price, I cannot think of anything from the Rhône more impressive or more delicious.

$9.95 PER BOTTLE $107.46 PER CASE

REVOLUTION IN THE BEAUJOLAIS

BY ITS VERY nature, this four-bottle sampler is limited to, well, what shall I call people like me? Wine nuts, wine connoisseurs (ugh), wine lovers, oenophiles (ugh), winos? (WINO = We Ingest No Other, or Wine Imbibing Never Over?) All I mean is, this is for those who take wine seriously (ugh).

There are stirrings of momentous changes in the Beaujolais. There are four winemakers who don't like herbicides or pesticides in their vineyards, who don't like to chaptalize or de-gas or filter their wines. And they *hate* SO$_2$!

In *Adventures on the Wine Route* I lamented the extinction of real Beaujolais (vinocide?), and I introduced readers to Jules Chauvet, who stood alone in refusing to accept the new formula grape-based concoctions. By the time my book appeared, 90-year-old Chauvet was gone. But years later, in one of life's miracle coincidences, an employee, Phil Sareil, tasted a bottle of Morgon at his French uncle's home. He liked it and sent me a bottle. It was made by Marcel Lapierre, who just happened to be resurrecting the philosophy of Jules Chauvet! Praise the lord and pass the Morgon.

Lapierre and his assistant Jacques Neoport wrote to me:

The desire to vinify wine without SO_2 started here in 1978. We noticed that we were getting more pleasure from wines that contained no chemical additives. Plus, there was the health question. Without SO_2 we suffered no morning-after head-aches, and we discovered later that the vitamins of Group B, present in all red wines, are preserved if no SO_2 is used.

In 1979 we made two cuvées without adding anything. One hundred percent pure wine. The results were so different that we kept those bottles for our own drinking pleasure.

We knew that Jules Chauvet had for years made wine without sulfur. Chauvet had the reputation of being the best taster in France, and we knew that he had worked with a Nobel Prize group in biology in Berlin. Intimidated, we did not dare make contact with such a personage. However, after reading some scientific articles on wine-making written by Chauvet and Monsieur Brechet of the Pasteur Institute, we made up our minds to visit Chauvet and ask him if we could do a stage during the harvest. That is why, since 1981, we fer-ment and raise and put our best cuvées into bottle without SO_2.

Lapierre followed Chauvet's example, and now he has followers, three of them, all at Morgon. There will be more.

Sulfur dioxide is used by almost everyone because supposedly it protects wine, a preservative of sorts. Yet, strangely enough, Lapierre's older wines with-out SO_2 have aged better than those *with* SO_2.

I thought you would like the opportunity to taste all four of these unique wines. They come from four quite different parts of the Morgon appellation. Because they are natural wines, each has a personality apart because each *terroir* is allowed to express itself through the wines.

Lapierre's is the lightest in color and body. It is slightly cloudy and has the most explosive Gamay nose. It also shows the most finesse.

Jean Foillard's is from one of Morgon's best sites, the Côte de Py. Also very Gamay, the color and aroma are much deeper and thicker. It is also a rounder, richer, more intense, more "serious" wine.

Guy Breton's bottle wears a very individual label. His Morgon vineyard is called Saint-Joseph. The most reticent of the four, "Breton's always takes more time to open up," Lapierre once said, and indeed, his 1990 and 1989 are currently more expressive than the 1991.

Thévenet has 80-year-old vines. Alcohol 13.2° without chaptalization! Deep robe. Spicy, floral bouquet leaps out with a hint of tobacco box. Sappy, complex, long, chewy.

All four age their wines in barrel, which is rare today in the Beaujolais where stainless steel reigns. They insisted I tell you, however, that they do not use new barrels, because the woody smell would mask the perfume of their wines. Each also insisted and re-insisted that I tell you that their methods were inspired by Jules Chauvet. And to keep their wines cool.

Quantities are limited, so I am offering them in a four-bottle sampler containing one bottle of each 1991 Morgon. The sampler is $54.00.

◊　◊　◊　◊　◊　◊　◊

1992 DOMAINE DE LA GAUTIÈRE *ROUGE*

Those of you who have read the chapter on Domaine de la Gautière in my book might be interested in this update: The happy couple, the once-happy Tardieu couple, split up last year. Paul remains at the domaine, working the vines with his son. Apparently the breakup was not entirely amicable, like the day Paul removed all the doors and windows from the house. That is a scene worthy of Marcel Pagnol, the great French writer and film director.

Anyway, I found Paul in top form when I went to make this blend in June. He told me he is dating an old girlfriend from his youth, 40 years later. Those of you mooning over some ex can take heart. Love is like baseball, and as Yogi said, "It ain't over til it's over."

This 1992 from the slopes of Haute Provence is quite special. It is a wine notable for its perfume and its thirst-quenching quaffability. The Grenache dominates the bouquet, giving its peach and apricot tones. The Syrah gives a hint of black pepper and Provençal herbs. The bouquet is open, pretty, springtime-like. I don't mean to suggest that it is complex in the sense of a *grand cru*. No, there is a simplicity, and that simplicity is a virtue, because you will want to serve this one cool and drink it, not study it. The palate seems drenched in perfume and suggests spice and cherry-like fruit. Don't look for power; this is all perfume and pleasure.

$6.95　PER BOTTLE　　　$75.06　PER CASE

LOIRE

1992 CHEVERNY · DOMAINE DU SALVARD

Introducing Domaine du Salvard and their first vintage imported to the United States, even though the domaine has existed since 1930. Old maps show a Château du Salvard on the site, but not a trace of it has been unearthed so far. That's alright, because there are plenty of other châteaux around. This is the heart of the Loire's château country, where the aristocracy came to play, and in fact there is a Château de Cheverny nearby, from which the wine takes its name.

Salvard makes the most drinkable, quaffable Sauvignon Blanc I have ever tasted. It does not have the weight of a Sancerre or a Pouilly-Fumé, but don't hold that against it, because it does have a fresh, inviting perfume and a balance and lightness of touch on the palate that allows it to flow. When I tasted it here with the staff, they not only liked it, they enthusiastically liked it. This wine begs to be drunk (if one is still allowed to use that word).

The 15 hectares of Cheverny vines are planted in soil of chalk, silex, and gravel, perfect for Sauvignon Blanc grapes. The wine is never heavy, but rather flowery and delicate, and slurping, smacking noises are part of the experience. Serve it nice and cold.

$7.95 PER BOTTLE $86.86 PER CASE

1992 SANCERRE · DOMAINE RAIMBAULT

During Paris stopovers I used to frequent Au Sauvignon, a hole-in-the-wall wine bar near the Sèvres-Babylone metro station, whose specialty is the cheese, the wine, and the charcuterie of the Sancerre region. I always loved their Sancerre, so honest and true, yet it was presented without a label, so I did not know who provided it. Perhaps they had a variety of producers. One day I simply asked. They buy from Raimbault, the waiter told me with a nasty sneer. So I went to see Raimbault (we call him Rambo) and imported his 1990. Then he had nothing in 1991. The big freeze, remember? Now I have his 1992. It has a fresh typical nose, not at all aggressive. There is a lovely floral note growing amidst the blades of grass. It has a good (not sharp) acidity that gives it length and vigor, and it is actually fairly rich for the vintage. Above all, let's face it, it tastes good and it is fun to drink.

Alas, Au Sauvignon was sold recently, I fear, because the quality of their *saucisson* sandwiches has deteriorated. The service remains as bad as always, however, and it is still a great place to people watch.

$12.50 PER BOTTLE $135.00 PER CASE

MATURE CHAMPAGNE

1985 COMTESSE MARIE DE FRANCE
CHAMPAGNE PAUL BARA

Uncorking this is an event. We are now in 1993, so the 1985 has been in bottle several years. That's a lot of ticks on the old clock. It exhales smoke when you pop the cork. The aroma has been gestating a long time. Almost long enough. Or could it get even better with more time? Watch out, though, because some claim that time waits for no one. Not for you, for example, or for me. Which might lead us to uncork one tonight.

This is Bara's finest cuvée, 100% *grand cru* from Bouzy. It has character, personality, grandeur. And to put it bluntly, the gigantic Champagne houses cannot compete. Incredibly complex, satisfying on the highest level. Try one before it is gone.

$49.95 PER BOTTLE $539.46 PER CASE

1985 CUVÉE ANGELINE · CHAMPAGNE LASSALLE

Robert Parker wrote in *The Wine Advocate*, "The ripe, buttery, apple smell, exquisite tiny bubbles, long aftertaste, and rich mid-palate and finish make this one of the most stunning Champagnes I have tasted in the last several years." *The Wine Advocate* lists the price at $65. In other words, here at KLWM you save $25. That is, $25 per bottle. A case holds 12 of them. 12 times 25 equals 300. Dollars. $300. Plus, we give a 10% discount for case purchases. That is why many people have grown rich shopping here.

Back to facts: This is such a gorgeously flavored Champagne, I find myself licking my lips long after I have swallowed in order to get every last drop.

$39.95 PER BOTTLE $431.46 PER CASE

SAINT JEAN-DE-BUÈGES

WE OWE THANKS to Jim Rule of Princeton's Institute for Advanced Study for these astonishing bargains. In a Languedoc sampler offer, I complained about the region's lack of decent restaurants and invited readers to send me recommendations. Jim Rule responded and also wrote, "In searching out excellent and inexpensive local production, you might want to talk to the people at the *cave cooperative* at Saint Jean-de-Buèges. They make a delicious rosé that I find indistinguishable from the best *Rosé de Provence*. They also do a lovely Syrah, the sort of thing that many of us would be delighted to drink for breakfast, lunch, and dinner were it available at comparably low cost here."

I have over the years visited a few *caves cooperatives*, and thereby tasted some of the most nightmarish wines of my career. But dutifully I went off to Saint Jean-de-Buèges, anyway, because you never know, right? And I found . . . a veritable paradise, lost and unspoiled. Nowhere to be seen are the ticky-tacky new villas that litter Provence. I loved the village, the landscape, the wines. I loved diving into the river Herault nearby; it was just me and the trout. I loved the landscape, including a cliff that, were it larger, would be worthy of Yosemite. No tourists, no ugliness. There are traces of the ancients here, including the Romans, of course, and there are incredibly steep, terraced slopes, proving that those ancients cultivated the vine and were willing to labor rigorously in order to obtain quality juice.

Here's to you, Jim Rule. Cheers.

I even liked the *cave cooperative*! Most of them are run by people who could not get jobs as communist bureaucrats. Here they were sweet and straightforward, all three of them working part-time.

At Saint Jean-de-Buèges there is not a single private domaine. Thankfully, the cooperative wines are wonderful. And if a *cave co-op* can do it this well, imagine what a Chave or Peyraud could do. I suspect an extraordinary *terroir* here.

1992 COTEAUX DU LANGUEDOC ROSÉ

Amazing! *There is nothing* WRONG *with it*. You know what I mean? This is flawlessly vinified, tender, pretty, and fun. Syrah and Cinsault. Nothing aggressive, nothing to bug you, just pure, simple pleasure.

$3.99 PER BOTTLE $43.09 PER CASE

1992 VIN DE PAYS *ROUGE* "CUVÉE LES CAPITELLES"

Merlot is combined here with traditional Rhône varieties. It is complete, balanced, and agreeable. The generous aroma contains hints of Rhône and Bordeaux. Fine robe; medium body with good tannin; long enough.

$3.99 PER BOTTLE $43.09 PER CASE

1992 COTEAUX DU LANGUEDOC *ROUGE*

Syrah 75%, Grenache 25%, from steep, stony hillsides. This is the wine that also proves that there is a great *terroir* here, especially for Syrah. It has been planted at least since the 10th century, which proves something.

Deep color. Lovely, intense nose of flowers from the *garrigue*, violets, spice, and a deep chocolate-like note. Loads of perfume on the palate, too. Richness and finesse. Lots of character. Unbelievable price.

$4.95 PER BOTTLE $53.46 PER CASE

◦ ◦ ◦ ◦ ◦ ◦ ◦ ◦

1992 DOMAINE DE BASSAC *ROUGE*

During a recent trip to the Languedoc, I visited the Domaine de Bassac, and three cuvées of 1992 stood out. I brought a sample of each back to Domaine Tempier, where François and Jean-Marie Peyraud helped put together a blend of Bassac's Syrah, Cabernet, and Merlot. The two latter varietals would have made a lovely Bordeaux-like blend, but the star of the show was Bassac's Syrah, with its vivid color and gorgeous nose of violets and black pepper. In fact, at first Jean-Marie argued for leaving the Syrah pure, and I was tempted, not only because it was good, but because "Syrah" on the label would not hurt sales in the varietal-conscious U.S.A. But a small dose of Cabernet added such complexity and the Merlot acted like a cello in a string trio, adding depth and richness, that finally, after an hour of trying this blend and that, we unanimously decided upon 66% Syrah with equal parts of the Merlot and Cabernet to finish it up.

Such quality at the price should attract a lot of attention. It gives enormous pleasure.

It was bottled unfiltered, so expect a healthy deposit sooner or later.

$4.95 PER BOTTLE $53.46 PER CASE

⊹ 1994 ⊹

SAVOIE SAMPLER

A T FIRST I thought it humorous when a winemaker in the Savoie asked me if the winter Olympics in nearby Albertville had generated a demand for Savoie wines in the United States. But then I heard the same question again and again. These folks feel overlooked, and they really harbored high hopes that the Olympics would bring them some attention.

The Savoie is located east of Lyon and south of Geneva. These foothills of the Alps are too tall to be called foothills, and I saw some of the steepest vineyards imaginable. The wines are sold at nearby ski stations and hardly anywhere else.

With no demand, and when even such an expert as Clive Coates thinks that Savoie reds are "light, thin, and of little consequence," why waste my time there? Why? Well, I like exploring. And there is a swell restaurant in Annecy called L'Éridan. The landscape is ultra-scenic, and there is a diversity of recreational possibilities. Plus, there is a gorgeous lake or two, and I like water sports. *And because Clive is wrong!*

Wait until you taste the three reds in this sampler, produced from a fabulous grape variety called the Mondeuse. If this is not Syrah's twin, it is its blood brother. However, like Syrah, Mondeuse needs steep, stony hillsides. On flatland soil it gives the insipid wines Clive Coates was talking about. On the south-facing slopes there is a microclimate where even sun-loving fig and almond trees flourish, and the Mondeuse produces reds that will astonish.

And there is a white variety, the Chignin-Bergeron, which turns out to be the Rhône's Roussanne. Same grape. It so happens that Bergeron is the name of an apricot variety grown around Tain-l'Hermitage. The winegrowers attached the name of the apricot to the name of their village, Chignin, long ago, probably because the Roussanne there smells and tastes apricot-like. Still, with such a wonderful grape, excellent examples are rare. I found only one. The problem is their vinification. Either the malolactic fermentation is blocked in order to preserve freshness and acidity, which means sterile filtration and lots of SO_2, or the wine completes its malolactic and comes out a bit flat and tired. Once this dilemma is resolved, we will see more grand whites from the Savoie. They already have the soil and the grape variety.

Of the hundreds of wines I tasted there, I bought only six to show you, but they were worth the effort and worth your attention. Be the first on your block! Discover the best the Savoie has to offer.

1992 APREMONT · PIERRE BONIFACE

A simple dry white for the thirst, this one is fun and easy going down. It is light, fresh, and gently perfumed, with a hint of natural sparkle to it. It is a white in the spirit of our Beaujolais Nouveau. Don't study it; quaff it.

$7.50 PER BOTTLE

1992 CHIGNIN · A. & M. QUENARD

This is not Roussanne. This is Chignin, not Chignin-Bergeron. This is less serious stuff. Very fresh nose, with rose petal and pit fruits. Light, round, perfumed, and lively on the palate. I serve it as an apéritif, or with *crudités* and charcuterie.

$7.95 PER BOTTLE

1991 CHIGNIN-BERGERON
LOUIS MAGNIN

Here it is, and it is more expressive than any Roussanne from the Rhône. Selected as one of the 500 best wines tasted in 1993 by the *Revue du Vin de France*, here is their description: "Beautiful golden color; ripe nose, apricot jam, candy, rose petal; palate rich and powerful. Splendid." This is an eye-opener.

$12.50 PER BOTTLE

1992 ARBIN · DOMAINE DE L'IDYLLE

The first of three reds from the Mondeuse, this has some of the purity and seductive pleasure of a good Saint-Joseph. It was raised in an oak *foudre* and bottled unfiltered for us. Fine nose with a ripe Syrah-like perfume. The flavor reminds me of violets, raspberry, and blueberry. Tannic but not too. Deliciousness is the attraction.

$7.95 PER BOTTLE

1992 MONDEUSE "VIEILLES VIGNES"
LOUIS MAGNIN

This one might shock. It is aggressive, rustic, alive, loaded with flavor. Deep, almost black purple. Peppery Syrah-like nose. Wild berry flavor. A palate-stainer with a tannic bite. Not for romance and candlelight, this one stands up and dominates one's attention.

$12.50 PER BOTTLE

1990 MONDEUSE · MICHEL GRISARD

Jancis Robinson writes in *Vines, Grapes, and Wines* that the Mondeuse from the steep hillsides can produce a "dense, deep, strong, chewy wine that is serious stuff indeed." Here is our third such selection. It has the depth and generosity of a great vintage. Excellent deep color; deep, ripe fruit with a touch of new oak; mouth-filling and structured to last. Plum, berry, spice. Taste it, then try to tell me the wines of the Savoie are inconsequential.

$14.95 PER BOTTLE

NORMALLY $63.35

SIX–BOTTLE SAMPLER $49.00

AMAZING BUT TRUE
1984 CHÂTEAUNEUF-DU-PAPE
DOMAINE DU VIEUX TÉLÉGRAPHE

THE BRUNIER family, Vieux Télégraphe, is one of my favorite visits. For one thing, I always get to stay for lunch and take advantage of Maguey Brunier's stunning Provençal cuisine.

However, my visit always starts in the cellar with a tasting of the newest vintage. The several cuvées will not have been blended yet or racked into *foudres*. Some are predominantly Grenache, others have more Syrah or Mourvèdre. I form a vague impression of what is to come. They also like to show me the cuvées that they do not consider good enough for the V. T. label, and which will be sold in bulk to the *négociants*.

Then comes the real work as I taste, select, and blend from the 18 to 20 *foudres* of the previous vintage that will be bottled as our Vieux Télégraphe. Of all the tasting I do each year, this is the most strenuous and demanding.

After that we taste a few older vintages, sometimes comparing our bottling to the filtered bottling everyone else gets. Ours always wins.

Then we select something to accompany Maguey's lunch. Last time, touring the bins, I noticed a big pile of unlabeled, mold-covered bottles. The vintage was marked in chalk on a little blackboard: 1984.

"Is that the French or American bottling?" I asked, because the French 1984 is tired while ours tastes great.

Daniel Brunier said it was neither. It is yet another bottling. He sells it bit by bit to the restaurant Beaugravière in nearby Mondragon, where they use it for sauces. Vieux Télégraphe for sauce?

"What's wrong with it?" I asked.

"It has a lot of sediment because I didn't filter it, and a lot of *gaz carbonique* because I didn't de-gas it. Shall I pull a cork?"

He did, and here the wine is, in Berkeley only, because some won't understand it. You've got to treat it right. Expend a little effort and you have a 10-year-old Vieux Télégraphe, at its peak, at a fabulous price.

It is simple. First, serve it cool, because when the wine is served cool the gas (natural CO_2) won't bug you. At room temperature it would seem a little too fizzy. Then decant it, because it has a sizeable deposit. There you are. Take a sniff of that! Sensational.

$9.95 PER BOTTLE $107.46 PER CASE

FINESSE

IN THE MAY 1993 issue of the *Revue du Vin de France*, France's most influential wine magazine, there is a valuable article entitled "The Return of Finesse." The author laments that many winemakers have been "led astray" by journalists, merchants, and consumers who judge wines too early and use questionable criteria. In order to earn high scores and make an immediate impact, weight and power are maximized at the expense of harmony and finesse.

Readers know that such sentiments coincide with my own. If I could convince you to value finesse, you would have a greater appreciation of the wines I select to import.

The article says, "Production of dark, fleshy wines, rich wines that end up proving soulless and monolithic, is too encouraged, mastodons that do not necessarily grow harmonious when becoming adults, wines that impress . . . then deceive and bore. In short, wines vinified for their weight!"

Today it is true that many winemakers vinify not in their own style, but in the style (extract, concentration, BIG wine) they know will win them high scores.

It is sad that in the U.S. *finesse* is often a code word for *light body*. That is a misuse of language that cheats the consumer. Finesse has nothing to do with body. It has to do with class, elegance, balance, the harmony of all the parts. Its presence is what makes us sometimes consider certain wines works of art.

I am not against full-bodied wines. I import, cellar, drink, and love them. But I do not select wines for their weight. Weight or body cannot be a factor when judging quality. It should play a role in one's judgment only at the moment you are deciding which wine to drink with which dish. If you are serving roast chicken, for example, you choose a light red. If you are having something hearty, you choose a full-bodied red. Hopefully both will show finesse.

A wine without finesse is tiring to drink. A sniff and sip can impress, but a second glass is not inviting. Your palate has been assaulted. A wine with finesse is not tiring; it will continue to reveal its qualities. A second and third glass is a pleasure, not a wrestling match.

Once journalists and buyers leave weight and power out of their scoring systems, we will be drinking better wine.

ATTACK OF THE BRETT NERDS

I F YOU HAVE never heard of brett, you haven't missed anything. Most have not heard of it, including the French winemakers, and they are doing just fine.

It used to be *ph*. Remember? All the hip tasters were talking about it. This *ph* means that, that *ph* means this. Most of us ignored *ph* and just wanted our wine to taste good. Now the *ph* types have discovered brett, which is short for brettanomyces. They think they demonstrate their discerning palate when, confronted with certain aromas, they can declare knowingly, "brett!" What sorts of aromas set off the brett nerds? Animal, undergrowth, mushroom, leather, earth, barnyard, dead leaves, etc., all long-valued wine aromas now shunned by the brett nerds.

Brett is a naturally occurring yeast. In many fine wines limited brett can appear during barrel aging and *contribute* nuances of these complexing aromas. Once in a great while there can be true spoilage, the fruit completely overwhelmed by these aromas, because of a brettanomyces fermentation in bottle. It is rare. It has happened to three of my wines in the past 22 years. Three times out of how many thousands of wines? Would an intelligent man sterile filter all wines because of those odds? I say STERILE filter, because that is the only way to thoroughly eliminate brett. I say if it is sterile, it is no longer wine. Let's call them grape-based beverages. So the brett nerds have their choice, sterile "wines" or an occasional runaway fermentation. As I wrote in my book, "If one loves natural wines, one accepts an occasional calamity. We would not castrate all men because some go haywire and commit rape. At least I wouldn't."

In his upcoming book about Domaine Tempier, Richard Olney describes their 1987s as "dominated by the aromas of older wines, game, humus, wild mushrooms, and black truffle." Sounds good to me. And it is meant to be complimentary, yet I've heard the brett nerds commence their chattering about those fabulous 1987s. Once the brett alarm sounds, any serious consideration of a wine is impossible for them, and it is written off. "Brett," so easy to pronounce.

It seems strange to me that here (but not in France), once this yeast was identified, it began to be treated by some as if it were a germ, as if it were dangerous. Or am I simply out of step in this era of AIDS? Is this an offshoot of the condom mentality? No, I think it is an American mentality. One of my very own grandmothers had the American preoccupation with and fear of germs. I remember shopping with her, and when confronted by a naked head of lettuce and one wrapped in plastic, she automatically reached for the plastic-wrapped. No hesitation. No logic.

Let the brett nerds retire into protective bubbles, and whenever they thirst for wine it can be passed in to them through a sterile filter. Those of us on the outside can continue to enjoy complex, natural, living wines.

But, what the heck, I don't even mind the static and pops on my old longplaying records. Out of touch and time and tune and fashion, obsolete, and soon to be accused of brett lust.

GRAY MARKET WARNING

THE COSTE-CAUMARTIN cellar contains some of Burgundy's greatest treasures, yet the quality is not consistent, nor is the bottling process always impeccable. I visit them several times a year in order to make sure you receive only the treasures. That means I do not buy every growth in every vintage. It means that I taste through the barrels to select the best, that the wines are bottled unfiltered, and that I never ship without making sure the final bottling was done well. After tasting the bottled 1991 Pommard Vignots, for example, I canceled our order even though it was already pre-sold pre-arrival.

National recognition was slow coming for Coste-Caumartin, but finally the 1989s and 1990s received rave reviews in *The Wine Spectator*. Afterwards (the highest compliment, if you want to look at it that way), Coste-Caumartin wines began to appear via the gray market, which means they began to appear in the U.S. imported by importers other than their exclusive importer, me. The problem is, the people who bought them without my import strip were buying wines that were completely different from the wines *The Wine Spectator* and I raved about, bottlings that were *not* from selected barrels, that *were* filtered, and that were shipped without prior tasting. They were not even purchased from Coste-Caumartin. They were purchased from distributors in England or other European countries, and some actually appeared wearing the French tax strip, meaning they came from French restaurants. They were not my wines.

And you must know by now that *all* my wines are shipped in temperature-controlled containers at 55°. Buying gray-market imports, who knows what temperatures they have seen?

For most of my selections, the story is the same. In 1992, for example, Amiot made two barrels of Montrachet. One was dazzling, the other slightly oxidized. I bought the good one and had him bottle it unfiltered. Amiot 1992 Montrachet also appeared via the gray market, but it was from the oxidized barrel, filtered!

Domaines that I represent whose wines you find without the K. L. import strip are often not at all the same wines that do wear my strip. Beware, lest ye get burned.

The gray marketeers are a sorry lot, trying to profit from the hard work of others.

TRAVEL NOTES

I RECENTLY completed my first tour of the vineyards since November. I visited the Loire, Bordeaux, the southwest, Languedoc, and Provence. The 1993s look good everywhere. The reds are well colored with excellent aromas, well-balanced, and striking in their typicity. They are less fleshy than vintage 1990. Some will fault them for that, others will appreciate the more streamlined style. The whites, easier to judge now that they have undergone their malolactic fermentations, have developed an excellent balance. They finish drier, more crisp and minerally than the 1992s.

Some highlights:

The 1993s from Charles Joguet include a stunning Varennes du Grand Clos. His 1991s were wiped out by hail, his 1992s diluted by rain. His 1993s are gems.

The 1993 Cuvée Spéciale from Château d'Epiré is a perfect summation of the Epiré potential.

My tasting at Michel Brégeon's finished with his fresh, classy 1987 Muscadet, seven years old and in top form!

From Château Fon de Sergay there will be a beautiful white Bordeaux, 1993, vinified in new barrels.

Château Perron sold their 1991 Madiran to *négociants* but offered 100 more cases of the gorgeous 1990. It arrives in August.

After skipping the 1991 Château de Pineraie, I purchased a good lot of their 1992 Cahors, which might be the best value of my trip.

I found a new domaine in the Minervois, Etang du Moulin. Explosive flavors dominated by peppery Syrah, gobs of cassis and cherry fruit, and the scent of the *garrigue*.

At Vieux Télégraphe it was too early to blend the 1993 and they were just putting our 1992 into bottle. We finished by comparing our original 1984, aged in *foudre*, with that recent batch, which was not. Two great wines. 1984! The wine raised in *foudre* was deeper, more ample, and expansive in every way. The other seems a little more square and hard-edged, in comparison. Long live the *foudre*.

In restaurants along the way I enjoyed many 1981 Bordeaux, my favorites of the decade. Ignored by the vintage chartists, they're relatively cheap. The grandest was Château Margaux, maybe the sexiest Bordeaux of my life.

Next week, I'm off to Burgundy.

◦ ◦ ◦ ◦ ◦ ◦ ◦ ◦

1992 CHÂTEAUNEUF-DU-PAPE
DOMAINE DU VIEUX TÉLÉGRAPHE

My wife pointed out that I have a favorite word for wines I really like to drink: pretty. I learned it from the French, who like to compliment wine by calling it *joli*. It is not an earthshaking pronouncement, pretty, but living on the San Andreas fault, earthshaking is not totally positive in its connotations. Commercially, I might be smarter to roll out such "compliments" as mind-boggling, mouth-wrenching, gut-splattering, but I think I'll roll over Beethoven instead.

If anyone compared a wine to Beethoven, I would think it ridiculous, so, given my mood, I might as well do it. The wine is Vieux Télégraphe. All right? Vieux Télégraphe = Beethoven. When most think of Beethoven they think of the stormier pieces like the mighty Fifth Symphony, or the soul searching of the late quartets, or the exquisite, profound longing of the late sonatas, but Beethoven is not always like that, and thank goodness. I want all of his frames of mind. Nor is Vieux Télégraphe always like the mighty 1990, and thank goodness.

I listen far more often to Beethoven's playful pieces, like his Fourth Symphony, music guaranteed to put me in good spirits.

So here we are. Vieux Télégraphe 1992 reminds me of Beethoven's Fourth but comes in fifths, tenths, magnums, and jeroboams. Well, why not? In this day and age I can't publicly compare wine to women anymore, which is the most fun, so why not music?

The symphony and the wine are playful, sprightly, upbeat, danceable. They are certain to animate me and alter my mood for the better. The wine smells fresh and happy. It tastes delicious and bright with no somber casts (unlike the sinister 1991), and it leaves a smile on your face just like Beethoven's musical jokes in the Fourth. And symphonic it is with its rich, full texture . . . that's enough. I quit. Pass the corkscrew.

$168.00 PER CASE

1993 CORBIÈRES "GRIS DE GRIS"
DOMAINE DE FONTSAINTE

During a heat wave recently I dropped an ice cube into my glass of this very rosé and it worked just fine, and I thought of the herd that drinks by the numbers ("I never drink less than a 95. Harumph."), and I thought of the pleasure they miss and the money they waste, and the time they spend trying to track down bottles of the high scorers, which often score or scorch the palate as well. ("Well, blister my tongue, that must be a 98.") Well, my taste is different, and I simply don't enjoy *swallowing* those wallapaloozers. Wine is not like arm wrestling.

Here is a perfect, delicious, pleasure-filled bottle of wine, rosé-colored.

$7.50 PER BOTTLE $81.00 PER CASE

1992 NORTHERN RHÔNES

EVERY SO OFTEN I invite the staff down into my cellar, and we start pulling corks to see what on earth has happened to the wines we sold when they and we were younger. It is enchanting to see how utterly useless a vintage chart would be in trying to predict which wines people end up preferring at these extemporaneous tastings. Living wines provide mystery and surprise.

One night corks started flying, one wine led to another, and we ended up comparing a range of 1984 and 1985 red Burgundies. The comments I heard were so out of synch with the vintage charts that I asked for a vote, and the 1984 won *unanimously*. 1984? What a shock. But it happened. They may be lighter, but the perfumes were finer and more captivating, and they gave more pleasure.

Recently we tasted through an array of northern Rhônes, going back from 1987 to 1969. Neither of the two I liked best would make sense to vintage chartists, because my favorites were from 1987 and 1981.

Côte Rôtie

The 1987 Jasmin was incredibly true to its *terroir*, unmistakably Côte Rôtie, and there was in addition a fresh, floral quality that prompted someone to say that it smelled like a field of flowers. It was giddily complex and seemed feminine compared to some of the others. Mostly, it was delicious.

I don't know if the vintage chartists think enough of 1981 to even list it anymore, but the 1981 Gentaz left everyone bedazzled and bewitched, and it was exactly the opposite style from Jasmin's: chunky, chewy, dense, deep . . . you get the idea. Gentaz in 1981 bottled a special cuvée for us, pure La Landonne, pure old vines, pure Syrah bliss. For me, along with the Jasmin 1987, it eclipsed the chartists' vintage stars like 1978, 1983, and 1985.

Anyway, now it is time to consider the 1992s from the northern Rhône. Here is my selection at pre-arrival prices. These are the tried and the true, the finest vineyard sites, raised in wood in the traditional manner, bottled unfiltered by the finest winemakers, rare treasures for any wine lover.

1992 CORNAS · AUGUSTE CLAPE

I would compare his 1992 to his 1982. Excellent color, densely flavored, but not hard or impenetrable. It is the sort of Cornas you can drink over several years, whenever the mood strikes, unlike the 1983, for example, which needed a decade before it started to open up.

$258.00 PER CASE FIFTHS $270.00 PER CASE MAGNUMS

1992 HERMITAGE *ROUGE* · J. L. CHAVE

Tasting it last year, I noted that it was perhaps the finest French red of the vintage! This year, for the moment, at least, it is better tasting than his 1991 or 1990. With time, no one knows. It has a smoky aroma that rises thickly off the wine's surface. Very intense, generous, complete. This is the master's rendition of the Syrah of Hermitage.

$498.00 PER CASE FIFTHS $534.00 PER CASE MAGNUMS

1992 HERMITAGE *BLANC* · J. L. CHAVE

To my taste, and judging by the number of bottles I cellar and uncork, Chave's is the finest dry white anywhere. The 1992 is rich, exotic, deep, and ripe. Don't miss it.

$462.00 PER CASE FIFTHS $492.00 PER CASE MAGNUMS

1992 CÔTE RÔTIE · RENÉ ROSTAING

Marked by a lovely, spicy, violet-tinged aroma, medium body, great finesse, a sense of outer beauty and inner structure. It consists of a good proportion of La Landonne, and is the bargain of the vintage.

$300.00 PER CASE FIFTHS $330.00 PER CASE MAGNUMS

1992 CÔTE RÔTIE "CÔTE BLONDE"
RENÉ ROSTAING

Some might call it seductive, some feminine, but I don't think that tells the whole story or captures what separates Rostaing's Côte Blonde from other Côte Rôties. There is also an expansiveness, a volume, an unusual depth to it, without any astringency or hard edges. The high proportion of Viognier accounts for the exotic bouquet. This Blonde is a deep, dark beauty.

$432.00 PER CASE FIFTHS

1992 CÔTE RÔTIE · ROBERT JASMIN

I don't know how anyone could resist our bottling of Jasmin's Côte Rôtie. It is always one of the greatest of the village and has a personality different from the others. A description from 1786 says Côte Rôtie is *un vin flatteur et fort delicat.* A later text remarks upon *la finesse de sa sève.* That pretty well sums up Jasmin's appeal.

$336.00 PER CASE FIFTHS

⋄ ⋄ ⋄ ⋄ ⋄ ⋄ ⋄ ⋄

1993 CORBIÈRES *BLANC* · JEAN BÉRAIL

When I am in France, I live not far from Richard Olney, author of *Yquem, Romanée-Conti,* and other delicacies, and sometimes I'll do the shopping (he doesn't drive), take the groceries over, and sit and drink while Richard prepares lunch. He always starts off with this Corbières *blanc* from Jean Bérail, nicely chilled, so I asked him if I could have a quote for this brochure.

"It is frank and fresh, with very pure fruit, peaches and apricot," he said. "It is an ideal apéritif wine, refreshing, a great pleasure to drink. I'd much rather have it at eleven o'clock in the morning than a Montrachet."

I asked him if we couldn't just say "Bérail's Corbières is better than Montrachet," but he said no.

$6.95 PER BOTTLE $75.06 PER CASE

1993 CHÂTEAUNEUF-DU-PAPE *BLANC*
DOMAINE DU VIEUX TÉLÉGRAPHE

Some people are good at finding precise aromas in wines, but I'm vague. When I had François Peyraud over the other night, I poured this Vieux Télégraphe white. I said it smells floral, and he said yes, it smells like *miel toutes fleurs,* which he explained is honey from bees that take the nectar from fields of mixed flowers. As he worked the grill (the perfect guest), preparing one of my favorite dishes, grilled mussels on the half shell, he also said there was a lemony touch to the wine, good *nervosité* for such richness, and a honeyed aftertaste.

His mussel recipe is simple enough. You get some coals going and grill mussels on the half shell, and just before their juices are evaporated, you dribble olive oil over them and powder them with ground pepper. The only hassle is opening all those expletive-deleted mussels, because you will want to eat an enormous plate of them once you get started.

$24.95 PER BOTTLE $269.46 PER CASE

❧ 1995 ❧

1993 POUILLY-FUMÉ "PUR SANG"
DIDIER DAGUENEAU

IF I OWNED vineyards in the Pouilly-Fumé or Sancerre appellations, I would vinify my wine exactly as Didier Dagueneau vinified this marvel, in slightly used (in order to avoid too much oak) *demi-muids*. A *demi-muid* is larger than a barrel, smaller than a *foudre*. He obtains all the positive qualities of wood aging and none of the negatives.

Pur Sang means "thoroughbred," and what a triumph it is. Excellent ripe fruit in the aroma, combined with smoke and gunflint. Rich on the palate, with great length and the desired nervosity. More than one critic on both sides of the Atlantic have called Dagueneau's the best Sauvignon Blanc in the world. He lives up to his reputation in 1993. Experience it for yourself.

Watch out, though. There are a herd of Dagueneaus in the region of Pouilly-Fumé. There is only one Didier. Also, his wine is now gray-marketed, but it is not our cuvée.

$35.00 PER BOTTLE $378.00 PER CASE

RED BURGUNDY

1991 NUITS-SAINT-GEORGES "LES CAILLES"
ROBERT CHEVILLON

I see that *The Wine Spectator* is revising upward its opinion of 1991, and they include Chevillon's Roncières as one of the 10 best. My favorite is Les Cailles, but it usually is. That is my personal taste. Cailles is Chevillon's leanest. The other day I read that Robert Parker considers "lean" a derogatory term. To me it is a compliment. Thin, no, no one wants a thin wine. Lean means muscular, intense, tight. With age Les Cailles can surpass the fat ones. It is not light, not thin, but lean. And what a glorious color, what fabulous intense flavors, what potential.

$42.00 PER FIFTH $453.60 PER CASE

1991 VOLNAY "LES BROUILLARDS"
DOMAINE BOILLOT

I have a French book about the origin of vineyard names that claims that "Brouillards" evolved from the first centuries of this era and indicates a family dwelling near some woods. In a modern dictionary, "Brouillards" means nothing more than fog. Yet the wine tastes nothing like foggy woods. No, wait, there is a suggestion of autumn to it, piles of humid, decaying tree leaves outside while Grandma's blackberries cook and bubble upon the stove inside . . . Aren't Burgundies fun?

$24.95 PER FIFTH $269.46 PER CASE

◇ ◇ ◇ ◇ ◇ ◇ ◇

1992 CÔTE RÔTIE "CÔTE BRUNE"
MARIUS GENTAZ

I have seen (and I tried to get it into my book) that the personal life of a winemaker can influence his wine. My pal Joseph Swan made the worst wine of his career the year his wife left him. Vintage 1993 was the last before the retirement of Marius Gentaz, and tragedy struck during the harvest when his son-in-law (his heir apparent) attempted suicide with a pistol shot to the head. He was left crippled and blinded. Is it coincidental that 1993 is the first vintage *chez* Gentaz I have tasted that is not up to par? Up to par for Gentaz means Côte Rôtie's best, thanks to his vinification and thanks to his old vines, which many consider the best of the appellation.

Those superbly placed ancient vines will be vinified now by René Rostaing, the nephew and neighbor of Gentaz, hopefully in a cuvée apart, which I am urging Rostaing to label *Cuvée Marius Gentaz*.

So, sadly, this current offering, vintage 1992, will be our last chance to have Gentaz vinified by Gentaz. Of additional interest, I convinced him to bottle his oldest vines separately for us, as he did previously in 1981 and 1984. Those so-called "off" vintages were right on, as good or better than other winemakers' so-called "great" vintages.

So, here is something to cellar not only for the quality, but also for a certain sentimental value.

$53.00 PER FIFTH $572.40 PER CASE

1992 JURANÇON "QUINTESSENCE"
DOMAINE BRÛ-BACHÉ

In a brochure more than 15 years ago I first recommended a wine for the jaded palate, meaning wine for adventurous people whose palates are tired of yet another Cabernet or Chardonnay, palates ready for off-the-beaten-path thrills.

Here is the ultimate jaded palate wine, and it is sweet. It is sweet because the grapes are left on the vine until early December. Super-ripe, shriveled, sticky Petit Manseng. The thick must was fermented in new oak. While it is as sweet as Sauternes, the flavors are much more exotic. Rich, concentrated body; ravishing flavors that I wish I could describe for you without sounding ridiculous, but I can't; great aging potential. In fact, I suggest tasting one now for the experience, and aging a few more *at least* five years.

Here is a neat quote from Colette about Jurançon wine: "I was a girl when I met this prince; aroused, imperious, treacherous, as all great seducers are."

$29.95 PER BOTTLE $323.46 PER CASE

SPRING SAMPLER

I WRITE THIS in Berkeley, looking out my window as the rain slashes down and the wind seems to pierce right through the glass panes. I just left my store, where the roof is leaking. Roads are flooded. People are evacuated. Bah humbug. In France this fall I ran into 40 days of rain and floods, and here it is again and again. Three lengthy inundations this year.

By my clock it is apéritif time. The only wine in the fridge is a rosé. This is not rosé weather, but it will have to do.

Looking at the pale, bright color, my thoughts turn to our next season, spring, which is not far away. Rosé will be appropriate. Spirits will rise. Flowers will blossom. Sleeves will shorten.

If you are seasonally sensitive, the change of seasons plays a role in your wine selections. Lightness and freshness matter more. So I am trying to will spring into being with a spring sampler, a personal selection of wines that complement our change of mood and stimulate a change of outlook.

Usually each April I go to Vinitaly, and that means Prosecco, the Veneto's lightly sparkling dry white, omnipresent by the glass in Venice and Verona. It means Soave, served under an arbor of grapevines.

In the south of France it means rosé: the bright sun, the pretty color in the glass, the chilled quaffer. And so I have included two bone-dry, ultra-tasty rosés.

Stoking the coals of your barbecue is best achieved with a glass of cool Beaujolais, although this has not been proven under laboratory conditions.

And there is a Syrah that fits the mood. Not a mighty Cornas. Not a regal Hermitage. It is Saint-Joseph, the seductress, and starting now, it too should be served cool. All the reds in the sampler should be slightly chilled.

April. Maybe the end is near. I'll drink to that.

I hope I'm not acting prematurely.

There is another reason, a less romantic reason, to buy the sampler. It contains a lot of good wines at a remarkable price.

PER BOTTLE

1992	Prosecco · Adriano Adami	$9.95
1992	Soave "La Frosca" · Sandro Gini	9.95
1992	Pinot Grigio · Pecorari	9.95
1993	Côtes du Rhône Blanc · Château du Trignon	7.95
1992	Sauvignon de Touraine · Domaine des Acacias	8.25
1993	Viognier · Domaine Saint-James	12.50

1994	Côtes de Provence Rosé · Château Maravenne	. . . . .	9.95
1993	Coteaux du Languedoc Rosé · Domaine d'Aupilhac	. . .	9.95
1992	Saint-Joseph Rouge · Roger Blachon	. . . . .	12.50
1993	Vin de Pays d'Oc Rouge · Domaine de Bassac	. . . .	4.95
1993	Beaujolais · Cuvée Kermit Lynch	. . . . .	7.95
1992	Coteaux du Languedoc Rouge · Château de Lascaux	. . .	8.25

NORMALLY $122.10

SAMPLER PRICE $84.00

◊ ◊ ◊ ◊ ◊ ◊ ◊ ◊ ◊

1993 BLANC DE BLANCS *SEC* · CLOS NICROSI

When Jean-Louis Chave was here we took him to dinner, and I grabbed several old northern Rhônes from my cellar, from appellations other than Hermitage, mainly to profit from his insights. I noticed a single bottle of Clos Nicrosi mixed in with other wines in a bin. The vintage? 1986. I grabbed it, too, out of curiosity.

I have always drunk Clos Nicrosi young, so that 1986 was a revelation. For me it was the wine of the night. Astonishing. It reminded me of Chave's own great white, honeyed but with more acidity and a dazzling citronelle note in the bouquet.

Those who think Corsica makes only plonk are mistaken. This wine received the *Revue du Vins de France*'s highest rating. They wrote, "Golden color; remarkable character and great length. A wine full-bodied and complete."

There is a tantalizing mushroom note in the aroma, fresh mushroom, still alive in the earth. The possibilities with certain dishes are obvious and mouthwatering.

$21.50 PER BOTTLE

BURGUNDY VINTAGES

THE OTHER DAY the lightbulb went on and I realized the extent of the problem. A lot of people have it plain wrong about Burgundy vintages, and their misconception, like blinders, keeps them from enjoying the very pleasure that Burgundy has to offer, a pleasure that can touch body, mind, and soul.

Everyone is concerned with the question "Is it a good vintage, or is it an off vintage?" Professional wine critics are happy to rush to print and provide the answer. It is almost a race. But if you study the ratings over the years, you will notice that Burgundy vintages are rated according to how hot the weather was, how ripe the grapes were. Using those criteria, why the hell not move Burgundy down south? Grow Pinot Noir at Gigondas. Bandol. Jerez. The grapes would really ripen every year, and you would have black, heavy, tannic Burgundies every vintage, which is what most people think they want. But it would not be Burgundy and it would not be as good as Burgundy. I like the statement Pascal Armand, grower at Pommard, made at the International Pinot Noir Celebration: "I'm not making Pinot Noir here, I'm making Pommard."

There is a reason why the ancients did not plant Grenache in Burgundy. Grenache would never ripen there.

There is also a reason they did not establish the Pinot Noir down south in warmer climes. It would overripen, and the result would not be interesting or harmonious.

Following the aesthetic criteria and advice of many, you would have to conclude that centuries of experience led to a monumental error in Burgundy, because Pinot Noir there only manages to make a huge, sun-soaked blockbuster about once every 10 or 15 years. But the fact is, Pinot Noir often loses its pizzazz in hot years. It is a grape that can make a dull, vulgar wine in hot climates. Centuries of experience proved to the ancients that Burgundy's ripening season and soil are perfect for Pinot Noir. But of course they were not looking for blockbusters. THEY WERE NOT LOOKING FOR BLOCKBUSTERS! That is not the Pinot Noir's talent. Pinot Noir at Burgundy is capable of more, you see. And when you open your mind and search for that "more," then you will get some satisfaction.

Yes, there is more to wine than size and power. But if that is what you seek, why buy Burgundy? Why not buy a Châteauneuf-du-Pape instead, or an Amador Zinfandel? It is easy to find big, black, tannic wines. The market is full of them, and at prices lower than you would pay for red Burgundy.

Joe Montana is expensive, but don't try to play him at linebacker. Ask the right things of Montana and you will get your money's worth. Same with Burgundy.

The weather in Burgundy is quirky. Maybe the quirkiest. And the resulting wines are full of quirks, and therein lies a lot of their interest. Interest. If a Burgundy is not interesting, it is not worth drinking. In a way, it is the quirks (and almost every vintage has them) that keep me passionate about Burgundy. Besides, some of the most thrilling Burgundies of my life have been from so-called off vintages, while some of the most boring have been from so-called great vintages. I will take experience over a vintage chart any day.

It occurred to me that perhaps we began applying the wrong aesthetic criteria to Burgundy because we were raised on domestic wines. We differentiated them based upon size and extract because the question of *terroir* was rarely applicable.

The *goût de terroir* is what gives Burgundy its underlying interest, what makes it more than simply fermented grape juice. The ancients stuck with Pinot Noir because in Burgundy there is a perfect combination of soil, climate, and grape variety. Listen to Henri Jayer:

> *The Pinot made its home here in Burgundy, and this is where it expresses itself best. It is a delicate little beast, the Pinot; it needs sunshine but not too much, rainfall but not too much. It is complex, all this, but it is here that the Pinot found the microclimate that suits it best. Burgundy is a wine that enchants with its perfume. It must be fine and elegant, which does not exclude a solid structure.*

Not a word about size, power, extract! Leave those criteria aside when you judge Burgundy. There are higher rewards in store for you if you do.

What are some of the words you might use to describe Burgundy's talent? Perfume, balance, harmony, nuance, complexity, finesse, grandeur, subtlety, fascination, character, breed, delicacy, mystery, and so on. And the neatest thing is, you can sometimes find several seemingly contradictory qualities in a single wine. That's interesting.

I never ask if it is a good or bad vintage in Burgundy. I ask, what is it like? What does it offer? And then the fun begins and lasts for years, because watching the evolution of the different vintages is a pastime full of surprises. For example, the 1982s. The first time I tasted them, right after the harvest, I told myself, "Here finally is a Burgundy vintage that I cannot buy." But as they aged they got better and better, and now they are some of my favorites. Especially the Maumes and Chevillons. Likewise, some vintages touted as black, tannic, *vins de garde* still have not developed such lovely perfumes.

If you are going to pay for a Joe Montana, shouldn't you play him at quarterback?

◦ ◦ ◦ ◦ ◦ ◦ ◦ ◦

BUGEY CERDON ROSÉ "LA CUEILLE"
PATRICK BOTTEX

Here is one of those curiosities we import that many people are afraid to try. Fear of the unknown? Well, it is a sparkling rosé from the Savoie made from a grape variety that no one has even heard of. Plus, it is ultra-light, only 7° alcohol! Strike four.

When I vacationed in Hawaii, Randy Caparosa, the ideal sommelier at Roy's Restaurant in Honolulu, invited my family to a picnic on the beach. He brought an ice chest of Bugey rosé. Of course, the sun and the waves helped, but I don't know that I have ever enjoyed a wine more. And even in the hot sun, at only 7° alcohol, this wine does not mount to the head. Next barbecue, give your friends an utterly unknown, utterly fabulous treat.

$14.25 PER BOTTLE $153.90 PER CASE

1994 MOSCATO D'ASTI
TINTERO

If I had 100,000 cases instead of 100, I could have a TV ad instead of a brochure: Married couples are gathered around a table in the garden patio. Everyone is joggingly fit. None smoke. No one is divorced. No one is wrinkled, although there is a bit of gray at the men's temples. All wear expensive casual clothes, though we can tell the men are more at home in executive fashions. They wear a look of satisfaction, of hard-earned success. There is a giant platter of cakes and cookies, and the most handsome of the men is confidently pouring Kermit Lynch's sparkling Moscato. Everyone gazes at the pretty bubbles glowing in the sunshine. They sip. Their faces light up, one by one. There are smiles, comprehension, a glow, while the announcer announces, "You and your friends *deserve* it." Fade to:

$6.95 PER BOTTLE $75.06 PER CASE

THE SOUTH

1992 CORNAS · AUGUSTE CLAPE

Who is the most consistent winemaker in France? Does anyone even care? Most people seem more interested in the latest palate gouger, the wine world's version of Warhol's 15 minutes of fame. Consistency is too boring. But listen, perhaps the rare fellow who has the quality of consistency is not limited to a single talent. Maybe he also has the talent to make a wine every year that you love to drink.

Auguste Clape, Cornas

Do you like Cornas? Clape's 1992 smells like Syrah from Cornas, nothing more, nothing less. It is all there—the size, the structure, the tannin. What a beauty! Auguste Clape deserves some kind of medal.

Plus, I like the guy. He's real, he's honest, with no egotistical b-s . . . like his wines, come to think of it.

$24.95 PER BOTTLE $269.46 PER CASE

1994 PIC SAINT LOUP *BLANC*
CHÂTEAU LA ROQUE

As long as I'm giving Clape the Lifetime Achievement and What a Swell Guy Award, I'm giving La Roque the long-awaited Progress Award. Boutin's planting of Viognier and Rolle, along with his Marsanne vines, is turning out a southern dry white more and more captivating. There is anise, honey, and citronelle in the bouquet and on the palate, all of which creates a perfect match with fish. You don't need a sauce or anything fancy. Leave the cookbooks on the shelf. Just the marriage of a fish grilled over coals with the flavor components of La Roque's white will be complicated enough for most of us.

$9.25 PER BOTTLE $99.90 PER CASE

* * * * * * * *

1994 CÔTE DE BROUILLY · CHÂTEAU THIVIN

A wine can have class, but what does class taste like? Obviously I bring it up here because of Château Thivin. Class is the first word that came to mind when I began writing this. *Class* means there is some style. There is restraint. It cannot be vulgar and showy. There are no cheap thrills, even if the wine is inexpensive, if you know what I mean. One wine writer described his favorite Beaujolais as having a sledgehammer-like feel on the palate. Fine, but I think that we can agree that sledgehammers have impact, but no class. Château Thivin's wine has class. It is our classiest Beaujolais. Does that mean it is our best? Best for what? Washing the dog? No, but if you are in the mood for class, it is our best. If you are in the mood for fizz, our own K. L. label Beaujolais is the fizziest. Flash? Try one from our Gang of Four.

Even though it shows restraint, by the way, it does not mean there is not a lot to the wine. It does mean, perhaps, that a little taste, intelligence, and refinement is necessary on the part of the taster. You might have to get involved. It won't hammer you.

The 1994 today has a ravishing, fresh Gamay aroma and flavor, beautiful not in the *Penthouse* style, no—think instead of Lauren Bacall in her first couple of films, with that freshness that almost crackles.

$13.95 PER FIFTH $150.66 PER CASE

Domaine de Trévallon

FRAPPEZ LA ROUTE
FROM ROCHEGUDE TO ORNAISONS

Business recently took me from the Côtes du Rhône region to the Corbières, and it was such an excellent trip in every respect, it seemed more play than pain. I kept thinking that the same route would not be bad as pure vacation. No work. All play. But still with its share of good wines, to be sure. So I put a vacation together, in case anyone is looking for one.

There is now a castle in the southern Rhône vineyards that rents rooms. It is near Orange, Sainte-Cécile-les-Vignes, Vaison-la-Romaine, not far at all from the vineyards of Châteauneuf-du-Pape and Gigondas. Part of the Hôtel Château de Rochegude (telephone 04.75.97.21.10) dates from the 12th century. Some of the rooms are quite spacious and furnished with antiques, the plumbing works, and there are views of the vine-covered Plan de Dieu with the Dentelles de Montmirail and Mont Ventoux in the distance. The restaurant is more than acceptable, with a good list of local wines and some overlooked, underpriced 1981 clarets. Don't hesitate phoning Faraud, Vieux Télégraphe, Domaine de Durban, or Château du Trignon for a visit, if you like.

At least one meal should be enjoyed at the Beaugravière, about 15 kilometers from Rochegude in Mondragon. The specialty is black truffles. Here also is the world's finest list of Rhône wines, including older vintages from most of the best

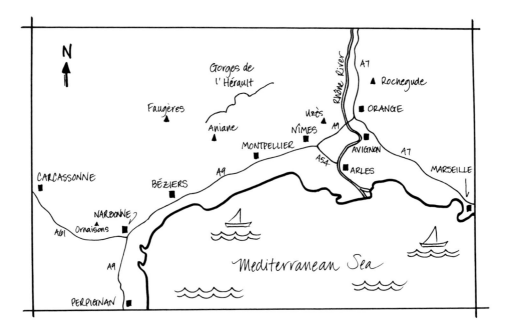

domaines. Here and only here could you possibly order a black truffle and a 1929 white Hermitage from Chave (5800FF). I am certain the marriage would be a good one.

It is really not far at all to Saint-Rémy and Arles. We are not talking long distances for this vacation. Down here in van Gogh country there are many wonderful places to stay, but the most curious is the Grand Hôtel Nord Pinus (I am not making this up), *centre ville* Arles, on the Place du Forum (telephone 04.90.93.44.44). Part of the hotel's façade is Roman. Later, the hotel was a favorite of Picasso and his bullfighter friends, and the inside walls show a lot of beautiful old posters from those heydays. In fact, the décor in the lobby is wild; the place has its own personality, believe me. The service is Provençal; relaxed. I like it.

Outside of Arles, after Fontvieille, there is the Bistro du Paradou for a simple Provençal lunch. I found it thanks to Pat Wells, but I'm not the only one who has discovered the place. Most tables now speak English or Japanese.

A few more kilometers and you can visit our olive oil source, the Oleicole de la Vallée des Baux, at Maussane-les-Alpilles, and if you cross the little range of mountains called Les Alpilles (spectacular scenery!) you are near the unforgettable Domaine de Trévallon. (At all wineries please call or ask your hotel to call for a rendezvous before stopping by. Etiquette prohibits visits unless you have previously consumed at least one case of their wine.)

There is so much to see around Arles and Saint-Rémy, give yourself at least a month. (Sure, Kermit.) But then head northwest to the Pont-du-Gard, an awe-inspiring Roman structure; plus, the river underneath can be jumped into. Then on to the village of Uzès with its fabulous old arcades, the village where *Cyrano de Bergerac* was filmed starring Gérard Depardieu, *bien sûr*.

A wonderful, little-known hotel is not far. Look for the village of Arpaillargues (if it ends in *-argues*, Romans were there, and they were), about five kilometers from Uzès on the D982. You want the Hôtel Marie d'Agoult (telephone 04.66.22.14.49), a rustic, 17th-century stone château. No trucks. No motorcycles. Here it is quiet, except for the happily swooping swallows. Pool. Tennis. Dine outdoors in the château's courtyard, where once in a while a grill is fired up right next to the tables. The cuisine is decent, with a good choice of wines. Last time there I had the white from Vieux Télégraphe and a red Faugères from Alquier.

In the morning, don't hit the road to go wine tasting. Stay put. Hang out by the swimming pool in their lovely park, and then leave around 11:30 A.M. for lunch outside a tiny village called Junas, near Sommières, near Montpellier. The restaurant Can Peio (04.66.77.71.83) is in no guidebooks. The name is Catalan and so is the cuisine. Don't go unless you love anchovies, red peppers, and olives. I want this chef cooking in my kitchen. I thank Anne Flaten Pixley for giving me the address. She wrote, "Can Peio was a favorite hangout for Lawrence Durrell. I like it at lunch with sunlight on the white walls and Spanish tiles. They will do an entire meal of tapas if you want a sampler of all their dishes."

Afterwards, from Sommières, take the D1 west and the D109 north to Fontanès, then follow the sign to Château La Roque for some wine tasting. This vineyard has proven its worth over the centuries. There were Romans here, there were thirsty monks, then aristocrats, and now it is the friendly Jack Boutin making the wine and welcoming you with a smile. The chilly, ancient, stone-vaulted cellar is a sight to see and feel.

From La Roque it is only about 10 kilometers north to Vacquières, a village made of stones, which is the site of Château de Lascaux, whose Syrah vines produce one of the Languedoc's most elegant reds.

Now, forget wine again and go sightseeing. Head for the Hérault River, due west, but you will have to zig and zag to get there. What a river! I cannot resist diving into it. Especially from the cliffs along Les Gorges de l'Hérault. Around here there is not much in the way of accommodations, but in Causse-de-la-Selle there is the funky Hôtel Vieux Chêne (04.67.73.11.00) with a surprisingly good cook. Then head south along the river (this is for swimmers only) near the Grotte de Clamouse, under the bridge they call the Pont du Diable, where the river is gorgeous and deep enough to do some serious diving from higher on the rocks. Be careful, though. Don't break your neck until you have visited two of the Languedoc's greatest domaines, Domaine d'Aupilhac in nearby Montpeyroux and the Mas de Daumas Gassac outside of Aniane. And you are close to one of my favorite restaurants, Le Mimosa in Saint Guiraud (04.67.96.67.96). Last week they served a *gigot de chevreuil*, and from the unbelievable wine list a 1988 Gentaz

Côte Rôtie, the best wine I have drunk this year. If you cellared it, pull one out, and if you are in the area, don't miss Le Mimosa.

From there I drive to Bédarieux, then south to Faugères to taste and buy Jean-Michel Alquier's superb red wine. I started with the father; now the son continues. There are rugged hillsides here, perfect for his Syrah, Grenache, and Mourvèdre. There is excitement tasting here, and you will find a true, consistent, Alquier personality in the wines. One of the best.

I still don't know of any wonderful hotels in the vicinity of Faugères, so I usually drive an hour or so, past Narbonne, to the Relais du Val d'Orbieu, near Ornaisons (04.68.27.10.27). I mentioned this place, somewhat critically, in my book. Since then it has changed hands. I like it there, and I will explain why. It is isolated, out in the vineyards, so it is quiet. Their blue-and-red-tiled swimming pool comes in handy when it is hot (and it always is, in the summer), and there are fruit, cypress, and olive trees. Last week, after a week on the road, I ordered a tenth of Tempier rosé to cure my homesickness, and it helped a little. Then I had a lovely white from Mas Julien and a fully mature 1979 red from Château Fortia in Châteauneuf-du-Pape. (No, folks, I was not dining alone.) The wine list is quite good, especially for the local wines. The hotel is also well located for day trips in all directions. Carcassonne is not far. The Corbières hills are wild and beautiful and barely populated. The Mediterranean is not far. The proprietor of the hotel asked that you mention my name should you call for a reservation. I cannot imagine why.

PAUL BERTOLLI
AND THE LOIRE

MUSCADET WITH oysters. I love Muscadet with oysters. It would, in fact, be a rare day that would find me refusing an offer of Muscadet and oysters. However, Muscadet with oysters. We have heard it so often it has almost grown into a one-word cliché. Muscadetwithoysters.

"My God, isn't there anything else that goes with Muscadet?" I asked author and chef Paul Bertolli.

In so many words, he replied, "Yes, give me a bottle of Muscadet and I'll uncork it in my kitchen and come up with an appropriate dish."

Well, one bottle led to another, and before you could learn how to pronounce *Loire* like a true Frenchman, Paul had created four recipes to accompany and show off the wines from the four Loire wine regions:

1. *The area east of Tours, including Cheverny, Pouilly-Fumé, Quincy, Sancerre, and other Sauvignon Blancs.*

2. *The area of the Pineau de la Loire, or Chenin Blanc, stretching roughly from Tours west to Angers, including Montlouis, Vouvray, Savennières, and Anjou* blanc.

3. *The great red appellations of Chinon and Bourgueil.*

4. *Muscadet, near the mouth of the Loire and the coastal oyster beds.*

Paul Bertolli is the talented fellow who creates the menu and cuisine at Oliveto Restaurant in Oakland. These four recipes are not at all difficult to realize, and they work. Author of *Chez Panisse Cooking*, Paul has had plenty of experience writing recipes and cooking great meals. I have personal knowledge. Follow his advice and watch the food improve the wine, and vice versa. And now, here's Paul.

1993 MUSCADET DE SÈVRE-ET-MAINE "SUR LIE" ANDRÉ-MICHEL BRÉGEON

Muscadet's greatest asset is its directness. This is simple wine that begs for a complement. Traditionally, oysters, which demand no great dimension of flavor in the wine, are its most authentic match. Recent trials proved that it is difficult to move beyond the realm of the ocean with this wine, so naturally wedded are its components to the flavors of the sea. I've always preferred slightly creamy oysters (those on their way to spawn), which are perfectly balanced by the appley tang and occasional spritz in this wine. Mussels and potatoes, tossed in a cream-bound reduction of the juices rendered in the skillet by the mussels, work in much the same way. Serve the Muscadet well chilled with the salad.

Warm Potato and Mussel Salad

1 pound new potatoes ("Red Rose")
1½ quarts water
1 tablespoon salt
1½ pounds small fresh mussels in the shell
1 shallot, 1½ ounces, finely minced
½ cup Muscadet
2 bay leaves
½ cup heavy cream
1 tablespoon chopped fresh Italian parsley

Combine the potatoes, water, and salt in a saucepan. Bring to the boil, reduce to a simmer, cover, and cook for 30 minutes or until soft in the center to the point of a knife.

While the potatoes are cooking, scrub the mussels. Place the shallots, wine, and bay leaves in a skillet. Add the mussels to the skillet and turn the heat on high. When the wine begins to boil, cover the pan and steam the mussels for about 5 minutes, shaking the pan from side to side every so often. When all the mussels are open, remove the pan from the heat and pour the mussels and their juice into a colander fitted with a bowl underneath. Discard the bay leaves. Pour the mussel juice through a fine sieve or through a sieve lined with cheesecloth to catch any grit or sand. Return the juice to the pan in which the mussels cooked. Place the mussel juice on medium heat; when it begins to simmer add the cream, raise the heat, and reduce by half. You should have about ⅔ cup. Set aside.

Pour off the water from the potatoes and allow them to cool for 10 minutes. Meanwhile, remove the mussels carefully from the shells so that they remain intact and pull away the "beard" clinging to the center of the mussel. Peel the potatoes while still warm and slice them directly into a bowl. Pour about one-half of the mussel cream over the potatoes and half of the parsley. Toss well with a spatula, taking care not to break up the potatoes. Arrange the potatoes on a platter, lay the mussels on top, and nap them with the remaining sauce. Sprinkle the remaining parsley over the top and serve.

For six persons

1993 POUILLY-FUMÉ "EN CHAILLOUX"
DIDIER DAGUENEAU
1993 SANCERRE · HIPPOLYTE REVERDY

Kermit reminded me that the village of Chavignol, known for its fine, firm-textured cheese, the Crottin de Chavignol, is in the heart of the Sancerre appellation. While this recipe does not utilize Crottin (a cheese not particularly suitable for melting), the association of goat cheese with this wine in the local tradition spurred me to come up with this dish.

Finding the right food pairing summons the aromas in the wine. Likewise, the wine can act as a condiment to the food, enhancing its flavors and providing a provocation to continue eating. In this case, the chalky pucker of the goat cheese draws out the flintiness in this wine and harmonizes well with its pungent grassiness. The soft, somewhat creamy effect of the omelette is also a good foil for the refreshing acidity in the wine (taken on its own it can appear "hard"), which washes it all away and further stimulates the appetite.

Goat Cheese Omelette

8 fresh farm eggs
1 heaping tablespoon fresh savory, finely chopped
¼ cup milk
Pinch of salt
3½ ounces soft fresh goat cheese (such as Bucheron)
Freshly ground black pepper
1 tablespoon unsalted butter
1 tablespoon fresh chives, finely minced

Preheat the oven to broil.

Crack the eggs into a bowl; add the savory, the milk, and the salt. Using your hands, crumble the goat cheese into the mixture and season with a few turns of the pepper grinder. Using a fork, mix until all ingredients are well combined.

Warm the butter in a 12-inch well-seasoned skillet or no-stick pan with a metal handle. Raise the heat; when the butter begins to brown, pour in the egg mixture. Scatter the chives all over the surface. Maintain high heat under the pan and cook the omelette for 2 to 3 minutes until just set on the bottom (the top will still appear quite liquid). Place the pan under the broiler on the highest rack in the oven. Continue to cook the omelette for an additional 4 to 5 minutes or until it puffs, is lightly browned on its surface, and is set in the middle.

Allow the omelette to cool for 5 minutes and serve at once.

For six persons

1993 CHINON "LES VARENNES DU GRAND CLOS" CHARLES JOGUET
1986 CHINON "VIEILLES VIGNES" · CHARLES JOGUET

It is not hard to imagine many dishes suitable with these wines although they are quite markedly different in style; the 1993, a much lighter wine with a Beaujolais-like appearance and nose, matched well with both a braised pig's trotter and a thick salmon steak seared dry in its own oils in a hot pan. We tasted the old-vines Chinon with a plate of venison salami, a braised stuffed shoulder of lamb, and the following sampler preparation with equal success.

Grilled Paillards of Beef
with Anchovies and Shallots

1¼ pounds aged beef loin or lean top sirloin
2 teaspoons whole black pepper
Salt
8 anchovy fillets, soaked in cold water for 5 minutes, laid to dry on a paper towel
1 clove garlic
4 tablespoons extra-virgin olive oil
Juice of ¼ lemon
1 shallot, 1½ ounces, finely minced
1 tablespoon Italian parsley, coarsely chopped

Prepare a charcoal or wood fire.

Cut, or have your butcher cut, four equally thin slices of beef.

Crush the pepper in a mortar and pestle, and salt and pepper each slice on both sides. Use all of the pepper.

Add the anchovies and garlic clove to the mortar and crush them to a paste. Stir in the olive oil, lemon juice, and shallots.

Grill the paillards to your liking over a hot fire and transfer them immediately to a platter or to individual warmed plates.

Using a spoon, spread the anchovy mixture over each paillard, sprinkle with the parsley, and serve.

For four persons

1993 VOUVRAY *SEC* · DIDIER CHAMPALOU

The slightly sweet note in the wine comes as a pleasant surprise and echoes a similar quality in sea scallops seared in brown butter and presented here relatively unadorned. Choose "day boat" scallops if you can find them; all the better if the roes are attached. The best, of course, is if you have the opportunity to purchase live scallops in the shell and shuck them yourself.

Sea Scallops with Brown Butter

1 pound very fresh sea scallops
Sea salt
6 tablespoons unsalted butter
Juice of ½ lemon
1 tablespoon chervil leaves

Lay the scallops out on a plate and salt each side lightly.

Warm a 10-inch skillet or cast-iron pan. Add 4 tablespoons of the butter and raise the heat to high. When the butter begins to brown, add the scallops broad side down. Maintaining the highest possible heat, sear the scallops on both sides. This should take about 3 minutes per side. The scallops will appear browned on their surfaces and crusted at the edges.

Transfer the scallops to four warmed plates. Add the juice of the lemon to the pan and the remaining 2 tablespoons of butter. Return the pan to a moderate flame. When the butter is melted and combined with the browned portion left over from the sauce, spoon a little of the butter over and around the scallops. Sprinkle chervil over each portion and serve at once.

For four persons as a first course

1994 MORGON · JEAN-PAUL THÉVENET

Taste this and you will see what I have been raving about. Our Beaujolais do not taste like others. You have real wine here. None of that super-polished tutti-frutti bubblegummy . . . And, yes, WE HAVE NO BANANA. We *never* sell wines that smell like banana. I do not regret a banana sliced onto Fanny's granola, but for heaven's sake, leave it out of my wine.

This is such a natural wine, you actually taste that it aged in barrel instead of stainless steel, that the grapes were grown organically, that no flavors, yeasts, or chemicals were added.

There is ripe black cherry evolving with aeration to black currant in the aroma. The surface is very appealing. First whiff, right off the bat, you are nodding and saying, "Wow, cool, far out, gimme five, that's zorch, sock it to me," then you notice the depth to it, all the interest that lies below that deceptive surface charm. There could be fiendish monsters lurking under there, but it is too dark to see.

As you taste it, you realize that you have quite a serious wine in your glass, the kind of wine that might, for your own good, someday be illegal; then you back off a step and remember, "This is a Beaujolais!" and the shock grows as the wine flows . . .

$18.50 PER FIFTH $199.80 PER CASE

1994 CÔTE DE BROUILLY
DOMAINE DE LA VOÛTE DES CROZES

Last month I got carried away trying to praise Château Thivin's Côte de Brouilly, fumblingly trying to define what class tastes like, making ageist remarks about Lauren Bacall, and suggesting that certain wines are more suitable for washing the dog than for drinking. Business must have been slow.

VIN DU BEAUJOLAIS

Côte de Brouilly

APPELLATION CÔTE-DE-BROUILLY CONTRÔLÉE

DOMAINE DE LA VOÛTE DES CROZES
Nicole CHANRION,
Viticulteur, "Les Crozes" CERCIÉ-EN-BEAUJOLAIS (Rhône) France

Well, forget class when you pull the cork on this dark, bright beauty, our other Côte de Brouilly. This one is a macho hunk. Closed. Dark. Rustic. Tannic. Chewy. Powerful. A macho hunk of *grand cru* Beaujolais vinified by Nicole Chanrion. Aged in oak *foudres*, bottled unfiltered, this makes an impression. It reminds me of Hemingway's description of tasting a wine in *A Moveable Feast*, "You could dilute it by half and still receive its message."

$13.50 PER BOTTLE $145.80 PER CASE

1993 BOURGOGNE *BLANC* · DOMAINE ROULOT

The Domaine Roulot in Meursault has always been one of white Burgundy's shining stars. Still, this Bourgogne represents a brilliant leap forward for them. It is their first trial bottling of a totally unfiltered wine. Jean-Marc Roulot was convinced to try it after an experience one night in the cellar below our office in Beaune, at a tasting attended by our white Burgundy producers, a tasting for the sole purpose of judging pairs of exactly the same whites, one filtered, one unfiltered.

The result is this super wine. It is luscious, lively, refined, subtle, and I ordered all I could get: 200 cases. The sheer perfection of it, everything *comme il faut*, vaults it over most more expensive bottlings of Meursault itself. Don't miss it.

Not once, by the way, did the group of winemakers prefer a filtered bottling to its unfiltered version. In fact, in the older vintages, we often found the unfiltered white at a rather glorious peak of maturity, while the filtered version of the same wine was over-the-hill. Yet some (most recently James Halliday in *The Art and Science of Wine*) wish to frighten us by claiming that unfiltered wines are less stable. If over-the-hill is stable, I'll take instability.

$16.50 PER BOTTLE $179.20 PER CASE

1993 HERMITAGE
JEAN-LOUIS CHAVE

Thomas Jefferson is one of my heroes. On each bottle I quote him: "Good wine is a necessity of life for me." That is not what I call beating around the Bush.

Jefferson traveled the French wine route in 1787 and 1788. When he was in Beaune, he might have walked by my office. When he took the coach from Marseille to Toulon, he most certainly passed by on the road down the hill from my house. He kept a journal of his trips, trips totally wine oriented, in which he demonstrates quite clearly that he possessed a remarkable palate.

He was a wine importer and president. Hmm. What a compelling combination. (No, no way. I inhaled.) He purchased French wines for Presidents George Washington, John Adams, James Madison, and James Monroe. For example, he advised Washington to buy "*Monraché*, the best kind of white Burgundy." He

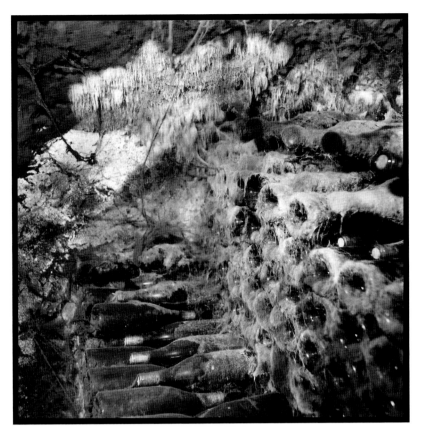

Chave's cellar

wrote to the Comte de Lur-Saluces directly, ordering 30 dozen bottles of Yquem for George Washington, and 10 dozen for himself. Those were the days! Where did we go wrong? Let's stop the film and run it back 200 years and figure out, where did we go wrong? Johnson (Vietnam), Nixon (Watergate *and* Vietnam), Carter (malaise), Reagan (-omics), Bush (league), William *Jefferson* Clinton (of all things). Who will be the next in line? Can't you just hear them campaigning? "No, I am not now nor have I ever tasted a Château d'Yquem, and if I had I wouldn't have swallowed."

Let's get back to Jefferson, please: Violinist. Harpsichordist. Author of the Declaration of Independence. Architect. Hermitage. Hermitage?

"Hermitage," Jefferson wrote. "This is one of the first wines of France. The white is much the best."

What is unclear is the white Hermitage remark. Is he saying white is better than red Hermitage, or is he declaring it the best white wine of France? We know he had an appetite for Montrachet and Yquem. To me it seems perfectly sound to place white Hermitage at the same level, but certainly not higher.

You, my clients, you purchase more red Hermitage than white. I always wonder why. Along with Jefferson, I consider Hermitage one of France's first reds.

But there are others, even nearby, like Cornas and Côte Rôtie. But in the world of great dry whites, after the top white Burgundies there is only Chave at the same level. And it is the single great white of southern France, so far. I would therefore expect you to buy more white than red.

Personally, I cellar twice more white than red Hermitage every year. And I wait on the white. I am patient, I can wait, yet I never seem to cellar enough. I am looking at my last bottles of 1974 and 1976, both of them in peak condition. Chave's is a white that ages dramatically and becomes much more than it was in its youth. The 1978 is still improving. It is the finest recent vintage for long aging, and I still have a decent supply as it opens up. I have not touched the six magnums. But the 1979? No white in my personal cellar has given me more pleasure over the years, and I must now face the cruel decision of when to open that last bottle. Since the beginning the 1979 has changed, of course, but it was never too young, never too old, a constant pleasure.

The 1993 has a nose of great purity. There is Marsanne honey to it, it is flowery, with a touch of anise and vanilla. Typical and classic, it is a great example of Chave's white.

His 1993 Hermitage *rouge* has a generous, irresistible, smoky nose, full of red fruits and that Syrah bacony aroma, and I think at this point it has the advantage of offering a lot of pleasure already, unlike the past several vintages. The 1988, 1989, 1990, 1991, and 1992 will not give the same pleasure until they have evolved longer in the bottle. Here is a vintage to help us keep our corkscrews out of them.

1993 Hermitage Rouge

$456.00 PER CASE

1993 Hermitage Blanc

$432.00 PER CASE

◇ ◇ ◇ ◇ ◇ ◇ ◇ ◇

1993 COTEAUX DU LANGUEDOC · CHÂTEAU DE LASCAUX

CHÂTEAU DE LASCAUX

1993

COTEAUX DU LANGUEDOC
APPELLATION COTEAUX DU LANGUEDOC CONTRÔLÉE
MIS EN BOUTEILLE AU CHÂTEAU
J.-B. CAVALIER
VIGNERON ELEVEUR · 34270 VACQUIÈRES · FRANCE

The Syrah of the northern Rhône has found a second home, and it is not in the southern Rhône, as everyone expected. In fact, it is such a flop around Gigondas and Châteauneuf-du-Pape that some growers are pulling it out. In my opinion, the second home of the true Syrah is around the mountain Pic Saint Loup in Languedoc. Those familiar with northern Rhônes can taste Château de Lascaux's 1993 and see why I say that. It has that ripe, smoky fruit that drives some of us to drink. There is a fullness but no roughness or bitterness. Everything is in place, balanced and fine. It has some of that Hermitage/Côte Rôtie raw game aroma (at least that is how the natives describe it). It is a bewitching, ravishing delight.

$8.95 PER BOTTLE $96.66 PER CASE

1992 BANDOL *ROUGE* "CABASSAOU" DOMAINE TEMPIER

SOMETIMES I WANT to say to hell with humility and let it all hang out. Me and Muhammad Ali. Forget the prissing around and just punch out the facts:

The greatest Chablis is Raveneau. *POW!*

Châteauneuf's tower of power is Vieux Télégraphe. Ka-*BOOM!*

Our Languedoc selections are the best value in the wine world today. Ker-BLAM!

The huge Champagne houses (factories) do not, cannot, and never will compete in taste with our estate-bottled Lassalle, Batiste, and Bara. Crrrunch! (Go ahead, sucker, throw your dough away on labels.)

Joguet? No one comes close.

Chave? Ka-Bam.

Clape? Ker-*SPLAT.*

See what I mean? Throw the gloves off. Drop the pretense. The truth and nothing but: Cabassaou is the finest expression of Mourvèdre the modern world has ever seen. Ker-*plooey!* Cabassaou! *Float like a butterfly, sting like a bee.* You want the best? Come and get it, wise guy. (Get smart with me and you'll be drinking your Mourvèdre with a knuckle sandwich.)

Just in case my uninhibited braggadocio is making you punch-drunk, I asked two objective sources to give me their tasting notes.

First, in the dark purple trunks, Jean-Marie Peyraud: "Lovely ripe cherry color. Fine and powerful aromas of *garrigue,* bay leaf, thyme, black currant, and blackberry. Good attack on the palate with a beautiful tannin/acid balance. Lots of fruit on the palate, and again I find cassis and blackberry. There is roundness and length. It is a wine you could enjoy already, but it should be superb in another five years."

And, in the dark purple trunks, François Peyraud: "Intense bluish purple color. Full deep aroma, rich in ripe fruits with a point of [illegible]. Palate rich, still quite youthful, but there is a certain roundness and fresh tannins—it is already good if you like this style, but it could wait another few years while it develops more complexity."

$29.95 PER BOTTLE $323.46 PER CASE

(This heavyweight is also available in magnums and jeroboams.)

MEET CHRISTEL FOUQUET

OUR NEWEST staff member is Christel Fouquet, but most of you will never meet her because she spends her time visiting and selling to restaurants. When I asked her to contribute to this brochure, she asked me to suggest a subject. Because Christel is French, I told her that our readers might be interested in hearing about the week she traveled with me in southern France, what it looked like through her eyes, the sight of an American importer buying in her native country. I must admit, I was curious, too. She wrote:

> *The first thing you notice traveling with Kermit is how in awe of him the French are. First, his accent is perfect. And then of course he is so handsome, and we French women cannot resist such a man; he is so debonair, like a young Maurice Chevalier. All the French women fall down when he flashes those deep, dark eyes on them, as if they are stricken by lightning . . .*

I said, No, Christel, that will never do because my readers might think you are only saying such things because I am your boss. They will wonder if you are really being objective. Try it again, but keep it on how I work, not personal stuff, and show me as I am, quirks and all, or it won't be credible when you do say something nice. She wrote:

> *In the old days Kermit Lynch might have ventured off the beaten path, hacking his way through the aboriginal forests of Chinon or the limestone swamps of Vouvray carrying only a backpack and sleeping bag, the first American to explore our bizarre little wines, what you call rotgut, that no one else wanted to buy, but now he has seen better days and he is just a fat cat who cannot wait to retire at the end of the day to his luxurious five-star hotel with TV and minibar. And nowadays of course he won't risk buying anything unless he's sure it will get high scores from . . .*

In fact, kidding aside, Christel did write something after visiting some domaines with me. I introduce now the real Christel Fouquet:

> *I am from the Cognac region. Just after leaving Opus One (where I worked for three years) and starting work for Kermit Lynch, I took a vacation and went back to France. I also spent four days in Bordeaux at VINEXPO, the big wine fair. What a change of pace I got when I met Kermit and discovered the wines of the Midi.*
>
> *Our tour took us through the country of the Romans, the Greeks, and the Cathars. It started in Arles when Kermit picked me up at the train station. By chance it was the day the* cigales *started singing this summer, so I really knew I was in Provence.*
>
> *It was fascinating to watch an American working with my countrymen. I enjoyed this unusual point of view. First, I expected a constant conflict between the chauvinistic French producer and the hard-headed American businessman.*

What a surprise when I realized that they mostly did business in the most casual, friendly way, going from one barrel to another, discussing the qualities, sharing opinions, and finally getting to the reservations. Where was the typical French arrogance? There they were, asking an American's opinion. It shocked me.

He has a way of telling them a wine could be better, or there is a problem, without being cruel or insulting. It is more like part of a quest they share. When he finds something he likes, the discussion turns more technical and he will turn to the bottling, to the fining, filtration, and, in white wines, the malolactic fermentation.

If the wines you like from KLWM are still alive and well in your glass, it is the result of hard work and long negotiation. Most producers today take filtration for granted and must be convinced not to do it. I could tell that with some it was an argument of years and years. That part is not easy. But everyone seemed intrigued by the subject, and most I met were ready to do what it takes to make the best wine they could.

I do remember one who finally said, "I know it would be better unfiltered, but my oenologist says it is not safe." Kermit asked him, "Who writes the check, me or your oenologist?"

Another asked for a letter signed by Kermit that promised he would pay for the wine if it dropped a sediment.

One day we went to taste at the Domaine du Vieux Télégraphe, where Kermit has bought for years. After Daniel Brunier gave me a tour and explained to me the details of his vinification, we had a beautiful tasting of the 1993 and 1994 vintages. Then we dined with the rest of the family at Henri Brunier's house. The conversation was so friendly that anybody walking in the door would have thought of a family dinner. That's what it was like! He is not just their importer anymore. I guess what I'm saying is that it surprised me to see respect and friendship where I expected to see confrontation.

I also thought that an importer represented certain wineries and sold what they had for sale. It surprised me, the intensity, how active the buying process can be. The trip changed the way I taste wine.

MICHEL GUÉRARD'S
CHÂTEAU DE BACHEN

ON ONE OF MY earliest trips to France I hit the town of Condom at lunchtime and happened upon a lively street fair. From one of the stalls I had a grilled sausage encased in a baguette (all right, a hot dog) and a glass of white wine that struck me as pretty decent for a wine purchased from a street booth, not to mention the screw cap. It was a wine called Tursan, and I learned that there was only one producer, a *cave cooperative*. I thought I'd better check it out because then as now decent cheap dry whites (what Richard Olney calls "mouth rinse") are hard to find. A fine palate demands perfection even from simple wines. So I drove out to the co-op and saw them filling plastic jugs from pumps with hoses and nozzles just like a gas station. Not for me, I decided, and hit the road again without even introducing myself. What a snob.

Years later I was in Margaux meeting with Bernard Ginestet about his translation of *Adventures on the Wine Route*. When he asked where I was headed afterwards, I said to the southwest, to taste the wines of Madiran. He told me to check

out a new winery owned by three-star chef Michel Guérard of Eugénie-les-Bains, because the first wines were quite intriguing. The wine: Tursan.

You see the parallels? From a street fair to a three-star gastronomic palace, *cave cooperative* to Guérard's breathtakingly beautiful Château de Bachen, from plonk to one of the greatest dry white wines of France, a gasoline nozzle to the gorgeous bottle, label, and capsule of the Bachen wines. This is a rags-to-riches story starring a wine.

What you will find inside the remarkable package Guérard has created is a white that compares in stature with the greatest the world has to offer, yet Bachen has certain advantages, including a comparatively reasonable price (for the moment), and a taste that is novel and singular. There are a lot of white Bordeaux, a lot of Chardonnays, etc., but no other white wine tastes like Guérard's Bachen. Everything about it, from start to finish, he accomplished with taste, style, and class. He hired American architect Patrick Dillon to design the *chai*, and it is worth a detour to visit next time you are in France, with its Greek and Roman touches, its perfect symmetry, its functional logic, and the beauty of the smallest details.

As you can see, Bachen is a great discovery, a characterful wine from a little-known grape variety, the Baroque (blended with Sémillon and Sauvignon), from a little-known *terroir*, Tursan. I hope you will try both cuvées to experience for yourself the excitement of discovering something new and wonderful.

1993 CHÂTEAU DE BACHEN

Lovely golden color. A touch of Sauvignon and a citronelle quality to the aroma that is characteristic. Fresh, lively, graceful, stimulating. This is a more forward, easier style than the more profound Baron de Bachen. In Burgundy, this would be the *premier cru*, and the Baron the *grand*.

$14.95 PER BOTTLE $161.46 PER CASE

1992 BARON DE BACHEN

Older vines; barrel fermented. Deeper color. Big, generous nose; full body. Complex, one-of-a-kind aroma with suggestions of passion fruit, ginger, citronelle again, honey, *pain d'épice.* The great achievement to me is the exotic quality you notice immediately, yet it is classically balanced and a model of finesse. It is, after all, the creation of a great chef who is used to combining ingredients to make a great dish.

$18.50 PER BOTTLE $199.80 PER CASE

SYRAH MASTERS
AUGUSTE CLAPE & GÉRARD CHAVE

1994 VIN DES AMIS · AUGUSTE CLAPE

A French wine writer by the name of Gérard Astier said that tasting Clape's wine gives him hallucinations. Hmm. And that you cannot describe a Clape Syrah without inventing words. (I find Clape's Syrah glibaciously pherique!) And Astier continues, "It is always good and it is always the year of the comet at Clape's place." And, "Clape must be a magician. He makes miracles on a daily basis." I think he likes it.

What a pleasure to bring you a bottle of pure Syrah from Auguste Clape at an ouchless price. If you don't snap this one up we will have you picking up debris at the edge of the freeway.

$9.95 PER BOTTLE $107.46 PER CASE

1994 SAINT-JOSEPH *ROUGE* · J.L. CHAVE

At first I could not have a case of the stuff. Then Chave visited Berkeley and loved his meal at Chez Panisse. Alice Waters and Stephen Singer then visited Chave and tasted his Saint-Joseph from his vineyard up behind Mauves. Chave then agreed to ship 1 barrel or 300 bottles or 25 cases per year, but I had to sell it all to Chez Panisse. Then he loosened up a bit more and shipped enough for Chez Panisse and for the crew of gastronautic guzzlers on the staff here at KLWM. And now there is enough to mention here. If you don't snap this one up we will sentence you to a preview tasting of 127 Australian Chardonnays.

Seriously now, what you should do is tell your favorite salesperson, "I want a few bottles of that Chave Saint-Joseph every year." That way we can keep a list and you will be notified of its arrival every year and you will be sure to have a bit.

$24.95 PER BOTTLE $269.46 PER CASE

° ° ° ° ° ° ° ° °

1994 CORBIÈRES "GRIS DE GRIS"
DOMAINE DE FONTSAINTE

This is the south, the sun-ripened fruits, the *garrigue*. Bring on the anchovies, the sardines, the oysters, the rosemary-scented grilled things, but above all this is hard to beat as an apéritif, a glass to precede the proceedings, a palate-fixer/pre-parer, an evening opener, a lovely rosé tinge upon one's outlook, a way to celebrate the division between day and night, a cold explosion of deliciousness upon a day-old palate, a toast to good health, a swallow of freshness . . .

$8.50 PER BOTTLE $91.80 PER CASE

1993 BOURGUEIL "CUVÉE LES GALICHETS"
VIEILLES VIGNES · PIERRE BRETON

For those who get satisfaction from appropriateness, get some now because the local name for the Cabernet Franc grape is *le Breton* and here it is vinified by Monsieur Breton. Oh, well. But I'll bet you would be impressed if I offered something from a Mr. Chardonnay.

I wonder what you will think of this one. My staff likes it, but they are not exactly representative. If someone who usually buys their wine from a super-market accidentally got ahold of it, their hair when they tasted it would prob-ably stand on end. Or even from looking at it. Some might call it opaque, some muddy.

Fifty-year-old vines. Gravelly hillside soil. *Culture biologique.* No SO_2 (La-pierre in Morgon gave Breton my phone number). Barrel aged. No filtration. In-tense wild berry sappiness. *Fraise de bois* and cassis. Good tannic bite (ouch!). Wiry, lean, promising. In two or three years I think it is going to explode (in the good sense, of course).

$13.95 PER BOTTLE $150.66 PER CASE

1993 SAINT-CHINIAN *ROUGE* · MAS CHAMPART

This year before I saw Isabelle and Mathieu Champart, partners in wine, I spoke with Bruce Neyers, our national sales director. He told me I should reserve more Mas Champart this year, three or four times more than we have been buying, be-cause their wines sell out so quickly. I told him that I buy every case they offer to me. Theirs is a small cellar. They don't make much wine.

Then when I visited them we took a tour of their vineyards, scattered little parcels in the rugged hills above Saint-Chinian. Isabelle pointed to one plot of Grenache and said, "That is ours but we sell the grapes to the *cave cooperative*."

Wow, I thought, not only will we be able to have more Mas Champart, but bottling all of the production will be much more profitable to them. Everyone will be better off except the co-op.

Lunching outside their front door under an olive tree, I proposed that they stop selling any of their grapes, that I could handle a much larger quantity if more were available.

Isabelle looked troubled. They stared at each other, communicating with their eyes for a long moment.

"But then, Kermit," she said finally, "the quality would not be the same. We are using only our best grapes for our own wine."

It is easy to get cynical these days. Here, however, is the product of a couple who could make more money but they prefer a profit of pride, pride in what they do and what they sell and what, hopefully, you will enjoy drinking.

$9.95 PER BOTTLE $107.46 PER CASE

FATHER-IN-LAW

By Jim Harrison

THROUGHOUT LITERATURE (and lower forms of entertainment) the Father of the Bride is an object of just ridicule, a ditherer with a hopefully ample wallet sweating on the sidelines while people actually competent in such matters orchestrate the wedding.

I recently proved to be no exception whatsoever during the marriage of my younger daughter, Anne, to Matt Kapsner in Livingston, Montana. I had no part in any of the central decisions that made the several-day party implacably smooth except in the area of food and wine, and even in the matter of food I deferred somewhat to my older daughter, Jamie, now a novelist, but formerly an employee of Dean and DeLuca in New York City. I was mostly the not very tiny voice yelling "more" and more we had including crab and shrimp from Charles Morgan's company in Destin, Florida, bread and cheeses from Zingerman's in Ann Arbor, Michigan, including Grafton Cheddar, Comté, Papillon Roquefort, triple crème l'explorateur, Vermont mountain cheese, Stilton, also roasted Italian olives. I almost forgot Dunn's Irish salmon, patés including splendid wild mushroom loaf. I also almost forgot the oysters and the actually *prime* Delmonico roasts, the Norwegian poached salmon, the two hundred pieces of duck confit made by the chef Mark Glass. There were about a hundred in for dinner and another 50 came along later.

Somehow they drank 19 cases of wine, not to speak of eating all the food. Years ago while cooking beef ribs at his house Jack Nicholson told me that "only in the Midwest is overeating still considered an act of heroism." We'll have to throw in Montana, too. Of course, drinking a lot is *de rigueur* at weddings except in the dourest confines of yuppiedom.

Since it was my sole delegated responsibility I gave the wine my full, somewhat manic, attention, testing 20 or so Côtes du Rhônes over a year's time in case lots, before settling on a Sablet *blanc* and Bandol for the red. I'm very good at this sort of testing compared to my miserable college years; my pratfalls in the arenas of the novel and movie making. The Sablet is quite wonderful though I drink very little white wine. The Bandol decision was easy, as I had been drinking and serving it for years. I rather like this sturdy, suggestive red with everything, and often with nothing at all. It invariably has made me happy, recalling as it does the primal flavors of sun and earth, rather than lightbulbs and supermarkets. It is also affordable if you can withstand the usual nagging of your accountant. Whenever life begins to crush me I know I can rely on Bandol, garlic, and Mozart. It will also be served in vast quantities at my funeral. This opinion was obviously shared by those at the wedding, the legion of the hollow-legged. I salute the Domaine Tempier for this pleasure which in geologic time is no more evanescent than life herself.

❖ 1996 ❖

COLLIOURE

THE BURNING question of my generation today is, Is falling in love possible after 50? Or are the arteries to the heart clogged and the outlook too jaded to feel the thrill again? After more than 50 trips to France I have fallen in love with Collioure, the ancient seaport located a few minutes from the Spanish border where the Pyrénées meet the blue Mediterranean. (What, you were expecting something more risqué? This is wine propaganda, not a tell-all.)

Dramatically beautiful from afar and close up, Collioure's only rival on the French coast is Cassis, near Marseille. Collioure is different, however, because the old town is closed off to cars, and what a relief that is, what a positive impact that has on the sights, sounds, and smells (no exhaust fumes!). And different from Cassis because this is not Provence, this is Catalonia. Not France, exactly, not Spain, no, this is Catalonia and the Catalan flavor is in the air, in the cuisine (lots of roasted peppers and local anchovies), and in the wine. Wine, of course, is what

Collioure

takes me to Collioure. Those parts of France without vineyards, well, I am not so familiar with them. Now, for next year's family vacation, I am trying to find an apartment to rent on one of Collioure's colorful, narrow streets, because two days in a hotel room is not enough.

The wine I buy there is produced by a very likable couple, Christine Campadieu and Vincent Cantié. I asked Christine to give me some inside info on her village for my next visit, and for those of you who might be tempted to check it out. She wrote:

> *For us, life in Collioure is separated into two main seasons.*
>
> *There is winter, when the village reveals its true dimensions, rediscovers its true character again while its touristic side is sleeping. This is the season in which we fully savor its Mediterranean character, gentle and violent at once, with the blowing mistral we call the Tramontagne, which sculpts our mountains, agitates our sea, and whips through our olive trees, leaving the entire countryside a shimmering silver shade. It is also in winter that the grapevines lose their foliage, exposing the*

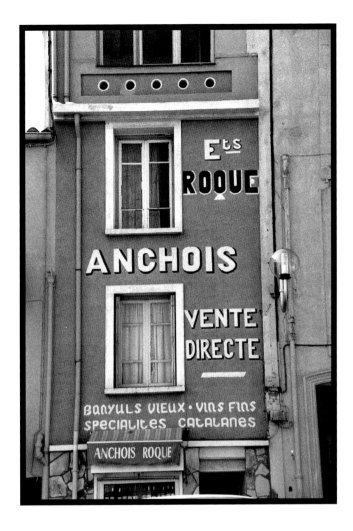

ancient dry rock walls and terraces. All at once the mountainsides, which tower up into the heavens, appear to have been finely sculpted by the backbreaking labor of our anonymous and courageous ancestors. We gather wild asparagus in March, then thyme in April while watching the flowering of the almond trees and the fragrant, bright yellow genet.

In summer everything seems crushed by the fierce Mediterranean sunshine. The contrast with winter is vivid. We desert the mountains and turn toward the sea. It is a season when we are no longer alone, and our rhythm of life is modified. We seek relief from the heat by setting a schedule for all activities, opening and closing the shutters in order to preserve the coolness of our Catalan houses for as long as possible, a dip in the Mediterranean (not far from anybody's doorstep) in the morning or late in the evening, because we natives avoid the broiling midday sun, then in the shadows of the afternoon we reopen our shops and businesses.

For all the above reasons, we have our own addresses, our own discoveries, places where we feel at ease and in harmony with each season.

In the winter we reserve a cozy booth at the Cave Arago, where chef Claude

Chazaud prepares fresh seafood dishes in the Spanish tapas style, accompanied by a judicious selection of local wines. Another favorite is the café-restaurant Les Templiers, which is decorated floor to ceiling (even in the upstairs hotel rooms) with paintings. The proprietor's friendship with famous and not-so-famous artists has contributed to make this bistro irresistible in any season.

In the summer we follow the narrow esplanade behind the church, which runs along the shore at the foot of the cliffs, to the little beach named L'Ouille. There, our favorite address (and again, little known) is called L'Imprévu. It is an open-air café on the water's edge where Richard Rimbau serves with much simplicity and authenticity fresh grilled sardines and an unforgettable gratin of mussels in Banyuls wine. I like to think that Hemingway would have felt at home here. Nothing is more beautiful after a dip in the sea and a wonderful meal than the walk back to Collioure, fifteen minutes along the seaside, and the sudden view of the medieval village with its unusual church built out over the water, and the massive yet harmonious structure of the ancient stone Château des Rois de Majorque, which juts out into the harbor and cuts the village in two.

Collioure is a place full of history where casual strolling is the best way to get around. Each stone seems marked by the past, sometimes humorously, like the inscription engraved above the church door that reads Liberté Egalité Fraternité, showing us a glimpse of the French republic's political agenda even on the door of a holy place.

Collioure is the birthplace of Fauvism, and since the time of Matisse and Derain generations of artists have set up their easels under the famous bell tower, endlessly duplicating the beautiful scene.

We have three current painters who remain dear to my heart. They have never faltered and they remain faithful to their original talent. The first, "Marco," seems to have landed in the wrong era. Using Chinese inks and watercolors, his finely detailed images in the 18th-century style are worthy of Hubert Robert. The second is an American, or was an American, because he has become an indispensable Colliourian. Kenneth Snodgrass paints abstracts in lovely pastel colors, never renouncing his native artistic influences, but he has imbued them with a feeling truly Mediterranean.

If these first two are easy to find in Collioure, the third hides himself. You've got to search for him in his delicious maison de pecheur (fisherman's house) in the charming quarter above the church called "Moré." When Charles Devarennes isn't busy sprucing up his little Catalan barque on the beach, checking out the evolution of his three barrels of wine, or harvesting his almond trees, he paints. Often he paints flowers or female sunbathers in the impressionist style, impressionist in the original sense of the term.

To profit from all these people who are the soul of present-day Collioure, you must take your time, have patience, and stop here in the off-season when the doors are left partly open . . .

CHRISTINE CAMPADIEU, WINEMAKER AT COLLIOURE, OCTOBER 15, 1995

Hello. It's me again. I guess the only thing left is for you to call your travel agent and for me to explain what a Collioure wine is and why you should buy one (apart from affording me an ascetic excuse for returning to my heartthrob).

The vineyards look like Côte Rôtie swollen to mammoth proportions. If you share my conviction that steep hillside vines make the best wine, you'll get a delicious sense of vertigo here. That broiling sun which Christine tries to avoid does not hurt the ripening process at all. Imagine a little touch of Bandol, a little remembrance of Côte Rôtie, but don't forget the Catalan accent.

At Domaine La Tour Vieille the varieties are Grenache, Mourvèdre, Carignan, and Syrah. The red is unctuous with a spicy, peppery aroma. Vincent says it comes into its own after three to four years in bottle.

There is also a *vin doux naturel*, appellation Banyuls, which is delicious served cool as an apéritif, shows brilliantly with blue cheeses, and works wonders when sipped with chocolate desserts.

You are invited to taste both wines with Christine and Vincent in person on Saturday, January 13, from 11:00 to 5:00, here at the shop.

DOMAINE DU POUJOL

Robert Cripps says he was bitten early by the wine bug while growing up in Oxford, England. He moved to California and worked with Saintsbury, Carneros Creek, Murphy-Goode, and Peter Michael. He also met Kim, a native Californian who was working in the wine business in the Napa Valley, and he proceeded to marry her. Amongst other things, they remember their enthusiasm tasting through a Languedoc sampler they purchased here at the shop.

In 1993 they moved to Burgundy, where Robert spent some valuable time working for Jean-Marc Roulot and Méo-Camuzet, and they began to dream of a place of their own. My office in Beaune got them in contact with Sylvain Fadat of the Domaine d'Aupilhac in the Languedoc. "His enthusiasm can be quite infectious," says Robert, and they began to consider buying a vineyard of their own in the Languedoc.

Almost too immediately they had a chance to buy the 50-acre Domaine du Poujol near Montpellier. With a courage I find remarkable, they jumped at the chance, just as the 1994 grapes were ready to harvest: Syrah, Grenache, Cinsault, Carignan, Merlot, and a little Carignan Blanc. Aiming to produce an interesting dry white, they are grafting some vines over to Rolle and Roussanne. The terrain includes some promising, well-exposed stony slopes.

Then, just three weeks ago, FLASH, EXTRA, READ ALL ABOUT IT, I grabbed the phone and called Robert and Kim because I was reading *Passions: The Wines and Travels of Thomas Jefferson*, by James M. Gabler. I had imagined I would be the first American to import the Domaine du Poujol, but no, there is evidence that Thomas Jefferson beat me to it! See page 107 in Gabler's fascinating book. (We stock it at $29.95.)

Robert's ambition is "to express in our wines both the domaine's French *terroir* and our California experience."

Well, I fell for their tasty first vintage, which you can purchase now or wait and taste with them when they visit the shop on Saturday, February 24. Note the date. It should be fun. They make French wine but speak English *and* American, so there will be no language problem.

1994 Vin de Pays de l'Hérault Rouge

$7.95 PER BOTTLE $85.86 PER CASE

1994 Coteaux du Languedoc Rouge

$9.95 PER BOTTLE $107.46 PER CASE

THE WORDS AND WINES OF
ANDRÉ OSTERTAG

ALAS, I BARELY have any memory of my previous lives, and although I am willing to bet that I was an innkeeper, a drunkard, or at least your common wine drinker, as much as I search my memory I cannot recall what wine tasted like back then.

Luckily, yet too rarely, I have at times had the opportunity to lower my nose into a glass of old Burgundy from the beginning of the century or a pre-war Alsatian wine, but each time a romantic dizziness swept me away from objective analysis.

One thing is certain, the wines of yesteryear have the power to set our spirits afire. Their rarity, their glorious age, and the weight of history, command our respect and impel us toward contemplation. Such tastings are always stamped by an almost religious emotion. And even if it should happen that such a wine shows a flaw or two, the emotion felt when drinking them renders the experience unique and unforgettable. Thus they will always seem superior to today's wines.

Nevertheless, wine has never been so intelligent as it is today. Our engineers, oenologists, and technicians of all varieties have made possible a spectacular leap in quality. Actually, good wine will soon become an everyday beverage found in bars, bistros, and shopping carts. Quality has democratized itself so much that Saint Marketing, who never ignores our weaknesses and who anticipates our desires, has finally cut us short of any sense of surprise. It is horrible to say it, but quality has become banal!

Above all, this kind of quality is a reflection of technical advances and consumer fads. However, true quality is that which succeeds in surprising and moving us. It is not locked inside a formula. Its essence is subtle (subjective) and never rational. It resides in the unique, the singular, but it is ultimately connected to something more universal. A great wine is one in which quality is contained. Such a wine will necessarily be uncommon and decidedly unique because it cannot be like any other, and because of this fact it will be atypical, or only typical of itself.

Modern man, in his eagerness to understand everything in order to master it, spends his time classifying, filing, and organizing. It is obvious that the indefinable, the unclassifiable, and the unusual confuse our modern thought processes. So it should come as no surprise that the notion of *terroir* suffers while the grape variety gains importance, or that the "commercially correct" spectrum of aromas is confined to the fresh, easy, and simple to the detriment of more unusual aromas (mineral notes, lees, and so on).

Today the definition of a quality wine is one that should give equal pleasure at any moment, night or day, from one's cradle to one's deathbed. As if wine were nothing but a vulgar consumer object, sleek and docile, a little pet devoted to not disturbing our moods or classifications. However, it seems to me that in the old days wine was more capricious, more erratic, no doubt, yet its personality was more pronounced. There were no clonal selections. Each plot of vines represented a variety of different rootstocks. A wine bore more than now the imprint of its vintage, because weather conditions and their direct consequences on a wine were less easy to remedy by treating the vines or correcting later in the cellar laboratory.

However, the real change took place above all in the relationship or exchange between man, his vines, and his wine. Before, a winemaker had to maintain an intimate, direct rapport with the elements. He had to link himself to things, allow them to become a living part of himself, to penetrate his soul, his gut, in order to feel and understand them.

Had he any other choice? There was no protection against disease or pests in the vineyard. No oenology lab, no research centers. Only the winemaker himself held the key to "*Le Grand Vin*." When scientific knowledge and technology are limited, our senses of observation, intuition, and sensitivity, all of which make up our subjective thought processes, are heightened.

In the old days the wine producer had few resources with which to defend himself against nature. He had to figure out how to come to terms with her.

ANDRÉ OSTERTAG

If I were to read something like that, I would want to taste the man's wine to see where such thoughtfulness led him. And I did. And now you can, too. "Wines that surprise and move us," as he says. This shipment marks the beginning of our collaboration with André Ostertag. You won't be bored.

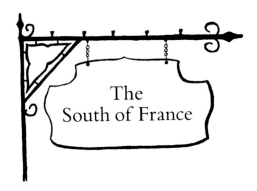

The
South of France

RARE
SOUTHERN WHITES

1994 CHÂTEAUNEUF-DU-PAPE *BLANC*
DOMAINE DU VIEUX TÉLÉGRAPHE

Wine as a time machine? I may have been under the influence of seeing *Twelve Monkeys*, but one sniff of this white Châteauneuf transported me back in time, before marriage, before kids, one warm springtime morning when I took a walk through the countryside in Provence with a lovely companion. Wildflowers, underbrush, yellow genet, the baked earth, and there is a little honey-like touch . . . leave the bottle open and bees will come buzzing around. The birds and the bees?

On the palate there is a sumptuous fullness, then the dry, austere, gunflint kicks in at the finish. As lush as it is, you will marvel at the delicacy of its aromas and their unfolding complexity. As you come back for more, there is always something new emerging in this bouquet.

Food! Tasting the wine with the staff, it inspired everyone to start calling out what they wanted with it: crab, calamari, cioppino, grilled fish, bouillabaisse . . .

$27.50 PER BOTTLE $297.00 PER CASE

1993 COTEAUX DU CAP CORSE "BLANC DE BLANCS"
CLOS NICROSI

In Provence one speaks of the *garrigue*. On the island of Corsica, it is the *maquis*, which my dictionary defines without a whiff of evocativeness as "Corsican brush." Like the *garrigue*, the *maquis* exudes aroma, and that aroma is in Nicrosi's great white. Don't ask me how this occurs. Just be thankful for it. Waverly Root described the aroma of the *maquis* as a "dry wilderness of hardy shrubs—arbutus, thorn, myrtle, juniper, heather, wild mint, and asphodel, the flower of hell." (Now some of you will probably want a full case.) Root continues, "The fragrance from these plants is so pronounced that it can often be smelled from sea as boats approach the island."

The wine (a dry white) also has a whisper of lemon/lime and of the juicy little golden plum called *Reine Claude.*

It has an elegant rusticity. It develops aromatically with bottle age. It is the world's finest expression of the Rolle grape.

$21.50 PER BOTTLE $232.20 PER CASE

°   °   °   °   °   °   °   °

1995 CÔTES DU RHÔNE *BLANC*
CHÂTEAU DU TRIGNON

Every time a vintage of his white catches on here, Pascal Roux of Trignon is sold out when I try to reorder, because he has no trouble selling his white in Europe. One day, though, he asked why we Americans buy such a high proportion of red compared to his white Côtes du Rhône.

His question was hard to answer. First, how do you explain to a Frenchman, especially one from the Rhône, the American craze for Chardonnay? Explain, that is, without making him think we are a nation of sheep that prefers monotony to diversity?

Secondly, how do I tell him that a lot of white Rhônes are so flat and flabby that they prejudice us? It is like the Beaujolais story. So many deserve to remain unbought, it scares us away. Once burned, twice shy.

And thirdly, citing the two reasons above makes me feel like I am shifting blame away from myself, because it is my job to explain to my clients why they should try certain wines, especially wines that are not on the Hit Parade.

Here is why. White wine dishes are sometimes adorned with garlic, olive oil, tomatoes, Provençal herbs, etc., the Mediterranean approach. Well, good dry white wines to accompany Mediterranean cuisine are hard to find. Chardonnay does not work. Sauvignon Blanc does not work. Forget Chenin Blanc, Riesling, and Gewurztraminer. Think regionally. Mediterranean wines with Mediterranean cuisine.

Trignon's white works. It is tasty, fresh, and possesses *élan.* It even smells good.

$8.95 PER BOTTLE $96.66 PER CASE

1994 TERRET *BLANC*
DOMAINE DE LA DONE

A simple little dry white. Good mouth rinse.

$5.95 PER BOTTLE $64.26 PER CASE

(P.S. When I tasted this in France I thought, My God, for the price this isn't bad at all, and everything else in the same range is flawed rotgut or rotmouth or throat pain, so I ordered a bunch of it and then like a nightmare I realized that no one knows what a Terret is, even whether it is white or red or dry or sweet, and how will I sell it now that I've got it. So I

decided to score it 92. Then I humbly thought, no, well, maybe 91. Then I tasted it with a pumpkin-fennel soup and wanted to give it a 96. Then I had this bizarre urge to give it a 97.778. Oh hell, I thought, why not round it off to 100 and sell it all in a day? But then I realized that no one would believe me and at my age I do not need a credibility gap. "Mouth rinse" avoids any credibility gap. Some people only want to drink wines that provide a mind-boggling, quasi-orgasmic Experience, but for those of you who know what I mean by mouth rinse, here's a good one.)

SOMEONE, PLEASE, OPEN A GOOD WINE BAR

MY FAVORITE is in Venice, but that's a long way to go to enjoy a snack and a glass of Prosecco.

You see, I don't want one of those TASTING bars where real connoisseurs sniff and judge and concentrate and compare and even take notes.

At Do Mori you eat and drink because it is fun and delicious. There is a short selection of reasonably priced wines by the glass; they don't even list the producers. You leave it to them to come up with drinkable wines, and they do.

Them. We might need them if we are to have the perfect wine bar, because they are masters of their métier. There are only two of them, yet I have seen them work the bar competently with 40 or 50 crowded into their small space. They can handle it. In other words, your glass is never empty too long.

Venetians love Prosecco and so do I, at least for starters. It is light, dry, and mildly sparkling. With rather neutral flavors, it gives a pleasant little zing. And with a glass of it, why not a saucer of fresh, marinated anchovy filets?

Yes, there is food. Sorry, no tables or chairs or waiters. You simply point at whatever looks good in the display cases (all is prepared in advance), and it is handed to you over the counter: octopus, sardines, shrimp, an assortment of Venetian white bread sandwiches called *Tramezino*, also marinated vegetables like artichoke hearts, eggplant, sun-dried tomatoes, and delicious prosciutto and salami. Bliss consciousness! And I cannot resist their garlicky salt cod purée.

The ambiance? Well, it is the sort of place where people stamp out their cigarettes on the floor, so I guess it would never work here. And when you leave, one of the barmen ponders a second or two before telling you what you owe. No bill, no cash register tape, so I guess it would never work here. I don't think they add it up item by item, even in their heads. They just decide, oh, all that must cost about such and such. And I'll bet the locals pay less than I do. I'm suspicious, but I DON'T CARE. Take me, I'm yours. Totaling things up precisely for everyone wouldn't give them time to keep the glasses full. And I do hate the sound of cash registers. (We have none, have you noticed?)

I wish I could import the whole place and the two talents who run it.

(Do Mori, 429 San Polo, Venice, Italy.)

CONFESSIONS OF A WATER DRINKER

By Wendell Berry

I HAD BETTER BEGIN by saying that I am primarily a water drinker. There are many pleasures in drinking water, the chief of which are to be found in a thermos jug, well-iced, when you're working outdoors on a hot day. But I don't mean just any water. I mean water with character and clarity, unmedicated, from a familiar source. For me, one of the happinesses of homecoming is a drink from my own cistern. Likewise, I love to drink the milk of a Jersey cow with whom I am personally acquainted.

Probably I will never become as much a connoisseur of wine as I am of drinking water and cow's milk, but I do take pleasure in good wine. As soon as you realize that some wines are better than others, you have the possibility of pleasure that you can think about, before and after. My own thoughts about wine improved a great deal after I read Kermit Lynch's *Adventures on the Wine Route*. All of a sudden, I saw much clearer than I had before how my interest in wine could be accommodated to my interest in good agriculture. *Adventures on the Wine Route* is, among other things, a fine book on agriculture. One of the best, really, for its interest is in the way the quality of place and soil and work are communicated to the quality of the final product. When these qualitative linkages are intact and are known, the result is a kind of trust that increases pleasure. Drinking wine from a good little vineyard such as Kermit describes and patronizes is like eating vegetables from a fertile, familiar garden, or lamb from the flock of an excellent shepherd whom you know. The immediate pleasure of taste is enlarged and enhanced by the pleasure that one takes in the life of the world and the husbandry of the soil.

An example of what I mean was in one of the recent Kermit Lynch catalogues. Kermit, visiting Isabelle and Mathieu Champart, discovered that they were selling some of their grapes. And then the following exchange took place:

> *I proposed that they stop selling any of their grapes, that I could handle a much larger quantity of their Saint-Chinian wine if more were available.*
>
> *Isabelle looked troubled . . .*
>
> *"But then, Kermit," she said finally, "the quality would not be the same. We are using only our best grapes for our own wine."*

Well, immediately I wanted to try a bottle of Saint-Chinian. Trust and a certain pleasure were already in place. I was ready to take a chance on the quality.

❦ ❦ ❦ ❦ ❦ ❦ ❦ ❦

1994 MONTPEYROUX · DOMAINE D'AUPILHAC

Someday when the wines of the Languedoc are better known, the vineyard of Montpeyroux will be rated one of the best for Syrah and Mourvèdre. Ironically, 20 prime acres of steep hillside with ancient stone terraces under the ruins of an old walled fortress are today not even planted in vines. Sylvain Fadat at Domaine d'Aupilhac would love to add the acreage to his small holdings, but he is too broke to purchase any of it.

His 1994 is the sort of wine I find myself calling a dark beauty. It is the biggest, chewiest wine he has produced so far. The aroma is reminiscent of a Côte Rôtie/Bandol blend. The palate is rich and tannic. I have been aging Fadat's Montpeyroux beginning with the 1989. It improves with time in the sense that it gains finesse and focus, but those who like it wild and wooly can drink it now.

$12.50 PER BOTTLE $135.00 PER CASE

THE TWIN PEAKS OF CORNAS

RECENTLY I had a totally satisfying meal at Willi's Wine Bar in Paris. Simple French cooking, excellent choice of wines, nice people, English spoken if you like. And at the bar I had the pleasure of sitting next to John Livingstone-Learmonth, who authored one of my favorite books, *The Wines of the Rhône* (a thicker, newly revised edition is available right here). It must be his name, but I always had it in my mind that Livingstone-Learmonth must be a craggy-faced octogenarian surveying the rest of us petty creatures from vast equatorial heights. Well, there is not a crag or a dent on him, he is not nearly as old as I am, and an easy-going, good-looking, straightforward chap at that. All wine bars could use one.

Noël Verset's cellar, Cornas

As you can imagine, two of the world's greatest Rhône fanatics meeting like that, we found one thing or another to chat about, and one of the subjects was: Isn't it a miracle that wines like the Corni of Clape and Noël Verset still exist?

In fact, in his book, Livingstone-Learmonth (to his face I called him John, which shortened our conversation appreciably) describes Noël Verset's Cornas as "very much the black strap wine of yore," and in another place he calls it "full-blooded," which I think is quite the good choice of word for Verset's vital, sapid, splendidly colored wine.

The twin peaks of Cornas: Clape and Verset. You really can taste the fact that their wines were "eked out" of a roasted, steep, granite hillside. Twin peaks because Verset has the finest vineyard and Clape is the most talented winemaker in the appellation. Those who cellar Clape and Verset each year drink well, I promise you that. I cannot comprehend *not* cellaring them.

1994 seems a perfect vintage.

NEW BURGUNDY ARRIVALS

1994 CHIROUBLES
DOMAINE MARQUIS DES PONTHEUX

Last November Bernard Diochon of Moulin-à-Vent fame guided me through the vineyards and cellars of the Beaujolais. Bernard is a bit of a hunk, with a thick, brushy mustache. He could model for those colorful postcards from the Beaujolais in which men and women find more to do in the vines and vats than just make wine.

I met some real characters that day, including a retired bicyclist (yes, in France that can be a profession) who now makes Beaujolais in his smelly racing shirt, yet whose new wine had a wild and fabulous black currant aroma. Already, however, during our visit, he was in the midst of *pre*-filtering (That's when you filter before you filter!). Diochon and I left shaking our heads. All the good was going, going, gone, just one month after the wine had been born.

At Chiroubles, however, I found a beauty, a wine totally different from Diochon's Moulin-à-Vent and our other Beaujolais *crus*. The domaine, the vineyard, all of it was the sort of place I tend to fall for: steep hillside, southern exposure, old vines, raised in *foudre*, bottled unfiltered by gravity flow.

The style is low-key, cool, reflective, unusually refined and classy. Cuvée *Deneuve*, as in *Catherine*. So taste a new addition to our Beaujolais list, this one a lovely combination of charm, deliciousness, and elegance.

1994 BOURGOGNE *ROUGE* "LA DIGOINE"
A. & P. DE VILLAINE

Here is a red Burgundy whose price, quality, and style will make it useful to you often. Fine and aromatic, medium-bodied, it is the sort of wine that works perfectly with, for example, a simple roast chicken. It also serves well at cellar temperature for luncheons and light dinners. It is not the kind of Burgundy that demands haute cuisine: bring on some sausages and boiled potatoes.

A beautiful progression, by the way, when you've enough people, is to commence with the Chiroubles (see above), then move on to de Villaine's La Digoine, and finish with a Gevrey-Chambertin, for example. You travel from one end of Burgundy to another (south to north), you go from lighter to chewier, but more importantly, you will get a view of the hierarchical nature of the Burgundy appellations, which accounts for a large part of Burgundy's pleasure and fascination.

One could do the same sort of progression musically. Listen first, for example, to Haydn's Symphony no. 99 (hopefully the old Beecham recording), then on to Mozart's no. 40 (lower numbers do not indicate inferior symphonies), and finish with a thunderous turn-me-up version of Beethoven's Fifth.

CLUES FOR THE FUTURE,
WHEN OUR PRESENT IS PAST

NATURE MAGAZINE reports that archeologists recently found ancient pottery containing wine residue, which proves that our ancestors were enjoying wine as early as 5400 B.C.

In one report a scientist is quoted as saying of this discovery, "It's possible this will be the earliest that will ever be found." Wait a minute. Doesn't it seem just as reasonable to say that this will *not* be the earliest ever found?

And what if wine predates mankind? It could. Imagine a wild vine with clusters of ripe grapes, and along comes Stegosaurus, who crushes them underfoot. The grape juice collects in a fissure in the rock, wild yeasts attack, and for a short time (before it turns to vinegar) wine exists.

"Earliest that will ever be found . . ." Bah, humbug. They call that science? I want my money back.

On a less grumpy note, one startling aspect of the discovery was the lack of a government health warning on the pottery containing the residue. After at least 7,400 years of wine drinking, it was our own relatively freely elected government that first required health warnings on a container of fermented grape juice. About time, right? Thank you, D.C. And to be objective, throughout history (excepting our current generation) everybody who consumed wine died, proving to some (like the scientist quoted above?) the plausibility of our government's requirements.

However, it must be said in wine's defense that despite drinking it, mankind itself is still alive, and probably enjoyed a giggle or two along the way.

Now, to return to one of my favorite themes, I would like to point out that what the archeologists found was residue. Sediment. In other words, if that wine had been filtered, we would not know that wine existed 7,400 years ago. We owe it to future generations to leave our own traces, our own little purple deposits, in order to ensure employment for future archeologists. Just one more reason for reasonable people everywhere to keep shopping at KLWM.

◊ ◊ ◊ ◊ ◊ ◊ ◊ ◊

CHAMPAGNE "BLANC DE BLANCS"
BATISTE-PERTOIS

With his 1992 Côte Rôtie we say good-bye to Marius Gentaz, and with these last 45 cases we say good-bye to Batiste-Pertois. In the new French style, the government has told them both that if they do not retire they will lose their rights to their social security. So in fact, it is not *their* social security after all, even though they paid into it all their lives. It is the government's, to use as it pleases to affect policy. The whole thing stinks. (Winemakers with children to take over can arrange things differently, by the way.) Can it happen here?

Gentaz survived on five acres of Côte Rôtie.

Batiste survived on 10 acres of 100% *premier cru* vines at Cramant.

What nasty threats to France's economic order! Kick them out. Fight unemployment. Make room for the young. Forget about what Kermit Lynch likes to drink.

Where will I find another in Champagne like Batiste, someone who abhors SO_2, who raises his Champagne in oak casks, who never filters or fines or cold stabilizes or pasteurizes this and neutralizes that . . . You would be amazed at some of the wine-making recipes in the big Champagne houses.

A dying breed. Gentaz and Batiste. Two irreplaceable jewels. I will cellar a bunch of each to enjoy over several years, and with each bottle uncorked make a toast to a concept called Government *for* the people, not people for the government.

1992 CRU BARRÉJATS · SAUTERNES

Listen, pal, I know what you're thinking right about now. You're looking at that vintage year and thinking that sly old devil of a wine merchant is trying to hoodwink one over on you, right? A Sauternes, vintage 1992, the worst year in the human race? Sure, here, Lynch, take my money, I don't need it.

But don't jump to conclusions right off the bat. This Sauternes, it's the straight stuff, rotten to the core.

Yeah, sure, I'm hip to the rap on the '92s. At Yquem they don't even want to talk about it. But what the hey, everyone's got some skeletons in their closet, wherever, secret-type things they don't want nobody to see. I'll bet you a fiver I got things I'm not proud of, too.

But wait, this wine is thick, and that rot, you know, it's the good rot, the kind that sends people off to do weird things.

Lemme put it this way. Don't you think Lynch knows that you don't even want to hear about a 1992 Sauternes, that it is the last thing you would ever even think of buying, even on your deathbed? He probably tried not to buy any of the stuff himself. He probably kept telling himself, "No, no, don't do it, not a 1992," and *bam*, the sucker goes ahead and can't help it, you know, like some guys are with some dolls, where they know they shouldn't, they know they're gonna get burned but they keep looking at the doll and she looks too good to be true and they go for it and then the next thing you know they're crawling around some dark alley with nothing on crying for their mama to help them.

Some guys are suckers for beauty. That's what this comes down to.

1995 MERLOT · DOMAINE SAINTE BRUNE

During my absence a spy took shorthand notes of my staff while they tasted the new Domaine Sainte Brune Merlot. And I quote:

SL: It's richer than the '94.

MB: Jesus, this smells great.

EC: He must have sold his soul to the devil to make this.

MG: Cigar box, tea leaf, deep, dark color.

MB: Mouth-filling, long, complete.

SL: It's thick, really.

MG: There's definitely a southern influence on the nose.

SL: But it has very elegant tannins.

MB: Soft, round, voluptuous, perfect.

GB: Complex.

MG: Bodacious.

EC: Larruping.

SL: I like that word, larruping.

EC: It's a word my grandmother used.

RK: What does it mean?

EC: I don't know. Darn good, doggone good, incredibly something. Like larruping good biscuits.

GB: That reminds me of a little Fronsac I once knew, a long, long time ago.

$6.95 PER FIFTH $75.06 PER CASE

CHAMPAGNE LASSALLE

You can have too much champagne but you can never have enough.

ELMER RICE

He behaved invariably as we would after a lot of champagne: light, capable, and happy. SIGMUND FREUD

The great thing about drinking Champagne is that you don't get a beer gut from it. VICTOR UBOGU (ENGLISH RUGBY TEAM)

Everybody ends up buying Champagne in December, often at the very last minute, requiring a dash into some liquor store to pay a fortune for one of the name brands.

Madame Lassalle lapsed into a state of shock when I informed her of this situation. "You mean," she said, "instead of buying Champagne Lassalle?"

So she and I cooked up a special price to entice you.

1988 "Cuvée Angéline" • *Champagne Lassalle*

$37.40 PER BOTTLE $396.00 PER CASE

JADED PALATE WHITE

1994 RULLY *BLANC* "LES SAINT-JACQUES"
A. & P. DE VILLAINE

How does a white Burgundy—a Chardonnay, no less—get into the elite Jaded Palate section?

"Has Lynch sold out?"

"He'll do anything to sell a bottle of wine."

"What does he take us for, anyway?"

"Chardonnay? I've had it."

"Let's boycott."

Wait a minute, wait one goldarned minute. A Jaded Palate is not anti-Chardonnay. A Jaded Palate is against Yet Another Faceless Chardonnay. One that seems to have rolled off the assembly line. A true Jaded Palate is dying for a Chardonnay that has class and differentness.

$18.95 PER BOTTLE

FOOD FIT FOR THE KING
GRACELAND WINES

DURING THE last half of the 20th century, few Americans intrigued their fellow Americans as much as Nixon and Elvis. Some see an only-in-America angle to their steep rise-and-fall stories: humble origins followed by a pretty heady dose of the American Dream that neither could handle. The President and the King. Damaged, they ended up disgraced or drugged. What could be more loathsome than the Nixon revealed in the White House tapes, or more pathetic than a bloated Elvis huffing and puffing through "The Battle Hymn of the Republic" at the end?

But we are not here to deepen our understanding of the dark side of the American Dream (what we might call its five o'clock shadow); we are here about wine.

Reportedly Nixon had a taste for Château Margaux and Zind-Humbrecht. He even had his own bin in the cellar of Lutèce Restaurant in New York. And haven't we all read that Nixon's favorite dish was cottage cheese and catsup:

TRICKY DICK'S COTTAGE CHEESE AND CATSUP

Cottage Cheese
Catsup

Serve one on top of the, uh, other.

I wonder how it *was* served. Did he keep some handy in the White House minibar and eat it right out of the carton? (Can you imagine Nixon, round about midnight, pounding on a recalcitrant catsup bottle, trying to coax out a glop?) Or maybe the White House chef served perfectly rounded little globs on White

House china. Or maybe it was not globs of cottage cheese but *globes* of cottage cheese with the continents sketched in with blood-colored catsup. Nixon could just sit down to table and eat Vietnam!

Wine goes with cheese, but cottage cheese? I fear that Château Margaux's fabled finesse might be lost in the midst of a big cold bite of cottage cheese. Tannins acting up, you know. And which Zind-Humbrecht with catsup? Riesling? Tokay? Rangen? Brand? Oh my, that sounds like a real clash, doesn't it? Yet another crisis for Tricky to cope with.

The only Elvis wine story is that there are none, unlike his competitor from

Louisiana, Mr. Jerry Lee Lewis, who has a repertoire full of wine songs: "Drinkin' Wine Spodeeodee," for example, or how about "The Alcohol of Fame," or these great lines,

> *Wine me up, turn me on, and watch me cry for you.*
> *Lately drinking warm red wine is all I want to do.*

My grandmother, like so many of the older generation, had a theory to explain away Elvis's success: "He wouldn't amount to nothin' without those Jordanaires," she told me. Poor Grandma. She missed it. Elvis didn't come out of nowhere, but it felt like it at the time. And if you were a song, and Elvis happened to you, it was like being hit by an earthquake from the inside out.

Why all of this? Because, thanks to Martin Aussenberg of Memphis, Tennessee, I now possess a personally inscribed book by Mary Jenkins, Elvis Presley's cook at his Graceland estate. Mary gives her detailed recipes of Elvis's favorite dishes, but, alas, there are no wine recommendations.

Right away in this book one is struck by the subtle nuances of Elvis's taste. For example, the *Ham Steak* recipe has a straightforward simplicity: "Sprinkle ham with brown sugar, place in foil and place in oven," while the complexly flavored *Baked Ham* combines molasses, Coke, and pineapple juice in the glaze.

One of his favorites when El and the guys hung out together was *Barbecue Bologna*. Here Elvis was touching on French *and* Italian culinary roots. The word *barbecue* comes from the French tradition of roasting an entire goat on an outdoor spit, cooking it from its *barbe* (beard) to its, well, one of those rear-end parts. "Punch holes in Bologna," Mary's recipe begins. Then it is basted, of course, with barbecue sauce, and cooked for an hour and a half. Obviously Elvis did not like his bologna undercooked! Still, the quality of the bologna itself is going to be crucial to the success of this dish, so I thought it might be helpful to organize an official Comparative Blind Tasting to judge for you the various bolognas on the market. Over the years here in Berkeley I have befriended some of America's top chefs, so I invited Judy Rodgers (Zuni), Jeremiah Tower (Stars), Alice Waters (Chez Panisse), and Paul Bertolli (Oliveto) to gather round the grill and evaluate available bolognas, but they had prior commitments. For the wine, however, it seems quite obvious: with *Barbecue Bologna*, why not a light, zesty Dolcetto to accentuate the bologna's Italian origins? Serve cool.

One truly challenging wine-and-food pairing occurs on page 107, where the principal (in fact the only) flavoring ingredient of *7-Up Cake* is 7-Up. What kind of wine goes with 7-Up? Or do you just can the wine idea and serve iced 7-Up? (Handy hint: Why not serve it in champagne flutes? *Yow!*)

Elvis had a favorite bedtime snack, the famous *Peanut Butter and Banana Sandwich*, as prepared by Mary on David Letterman's show, and Mary divulges the actual recipe in this, her book. I was struck by Elvis's lavishness. For a mere three (3) white bread sandwiches, the recipe instructs that they be "browned until golden brown" in one entire stick of melted butter! The obvious wine would be a Duboeuf Beaujolais to marry with both the peanut butter and the mashed banana. But then I had a mild insight. This is the King's favorite *bedtime* snack. Might not a youthful Beaujolais excite the King and keep him awake? Also, Elvis was not budget conscious. He was loaded in more ways than one. For example, he bought a car for Mary and one for her husband, Sleepy, bought them a stone house, bought a Pontiac apiece for the three (3) lady real estate agents who handled the deal, plus a nifty finned Cadillac (pictured in the book) for Mary's foster brother, Willie Payne. So Elvis did not mind a splurge now and then. Therefore, with the *Peanut Butter and Banana Sandwich*, I'd recommend a 1921 Yquem.

This is an altogether fascinating book, but my favorite part is when Elvis would bring his guitar into the Graceland kitchen and serenade Mary with B. B. King and Howling Wolf songs while she worked. Wow, for that I'd have sommeliered for free, because Elvis was one white boy who could sing the blues so that the only color that mattered was blue. Plus, in my opinion, he caught a lot of rabbits.

✦ 1997 ✦

◇◇◇◇◇◇◇◇◇◇◇◇◇◇◇◇◇◇◇◇◇◇◇◇◇◇◇◇◇◇◇

SPECIAL EVENTS

Saturday, February 8, 11:00 A.M. to 5:00 P.M.

Aubert de Villaine will be in our shop with samples of upcoming vintages of his red and white Burgundies. He speaks English quite well (perhaps because he married a California girl?), so you won't need to use sign language. Aubert is a man of charm, intelligence, a great sense of humor, and, joy to behold, no big ego. He splits his time between Domaine de la Romanée-Conti and his home in the village of Bouzeron, where he produces heavenly wines that I consider the finest values Burgundy has to offer. See for yourself.

Thursday, February 13, 3:00 to 6:00 P.M.

Henri Roch, Aubert de Villaine's partner at the Domaine de la Romanée-Conti, also has his own domaine, Domaine Prieuré-Roch, where the vinification is handled by Marcel Lapierre's nephew. Henri Roch is bringing 1995s and 1994s with him to taste. Burgundy fans, do not miss this.

Saturday, February 15, 3:00 to 6:00 P.M.

Jean-Nicolas Méo from the great Domaine Méo-Camuzet will be in the shop to discuss and taste Burgundy with us.

Most of the Henri Jayer wines we imported were from Méo-Camuzet's vineyards. When Jayer retired, Jean-Nicolas Méo took back the vineyards and began to vinify the wines with Jayer's advice. However, Jean-Nicolas has his own taste and vision, and with vintages 1993, 1994, and 1995, we see fabulous triumphs that, while not precisely in the Jayer style, are of equal brilliance.

And what superb holdings, including three *grands crus*: Le Corton, Clos de Vougeot, and Richebourg.

Saturday, February 22, Noon to 5:00 P.M.

The **Gang of Four** plus two equals the Gang of Six: Lapierre, Breton, Thévenet, Foillard, and Métras, with their white wine–making friend Jean-Jacques Robert from Domaine Robert-Denogent. Meet them here in the shop and see what they're like.

Sunday, February 23

The **Gang of Six** likes to live it up, so we are taking over Chez Panisse to show them how we do it in California. They are bringing a few odds and ends to taste, and their new vintages will flow when we all sit down to lunch. These guys are carnivores, mainly pig crazy, but I'll bet in France they're never tasted great beef, so one of our courses should be aged Niman Schell steaks grilled over vine branches. Call (510) 524-1524 for reservation information.

CHÂTEAU DU TRIGNON SAMPLER

CHÂTEAU *de* this and Château *de* that, but why Château *du Trignon*? Because it is on the banks of the Trignon, a small stream that runs between Gigondas and Sablet until it flows into the larger Ouvèze, which consequently empties into the mighty Rhône. Château? Well, it is a nice house, but if you are used to Loire or Bordeaux châteaux, you've got to lower your expectations a few hundredfold. Funky Provence has lower standards. But what an idyllic setting with the stream gurgling by, the rows of vines, and a lovely view of the Dentelles de Montmirail up behind Gigondas. There is an absence of road or city noise, although in the summer the cicadas' whirring roar is pretty impressive.

I like Trignon's wines because they don't put new oak where it does not belong, because their Rhônes taste like Rhônes yet show freshness and balance, because their Bois des Dames soil produces the finest appellation Côtes du Rhône I have ever tasted (it's the stones!), because their Mourvèdre at Rasteau gives a red that tastes good young or old and has a handsome Côte Brune character you can depend on, while their Syrah at Sablet gives a prettier, less tannic, Côte Blonde style, and because they recently added 20 acres to their Gigondas holding and changed the vinification dramatically for the better. There is an exciting ambiance of tradition and creativity. Château du Trignon is one of the Rhône Valley's great properties.

Our Trignon Sampler will give you various pleasures of the mind, eyes, nose, and palate, enhance your appreciation of Rhône wines, and, if nothing else, it adds up to one big juicy bargain. Limit: 10 samplers per family member.

Special Sampler Case Reduced 25%

$114.00

GAIN GARRIGUE POWER
FROM OUR GARRIGUE SAMPLER

EVERYONE HIP TO the garrigue but you?
Then it is time to GET HIP so you can win friends and impress your boss next time you are at table together. Imagine this: You pull the cork on one from our Garrigue Sampler. You pour. Your boss swirls, sniffs, exclaims, "Holy smoke! What in heaven's name is that utterly captivating perfume?" You sniff yours and coolly reply, "That there smells like Lou Gehrig." No, no, try it again:

"That is a perfect expression of the Provençal garrigue." Instant raise in salary; you have more bucks to blow on wine; we all win.

Richard Olney has lived in Provence in the midst of the garrigue since the 1950s, so I asked him to define *garrigue*. He answered:

> *Arid limestone hillsides populated by scrub oak, cade (wild juniper), wild asparagus, sweet-scented broom, aromatic herbs —thyme, savory, oregano, rosemary, aspic (wild lavender), fennel—and more elusive, related essences. The garrigue is the air of Provence. What can I say? Without the garrigue, the fruit would fall flat.*

I also asked Lulu Peyraud from the Domaine Tempier for help:

> *Provençal writers and poets were right to draw our attention to the fragrances of the garrigue. Actually Daudet like Giono, Pagnol like Magnan, and of course Frédéric Mistral, have charmed their readers with their thorough descriptions of the garrigue.*
>
> *In Provence, there are still many hills covered with small trees and plants whose scents are extremely potent, especially in the morning when the dew evaporates in the heat of the first burst of sunshine. Then one can distinguish lavender from broom, rosemary from thyme and savory, which competes with sage, and distinguish heather from wild fennel. These plants all grow at the base of pine trees, junipers, and oaks. In Corsica it is called the* maquis, *where it grows so thick that they say even the police wouldn't be able to find you hiding in it.*

Vieux Télégraphe's Châteauneuf-du-Pape often shows aromas of the garrigue alongside its typical stony gunflint and ripe fruit, so I called upon Daniel Brunier for some help defining the garrigue:

> *The garrigue. That's the place where nothing else will grow. It is the domaine of wild lavender, wild rosemary, and scrub oak. It is a place austere and hospitable at once. With nothing more than your nose, you'll know you are there! But if it is possible to stretch out on the ground without getting jabbed in the back or rear end, you are not really in the garrigue, because in the true garrigue, you'd need to find a flat rock just to sit down. The garrigue smells so good, I can smell it just thinking about it. And in the summer heat, if you piss in the garrigue it is as if you had prepared an herb tea. It is so fragrant, but the garrigue is never silent because it is teeming with life. It is* Manon des Sources, Jean de Florette, *it is Pagnol . . . c'est un accent.*

When southern French winemakers smell the garrigue in a wine, they light up with pleasure. It's a plus, and now that such wines are imported, we don't want to miss anything. We want to recognize it when it is there.

The smell of it can be a shock to those who are accustomed to straightforward mass-market wines that smell of jammy fruit and new oak. The garrigue is much more complex, more funky, more earthy (as in "of this earth"). You have the sun-baked aspect, the roasted herbs (*not* herbaceous), and you also have a resiny aspect (as in rosemary or pine needles). You have all those god-given scents from the Provençal countryside. Alongside, your jammy/oaky wine might seem banal.

Try this simple treat to see how useful a garrigue-laden wine can be at table. Dress your favorite noodles with a tasty olive oil, good salt, and Parmesan. Alongside it, pour a selection from the sampler. What could be simpler to prepare? Yet the pasta with a taste of garrigue-scented wine makes an ensemble of complexity and deliciousness.

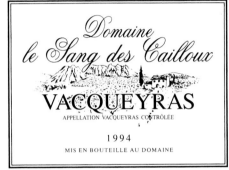

How does the perfume of the garrigue get into wine? See page 37 in my book *Adventures on the Wine Route* for one theory. See page 168 for another. I simply call it magic, and thank goodness for it.

I browsed through the store and re-tasted a lot of our southern reds in order to find those that really express the scent of the garrigue. Work your way through this six-bottle sampler at your leisure and afterwards, when you run across a wine that smells of the garrigue, you will know it.

(P.S. No matter what they say about morning dew and stuff like that, do not add liquid hot or cold to your sampler wines.)

1994 Bronzinelle · Saint Martin de la Garrigue
1994 Rasteau · Château du Trignon
1994 Faugères "Les Bastides" · Alquier
1994 Vacqueyras · Domaine Le Sang des Cailloux
1993 Saint-Chinian · Domaine Fonsalade
1991 Bandol Cuvée Spéciale "La Tourtine" · Domaine Tempier

Six-Bottle Sampler

SPECIAL PRICE $80.00

NORTHERN RHÔNE

INTRODUCING 1995 OFFERUS · J. L. CHAVE SELECTION

This release is the culmination of several years of discussion and effort. In 1979 Gérard Chave opened my eyes to the potential of certain Saint-Joseph hillsides by taking me to the top of one, where I purchased Trollat's 1978. I have had a passion for Saint-Joseph ever since, even to the point of entertaining the notion of purchasing one of those steep, terraced slopes for myself.

Whenever Chave and I got together we would spend a little time lamenting the fact that the potential we saw was seldom realized. One day he told me that no one ever tastes the greatest Saint-Josephs because they are produced in small lots by farmers who don't make enough to justify bottling it. Chave knows practically everyone in the heart of the appellation, went to school with them, knows who has the best vineyards, the oldest vines, etc. But their cuvées are sold to *négociants* who blend them with flatland wines.

I said that there must be some way out of such a ridiculous situation, that I could pay the growers in advance, pay more to have the best, buy them the bottles, corks, labels, etc., and have them bottled for me.

No way, Chave said, because these growers are really farmers with orchards and other crops, not polished winemakers. You would have to get the wine as soon as it fermented and raise it properly.

Great Syrah going to waste! The idea bugged me.

The next time I showed up he and Jean-Louis had two 1994s for me to taste, two of the most splendid Syrahs of my life. It was like discovering a Clape, a Gentaz, or a Chave, but it was a Saint-Joseph! If I had known how to say "We are going to blow people's minds" in French, I would have said it.

Chave told me that his grandfather long ago had obtained a *négociant* license, but the family never used it. Was I seriously interested in those Saint-Josephs? *But of course.*

He then learned, however, that French law does not permit him to bottle purchased wine in his domaine cellar. So, good-bye to the 1994, the one that got away.

Fast forward to today, all bureaucratic problems solved, as I proudly introduce Offerus to the world of fine wine. (The name *Offerus* is explained on each bottle.) For the 1995, Gérard and Jean-Louis selected barrels (20 of them) from seven of Saint-Joseph's top *terroirs*, and then one day I watched them tasting and blending until they had assembled a cuvée quite amazingly superior to any of the separate lots.

Top vineyards, top vintage, the master blenders' touch.

Chave works his own Saint-Joseph vines at Mauves. Offerus is different. Because of his *terroir*, his domaine-bottled Saint-Joseph is more of an ultra-delicious quaffer. Offerus will always be darker, more intense, chewier, more serious an event. Especially the 1995, which has, as Clive Coates would say, good grip.

I took everything that Chave bottled. Wouldn't you?

$19.95 PER BOTTLE $215.46 PER CASE

1996 COTEAUX DU LANGUEDOC ROSÉ
DOMAINE DU POUJOL

What I remember so vividly about this rosé is how quickly the first bottle was empty. Robert Parker uses a 100-point scoring system. Hugh Johnson likes the Sniff System, as in, "I don't like it; I only gave it one sniff." So, what about the How-soon-was-it-drained Scoring System?

Anyway, it was sundown when Robert and Kim Cripps (our Anglo-American winemakers in France) drove me up to the top of their vineyard in a 4 × 4 Land Rover. The so-called road and the vertiginous precipices were so scary that my throat began to parch up on me. At the summit we scrambled out, gazed across the valley and the *garrigue*-covered hills to a distant blue patch of Mediterranean, and slurped down their newly bottled rosé like greedy pigs at the trough.

I don't think it was one of those you-had-to-be-there things. Their rosé is delicious at sundown here, too.

$7.95 PER BOTTLE $85.86 PER CASE

AN EVENING WITH
AUBERT DE VILLAINE

Bouzeron, population 151, is a little tail's end of a village in Burgundy where winter's night can fall with an especially icy clunk. Its three or four streets were already dead and deserted when I drove up to Aubert de Villaine's iron gate last November. Actually, I was running a bit late, so after a handshake we descended straightaway into the cellar and its heady smells of earth, oak, and newborn wine.

Aubert de Villaine has a ready sense of humor and an enviable combination of lucidity and discretion. When I picture him, I see him just breaking into a smile, a playful gleam in his dark, intelligent eyes. Having known each other for more than 20 years, we always have too much to talk about, so our tastings

bounce chaotically from comic asides to catching up on friends and family to wine trade gossip and a no-holds-barred critique of whatever we are tasting.

Of course we begin with his Aligoté de Bouzeron, considered Burgundy's best, and Aubert said that personally he prefers 1996 to 1995. I said 1996 ($14.95) seemed leaner than the 1995. "*J'aime bien les vins austères*," he said, contradicting almost the entire American wine establishment.

Then he announced that for the United States he left his 1995 white Burgundy Les Clous ($16.50) completely unfiltered. A true

Aubert de Villaine

stony hillside wine, Les Clous always shows more race and structure than flatland Bourgognes, and I must say that it gains by remaining unfiltered because there is more flesh left on that impressive bone structure. He uncorked a 1993, too, which has opened up beautifully. If ever I make a wine, I would hope it shows such subtlety and class.

Aubert's newest acquisition, a *premier cru* from Rully, Les Saint-Jacques, is a real prize. (But then, could a de Villaine settle for an ordinary *terroir*?) The 1995 has a delicious pear-skin aroma and a firm, full palate. The 1994 ($18.95) has so much personality that I made it a Jaded Palate selection, and the 1995 shares that same *goût de terroir*.

My tasting notes on the 1995 red Burgundy La Digoine ($18.50) begin with the word wow and then I repeat it at the end, too, which isn't like me. Due to 1995's short crop, I had to settle for half the quantity I wanted.

His 1995 Mercurey Les Montots ($19.95) is something else entirely. La Digoine is so pretty a wine, but the *terroir* of Les Montots produces a more tannic, old-fashioned style. "*Un vin d'autre fois,*" Aubert said. But it also seems to smell of grape skins and stems and freshly crushed Pinot Noir. "That is one reason I love the Mercurey," Aubert said, "because it always recalls that smell of the harvest, you know, working the grapes, the crush."

Something about the 1995 Les Montots made me think of Conrad's title *The Heart of Darkness*, and the title would occur to me again before the night was over.

Right about then, as Aubert poured a taste of the 1994 Mercurey, I mentioned that I was wearing espadrilles from Provence, and that my toes were chattering. During wintertime that earthen cellar floor is like standing on an iceberg, so carrying along the 1994 Rully *blanc* to serve as our apéritif, we walked out into the darkness up to his house.

He built a fire first thing, poured that wonderful Rully, then showed me two new recordings of the Bach Cello Suites, one by Yo-Yo Ma, the other by the Russian Mstislav Rostropovich. We decided to "taste" and compare the two performances.

I grew up with the Pablo Casals version of the suites, one of the great recorded performances of the century, so truthfully I was prepared to be a little underwhelmed by the new recordings. The Casals seems soulful, existential, the Rostropovich emotionally vast. How their cellos seem to sing and speak. The Yo-Yo Ma is more lively, dance-like, but not as subterranean.

Right about then Aubert left to search for another white. Many of you might not be aware that he owns part of another winery farther north, in Vosne-Romanée. Anyway, he returned with a 1967 Montrachet from his other winery, which really hit the spot as we listened to the second cello suite *à la* Rostropovich.

Aubert began to tell me what he had heard about the actual recording of the suites, which the Russian must have believed will remain his foremost legacy as a cellist.

Rostropovich chose to record the suites in France in the ancient cathedral at Vézelay from which the Crusades were launched because, he wrote, "I saw the rhythm of the internal architecture shorn of all superfluity, with none of the gilt and ornamental trimmings of the Baroque style. I saw the severity of line and the rhythm of this vaulted construction, which reminds me so powerfully of the rhythm of Bach's music."

Recording took two months. He recorded at the midnight hour, the cathedral silent, empty, except (I've been there) for whatever spooky stuff might be emanating from its crypt (which is said to have contained some remains of Mary Magdalene). Imagine the texture of the cello's sound in that vast, dark, stone cathedral! And my God it is fabulous as it growls and soars.

We listened to the Sarabande from Suite no. 2. (Film buffs, didn't Ingmar Bergman use this piece in *Through a Glass Darkly*? I seem to recall hearing it during a scene in the dark hull of a wrecked ship, with . . . was it incest, sexual initiation, both?) Is there music that searches deeper? It is terrible and magnificent. The cello's bow seems to scrape right across your own guts.

While recording, the Russian and his wife lodged with Marc Meneau, who has the three-star restaurant L'Espérance just down the hill from Vézelay. A cellist who apparently has a healthy appetite, Rostropovich might have enjoyed some of our Bourgogne *blanc* Henry de Vézelay from Bernard Raveneau ($12.50), which is made practically next door. I like to think he did.

Back now, though, to Bouzeron, where dinner is served with a 1961 Romanée-Conti. I have, I admit, during my career, enjoyed many an old vintage, but this, this!!! I told Aubert that it has a *goût de terroir, mais pas de cette terre*. It is from another planet. Tasting notes? Are you kidding? I am in no mood to attempt the impossible. But what a culmination to the evening. Would I have been so receptive to the glorious intricacies of the 1961 Romanée-Conti had it not been for our passage through the Bach Cello Suites? Forget wine-and-food marriages. Here was a fusion of music and wine. The only way I could describe the wine would be to play the music.

And what a voyage the entire evening had been, starting with that first innocent burst of fresh Aligoté.

◦　◦　◦　◦　◦　◦　◦　◦

1996 MORGON "CÔTE DU PY" · JEAN FOILLARD

Last March at Foillard's I tasted the various components or cuvées that would be assembled to create this bottling. They were hard to judge because I had to taste alongside a visiting French recording artist, a kaftan-wearing, jewelry-laden *accordéoniste* who must have just emerged from a few healthy laps in a swimming pool of aftershave. Then this summer I kept trying to get Foillard to send me a sample of the finished wine, but I guess he couldn't get out of his comfy new backyard hammock long enough to go to the post office. And now in Berkeley the ship delivering it docks after this brochure's deadline. I don't know what we have here.

$16.50 PER BOTTLE　　$178.20 PER CASE

CHINON

W̲E̲ A̲R̲E̲ N̲O̲T̲ yet presenting the big agers from the Loire's sun-soaked 1996 vintage. They are still in barrel. Here we have two *vins de plaisir*, and by that I do not mean light and superficial. I mean that they give immediate pleasure, and they are easy to love. I mean you will have fun with them because of the way they taste.

These two wines are quite different, however, presenting us with two distinct personalities. You needn't choose. This is not like marriage. With wine you are allowed to enjoy diversity.

1996 CHINON "CUVÉE TERROIR"
CHARLES JOGUET

This would probably be easier to sell if Joguet had called it *Symphony* or *Vibrato* or *Cadanza* or *Gigue* or *Anthem* or *Cantata* or something like that. (How about *Vibrator?*) Who can resist wines with sappy names? (KLWM customers, that's who!)

I'll bet Charles Joguet calls this new cuvée *Terroir* because it is rustic and earthy. The color is deep and so is the aroma. On the palate, quite chewy with wonderfully ripe tannins. This is his press wine, and you will enjoy the extract.

$11.50 PER BOTTLE $124.20 PER CASE

1996 CHINON "LES GRANGES" · BERNARD BAUDRY

The Joguet plays bass. Here is the violin.

Joguet's *Cuvée Terroir* plays like Côte Brune, *Les Granges* Côte Blonde.

Terroir with the lights down low in the midnight hour, *Les Granges* for your picnic on a blanket under the boardwalk.

Oh well, no one can be serious with this bright, grapey piece of work soaring out of the glass. Serve it cool!

$11.50 PER BOTTLE $124.20 PER CASE

° ° ° ° ° ° ° °

1996 MÂCON-VILLAGES · "CUVÉE KERMIT LYNCH"
1996 BEAUJOLAIS · "CUVÉE KERMIT LYNCH"

How can I recommend wines wearing my own label without sounding conceited? I suppose I simply try to honestly represent the actual quality of the wine in the bottle and hope that you don't consider the source.

The 1996 Mâcon has a Montrachet-like presence and a Corton Charlemagne–like attack on the palate, although certain aspects of it may remind you more of the 1929 Yquem without precisely the same color, aroma, or flavors. Conspicuously aromatic, it is an atomic bomb concentrate waiting to blow your palate to smithereens, yet what tender finesse! The complexity achieves grandiose parameters, and then, *then*, that aftertaste: Lucy in the Sky with Diamonds! Truly a mind-bending gem. Expected maturity: tonight.

$9.95 PER BOTTLE $107.46 PER CASE

The 1996 Beaujolais towers majestically over every other red on the market today yet retains the quaffable *légèreté* we demand from this monumental appellation. At the same time, how can one ignore its eyeball-riveting color, its super-concentrated body engorged with blackberries, blueberries, raspberries, olallie-berries, boysenberries, cinnamon, cherry pit, violets, petunias, red currants, black currants, elderly currants, and graham crackers?

$8.95 PER BOTTLE $96.66 PER CASE

1995 CHÂTEAU HAUT-PLANTEY SAINT-EMILION

BORED BY BORDEAUX? (Hey, that's catchy.) I used to like Bordeaux. I still do when I can get my hands on an older one, preferably pre-1982. My idea of great Bordeaux is summed up by this quote from Alexandre Dumas, speaking in the voice of Cardinal Richelieu:

They are neither generous nor vigorous, but the bouquet is not bad, and they have an indescribably sinister, somber bite that is not at all disagreeable.

Bordeaux today seems to have lost that sinister bite, that somber or *noir*-ish undercurrent. How many have real personality lurking behind their Cabernet fruit and oak dressing? Instead of a sinister bite, you expect them to flash you the peace sign and tell you to have a nice day.

Yes, I like wines that have stuff *lurking* in the background, wines that show their *terroir*, wines with soul, wines that stand apart.

If you are going to buy only one 1995 Bordeaux, make it Haut-Plantey. It is an amazing wine. It deserves to be *Banned in Bordeaux*. It is a classic in the old style, intense, full of intrigue, packed with the kind of good stuff you just don't see anymore.

Sinister bite? You'll want to bite right back.

$249.00 PER CASE FIFTHS

⇢ 1998 ⇠

LUCIEN PEYRAUD
1912–1996

At lunch this summer at Domaine Tempier, Jean-Marie Peyraud poured a 1953 rosé. He said he found it stashed behind a clutter of stuff in the domaine cellar. He figured we should at least take a whiff of it out of curiosity before he emptied it down the drain.

A 1953 rosé, drinkable? Impossible. Lucien Peyraud made that 1953, and it lit

Lucien passing on to his granddaughter Valerie his secret recipe for vin cuit

Lucien and Lulu, 1935

up the table. It was better than drinkable. A series of decanted older reds awaited us, but we took a little detour and drained that rosé to the last drop. Everyone was awed. It was old only in the best sense.

A week later François Peyraud opened Lucien's 1957 *rouge*. It is the finest wine I tasted this year along with a 1978 Côte Rôtie from Marius Gentaz that Stephen Spurrier served in London. The 1957 Tempier, 40 years old, from a vintage considered unexceptional, was exceptional, middle-aged, vigorous enough to go another 40. It did everything a red wine can do.

I asked François to explain such quality and longevity. How did Lucien do it? He said that his father was strictly a non-interventionist winemaker who had faith in nature. He did not like SO_2, nor did he like to rack his wine. He was especially scornful whenever he encountered a good wine masked by new oak. And Lucien did not mind if his wine had some CO_2, which he considered nature's own protection against oxidation. So just after Lucien bottled his wine, it remained a wild thing, not exactly civilized. François said that today, when critics rush to judge a wine right out of the gate, Lucien's 1957 would probably be considered defective.

Last fall Lucien would not be hospitalized. He died at home with his family five minutes after the last grapes of 1996 were harvested, as the harvesters were walking by outside his window on their way home. At the funeral I spoke with the village priest, and when I mentioned the coincidence, Lucien waiting to die until the grapes were in, the priest said no, it was not coincidence, he had seen it before with other old vignerons. My my.

I remember in the early years, I was truly intimidated by him. There I was, a young whippersnapper from the Wild West. Whenever it came time to open my mouth to speak, I wanted to run away because I was sure Lucien could see right through me, see my inexperience, see how superficial my knowledge was. His vision seemed so clear, so penetrating.

But then when I was on the road, tasting wines and buying, I found myself posing a question: Would I serve this wine to Lucien Peyraud? You would not want to serve a trickster's wine, a contrivance, to Lucien. It would have to be an honest, natural wine with its roots in the earth, and more than that, the right roots in the right earth.

He saved his strongest venom for the wines of the Beaujolais. He sneered at the over-chaptalized recipe wines that dominated the region. They did not deserve to be called wine. One day with much trepidation I had him taste Marcel Lapierre's Morgon. What a relief when he clinked glasses with me and said, "*Ça, ça c'est du vrai vin.*"

As the years fluttered past way too quickly, our relationship deepened, and Lucien began to refer to me as his adopted son. He and Lulu had seven living children, but they had lost a baby boy shortly after birth in 1941, my birth year, and as Lucien grew older and more sentimental he began to think of me as having been sent to replace the son he lost. Neither of us took it too seriously, but it was there.

Lucien was a *guiding light, an inspiration, a blazing star whose wine was and remains the raw essence of individuality in a sea of conformity.* He is known as the father of the Bandol appellation, but he was more than that. *His wine was as mystical* as it was delicious, *as humbling* as it was uplifting. *His message was* in his wine and *it gets into the mystery of life.* It links us up with the primordial.⋆

Raise your next glass to salute Lucien Peyraud. I doubt that he can appreciate the gesture, but if he can, he will.

⋆ *I lifted most of this paragraph from Bob Dylan's tribute to Jimmy Rodgers in the CD* The Songs of Jimmy Rodgers: A Tribute *because the words seem so appropriate.*

LATE-HARVEST MASTERWORKS
FROM ANDRÉ OSTERTAG

WHILE I WAS visiting Alsace in September, my palate collapsed on me. Alsace is an endurance test because of the number of wines to be tasted at each domaine. Think about it, the multiple grape varieties, each coming from several vineyard sites, then the range of styles from dry through the *Sélection Grains Nobles*, or SGNs. When I arrived at André's, we went through all the dry wines and then I called it quits, because I knew I could no longer physically perform as a taster. Tired Palate Syndrome.

A week later, at home, refreshed, I opened a case full of André's late-picked beauties and telephoned him. We proceeded to taste the wines together, *on the phone*. Why not? Phone sex appears to be all the rage, judging by the number of ads, so why not phone tastings?

We traded perceptions and opinions and philosophies, and I noted down some of André's ideas. Here's one to gnaw on as you consider our offering of Vendanges Tardives and SGNs: "I don't like sweetness," says André. I mean, here is a man offering me his sweet wines and he starts off like that!

"Sugar in wine can only be justified by the nobility and potential of its origin."

Obviously he does not make late-harvest wines to satisfy a sweet tooth. But, of course, they are sweet. The sweetness is a result of a super-maturity obtained only in exceptional years. And when nature declares its inclination to permit such a rare event, André still sticks to his guns: "I believe that in wine there is only one truth, that of the empty bottle!" Which is to say, if I can interpret, that late-picked wines must be balanced and harmonious, must hold our interest to the last drop, must not paralyze our taste buds, and must reflect a noble *terroir*. It is this notion of *terroir*, after all, that makes a second sip more interesting than the first and the last glass more interesting than the first. Without a *goût de terroir*, you get what there is in one whiff, and there is no mystery to unfold taste after luscious taste.

Enough philosophy. I selected the following:

		PER BOTTLE
1995	*Riesling Heissenberg · Vendanges Tardives*	$44.25
1995	*Riesling Muenchberg · Vendanges Tardives*	51.00
1994	*Gewurztraminer Fronholz · Vendanges Tardives*	46.80
1994	*Pinot Gris Muenchberg · Vendanges Tardives*	54.00

		PER TENTH
1995	*Riesling Heissenberg · SGN*	$54.00
1994	*Pinot Gris Muenchberg · SGN*	52.00

NEW DISCOVERY
DOMAINE SAINT-ANDRIEU
AT MONTPEYROUX

MONTPEYROUX?

Hardly anyone knows that Montpeyroux, off the beaten path north of Béziers, possesses one of southern France's most interesting *terroirs*. It is barely beginning to attract attention. For intelligent wine drinkers, that means *great wine* and *great bargains*.

Did you read in *The New York Times* the other day about all the $100 to $250 Cabernets on the market? Think about it. I wonder how many of them are as interesting and delicious as these two reds from Montpeyroux. Cabernet = cliché, fatigue. Montpeyroux = originality, discovery. Do you pay a fortune to jump on the Cabernet bandwagon, or will you be the first on your block to enjoy Montpeyroux? One hundred bucks for an oaky fruitbomb? One hundred smackers for been-there-done-that? People, please. Wouldn't humankind be better served if you drank Montpeyroux instead and donated the extra bucks to charity? If everyone drank Montpeyroux we could save the world, maybe.

The only trouble is, there is a lot more Cabernet than there is Montpeyroux. In fact, our total allocation here is 125 cases. Oh, well. My intentions were good. Instead of saving the world, maybe I'd better concentrate on the deliciousness factor.

We are talking about arid hillside vineyards up in the *garrigue* and small yields from Mourvèdre, Grenache, Syrah, and 70-year-old Carignan, aged in barrel and bottled, guess what, unfiltered.

$\diamond$ $\diamond$ $\diamond$ $\diamond$ $\diamond$ $\diamond$ $\diamond$ $\diamond$

1996 "LE CARIGNAN" · DOMAINE D'AUPILHAC

A mere seven acres of old, old Carignan vines with deep-searching roots in decomposed oyster-fossil and limestone hillside soil. OLD Carignan vines, nothing less than 50 years old. The vines are gnarled and thick; each would make an evocative photo portrait.

Why do I always bring up *hillside* vines? Drainage, man. You don't want your wine to taste like a water table.

The fact is, even old Carignan tends to overproduce, hillside or not, which is why a lot was ripped out and replaced in the Languedoc. Carignan is a grape variety that tends to spend itself frivolously, that refuses to concentrate on the qualities that concern the discerning wine drinker. However, the idea of uprooting 50- to 100-year-old vines bugged Sylvain Fadat. What a waste, he thought. So he took another approach, pruning, hacking his Carignan vines into submission, and ended up producing a Carignan that has captured the attention of the wine world. In the winter, he prunes back mercilessly, limiting yields, and then he attacks again during the summer, lopping off *two-thirds of his crop!* All the old vine sap goes into the few grape bunches left on each vine.

The ripe, succulent juice is vinified in oak *foudre* and bottled unfiltered. Fadat has been quoted as saying, *vin filtré = bon; vin non-filtré = super bon.*

This splendid, deep-colored, sappy red is an insider's wine, not for the masses, not for label snobs.

This 1996 is the best yet (he began in 1989). First, there is a fabulous depth and complexity. It seems alive and kicking beneath its gorgeous surface. Second, the 1996 has a length on the palate normally found only in the greatest growths.

The flavors? A lot of tasters find blueberry. Maybe so. Whatever berry you find (Carignan berries?), you will love that juicy, sap-like quality, and what the French call *ampleur*.

$14.95 PER BOTTLE $161.46 PER CASE

OLDER WINES

AT THE BEGINNING of February I collaborated with chef Paul Bertolli at Oliveto restaurant in Oakland for three nights of wine and black truffle dinners. As part of the preparation we studied and analyzed the interplay between different wines and black truffle dishes. Even though it was our day off, Sunday, my staff bit the bullet and showed up at Oliveto for a trial run luncheon with the Oliveto staff.

The highlight wine for me came from my last magnum of 1982 Meursault Charmes from François Jobard. It was high-toned with good nervosity and that complete openness that mature wines possess. Those white Burgundies from 1982 have aged beautifully—even better, I think, than the higher-rated 1983s. If I had another magnum left, I'll bet another 10 years wouldn't do it any harm. With the truffles, it soared.

In November on my way back to California I stopped in London and dined at the Turf Club with wine writers Stephen Spurrier, John Livingstone-Learmonth, and Simon Loftus. It was my first visit to one of those old English private clubs, and it was an un-American, politically incorrect treat: big leather armchairs, horse art on the walls, a lot of middle-and-older-aged men smoking and drinking guiltlessly. In fact, there was only one woman in the dining room and she stood out as even more foreign than I, her cleavage gleaming in the masculine atmosphere like a beacon.

The menu was loaded with various game, so I ordered the first grouse of my life.

My hosts brought along old Rhônes. There was

a gorgeous white from Château Rayas, Châteauneuf-du-Pape 1973. Do not underestimate the ability of white wines to age: 1973, that's 24 years old! A 1957 Mont Redon red was brimming with Châteauneuf character, perfectly mature. Then they served two Côte Rôties. The 1978 from Marius Gentaz is a wine I know well, but it was the best bottle of it I have ever tasted, and one of the two or three finest wines I tasted last year (the 1961 Romanée-Conti being another). The second Côte Rôtie served was a 1969 from quite a famous vineyard and producer, and was undrinkably over the hill. (Now why did that please me?)

At one in the morning the Cognac was served, but I headed for my hotel. In the Olympics of drinking, yours truly brought home no medals.

Whenever a shipment arrives, my staff sticks around after hours and we taste all the new arrivals. When the 1995s from Chave arrived, Hermitage red and white, I brought in bottles of his 1983, 1979, and 1976 reds to show these young whippersnappers how Chave's wine ages. We were struck by how alive all three are today, not merely wonderful, but alive and kicking in the glass, never a dull moment, changing and developing right under our noses.

The 1983 is big and brawny, and I will save my remaining bottles for wintry nights and, hopefully, game on the plate.

The 1979 was my favorite because it was the most harmonious and complete, a dazzler in every respect. But this is a wine that has given pleasure at all stages, even the year it was released.

The 1976, from a big, hot, dry year, was the first Chave to wear my import strip. Following the velvety 1979 it looked closed and still hard after two decades, but 15 minutes later it seemed to rally, blossoming and softening and growing more and more complex until . . . my glass was empty.

None of them is close to going over the hill. On the contrary.

Vintage charts label 1987 a lackluster year, but a 1987 Cuvée Spéciale from Domaine Tempier the other day showed all the signs of an extraordinary year. It is still young, rambunctious, chewy, and loaded with flavor. Those of you who cellared it, don't hurry through it. It has another 20 to 30 years of life ahead of it, but it tastes great now, like a handsome adolescent with an unusually complex personality.

The other day I was invited to lunch with Alice Waters and Terry Thiese. He's the importer who has earned quite a reputation for his Austrian and German selections. Needless to say, I wanted to pour something impressive. We started with a 1995 Raveneau La Fôret that whispered its stony *terroir* in a most seductive voice. Then I poured a 1978 Échezeaux from Henri Jayer. It was corked! And there we were in a restaurant. When it happens at home you can run down to the cellar and get another bottle, so the disaster is quickly forgotten, but there we were with nothing to do but order from the wine list, our great expectations dashed.

And finally, for those of you who buy Zind-Humbrecht wines and drink them right down, you might consider the 1976 Gewurztraminer Hengst Vendanges Tardives that I enjoyed recently. A powerhouse in its youth, it has developed remarkable subtlety and exquisite finesse.

Great winemakers, great *terroirs*, there is never any hurry. And I no longer buy into this idea of "peak" maturity. Great winemakers, great *terroirs*, their wines offer different pleasures at different ages.

◊   ◊   ◊   ◊   ◊   ◊   ◊   ◊

1996 MOULIN-À-VENT "VIEILLES VIGNES" BERNARD DIOCHON

French wines can be so multidimensional, contain and offer so many qualities at the same time in the same wine, that they can make the rest of the world's wines seem dimensionally dysfunctional. Some will say that I am not objective, that I am prejudiced because I sell only French wine, but no, I did not start importing French wines and then in a sudden blaze of self-interest decide that they were the best. My specialization is no which–came–first–the–chicken–or–the–egg conundrum. The way it happened was this:

1. *First I opened a wine shop.*
2. *More and more I was interested by French wine.*
3. *I decided to specialize.*

See, I might be opinionated, but I am not prejudiced. Hell, nobody's perfect; if prejudice were one of my imperfections, I'd tell you.

Sometimes a wine possesses qualities that even seem to be opposites. You would think they would rule each other out. For example, Diochon's 1996 is juicily delicious, yet there is a majesty to it. It is full-blown and full-bodied, yet it has a lush, supple, swallowable texture. No hard edges. No astringency. No heat. Moulin-à-Vent is supposed to be the grandest of the region's *grands crus*, and here you sense a certain grandeur throughout the taste experience.

And don't overlook the visuals. Diochon's color is always a sight to see. The color, like the flavor, is cassis-like.

$14.95 PER BOTTLE $161.46 PER CASE

1995 COTEAUX DU CAP CORSE *BLANC* · CLOS NICROSI

I retain two vivid memories of this golden dry white from Corsica.

One was just last year when I served the 1986 to Jean-Louis Chave at Oliveto. He had never even heard of the wine. The quality amazed him, including the incredibly expressive, complex bouquet it still showed after 10 years in bottle.

Corsica

The other memory goes back to the early 1980s when I went to Corsica in search of treasure with Domaine Tempier's winemaker, Jean-Marie Peyraud. Jean-Marie recently wrote, congratulating me for my business's 25th anniversary, and he reminisced about that long-ago trip to the wild island of Corsica:

> *After having driven all day long upon the tortuous little roads of Corsica, we were both exhausted. We had visited several domaines and tasted a lot of wines and our deception was as big as our discouragement. We had tasted nothing interesting!*
>
> *It was already eight P.M. and I suddenly realized that we were not through yet, that we had one more rendezvous 20 km further along, an address my father Lucien had given you. But we were both thinking, My God, not another lousy wine to taste.*
>
> *We got there and Monsieur Luigi served us his white. Hmm, pretty color. I raised it to my nose and what a shock, what finesse, what fabulous subtlety in its aroma. I turned to you and I saw your expression sparkling with pleasure. We were anxious to taste it and with the first swallow I knew it would soon be in your cellar and in that of your clients. That wine took us straight to paradise!*

$18.50 PER BOTTLE $199.80 PER CASE

1996 HAUT-BARSAC · CHÂTEAU ROÛMIEU-LACOSTE

I enjoyed my first glass of Roûmieu-Lacoste back in the mid-1970s when I was beginning to shop for French wines. I would lay over a couple of days in Paris each trip, trying to get my brain adjusted to French time while seeking out new addresses to visit on the wine route.

At that time, Jon Winroth, an American in Paris, wrote about wine for the *International Herald Tribune*, and he liked to eat and drink. We met at Au Sauvignon, a teensy wine bar featuring great Beaujolais and Quincy by the glass with platters of fabulous *saucisson* sandwiches on Poilâne's perfect levain bread.

For more serious fare, Jon liked Chez Serge, out near the Porte de Saint-Ouen. I got to his apartment on the rue du Vieux Columbier at noon one day just as he was unplugging himself from his dialysis machine. We took the *métro* out to Chez Serge and the bartender immediately set up four or five water glasses and a spoon for Jon, who proceeded to stir up various powders, potions, and pills. He downed each one and off we went to table.

One of Serge's specialties was foie gras with Sauternes, a French favorite no matter what region you are in, and Serge's Sauternes was the 1967 Roûmieu-Lacoste.

At the time it was vinified by Madame Dubourdieu, and she did not like the taste of wood, so she raised it in *cuves* of stainless steel. Her son Hervé now vinifies Roûmieu and the cellar is filled with handsome oak barrels. His 1996 is wonderful. In fact, if you compare it one-on-one to Château d'Yquem, you will find that the only difference—besides, of course, the label—is in price and quality.

I ordered a good supply of half-bottles because they are so practical.

Back to Paris and Chez Serge. We ate and we drank and with jet lag the wine went straight to my sleep control center. Jon was disappointed in me. He was raring to go. He was on his way to a tasting of some incredible number of interesting wines and then apéritifs with some publisher and then a dinner with a winemaker from the Loire who was bringing a bunch of ancient vintages . . . What was in those medicines that gave him such stamina? Sometimes, in my business, a dose of it would come in handy.

$27.50 PER BOTTLE $297.00 PER CASE

1996 CÔTES DU ROUSSILLON *ROUGE*
DOMAINE LA CASENOVE

Quiz: What is the difference between Catalonia and Catatonia?

Catalonia. Barcelona, Perpignan, Casals Festival at Prades. A nugget now of France and Spain, right there where the Pyrénées meet the blue Mediterranean. Hip yourself to Catalonia: Anchovies, sardines, garlic, snails, tomatoes, garlic, eggplant, red peppers, garlic, garlic, wine . . . Wine? Did someone say wine?

A favorite Catalan breakfast, according to author Waverly Root: a slice of bread rubbed with garlic and moistened with olive oil. Now tell me, do you think the Catalan people ate bread, garlic, and olive oil without a glass of wine? Even for breakfast? Breakfast it may be, but if you are going to break a fast, you'd be crazy not to wash it down with a celebratory glass of wine. People used to once upon a time enjoy a little wine in the morning. Our third president (it is on record, folks) was known to have "breakfasted" on wine. So I'm thinking, IT USED TO BE NORMAL. Do you really believe that in olden days they wanted to spend all morning stone-cold sober like we do?

Back to Catalonia: Get to know our small selection of Catalan wines because they have flavors you don't find elsewhere, a sun-baked earthy ripeness of flavor that goes beautifully with Mediterranean-style cuisine. Toast a slice of levain, rub with garlic, place upon it an anchovy filet or a strip of roasted red pepper or both, a little *huile d'olive*, then take a bite. Then have a swallow of Casenove's deep, vibrant 1996. See?

$12.95 PER BOTTLE $139.86 PER CASE

HARVESTING MORGON

Alison Rosenblum and Erin Cannon, two women on the KLWM staff, spent a day harvesting grapes in September for Marcel Lapierre in the Beaujolais vineyards. I took their reports and edited them to make this composite. K.L.

I WANTED TO return to Morgon and help with Marcel Lapierre's grape harvest again because of the sense of pride and accomplishment that comes from grueling, backbreaking labor. NONSENSE! I went back because it was so much fun last year. The scene there is so different from the rest of my life—it feels like I'm on a movie set or having a hallucination.

Twenty-one grape pickers bunk at Lapierre's for the harvest, and at 7:00 A.M. they all shuffle sleepily into the dining room for bowls of hot coffee and croissants. No one says much, close to zero, in fact, and they all wear a dazed sort of "day after" expression. Drop your spoon too loudly and you could get clobbered.

By 7:30 Marcel's wife and his sister are rounding up everyone to head for the vines. Those two are women of steel. They have already been up for hours shuttling kids around and preparing food for the troops.

Two vans deliver all of us to the vineyard, where buckets and blades are handed out. There are no harvesting machines at Lapierre's, and I have the scars to prove it. We were lucky because it was a glorious, clear sky with a rosy glow toward the east. We could see all the way to Mont Blanc, and it was a very special moment.

Our instructions were to pick only the two or three ripest bunches from each vine; then the team would go through again after an additional week of ripening. The grapes were small and thick-skinned, deliciously sweet with a tart kick.

In the Beaujolais the vines are grown knee-high. That's low. To pick efficiently either you bend over constantly or you employ a slower up-and-down squatting technique. There is an undeclared race to finish each row, so in order not to embarrass myself, my country, or KLWM, I chose the backbreaking method.

Quite rapidly I began to wonder why I had volunteered to take part in such physical torture, but then around 9:00 a flatbed truck pulled up with baskets of bread and platters of sausage, terrines, and cheeses. Marcel, who had been working in the winery, appeared before us corkscrew in hand and started pulling corks. Yes, folks, at 9:00 A.M. True, some harvesters opted for hot coffee instead, but the wise ones go for the vino because it also dispels some of the ache in one's back. (I chose the path of wisdom.) I'm thinking Kermit should provide the same kind of morning break, because the workers really come alive, laughing and joking, suddenly in great spirits under that gorgeous sky. (I hate to think of the same work in the rain, which happens.)

When Marcel splashed more Morgon into my glass, I asked him what he thought of the 1997 vintage so far, and he said that because of uneven ripening it was crucial now to pick only the ripest bunches, then pass through later a second, even possibly a third time when the rest have achieved a similar maturation. This is unheard of in the Beaujolais, I am told, because it is so easy and more common to pick underripe grapes and then chaptalize, which means to add sugar to the fermenting wine to make up for the ripeness lacking in the grapes.

Back to work! As we resumed, one of the girls who had earlier seemed to be in a zombie-like trance broke into song, decidedly off-key. She withered under a hail of tossed grape clusters, but then someone else took up the song and soon everyone joined in. It was "Love Me Tender" with a French accent. It was less painful to join in, too.

At 12:00 sharp, and I mean on the dot, everything stops. We clamber back into the vans and down to the winery for a classic Burgundian *coq au vin* and several unlabeled bottles of Lapierre, what turned out to be his 1996 rejects, the cuvées he did not put into the blend he sold. Still, it showed that one and only Lapierre style, and it was satisfying to think that the grapes I picked would end up tasting good, that I would one day enjoy drinking the fruits of my labor.

At the end of a long, hard afternoon we heard Marcel's final order: "Someone find us a corkscrew!" Bottles of the veritable 1996 Morgon were uncorked for evening enjoyment. When dinner was served it was *tête de veau* (calf's brains), my first, and I was hungry. With it there was a ceremonial glass of the new wine, what the old-timers call "paradise," right out of the press. Someone kindly advised me not to drink too much paradise or I would spend most of the night in the WC. Dinner was followed by singing and dancing and plenty of bright purple Morgon flowing.

The Beaujolais region has a reputation for ribaldry, maybe because of all the bawdy postcards for sale in every *tabac* and *maison de la presse* showing naked women in the cellars, couplings in the vines, four naked legs sticking out from behind a barrel, stuff like that, but I didn't see any of it. Well, someone did end up in an oak fermenter, but no one need get puritanical because when she emerged she was coated with grape parts. You might say you couldn't see the nips

for the pips. Just kidding. (*Dear Grandma, this part is what Kermit calls editing, love, Alison.*) My goodness, wine is considered sinful enough in the U.S. without adding raw sex to the brew. Details from the rest of the evening are pretty foggy. An old French hippie co-picker picked my brain about the Grateful Dead. He had seen them on a 1972 European tour. I remember a lot of Beaujolais-inspired merriment, and that I did nothing to be ashamed of, nothing to tarnish our image of seriousness and sobriety.

FOUND:
A SMALL CACHE
OF WHITE BURGUNDY

MONSIEUR CAILLOT had just pulled what must have been the 30th cork from a series of young and old Meursaults and Pulignys, some quite old, and I was pinching myself to see if I was dreaming some version of Wine-Hunter's Heaven.

"My father doesn't like to sell," Caillot said, explaining the endless piles of older bottles that littered that part of his cellar. "He believes it is better to have wine than money."

Some days the sun seems to shine on your side of the street, you are glad you got out of bed, you didn't even burn the toast, and at the end of the day you have something to show for it, something tangible, a tangible accomplishment.

I did not get away with a lot of wine, but I got the beauties, the pick of the bunch. Here they are:

DOMAINE CAILLOT

		PER BOTTLE	PER CASE
1995	*Santenay* Blanc	$19.95	$215.46
1992	*Puligny-Montrachet "Folatières"*	69.95	755.46
1990	*Bâtard-Montrachet*	120.00	1,296.00
1989	*Bâtard-Montrachet*	120.00	1,296.00

SUM-SUM-SUMMERTIME

1997 APREMONT · PIERRE BONIFACE

Oh, the pleasure of "little" wines! A lot of people don't really get it, you know. The appeal passes right over their heads, or palates. "Why have a BB gun when you can have an atomic bomb?" is, I suppose, the way they look at it. Bigger is better. Always better. Even when it's not.

Have you ever told a kid to taste something good and the kid says he doesn't like it without even trying it?

Apremont is a light, barely effervescent dry white from France's Savoie region between Lyon and Geneva. The other day when it arrived we dutifully chilled one and, to make sure it was good enough for you, we tasted it after work. Everyone seemed to brighten up, and we all noticed each other brightening up, and it was good.

Light in alcohol, dry and crisp, fresh, exhilarating, even tasty, we all urge you to try it.

$9.95 PER BOTTLE $107.46 PER CASE

DOMAINE OSTERTAG

MOUTON MASQUÉ

Mouton is French for lamb, or sheep, or . . . but of course, mutton! *Mouton* means "mutton" and *masqué* means "masked." You've heard of that famous masked man, the Lone Ranger? Well, here we have the masked mutton. (It is to be drunk. It is wine, white wine, dry white Alsatian wine.)

André is insisting that we all accept this in the sense that wine remains, basically, something to be swallowed, digested, and *pissé* (if you'll pardon his

French). He also points out that the year 2000 is fast approaching, so it is growing urgent that we change our entire system of values. He also beseeches us to speak of wine, when we speak of wine, with humor and poetry, as if we were speaking of life itself.

This is only the second Mouton Masqué in world history. A few years back the first was refused entry because someone from our government noticed on the wine's cartoon label a person's chest upon which were two naked dots about the size of the period at the end of this sentence . . Oops, don't gaze upon those dots too long. They might cause . . heavy . . breathing . . lust in your parts . . unspeakably un-American urges . . Wait, maybe three is better . . . If the chest had sported three dots, I wonder if it would have been permitted entry into the U.S. Maybe that's just a fine point. So to speak. But how many dots are dirty, how many not? Only Washington can decide what is really good for us, right?

Thankfully, André learned self-control in between his two Mouton Masqués, and his new label was permitted upon our shores, keeping our nation pure.

This wine is fun to drink. That's all, folks.

$9.95 PER BOTTLE $107.46 PER CASE

° ° ° ° ° ° ° °

1996 BOURGUEIL "CUVÉE BEAUVAIS" THIERRY BOUCARD

In 1978 I bought some 1976 Beauvais from Boucard. It is still a dazzler, 22 years old, with a healthy deposit.

Then he began filtering. Yikes. Abandon ship!

Now I convinced him to stop emasculating his prizes, 20 years later, and I'm back in a Bourgueil mode again.

$12.50 PER BOTTLE $135.00 PER CASE

PROVENCE

1996 CASSIS *BLANC* · CLOS SAINTE MAGDELEINE

Sometimes I feel underappreciated because some people think my life is one big vacation. They don't realize the effort it can take to obtain a decent bottle of wine.

Yesterday, for example, I had to spend practically the entire day at Cassis. It is not like I can just taste the wine, agree on a price, and go home. No, I had to drive down to the harbor with the winemaker, jump from the pier onto his bobbing boat, and motor out onto the Mediterranean, scene of countless shipwrecks. The sun's heat was blazing. I tried not to think of ozone depletion, sunburn, skin cancer . . . We had no choice but to jump into the cooling sea. Luckily I happened to be wearing a bathing suit. Just as I was about to dive in, I noticed a

school of inch-long jellyfish floating by. Their sting can momentarily paralyze you and leave you in pain for days. I wondered, is this really worth it? We motored out to safer waters and, finally, almost faint from heat prostration, I plunged into the cool blue water, a blue so beautiful I could barely stand it.

But still it was not over. Back at the domaine with its panoramic view of the cliffs and beaches of Cassis, I had to shelter myself under a tree and wait until the coals were ready for grilling a few local fish. Once they were cooked, we washed them down with some Cassis. (Of course. What do you think, a winemaker is going to serve me any wine other than his or her own? I told you this job is no vacation.)

But sitting there I finally got something accomplished. I was working it out in my mind: fish, Cassis, wine, Cassis wine, fish, fishing, etc., and all of a sudden it came to me. The white wine of Cassis was not invented to be shipped all over the world. It exists because once upon a time long ago the population of Cassis, a simple fishing village, needed something to drink with their catch, or seafood, as we call it. I thought to myself, why not recommend to my clientele that the next time they eat seafood, they drink a wine created to drink with it, Cassis. It works.

$16.95 PER BOTTLE $183.06 PER CASE

◦ ◦ ◦ ◦ ◦ ◦ ◦ ◦

1996 BOURGUEIL "GRANDMONT" · PIERRE BRETON

Tasting in Breton's crowded little cellar, well, it was one of those exciting moments where every wine sings and I was flabbergasted and he could see that my flabber was gasted, and we couldn't stop and say good-bye and head out into the sunlight just like that, so he pulled the cork on an older bottle. He asked me to guess what it was. I looked at it and guessed red, which he confirmed. I sniffed and guessed Bourgueil. Yes! As for the vintage, it was clearly from a big, ripe one.

It had the color, the magnitude, the dramatic impact of his 1996s, but older, so I guessed 1990. It seemed logical, but no, folks, it was a 1964. Your master taster missed it by 26 years. Oh well, back to the training room.

Do not underestimate the aging potential or the potential glory of our unfiltered old-vines cuvées from the Loire.

And here is one, all 50 cases of it, that I am certain of. Collectors with good cellars for aging, snap it up and put it down!

$14.95 PER BOTTLE $161.46 PER CASE

1996 RACINES · LES CAILLOUS DU PARADIS

In June I was in a Paris wine bar where the barman knows me. He served me a red and wouldn't tell me what it was. I guessed it to be a Rhône wine because it was so ripe, thick, and substantial, plus there was something about the aroma . . . No, folks, it was this very red from the Loire. *I wish people would stop making me guess what I'm tasting.*

Anyway, it is from ungrafted Cabernet Franc and seven other grape varieties whose names I did not write down. I did, however, drink it. Then I visited the domaine south of Blois (pronounced *blah*, sort of) where Racines is made by a hippy-looking organic farmer/winemaker named Claude Courtois. His wines don't taste like anyone else's. He's not like anybody else, either.

Racines is French for roots. You've heard of roots music, roots reggae? This is roots wine, and it rocks.

$14.95 PER BOTTLE $161.46 PER CASE

1997 BOUZERON ALIGOTÉ
A. & P. DE VILLAINE

When you consider de Villaine's Aligoté, does it matter that he also makes wine at Domaine de la Romanée-Conti? I would say yes, only in the sense that he starts from a lifelong habit of high standards and would abhor lending his name to anything second-rate.

Aubert (my seven-year-old son calls him "old bear") de Villaine is a perfectionist. When I told him that he must be proud of the rave reviews he has received for his recent Romanée-Conti vintages, he hesitated before saying, "Now that you mention it, it is unfortunate that I never feel such a sense of accomplishment because I'm too busy thinking about how I might have done better."

Aubert's Bouzeron Aligoté, *the* Aligoté of France's starred restaurants, really shines in 1997. It is the best since he shipped us a special old-vines cuvée of 1979, unfiltered. The 1997 has great beauty from start to finish. Everything is there in harmony, an absolute perfection.

He wrote about 1997, how the summer sun and heat lasted all the month of September without a drop of rain:

The grapes were picked admirably ripe and healthy, gorged with sugar, which produced a wine that combines a beautiful structure and dazzling fruit, but without heaviness thanks to the natural vivacity of the Aligoté grape. It has an opulent aroma and it is fulsome, you might say curvaceous, typical of the Aligoté from the Bouzeron slopes.

If I had a restaurant, I would not only offer Bouzeron Aligoté by the bottle. I would pour a few swallows for each diner as they were seated. You sit down, you swirl, you sniff and swallow and *voilà*, let the evening commence. Bouzeron Aligoté acts like a stimulant. It gets the conversation flowing, the appetite aroused, one's mood on course.

$14.95 PER BOTTLE $161.46 PER CASE

GIGONDAS
DOMAINE LES PALLIÈRES

TWELVE YEARS ago I wrote, "What a wonderful place for a wine merchant to retire, surrounded by vines, olive and fruit trees, wild herbs, ruins of the medieval fortified city on the hillside, and a population of only 750 with whom to share it all."

I was writing about Gigondas.

And 10 years ago for the cover of my book I chose a photo of a vineyard beneath the beautiful rock cliffs called Les Dentelles de Montmirail up above Gigondas.

So you see, there has been an attraction for a long time.

I am not ready to retire, but my dream came closer to reality the other day when I purchased a domaine, appellation GIGONDAS.

Don't worry, I am not going to turn into a winemaker. I will not subject

you to that. My hands will never be stained purple unless I swirl my wineglass clumsily.

It all happened like this: This past May, Daniel Brunier joined me for lunch at Chez Panisse. He mentioned in passing that an interesting domaine was for sale at Gigondas. I think my excited reaction shocked him. What, where, which, when, how much?

It was the Domaine Les Pallières, Daniel said.

It might interest you to read about Les Pallières in Robert Parker's *Wines of the Rhône Valley*, Livingstone-Learmonth's *The Wines of the Rhône*, or *Rhône Renaissance* by Remington Norman. Some samples:

The domaine is tucked away in the north of the appellation, on the way towards Sablet, and on a hot summer's day is enveloped in a stillness and a mantle of sweet Provençal aromas that make the visitor feel he is entering an enchanted garden. (L.-L.)

This is one of the more splendidly situated properties in Gigondas, with vineyards planted on the clay/limestone terraces tucked under the craggy needles of the Dentelles de Montmirail. (R.P.)

When Rhône wine dynasties are discussed, it is invariably the 500-year unbroken succession of Chaves at Mauves which catches the imagination. Yet, the Roux family have been farming Les Pallières, in the hills between Gigondas and Les Sablets, from father to son since 1400. (R.N.)

Daniel said that now, after all those centuries, there is no successor to inherit the domaine and that the proprietor wanted to retire.

I thought of the magical site, the old vines (the youngest are 30 years old, the oldest were planted in 1905), the fact that the wine of Gigondas is undervalued, and above all that I had, right in front of me, the man I consider (working with his brother Frédéric) the most talented winemaker in the southern Rhône. Take any southern Rhône and line up 5 or 10 vintages of it and the same 5 or 10 from Vieux Télégraphe and you will see what I mean. Also, the Bruniers, father Henri and sons Daniel and Frédéric, share my philosophy of realizing and preserving a great *terroir*'s typicity. I imagined tasting one of the Rhône's great *terroirs* at Gigondas vinified by the Bruniers.

"It is almost *too* perfect," I said. "Let's do it, let's buy it together."

Well, it wasn't easy. We weren't the only ones who prized Pallières. Offers were pouring in from the likes of Guigal at Ampuis, the Perrins at Beaucastel, from nearby Château du Trignon. Even a Bordeaux château entered the bidding. It could have gotten too expensive for us, but after all, I am of the opinion that the chemistry between old man Brunier, Henri Brunier, and the seller, Pierre Roux, clinched the deal for us. Both are of the old school, *vieux vignerons*, and I believe Monsieur Roux liked the idea of the Bruniers continuing his work and tending the vines and wines. (Plus, it probably didn't hurt that we agreed to let him stay and spend his retirement at Pallières. ("It will be helpful," Daniel said, "because he grew up here, he knows every vine.")

There are 25 hectares of vineyard. It does not take much effort to keep yields low from the old vines, and we expect to average around 6,000 cases per year. As you read this, the first vintage of Gigondas Les Pallières vinified by Brunier is happily fermenting away.

BOMBS AWAY

ATTENTION, wine lovers! Head immediately for your wine shelters. Somebody just dropped another hedonistic fruitbomb.

Hedonistic fruitbomb. Those of you who do not follow wine jargon have missed what has become a journalistic favorite. I remember seeing the words used separately for a while, hedonistic wines and wines that were called fruitbombs, then someone put them together and it really caught on. Hedonistic fruitbomb is intended to be a compliment! Not only that, a large part of the press would have you believe that the goal of all winemakers is to create hedonistic fruitbombs, and that a winemaker who does not, falls short.

Nonsense. Discussing this bizarre, even vulgar turn of events, a winemaker said to me the other day, "You know, anyone can make a wine like that. All it takes is bad taste."

Let's face it, *hedonistic* has turned into a code word for high alcohol, freakishly high alcohol. Recently on a restaurant list I saw a Châteauneuf-du-Pape one critic had awarded 96 points (today it seems only hedonistic fruitbombs rate high scores), so I ordered it out of curiosity. One smell, one swallow, and I asked for the wine list again to look for something drinkable. (According to my aesthetic a wine should, above all, be drinkable.) The Châteauneuf weighed in at 16.5° alcohol. It tasted like prescription cough syrup. It hurt going down. And of course it was impossible to taste food alongside it.

Now, on to *fruitbomb*, which sounds like something that smells like Carmen Miranda's headgear looks.

While I have never experienced one firsthand, I imagine that by its very nature a bomb lacks finesse. Fruitbomb signifies gaudy, overdone, overblown, designed to appeal to one's baser, not finer, instincts.

And one more thing: How many of those hedonistic fruitbombs are bottled with sweetness remaining in order to hide the acrid flavor of their high alcohol? Then you've got to add some acid to make up for the flabby flatness that results from harvesting overripe grapes.

Another thing: you never see a Muscadet described as hedonistic, yet what is more hedonistic than a platter of shellfish and a bottle of Muscadet? WHAT IS WINE FOR?

Next month we will examine another popular term: *highly extracted*, which always reminds me of a trip to the dentist.

✦ 1999 ✦

ALSATIAN WINE SAMPLER

FOR SOME TIME I have wanted to organize a sampler that would demonstrate *in your very own wineglass* the depth and diversity Alsace can offer, but I never seemed to have together *all at one time* the wines appropriate to make a sampler meaningful.

This one works. There are several reasons to purchase it. To learn, to enjoy, and to save money, for example.

Can it be, 25 buying trips to Alsace? My goodness. And here, working by the fire on a cold February day, when I think of Alsace I see the ruins of castles along the string of mountaintops above the *route du vin*. I remember the numerous pristine medieval villages, their half-timbered houses all dated above the doorways, and the warren of cellars underneath. Listen, by the year 800 there were already over a hundred wine villages in Alsace. The past seems to reside in its narrow cobbled streets alongside the current population. Don't take your kids to Eurodisney. Take them to the fairy-tale villages and castles of Alsace, where a parent can escape underground now and then for a restorative glass of wine(s).

So many memories. A perfect bottle of 1966 Riesling Herrenweg on a restaurant wine list. A 1981 Château Cheval Blanc for 800FF at the Auberge du Cheval Blanc in, was it Ribeauvillé? A picnic on a blanket up in the vineyards while a brass band played in the streets of the same ville below. The trout pulled out of an icy stream and pan-fried up in the forest with a cold pitcher of electric Riesling.

Alsace is cluttered with starred restaurants and I've been to several . . . once. The hell with them. I like the basics, the family-style cuisine, not the hoity-toity designer versions you are subjected to in the starred shrines. Wander around, ask the locals, sniff at the kitchen doors of taverns and the like—that's how to find the best food in Alsace.

I had a favorite for years to which I was faithful. I would resist *choucroute garnie* all year long, saving my hunger for the best, for those great sausages, chunks of pork, and sliced ham, that delicious pot of mustard, the restaurant's "Who's Who in Alsace" wine list . . . Then they got a star in the *Guide Michelin*. All of a sudden a reservation was required, the prices jumped, the massive old beams were *painted*, of all things, and then to top it all off, *pink tablecloths*. The food? Well, there was no kiwi in the sauerkraut, but it had been, to put it kindly, refined. Choucroute Lite!

But lucky me, since 1981 I have been a client *chez* Zind-Humbrecht, which means that every so often I eat the home cooking of Olivier Humbrecht's mother and grandmother. There was a soup of frog legs and watercress that I shall never forget, an incredible plum (*quetsches*) tart served with an extravagantly flavored late-harvest Gewurztraminer, plus rustic classics like *choucroute garnie* and *beckenoffe* that make the starred versions look canned.

The sampler contains wine from three domaines. Zind-Humbrecht is considered (with reason) the genius of Alsatian wine and André Ostertag the artist, and the venerable firm of Kuentz-Bas delivers us beautifully classic renditions at great prices, wines that are known for blossoming with age.

Please serve these sampler wines in sequence, as listed, whether you serve one of them per night, a flight per night, or you invite friends over to taste all of them in one go, and if that's the case, take a little bread break when you change from one grape variety to another. If you don't, it will be too difficult to change gears, to go, for example, from the extraterrestrial Rangen to the nifty little Gewurztraminer from Kuentz-Bas. Give your delicate palate time to regroup between rounds.

Here we go:

1996 PINOT BLANC "BARRIQUES" · ANDRÉ OSTERTAG

Barrique? You probably expect an oak bomb. No way, André. Our sampler starts with a classy whisper, a whisper like Marilyn Monroe whispered. And I know what would be good to munch on with it: that fried Hama Hama oyster sandwich, spread with coleslaw and tartar sauce, that I devoured upstairs last week at Chez Panisse.

This wine's compass points to Burgundy. Hama Hama!

$13.50 PER BOTTLE $145.80 PER CASE

1996 PINOT BLANC · KUENTZ-BAS

Keep one in the fridge for a ready apéritif. Promise? All the staff thinks it smells like white blossoms, but each comes up with a different flower. Creamy texture, vibrant core, long on the palate.

$9.95 PER BOTTLE $107.46 PER CASE

1996 RIESLING "TRADITION" · KUENTZ-BAS

The aroma takes me back to that mountain *auberge* where they pulled my trout wriggling out of the stream. Riesling, Alsace's noblest variety. This is classic! Notice the hint of rose petal, tangerine, and that sleek mineral finish.

$11.95 PER BOTTLE $129.06 PER CASE

1997 RIESLING D'EPFIG · ANDRÉ OSTERTAG

Here you enter the aromatic opulence of 1997's extraordinarily long, sunny harvest. Given the lush aroma, you might be surprised when it finishes . . . *d-r-y*, with a racy acidity. Perfect for *choucroute*, if ever need be, or fish, or fowl: charcoal-roasted game birds, for example.

$15.95 PER BOTTLE $172.26 PER CASE

1996 RIESLING "HERRENWEG" · ZIND-HUMBRECHT

It is almost as if someone turned up the volume, and that someone is Olivier Humbrecht. But it's not blaring. It is subtle and fine and you cannot help wondering at the outsized talent of its winemaker. Gorgeous, complex fruit with a puff of gunflint. Totally versatile, but when we all went through these wines, Steve Ledbetter dreamt aloud of sweetbreads, and we all said, "Yeah, wow, ooh, amen, STOP IT," and stuff like that.

$27.50 PER BOTTLE $297.00 PER CASE

1996 RIESLING "CLOS HÄUSERER"
ZIND-HUMBRECHT

A soil of marl and limestone gives a strong minerality here. *Not* for beginners. Experience required. This is like a youngster, a newborn, best decanted to liberate what is an incredibly complex aroma. A grape can do *this*? "Crisp and powerful," says Olivier. It's a knockout.

$29.95 PER BOTTLE $323.46 PER CASE

1995 PINOT GRIS "BARRIQUES" · ANDRÉ OSTERTAG

Barrel aging even for wines of the Pinot family is rare in Alsace. André finds that if you can do it without smothering the wine with oak flavors, it develops, liberates, expands, and deepens a wine's personality. His 1995 is full-bodied and firmly structured with good nervosity. It shines with steamed, poached, or stewed fish preparations. For ultra-impact, serve it with sushi.

$19.95 PER BOTTLE $215.46 PER CASE

1996 PINOT GRIS "FRONHOLZ" · ANDRÉ OSTERTAG

Ripe, ample perfume. Campfire smoke and dried fruits. Huge, luxurious palate. All flavor. Nothing wasted. And then, thankfully, those flavors linger on and on and on.

$29.95 PER BOTTLE $323.46 PER CASE

1996 PINOT GRIS "RANGEN" *GRAND CRU* ZIND-HUMBRECHT

Nothing can prepare you for a wine like this. And only ZH makes them. Here is your chance to experience what many consider to be the Romanée-Conti of Alsace. Volcanic soil. Harvested in November. Botrytized Pinot Gris. Great vintage. Power and majesty. I will not try to describe the aromatic complexity.

$58.00 PER BOTTLE $626.46 PER CASE

1997 GEWURZTRAMINER D'EPFIG · ANDRÉ OSTERTAG

Simple, fresh and youthful, rich in body, this would be ideal served outdoors, well chilled as an apéritif. Delicious by itself, it seems luscious and ethereal all at once.

$22.50 PER BOTTLE $243.00 PER CASE

1996 GEWURZTRAMINER "RÉSERVE" · KUENTZ-BAS

Deep, dive-into-me aroma with serious spice. Powerful, solid, dry Gewurztraminer. You could say textbook, but it is livelier, better balanced than most. It works beautifully with a cheese platter. Mmm, the spice and pear skin linger.

$18.95 PER BOTTLE $204.66 PER CASE

1995 GEWURZTRAMINER "HERRENWEG" VENDANGES TARDIVES · ZIND-HUMBRECHT

There is a symphony of aromas roaring out: smoke, spice, nuts, mineral, concentrated fruits . . . What a brilliant wine. But what to serve with it? If I smoked, I'd pour a glass and simply light up. No, let's do some grilled almonds instead. Nothing *too* complicated because you don't want to interfere with the complicatedness of the wine.

$72.00 PER BOTTLE $777.60 PER CASE

That's it, our Alsatian Sampler. What a long, strange trip it's been. Unbelievable, the voyage from wine one to the late-harvest Gewurz, isn't it? From a comet to a universe.

Price Before Discount
$330.15

Special Sampler Price
$240.00

REST IN PEACE

Recently, well before his time, the jovial, unspoiled, well-loved Robert Jasmin was hit by a car and died instantly. I sent Erin from our Beaune office to the funeral with condolences on behalf of the KLWM staff and clientele. More than a thousand people showed up to mourn in tiny Ampuis, where Jasmin lived between the Rhône River and the Côte Rôtie.

When I first visited the northern Rhône in 1976, I identified a sort of core group of talented *hommes de terroir*: Clape at Cornas, Chave for Hermitage, Trollat for Saint-Joseph, Gentaz and Jasmin at Ampuis. I was attracted to something timeless about their wines, wonderful Syrahs that managed to express quite clearly their individual *terroirs* yet at the same time bore the personal imprint of each winemaker.

Robert Jasmin

The Côte Rôtie Jasmin made tastes like no other. Those in search of heavy blockbusters disparage his efforts, but even though Robert was pretty macho, macho is not what he liked in a glass of wine. Yet, in the cellar, his Côte Rôtie ages longer and more cleverly than the inky blockbusters. The delicacy of a Jasmin Côte Rôtie is almost like a disguise that masks a wine of great vigor and muscle.

Of course, as is pretty well known, my cuvée was different from other Jasmin bottlings, and each and every year he would put me through my paces before giving me exactly what he knew I wanted. One year he told me I was too late, everything had been filtered, and it was ready to ship whenever I wanted. I fumed and snarled and finally told him, well then, I won't be a buyer for this vintage. Today I can see him clearly, standing there in that silly undershirt of his, laughing with gusto. He threw a big arm around my shoulder and steered me into the deepest part of his cellar where he had a *demi-muid* and a couple of barrels marked "KL" in chalk.

"Those are for you if you want them," he said, "and I'll bottle them for you unfiltered. But personally," and a big smile spread across his face, "personally I prefer the filtered!"

Suddenly, abruptly, there is a big empty space in that part of the world.

I would have expected him to kill the car.

◦ ◦ ◦ ◦ ◦ ◦ ◦ ◦

1997 CÔTES DU RHÔNE *ROUGE* "BOIS DES DAMES" CHÂTEAU DU TRIGNON

Q: I want to drink Châteauneuf-du-Pape all the time, but wouldn't that get expensive?

A: Expensive is relative. Bill Gates can shower in Châteauneuf-du-Pape if he wants. Something tells me that you cannot. Therefore, heed this KLWM insider info: Every so often Trignon vinifies their Bois des Dames apart. This is their first since the 1993. Bois des Dames has the same glacial-era rolled-stone terrain as Vieux Télégraphe, called *galets roulés*, and those stones influence the taste of the two wines. Bottled pure, I consider it the finest A.O.C. Côtes du Rhône on the market. Try it. It might solve your dilemma. Oh, and Bill, next time you need a shower, see our Vieux Télégraphe pre-arrival offer.

$11.50 PER BOTTLE $124.20 PER CASE

1998 COTEAUX DU LANGUEDOC ROSÉ DOMAINE DU POUJOL

The wine world is amumble after Master of Wine Rosemary George of London called Poujol's 1998 rosé "scrummy." Is that short for *it's crummy* or short for *scrumptious*? My dictionary has *scrummage*, but no *scrummy*. But wouldn't *scrumpy* be short for *scrumptious*?

Another critic called it *unabashed*. An *unabashed* rosé. That's from Boston. Yet another says it has *spunk*. Weird, isn't it, the choice of words this clytemnaceous little rosé inspires. But none of them inspire THIRST. I mean, who wants to drink scrum?

How's this? The heady strawberry and watermelon-like fruit and a crisp, minerally, lip-smackingly dry finish keep you coming back for one unabashed swallow after another.

$8.95 PER BOTTLE $96.66 PER CASE

1995 GIGONDAS
DOMAINE LES PALLIÈRES

There was wine still in cask in the cellar when I purchased Les Pallières with the Brunier family. We tasted through the casks several times and selected two *foudres* of 1995 to keep, then sold the rest off to *négociants*. So what you have here is our selection of Pallières at its best under the direction of the previous owner, Pierre Roux.

It had just been bottled when I arrived for a two-week buying trip in mid-March, so I carried 12 bottles along with me in the trunk and uncorked them for various winemakers along the route. All agreed that it is the best wine they have ever tasted. No, just kidding, but I was pleased and impressed by how quickly the bottles grew empty once uncorked. Always a good sign, right? Often the winemakers remarked upon the wine's finesse, unusual for the appellation Gigondas.

Rooftops of Gigondas

And many found a distinctive perfume of *réglisse* and violets that lingers on the palate. The Bruniers and I find the same perfume in our first vintage, the 1998, and wonder if *réglisse* and violet might be typical of the Pallières *goût de terroir*.

Réglisse is translated in my dictionary as "licorice," but the flavor in the wine is not of the black candy but of the sweet, distinctively flavored root of the plant, *Glycyrrhiza glabra*, a Mediterranean perennial. French kids grow up chewing on branches of the stuff. You can buy it like candy in France. The dry, wild, sweet, branchy taste of it stirs up remembrances of things past in the consciousness of French wine drinkers, so the perfume is highly prized.

Violets were in bloom when I was at Pallières, and the wine does have a suggestion of the little blue violets that grow wild around there.

The vineyard at Pallières is in parcels scattered about different levels of the hillsides in the midst of 240 acres of woods and *garrigue*, and that outdoorsy aroma is present in the wine, too.

The 1995 is open and perfectly developed for current enjoyment.

$22.50 PER BOTTLE $243.00 PER CASE

LONELINESS

ALMOST THE worst thing about traveling alone is dining alone. Some people apparently feel self-conscious: *Everyone in the restaurant must be thinking I'm too much of a jerk to get anyone to eat with me.* But dining alone makes me feel incomplete, because there is no one to ooh and aah with if it's good, and no one to gripe with if it's bad. And the other thing is, I don't know what to do with my eyes. You can only stare at other diners so much without provoking an incident. Studying the tablecloth gets old and studying the ceiling *does* make me self-conscious. *What's he see up there? What's wrong with his neck?* Once in a while I will take a book to table, but my mother must have trained me as a pup, because a voice keeps telling me it is rude to read at table, so total concentration is never possible. Thanks, Mom.

If you are dining alone in France, here are three favorite addresses. At each you will find a show outside to keep your eyes busy.

In Paris I go to Au Sauvignon, a little wine bar in the 7th, 80 rue des Saints-Pères. Seated at one of the outdoor tables, you can watch a great parade of Parisians go by. Indoors the walls and ceilings are filled with wonderfully accomplished, hilariously lewd sketches of Beaujolais wine scenes. *Ooh, look where he's got his hand!* But let's get back to the street, weather permitting. There are a lot of chic boutiques for women in the neighborhood, so you get a fashion show, and I must say the fashions you witness are remarkably different from our Berkeley-type clothing and accessories. And there must be an art school nearby (the Beaux Arts?) because you see a lot of students with portfolios, late for class with wet hair and cigarettes.

Au Sauvignon offers seven or eight wines, bottled on site, beautifully chosen.

I especially like their Quincy and Beaujolais. There is no real cooking. Try the *saucisson* sandwich, bread by Poilâne. And I urge you to try their goat cheese from Sancerre, the Crottin de Chavignol, with fresh butter and slices of Poilâne. Yes, cheese with butter. I know, I know. It is almost un–American.

If alone near Arles, head for the restaurant Vaccarès on the Place du Forum and request a table on the terrace. You look down on a lively scene and no one looks back up at you. You will see a big hunk of Roman ruin on the corner of the Hôtel Nord Pinus, a statue of Frédéric Mistral, a bright café that van Gogh painted by night, plane trees, birdies, and lots of people down in the square, too. Meanwhile, the cuisine is Provençal and you have a choice of several vintages from Domaine Tempier, Trévallon, and Clape, just to name a few. Hmm, dining alone gets better by the glass.★

Lately I have to go to Collioure once a year to select wine. I time my visit carefully in terms of weather because Collioure is on the Mediterranean, and I like to jump in. June through September works. I like to eat outside at the restaurant Les Templiers, which is on a street closed to cars, so again you can enjoy a pedestrian parade, and this time they are dressed for the beach! Sure, most are in today's tasteless, brand X T-shirts, but once in a while something eye-catching goes by. Here I usually order nothing but starters for the whole meal, because the starters are truly Catalan, and well made. For example:

> *Salade de Pêcheur*
> Marinated anchovies
> Marinated anchovies with roasted red pepper
> *Jambon Serrano* from Spain
> Squid with aioli
> *Friture* of little local fish
> Red peppers stuffed with squid

And you can wash it all down with the 1997 Collioure *rouge* from Domaine La Tour Vieille. Come to think of it, we actually sell that exact same wine right here in Berkeley, too.

★*As noted elsewhere, the restaurant Vaccarès has closed its doors.*

◊　◊　◊　◊　◊　◊　◊　◊

1998 CÔTE DE BROUILLY · CHÂTEAU THIVIN

In 1976, when I was busy being born as a wine importer, Richard Olney guided me through the French vineyards. In the Beaujolais we visited Château Thivin and Georges Duboeuf. I chose to pursue Thivin. Had I gone the other way, I would have lived an entirely different life. Instead of importing hundreds of cases of Thivin every year, I would have had hundreds of thousands to work with. Instead of writing this memory right now, I might be retired, uncorking a Tempier rosé on my yacht, anchored off some Greek isle. But Monsieur Duboeuf would probably have seen that I wasn't suited for the job and selected another importer anyway. It would never have worked for either of us. At the time, of course, I did not foresee the consequences of my choice. I was at a crossroads without really knowing where each road led.

Anyway, I fell for Thivin, and today, still, it stands out in a crowd. Is it not the aristocrat of the Beaujolais? I don't mean that in the foppish, nose-in-the-air sense of the word. The wine of Thivin is like a country squire who is not afraid to get his boots muddy. Handsome, virile, earthy, *and* an aristocrat.

In this newly arrived vintage 1998, you really notice the wine's breed, because it is not a vintage of amplified fruit. It is what André Ostertag in Alsace calls a *vin de Pierre* instead of a *vin de fruit*. I mean, of course there is fruit, this is Beaujolais, but you also sense the wine's mineral birthplace.

Thivin is a connoisseur's wine. Serve it at a cool temperature. I believe you will be amazed at how classy it is, from its vivid color all the way through to its elegant finish.

$13.95 PER BOTTLE $150.66 PER CASE

1998 VOUVRAY SEC · DOMAINE CHAMPALOU

After a monumental 1997 so rich and unctuous that I could only get it down spoon-fed by harem girls, here we have an entirely different style in 1998. Thank goodness. I like variety! Why else keep a harem?

(*Oh, my darling wife, I'm only joking. Even if I had a harem, I wouldn't want one.*)

After three *vins de garde*, 1995, 1996, 1997, here is one you can dive right into starting now. What I like about it has to do with its freshness, both in the bouquet and on the palate. There is very little acidity this year. This is a smooth one. The liveliness comes from its freshness, and it quite ripely slides down the gullet. Very seductive from start to finish.

$12.50 PER BOTTLE $135.00 PER CASE

CHÂTEAU LA ROQUE · PIC SAINT LOUP

There is a story in the wine literature whose punch line goes something like this: The girl, I no longer remember her name, but the wine, the wine was Chambertin.

In my story, however, I remember the woman's name *and* the name of the wine. The wine, the wine was Bandol, and the woman, the woman had on a blouse that Jean-Marie and I still . . . oops . . . the woman was Christine.

Jack Boutin, proprietor of Château La Roque, has a lot of Mourvèdre planted, but he had never visited the capital of Mourvèdre, so one summer day we arranged to meet at Domaine Tempier for a tasting with Jean-Marie Peyraud. When I pulled into the grassy parking area, I was not really surprised to see a couple necking in a little Renault under one of the cherry trees. Over the years, I have seen a lot of funny business at Tempier because their wine inspires people to kick off their shoes and let their hair down. But this couple turned out to be Jack

The cellar at Château La Roque

Boutin and his girlfriend I'd never met, Christine, and they had yet to down a single taste of Tempier at ten o'clock in the morning.

During our tasting, Jack had a lot of fun chewing on various vintages of Cabassaou, while Jean-Marie and I kept trying to appear nonchalant while stuffing our eyeballs back in their sockets. What silly nincompoops doth God's beautaceous creations create.

Now I know that you are more interested in getting to the history of La Roque (Romans were there even before Jack), the grape varieties, vinification, how much new oak, and all that important stuff, but my story has a moral, which is that Jack Boutin, or better, Jack's wine, or in fact maybe I don't know the precise moral of the story. I do know that there is nothing *im*moral about this story. I suppose I am trying to say that anyone who sits around necking under a cherry tree with Christine may be the kind of guy, whatever grape varieties he has, whose wine tastes good. See for yourself.

NEW VINTAGE

1998 PINOT BLANC · KUENTZ-BAS

Back in the early 1960s I spent some time on NY's Lower East Side and lived to tell about it. My favorite bar was named The Old Reliable, on East 4th near Avenue C. You had to knock to get in. They'd slide open a little slot to check you out first, just like in the movies. (That didn't stop a guy from getting knifed one night.) The Old Reliable had out-of-this-world hand-cut *free* French fries. No orders accepted. Orders resented, in fact. Now and then an old tramp would mosey out from the kitchen and place a hot, glistening platter on someone's table. Your table, if you were lucky. It was random. And they had a great house band, ahead of its time. What was the band's name? The leader was a singer, a guitarist, and a painter, too. If I'd had any money, I'd have bought a painting from him.

The Old Reliable. What a great name.

Which reminds me of . . . er, the Kuentz-Bas Pinot Blanc? How do we get from Avenue C to Husseren-les-Châteaux? Why, Old Reliable, of course. I trust that this transition requires no further justification.

Whenever I taste KB's Pinot Blanc, I forget to appreciate its winemaker. After so many good bottles, I take its class too much for granted. The fashion today is to make every wine a flamboyant statement, the fist-in-the-face style. But you know what it feels like when a lover whispers in your ear, don't you? Well, that's what this tastes like. Instead of your mouth falling open in awe, it opens for another taste. The wine expresses classic Alsatian Pinot Blanc, but we should not forget that it is thanks to the winemaker that the classic is delivered with such delicious perfection.

$11.50 PER BOTTLE $124.20 PER CASE

NEW RED FROM BANDOL

1997 DOMAINE DU GROS 'NORÉ

The winemaker is Alain Pascal, a living, breathing hunk of Provence. This 1997 is his domaine's debut bottling.

Alain's father, who planted the vineyard at La Cadière-d'Azur, was named Honoré. Locals called him 'Noré for short. He was a massive, broad-backed fellow.

 I live nearby and remember seeing him around. How could anyone forget seeing him? He seemed to fill the landscape. Alain inherited his dad's chiseled features, fit for a Provençal Mt. Rushmore. And Alain named his domaine after his dad. *Gros* 'Noré. Big 'Noré.

Several times this summer I crossed the little valley that separates my house from his. He's a hunter, too, so along with the wines I have been served bloody, barely cooked little birdies (you are supposed to eat them crunchy bones and beaks and all), delicious homemade pâtés, and a sickeningly flavored leg of wild boar that I could barely cut through with knife and fork, much less chew, much less (gag) swallow. Folks, I do it for you, to score for you that rare prize, a natural wine.

Alain is a naïf when it comes to wine. He does not know where Chablis is, for example. And he thinks Côte Rôtie is a blend of Syrah and Mourvèdre! But you should see the look on his face, the glow, the boyish excitement when he runs off to find us an old bottle he and his father made for their own drinking. (They sold most of their grapes to domaines Pibarnon and Ott and the local co-operative.) It is rustic, oh yes, rustic in the good sense. Of this earth, of our sun. Those older bottles, 1993, 1989, 1985, are totally convincing Bandols. He loves big, old-fashioned wines and seems pretty happy to have found a client who wants to buy the kind of wine he likes to make.

$22.50 PER BOTTLE $243.00 PER CASE

1997 VENDANGES TARDIVES DOMAINE OSTERTAG

WHEN ANDRÉ Ostertag and I tasted the three wines offered here, my goodness, I began to hear music, but he said that he had never thought of them musically, that he sees these 1997s architecturally. Well, there is a word that brings it all together: architectonics. We were both seeking to describe the (outward) style given each wine by its (inner) structure.

1997 RIESLING *GRAND CRU* · "MUENCHBERG" V. T.

Late-harvested wines are sweet, of course. That is expected. And sweet means luscious. I told André that what sets this Riesling apart and really makes one's heart skip a beat is the lovely violin solo that seems to soar out from the rich, luscious body. André says that he sees a cathedral, a Gothic cathedral. Look at the Strasbourg Cathedral, he said, the way the steeple spires up into the heavens from its substantial foundation.

This is only 9.6° alcohol, so the great subtlety and nobility of the Riesling and the *grand cru* vineyard are not obscured by high alcohol. That's neat. It was harvested at the end of October under Rhône-like sunny skies, but despite the extraordinary ripeness, the Riesling delivers the minerality of the Muenchberg *terroir*.

If you have Beethoven's Violin Concerto, listen to the initial entry of the solo violin. That will give you an idea (while you look at a picture of the Strasbourg Cathedral) of the nature of this wine's style.

$41.50 PER BOTTLE

1997 PINOT GRIS *GRAND CRU* "MUENCHBERG" V. T.

I hope you can experience the two Muenchbergs side by side. When you do, the Riesling seems floral and mineral, while the Pinot Gris evokes ripe fruits baking in the sun on the ground in an orchard. Also in this Pinot Gris, there are aromas of humus, quince, and smoke. You see all of the two wines with CLARITY when tasted side by side.

André describes its structure as Romanesque. Thick, solid, large-scaled, weighty. I was hearing the rumble and growl of Pablo Casals's cello.

$44.00 PER BOTTLE

1997 GEWURZTRAMINER · "FRONHOLZ" V.T.

The soil is clay and quartz. André believes that Gewurztraminer is a grape variety with a tendency to seem flagrant or blatant. A lot of wine lovers adore that over-the-top quality, but André finds it too often vulgar or ostentatious. The quartz at Fronholz, he says, keeps the Gewurztraminer's questionable tendencies in check. You will see what he means in this super-ripe (130 grams of residual sugar) example. He almost makes an honest woman of her!

What a wild variety of aromas. It is explosive, exuberant, complicated. Architecturally, André says, it is Baroque. You will be amazed by how filled with flavor and perfume it is. Really super-charged. *The Wine Advocate*'s comment: "It has loads of concentration, power, and depth of fruit yet maintains surprising elegance."

These are three wines for the kind of client I like to think I have, wines that satisfy on many levels, including (mere) deliciousness.

$39.25 PER BOTTLE

STRANGER THAN FACT!
THE BIZARRE LEGEND BEHIND THE NAME
PIC SAINT LOUP

After my recent brochure about Château La Roque and the Pic Saint Loup region north of Montpellier, your cards and letters kept piling up until practically all other endeavors at our office ground to a halt. A decision was made. We would respond to your question "Why did they name the peak Saint Loup?"

Well, it does not mean Saint Wolf's Peak, as I hypothesized (loup meaning "wolf" in French). I had to spend weeks scouring moldy archives in ancient monasteries eating bread and water until, eureka, I held in my hands a tattered few pages from the Dark Ages that shed light upon the origin of the name Pic Saint Loup.

ONCE UPON A TIME near Vigan in the Cévennes, a certain Count Rénaud died of grief shortly after his wife's untimely demise. The unfortunate couple left three sons, the Seigneurs d'Esparon, in the family castle.

The firstborn, Guiral, was quite a dashing young knight—tall, dark, and handsome with long, wavy hair. Pumping iron had given him an imposing musculature and no one could compete with him at the tourneys, where all the

Pic Saint Loup

women recognized his physical prowess and burst into passionate applause after his victories.

His younger brother, Loup, was also a handsome knight, with delicate features and silky blond hair. He devoted himself to his studies: grammar, speech, music, and philosophy. As a troubadour he knew how to compose sweet melodies, and when he sang, all the ladies were touched very deeply and responded with adoration, their hearts aflutter.

Alban, the youngest brother, might have been less of a hunk than the other two, but what a heart of gold. His kindness and charity to the less fortunate impressed many a young girl who appreciated his sweet disposition and understood that it would come in handy in a husband. "He's neither a lout nor a pig," they muttered amongst themselves.

So the three knights spent wonderful nights until one day, touring the countryside, they decided to visit their cousin Irene, Countess of Bévieures. Gracious, young, pretty, awesomely constructed, and quite rich, she possessed all those qualities that turn men into drooling nincompoops and screw up their lives forever. Yes, even handsome knights in shining armor.

Alas, just like that, our three brothers were unanimously burning with love for the countess. They tried to get her attention with gifts, flowers, perfume, poetry, songs, and free visits to Guiral's gym.

Irene, how shall we say, was not blind to their attentions. Trying to keep your toes warm night after winter night in a cold stone castle gets old quickly. As hard as it may be to imagine, Irene fell for the three of them exactly equally. (It is stuff like this that makes some stories become legends; if she'd picked one, we wouldn't be here right now and you could get on to buying some wine.)

Then, to make matters worse, the boys not only agreed that they would never marry anyone but Irene, they also *swore* it. What a scene! Three brothers, one cousin. Even if they hadn't been related, it just wasn't done.

Then something happened in a land far away that promised to bring matters to a head: the three young knights were ordered to accompany their sovereign on a crusade to the Holy Land.

On departure day, while the wind howled and the horses stomped their hooves in the icy ground, Irene descended the castle stairway in a diaphanous gown, and *mon dieu*, her charms were splendidly evident. Waving fervently, she bade her suitors farewell and promised she would choose between them upon their return. This vision of Irene haunted the three of them all the days and nights of their crusade.

Five long years the war lasted in Palestine, and Irene waited and waited, dating no one, watching from the highest tower of her château for the safe return of her lovers, because even in those days the French mail service was unreliable.

Finally our three heroes returned in triumph, loaded with the spoils of war. However, when they arrived at the foot of Mount Hortus, they noticed a procession advancing slowly toward them: a priest followed by monks carrying a coffin, and a group of wailing women dressed all in black.

It is impossible to describe the pain the brothers experienced when they learned that the funeral was their fiancée's. Irene had fallen ill waiting for them year after year, hanging out in that icy tower without a fireplace, losing her appetite until she was too frail to escape the clutches of death.

For a year the brothers lived in their château together, drinking coarse wine into the wee hours and singing chorus upon chorus of "Goodnight Irene" until they would stagger off to their spacious, lonely beds. Life had no meaning, so they voted three-zero to devote the rest of their days to the Lord. They sold their château and gave the proceeds to their servants and to the poor. They separated and became hermits.

Guiral went north and settled on a snowy summit, living an austere existence to atone for his sins.

Loup (remember Pic Saint *Loup*, the reason for all this?) went south, climbed a peak (peak = *pic* in French) across from Irene's old place, and spent his time composing corny poems about ideal love.

Alban moved into the rocky crevice of another nearby mountain, his only companion an ivory crucifix, which he kept moistened with his tears.

Upon separating they had vowed to light a fire every year on the anniversary of their beloved's death. The fires, blazing upon the summits of the three peaks, would be the only tie that united them.

And thus it was. Each year the three hermits lit their fires in memory of Irene, and each could see two lights from afar when night fell and the first star appeared.

For several years they renewed their ceremony until one year Loup could see no light to the north. Guiral, the strongest, had died. The next year there was no sign of light from Alban, for he too had ascended to heaven. Loup understood that his own fire would be extinguished next.

The following year he still had the strength to gather enough wood to light a fire, and while the last embers burned down, Loup stretched out on the straw bed of his hermitage and gave up his soul. With his last breath he urged all U.S. citizens to remember the purity and fidelity of his love for Irene by consuming copious amounts of the dark-colored, fleshy wine from vineyards at the base of the Pic Saint Loup.

And as we raise our glasses, dear reader, let us try to forget just how dumb Loup and his brothers really were. What a ridiculous waste. What if they had, right at the beginning, simply flipped a coin? We would have been out of here with a "happily ever after" pages ago. Sometimes I think a tree or a fly has more sense than a human being. Then I realize that trees and flies do not know how to vinify.

⇴ 2000 ⇷

WINE, WOMEN, AND DOG

1997 MADIRAN · CHÂTEAU DE PERRON

WHEN I ENTER the courtyard of the inconspicuous Château de Perron and climb out of my car, two events always occur. First, a mammoth, grizzly, out-of-shape German shepherd comes bounding up and sniffs around, deciding whether to wet one of my tires or chew me into bloody pieces, so I act like everything is normal. "Hi, boy. Nice dog." Then I start sniffing, too, to see if my fear has a scent. Then finally (seconds seem like minutes, *nice doggy*, minutes seem like hours, *good doggy*), the couple who own Perron emerge from their château, out a side door. Why do I always have the impression that I have interrupted them at play? The expression on their faces, that's why, as if they are not yet quite capable of focusing their attention on an intruder, even if he has an appointment. And what kind of smile is that on her face? I'd call it mischievous, playfully mischievous, and I like it. I want to say, Go back, this wine stuff can wait, get back to your funny business. Wine, women, and dog, that's what Château de Perron means to me.

But what will it mean to you, deprived as you are of Madame's elfin expression? Here I present their 1997, which is a very special vintage at Madiran. You like black wine? Here's black. Then you sink your nose into a huge, smoky, dense, cassis bouquet that'll knock your socks or some other article of clothing off. A big, round, powerful impression on the palate. You'd best chew it around a bit before swallowing. In fact, this is the one to pull when you are in the mood for a full-throttle tannic presence. Fabulous stuff.

$9.95 PER BOTTLE $107.46 PER CASE

THE HORMONE/BLACK TRUFFLE WAR

BECAUSE WE are in a trade skirmish, black truffles—one of the two or three most haunting, captivating, delicious flavors in the universe—are doubly expensive this year. We pay a 100% tariff to import truffles because the French will not allow U.S. hormone-fed beef into their markets. Our government responded, "You won't eat our hormones? Then we won't eat your truffles. Take that!"

We, however, are going to do some fresh truffle dinners with Paul Bertolli at Oliveto anyway, not in protest, but because we deserve it. And we are not going chintzy with little flecks of truffle. We are going to do it right, truffles all over the place, truffles you can smell and taste and feel and ooh and aah over, black truffles that make our wines taste even better.

If the French don't want to eat hormones, they shouldn't have to, right? They still won't allow English beef, either, because of mad cow disease. But before you begin admiring the French government for protecting its citizenry, think about this: French livestock is fed sewage-enhanced feed. And then there is the fact that 80% of French electricity is created by nuclear power. They make so much excess that they export it to their neighbors. So, no U.S. or English beef, but the danger of a French Chernobyl isn't even discussed in France.

Let me vote and I will vote no on hormones, no on nuclear power plants, yes on truffles.

But honestly, our truffle dinners are a hedonistic, gastronomic extravaganza with zero political content. I am just explaining here why this year's truffles are more of a splurge than usual.

The truffly dinners are coming right up, Thursday, Friday, and Saturday, February 10, 11, and 12, and we are flying in the best black truffles money can buy. Call Oliveto in Oakland to secure a table.

ITALY'S PIEDMONT

1998 DOLCETTO "PARLAPA" · ALDO MARENCO

A couple of winemakers drove me up into the hills above Alba one night to a restaurant "the tourists don't know about." Diners seemed to consist largely of wine people. Bottles and magnums circulated from table to table, Barolos and Barbarescos, new vintages and old. The air was full of the scents of wine and white truffles. But according to my swallow meter, the best wine of the evening was this incredible Dolcetto. Everyone wondered at my fidelity to it in the midst of much more expensive bottles. I proclaimed, "Better a perfect Dolcetto than an imperfect Barolo." Applause was not rampant, but as Jim Harrison writes elsewhere in this brochure, "I've never been interested in differentiating between genres. The best is the best and we must take it on the rare occasions that we find it."

Here is a champion in that most important category of all: Deliciousness!

$16.50 PER BOTTLE $178.20 PER CASE

RICHARD OLNEY'S
FINAL BOOK, *REFLEXIONS*

Commentary by Jim Harrison

I WAS THOROUGHLY swept away by Richard Olney's *Reflexions*, which made me all the more saddened by his death this past July. There is ample evidence in *Reflexions* that no one on the planet has sat at better tables, most especially his own, or drank consistently better wines than Richard Olney. The evidence is here and in his many other books, all of which I revere for their lucidity and range as books about food and wine that suggest, but not obtrusively, that there are standards that must be kept, no matter how implausibly high these standards might be. And this is all against a backdrop, a diorama, of a life lived with devotion and honor, of life lived as art itself.

If I have ever been to a home that may suitably be called magic it must be that of the Peyraud family in Bandol. The place has all the delicate mystery one senses in reading Alain Fournier's *Les Grandes Meaulnes* (in English, *The Wanderer*) but also the very visceral, sensual quality of the best food one is likely to eat, prepared by Lulu Peyraud. Once there, there is not the slightest desire to ever leave, not for Paris let alone home.

I had been to Lulu Peyraud's for lunch once before I met Richard in the spring of 1996. In the earlier trip I was with a Franco-American, Guy de la Valdène, who had taught me a great deal about both the French and their cooking. I was very excited at the time to learn that Richard lived in the area because I was so devoted to his work, much in the manner that I would have been in Mississippi had I known that Faulkner was down the road frying bacon for lunch to go with his bourbon. I've never been interested in differentiating between genres. The best is the best and we must take it on the rare occasions that we find it.

So in 1996 when I was on a French book tour, no more delightful than an American book tour except that, unlike in America, the food will carry you through, I drove to Lulu's for lunch with my friend the French literary fixture and translator, Brice Mattieussent. I was a bit flustered, actually stunned, to find that Kermit Lynch and Gail Skoff were there with the fabled Richard Olney. In a curious, not improbable way, I had the same set of feelings I had had years before in London on spending time with John Huston. Were either of them still alive the comparison might strike them as far-fetched, but I can guarantee they would have been drawn to each other. In both cases I knew the work thoroughly before I met the man. And in both men there was an uncompromising, tenacious, and indefatigable pursuit of excellence, an implicit splendor that accompanies Kierkegaard's "purity of heart is to will one thing," whether it be the art of food and wine or the art of cinema.

In *Reflexions* and in person one senses that like many artists Richard was quite human, only more so. He was perhaps too indulgent with some of his friends but that is part of the territory, and I remember his laconic twinkle when I was carted

away after a four-hour lunch and a great deal of wine to address a large audience in Marseille. He was sympathetic but knew the situation was comic. Luckily with a gallon of excellent Domaine Tempier Bandol in my system the audience became a flowery blur.

The next morning on the train from Marseille to Paris I remember reflecting that there was a specific grandeur to Richard Olney. This was a largehearted man, and his largeheartedness is everywhere in *Reflexions*, from his single-minded devotion to his work, to his lifelong love for his five brothers and sisters and his many friends. One can only imagine the loss felt by his close friends such as Kermit and Gail, Lulu Peyraud and Alice Waters, and his brothers and sisters and their children who were so close to him. *Reflexions* is an enchanting memoir of this life.

SEE LIFE THROUGH
ROSÉ-COLORED GLASSES

ONCE UPON A TIME I took a flying leap and imported 25 cases of rosé, the 1975 Bandol rosé from Domaine Tempier. Few of my customers were willing to try one. It took over a year to sell the 300 bottles, even though I drank a good share of it. The attitude was, "No, I like good wines, I wouldn't be caught dead drinking rosé." My, my, the arms I twisted, with little success, and actually everyone had reason to be wary because they'd been turned off by California rosés. In those days wineries set aside their rotten grapes for their rosé and then left sweetness in the wines, hoping to cover up the rotten flavors that resulted. No thanks!

Today, however, we cannot obtain enough Bandol rosé and we hear from angry clients who don't understand why there is not enough. I would venture that it was Domaine Tempier that made drinking rosé aesthetically correct here at home.

But Tempier had help. We were aided by my comrade-in-arms, or comrade-in-rosé-colored-glasses, Alice Waters, who insisted from the start that Chez Panisse's supply of Tempier rosé never run dry.

Robert Parker gave it a boost when he called it "France's finest rosé."

My old friend Joseph Swan, whose 1968 and 1969 Zinfandels still taste as good as ever, wrote here that Tempier's was "the best rosé in the world."

And then my very own wife, loftily free of even a sliver of wine snobbishness, added her opinion that Tempier rosé is the best wine in the world. As for wine, the only thing she likes better than a glass of Bandol rosé is a glass of Bandol rosé followed by a good red.

Now that wine drinkers have been seduced by the pleasures of good rosé, more winemakers are putting their talents to it, and some of them learned from the vinification at Domaine Tempier.

Four freshly bottled 1999 rosés just arrived from southern France.

		PER BOTTLE	PER CASE
1999	*Vin de Pays de Vaucluse Rosé*		
	Le Pigeoulet en Provence	$9.95	$107.46
1999	*Coteaux du Languedoc Rosé · Domaine du Poujol*	9.95	107.46
1999	*Bandol Rosé · Domaine du Gros 'Noré* . . .	19.95	215.46
1999	*Saint-Chinian Rosé · Mas Champart*	12.50	135.00

1998 DOMAINE ZIND-HUMBRECHT

T HE AVERAGE yield at Zind-Humbrecht in 1998 was 40 hectoliters to the hectare. The average in Alsace was 90. Consider the concentration of flavors, given those figures. I tasted the difference on the vine during the harvest, and you will taste it in the wine.

A winemaker friend spent a few days with Humbrecht recently on a wine tasting trip. "Never have I met anyone so knowledgeable, devoted, and passionate about the concept of *terroir*," he told me.

I tasted the 1998s with Olivier and his father, Leonard, in their tasting

ALSACE

Clos Windsbuhl

HUNAWIHR

APPELLATION ALSACE CONTRÔLÉE
PINOT GRIS

DOMAINE ZIND HUMBRECHT
Léonard et Olivier HUMBRECHT - TURCKHEIM (Haut-Rhin) FRANCE

Leonard Humbrecht

room with an open view down to the vinification cellar. Some wines were bubbling away, still fermenting, which creates a background sound something like a Philip Glass concert. Blup, ploop, blurp, bloop . . . The cellar is full of oak *foudres*, some with hand-carved fronts. You gaze down upon their cellar, you hear it, you smell it, you *know* it is going to make great wine.

Then Leonard speaks up. "If I had to work with stainless steel instead of oak *foudres*, I would have chosen another occupation." I second that emotion.

He also said, "Vintage 1998 is our vintage of the century for the Rangen vineyard." The Riesling Rangen shows an almost toasty nose, so I asked if it had seen any new oak. No, that impression comes from the roasting of the grapes on the slope, and the volcanic soil.

Another fascinating comment: "The consumer can participate in the creation of a great wine if he will put aside some bottles of the single vineyard wines like Hengst or Clos Windsbuhl and allow them to evolve further."

It is a vintage so stunning, so deliciously ripe and often packed with botrytis, that it is difficult to find words enthusiastic enough to fit the quality of these wines. All I can promise is that you will kick yourself later if you go conservative today.

BIRD PROGRESSIONS

I HAVE BEEN working on a piece trying to explain (so far without success) Richard Olney. He was my friend and, in a casual sort of way, my mentor, and I liked his attitude about food and wine. Richard died last year, and I think about him a lot.

To mention Richard here, where the subject is Thanksgiving, does not seem thoroughly appropriate. I can see him loving the event, the reunion of his large family, enjoying the progression of wines that a long meal and lots of people would occasion, but when the huge stuffed bird is placed on the table, I can see Richard wince. There were two American favorites that Richard really could not stomach: turkey was one, and he hated watermelon. So I think of Richard in this context not as he might relate to a turkey, but because of his genius for wine progressions. To put it simply: dry to sweet, light to weighty, simple to complex, young to old.

Thanksgiving provides us an opportunity to riff on his theme, because there are a good number of glasses to fill and refill, several courses that need accompaniment, and, because almost all wines go with Thanksgiving fare, we can get into some nifty improvisations.

After studying our current inventory, I composed four wine menus to serve with traditional Thanksgiving fare. Those of you with wine cellars might, of course, prefer to dig out some older treasures.

"The genius of champagne seems to me best expressed at the apéritif hour," Richard wrote in *Ten Vineyard Lunches*. And, "as long as the champagne glasses are kept filled, no one minds lingering before going to table."

Champagne or other sparkling wines are a festive way to open holiday ceremonies. Spirits brighten, tongues loosen, stomachs start to growl.

As you will notice, I like themes and variations. Also, I find that Alsatian wine is in the right spirit for this holiday. Beaujolais, too. Both, in their perfumes, contain memories of the past harvest's bounty, which is what we are giving thanks for, right?

With several bottles needed, it is the opportunity to open your white wine service with, for example, a drier, simpler Riesling or Gewurztraminer and move to a finer, more complex and expansive wine from the same grape variety.

Menu three riffs on a Chardonnay theme, working south from Lassalle's Blanc de Blancs to Bernard Raveneau's white Burgundy from Vézelay to Roulot's richer, deeper Bourgogne *blanc*. Or you could draw from your cellar a 1988 Raveneau Chablis and follow it with a 1982 Meursault from François Jobard, or something like that. It is fun to mull over the possibilities (it involves defining the

character of the wines you are considering) and fun to enjoy the results of your decisions later at table.

Notice that two of the menus include reds from Beaujolais and lead to red Burgundy. I love that progression from a flashy, fruity, youthful red to something older and nobler. Gamay and Pinot Noir are good choices for Thanksgiving. They shine.

The flavors of reds from Chinon and Bourgueil (menu three) seem to bring out the wild fowl/Pilgrim origins of the holiday bird. It would also work to open the reds with a Chinon or Bourgueil and follow with an older Saint-Emilion, which usually has Cabernet Franc in its blend. If you have a Joguet Chinon from the 1970s or '80s, follow it with a Saint-Emilion from the '60s or '70s. Nice.

Menu four is for Rhône addicts, but the Champagne is for getting your mouth wet. First things first. Then you have a white from the far south, hopefully with some Marsanne in it, like Trignon's Cuvée Célestine or Alquier's Marsanne/Roussanne blend, then you head north for the Rhône's greatest white, Chave's Hermitage *blanc*, which you will have to provide, because we have none left in stock. The 1989 and 1983 are doing well, for example. Sink your nose into one of them and you'll find yourself laughing out loud even though your father-in-law has not attempted a joke. As for the reds, the Châteauneuf follows the Côtes du Rhône Villages beautifully. Hierarchy, man! French wines have hierarchy, and if you know how to use it, you can orchestrate a symphonic progression.

MENU 1

		PER BOTTLE
NV	Vouvray Pétillant · Champalou	$14.95
1999	Riesling d'Epfig · Ostertag	17.50
1998	Riesling Herrenweg · Zind-Humbrecht	29.95
1999	Morgon "Vieilles Vignes" · Thévenet	19.95
1998	Bourgogne "La Digoine" · De Villaine	22.50
1997	Sauternes · Roûmieu-Lacoste	29.95

MENU 2

		PER BOTTLE
NV	Prosecco Brut · Adami	$12.50
1998	Gewurztraminer Cuvée Tradition · Kuentz-Bas	16.95
1998	Gewurztraminer "Clos Windsbuhl" Zind-Humbrecht	48.95
1999	Moulin-à-Vent "Vieilles Vignes" · Diochon	16.50

1994	Mazis-Chambertin · Domaine Maume	87.00
1994	Pinot Gris "Clos Jebsal" SGN Trie Spéciale	
	Zind-Humbrecht	250.00

MENU 3

PER BOTTLE

1990	Champagne "Blanc de Blancs" · Lassalle	$54.95
1998	Bourgogne Blanc · Vézelay	14.95
1998	Bourgogne Blanc · Roulot	21.50
1999	Chinon "Cuvée Terroir" · Joguet	15.95
1997	Bourgueil "Les Perrières" · Breton	27.95
1996	Jurançon "La Quintessence" · Brû-Baché	29.95

MENU 4

PER BOTTLE

NV	Champagne Brut Rosé · Bara	$39.00
1999	Côtes du Rhône Blanc "Cuvée Célestine"	
	Trignon	19.95
????	Hermitage Blanc · Chave	out of stock
1998	Côtes du Rhône Villages · Saint Luc	13.50
1996	Châteauneuf-du-Pape · Charbonnière	22.50
1998	Muscat de Beaumes-de-Venise · Durban	19.95

1998 ZIND-HUMBRECHT
LATE HARVEST

ONE OF RICHARD OLNEY's books was about Château d'Yquem, and he had a few bottles of it in his cellar. Thanks to him I have had the good fortune to taste several old vintages of that grandest of all Sauternes, including the 1921 and 1947. When I wrote a few years ago that one of Zind-Humbrecht's late-harvest wines showed the quality of a great Yquem, I wondered if I would hear from Richard, telling me I had gone too far.

Last night my wife and I uncorked a half-bottle of the 1994 Pinot Gris Rangen Vendanges Tardives. I felt better (in more ways than one) because the thick, heavily botrytized, ravishingly beautiful Zind-Humbrecht was the equal of a great Yquem. There is room for two at the top.

Now we are in luck, because Zind-Humbrecht's grapes were loaded with noble rot in 1998, and you have the opportunity to obtain some of the most fabulous dessert wines ever created. Opening one will be among the greatest wine events of your life.

At the same time, Zind-Humbrecht is releasing his SGN from 1997.

If you are new to ZH and wonder what all the hoopla is about, taste one of these wonder wines. They might be from another planet.

✦ 2001 ✦

CORSICA

1999 AJACCIO *ROUGE* · COMTE PERALDI

Tᴴɪꜱ ɪꜱ a blend that I made, and some people will take a sniff and say ɴᴏ ᴡᴀʏ, ᴊᴏꜱᴇ́, and exit quite quickly. Maybe even prematurely? Others will do their duty and stick to it but never warm to it. Others, you know who you are: Calling all Jaded Palates; here's one for you.

First, this is a light-colored red, and my oh my, it is almost sinful for a red to look light these days. But this wine is made from the Sciacarello grape, an ancient Corsican native that is characterized by a lack of pigment, and the color has nothing to do with the wine's flavor, which is big enough.

Then the nose. It smells brambly, *sauvage*, tarry, smoky, weedy, black peppery, and even worse, it smells like no other wine, which means that it cannot be compartmentalized, and that makes some people uncomfortable, shaky, queasy . . . Many will seek shelter in an oaky fruitbomb.

On the palate, finely tuned with a down-home rusticity, whatever that means. Never mind. Just serve it with a sausage, chard, and bean stew, that sort of thing, or any dish full of garlic and/or tomatoes. Or why not thyme-and-rosemary-perfumed lamb, or Richard Olney's recipe for chicken with 40 cloves of garlic? That'll work. That will really work.

$16.50 ᴘᴇʀ ʙᴏᴛᴛʟᴇ $178.20 ᴘᴇʀ ᴄᴀꜱᴇ

REMEMBERING RICHARD OLNEY

By Lulu Peyraud

Wʜᴀᴛ ɪꜱ ᴛʜᴇ ꜰɪʀꜱᴛ thing I would say about Richard Olney? That he was a handsome man, very elegant in his bow ties, discreet, considerate, a careful listener, and a good friend.

We met him, my husband Lucien and I, thanks to Magdeleine Decure and Odette Kahn, publishers of the magazines *Cuisine et Vins de France* and *Revue du Vin de France*, back in the 1950s. In view of Richard's remarkable aptitude for wine tasting and his innate understanding of the cuisine of the great chefs (to whom Magdeleine and Odette introduced him), there was no way they were going to leave Richard free to focus on the passion that had originally brought him

Richard Olney's kitchen

to France: his painting. Speaking perfect French with a lovely American accent (which added to the charm I found in him), schooled by entering a circle that presented prestigious tastings in the noblest cellars of France and at its most celebrated tables, Richard acquired, with the seriousness and unaffectedness that came naturally to him, a competence rare for a foreigner who had so recently arrived in that privileged milieu. Accepted in the world of gastronomy and oenology in Paris as well as in the provinces, he began writing articles for *Cuisine et Vins de France*.

Then he created the Lebéron College for foreigners seeking food and wine instruction, with classes and practical experience at certain wine domaines and restaurants. After that he spent seven years, mostly in London, where I sometimes visited him, working on the Time-Life series *The Good Cook*. Several other books followed, which have been translated into several languages.

Before that, however, he had left Paris for Provence and moved quite close to us, and thus the ties between us grew stronger. He would visit our home at Domaine Tempier, which was filled with children that he watched grow up, and full of our friends with whom he shared parties, banquets, tastings, and celebrations. All these events gave us the occasion to go pick him up, because Richard never learned to drive. Or, we would go up to his hillside home to dine outside in the shade of his vine-covered terrace. He would prepare succulent meals all by himself, including vegetables and salads from his own garden. We shared the feasts with friends we had in common, like Michael Lemonier, Jill Norman, Aubert de Villaine, Alice Waters, and Kermit Lynch and his family. Richard would always give us his enlightened, to-the-point opinion when wine tasting, whether we were judging the newest vintage or enjoying an old treasure.

His rigorousness, his candor, and the friendship that grew between us were a source of great happiness, because whether times were good or bad, we could count on each other.

He did Lucien and me a great honor when he wrote his book (*Lulu's Provençal Table*) about Domaine Tempier, which featured recipes from my kitchen.

We met his numerous brothers and sisters, who gathered every summer at his house here in Provence, and we enjoyed entertaining them with luncheons at the domaine. We also received Richard's parents from Iowa, the time they traveled together to France to see him, and I still have the charming painting his mother did of a vase of flowers, which hangs in the entry hall at Domaine Tempier.

During his health problems, we kept his family informed, right up to the final, fatal attack. But Richard's spirit is so alive in all of us that we will never stop honoring his memory when we get together.

◦　◦　◦　◦　◦　◦　◦

2000 APREMONT · PIERRE BONIFACE

This is as fresh as wine gets, the wine version of bubbling, crystal-clear springwater. It is light in body, light in alcohol, alive and kicking on the palate, bone-dry, and crisp at the finish. It reminds me of green apple, granite cliffs, and alpine meadows inhabited by of-age nymphs. Perhaps it is better not to get too carried away, however. It is only a bottle of white wine.

$12.50 PER BOTTLE $135.00 PER CASE

LOIRE

2000 REUILLY *BLANC* "LES PIERRES PLATES"
DOMAINE DE REUILLY

Here is a new addition to our Loire list. Reuilly is in Sauvignon Blanc territory, an ancient wine-making village that today has only about 300 acres in vines.

Our bottling, Pierres Plates, is from a specific vineyard with Chablis-like soil full of chalk, fossils, and seashells. Try to imagine Sancerre grown at Chablis.

The fruit is lovely, with white flower perfumes, citrus, and minerality. It has finesse and precision.

If you want to experience what I mean when I say minerality, notice the first impression on the palate, which is of fresh, cushiony, Sancerre-like Sauvignon Blanc. Then, immediately, there is a firmness, a stony firmness that appears from within the wine. Let's call it *Terroir* to the Rescue, because a wine with nothing but pure fruit seems banal.

$14.95 PER BOTTLE $161.46 PER CASE

2000 POUILLY-FUMÉ "VIEILLES VIGNES"
RÉGIS MINET

I leafed through some old wine books looking for some insight before presenting Minet's old-vine cuvée. Let's see if any of these quotes make you thirsty:

Pouilly-sur-Loire produces spirited white wines that have good body, a suggestion of gunflint, and a highly agreeable taste.   JULLIEN (1816)

Pouilly-Fumé remains the most naked of wines. No other wine presents itself so naturally without artifice or anything to hide its true nature.

PIERRE BREJOUX (1956)

Empty your full glass. Fill your empty glass. I cannot bear to look at you with your glass empty or full.   RABELAIS

Okay, I admit it. Rabelais was not writing about Pouilly-Fumé. He meant wine in general, but he was from the Loire, and it is a pretty neat quote.

Minet's 2000 floats and stings, persists and crescendos. It leaves the palate fresh and eager, which feels good.

$16.95 PER BOTTLE $183.06 PER CASE

1999 BOURGUEIL "CUVÉE BEAUVAIS"
DOMAINE DE LA CHANTELEUSERIE

Boucard ages his cuvée Beauvais (one of Bourgueil's best Cabernet Franc sites) in stainless steel, new barrels, *demi-muids*, and *foudres*. Each container starts out as the same wine but develops differently, so it is fun to taste each and make what I believe to be the best blend. A little of this, a little of that, a *lot* of that one, etc. In 1999 I could not improve on Monsieur Boucard's blend, so the bottle here for a change contains the same wine that you would find in France . . . well, almost the same. Ours was not filtered, so in their version the French don't have as much color, nose, body, flavor, texture, length, or aging potential.

$13.95 PER BOTTLE $150.66 PER CASE

2000 VOUVRAY "LA CUVÉE DES FONDRAUX"
DOMAINE CHAMPALOU

I really respond to this bouquet, because I have been going to Vouvray at least once a year for 25 years, and a sniff of this takes me back underground to Vouvray's limestone caves, the air thickened by the smells of earth, wine, and wood.

It has a "name-that-fruit" sort of nose. Is it Mirabelle? Quince? Almond? White acacia blossoms? A French couple, customers here in Berkeley, told me that it smells like the aroma of fruit tarts from their youth, cooking in Grandma's kitchen.

Les Fondraux in 2000 is round and minerally on the palate; while not really sweet, it could be called a sweetie pie.

This wine is very French. It could, in fact, come only from the French vineyards. The quality that sets French wines apart from others is abundantly present here.

$14.95 PER BOTTLE $161.46 PER CASE

⁘ ⁘ ⁘ ⁘ ⁘ ⁘ ⁘ ⁘

1999 CASSIS *BLANC* · CLOS SAINTE MAGDELEINE

The fact that the restaurant Le Sourd in Toulon does not carry Clos Sainte Magdeleine's Cassis is not its only flaw. It is practically crawling with flaws. Yet when I am in the Bandol area, it is the only restaurant I keep going back to.

Maybe I'm spoiled. During the Berkeley part of my year, Chez Panisse is only a few blocks from home, and all over the Bay Area it is so easy to eat well. You might think it is easy in Provence, too, but after 15 years living there part-time, I do not have one single restaurant recommendation for you. The last time I went to the most acclaimed restaurant in the area, their aioli was as runny as heavy cream and they denied that a corked wine was corked. Swell!

But back to Le Sourd, which is behind the theatre in *centre ville* Toulon. Another problem is the service. The kid who clears the plates between courses, for example, approaches each plate as if it had a rattlesnake coiled up on it. Removing the plates can run to an hour. The expression on his face says, Rocky Marciano just caught me with an uppercut. And it might require three or four reminders to get that second bottle of wine, or to get the bill when your kids are sleepy and you are ready to leave. Another problem is the cooking. You must stay away from anything that requires cooking talent.

CLOS Sᵗᵉ MAGDELEINE

CAVES DU CLOS SAINTE - MAGDELEINE A CASSIS
COSTIA ZAFIROPULO. PROPRIÉTAIRE - RÉCOLTANT

APPELLATION CASSIS CONTROLEE
MÉDAILLE D'OR - EXPOSITION UNIVERSELLE 1900

An old label from Clos Sainte Magdeleine

There is only one reason to suffer through it all: seafood, Mediterranean seafood, the freshest, finest, rarest products the local catch is capable of producing. The proprietor is a genius at obtaining from the sea that which has become all but unobtainable, and for that, I am willing to forgive him a lot.

Oursins (sea urchins), *vioulets* (a strange beast with neon yellow flesh that seems to exist only between Marseille and Toulon), wild oysters, sea snails with an erect aioli, tiny eat-'em-whole shrimp, and don't miss the *friture* of bite-sized fish and squid.

Then the proprietor arrives at your table to talk fish. You are a party of four? He has a *loup de mer* for four. Or a *sar* for two, and a *dorade rose* for the other two. Or a *rascasse*, or little *rougets* so tiny they are illegal, so they cannot appear on the menu. Were you surprised when I mentioned "wild" oysters? The oysters we eat almost everywhere in the world are raised, or farmed, which is common knowledge. Le Sourd sometimes has wild oysters from the waters near Toulon. They taste different. But are you aware that it is not easy today to find "wild" fish along the French coast, that almost all the fish in those pretty little ports are farmed? Raised on feed? Fed who knows what? Of course the flavor of wild fish is completely different from that of farmed fish, as is the texture of their flesh. Most restaurants will lie if questioned about their "catch."

Anyway, once you choose your fish, he brings out the poor glorious beast for you to inspect before he cooks it. He might tell you the name of the fishermen at Bandol who fished it. He shows you the eyes, the color inside the gills, then he moves it under the light so you can appreciate how brilliantly it shines. Later it comes back grilled, plainly and perfectly, and the proprietor deftly bones it in front of you.

The last time I went, the food was stunning, the service worse than ever, and the white wines less than mediocre. We gave up and ordered a Tempier rosé. Old reliable. But we missed Clos Sainte Magdeleine's Cassis. It would have been perfect.

$20.00 PER BOTTLE $216.00 PER CASE

NOW I'VE HEARD EVERYTHING

Someone showed me an article that says, "Alice Waters credits Lynch with influencing her cooking." Oh yes. Of course. That must have been my special Charred Pork recipe. I might as well give it to you straight, because Alice has never forgotten it, and she mentions it to me usually in public at least once a year. I can just hear her introducing me to somebody like Julia Child, for example, saying, "And this is Kermit Lynch, the wine importer. Once he invited me over for dinner and . . ."

CHARRED PORK

Season ecologically correct pork filet. Place filet on grill over red-hot coals. Start gabbing with Alice about the food and wine scene. Get carried away. Smell burning pork flesh. Run. Remove flaming filet from grill. Look in fridge for something to eat.

No, really, it is true that I have now and then prepared meals that Alice has eaten, somewhat, but influenced her cooking? I am flattered, however, and will now probably make the history books. Unless . . . unless it was my:

SLICED HOMEGROWN TOMATOES

Slice homegrown tomatoes into slices. (By no means shall you slice them into quarters.) Allow ground salt and pepper to descend by gravity flow onto each slice. Serve immediately.

I don't know. I'm sure Alice's future biographer can safely say that she influenced my cooking more than I did hers.

But now you see perhaps the difference in personality between me and Alice. She seems driven to revisit my Charred Pork, but I would never, ever reveal the recipe for her Fish Soup on the Floor.

WINE NOTES

By Jim Harrison

MUCH ABOUT WINE is problematic and open to nearly infinite conjecture. For instance, what is the sex of wine, and are we falling into a sump when we consider the question, a trap of silliness that professional wine tasters so easily fall into? Wine tasting is susceptible to parody, but so are other professions of great intrinsic value, from mad scientists to virtuous strippers to pure-hearted politicians.

But then it is always good to question the terminology of our enthusiasms. We can say that wine is essentially female because it comes from the earth and we don't say "father earth." The best things are female, including females, and allowing this characterization energizes our imaginations in ways not possible to other terminology. Blatant, loud-mouthed, bad wines are, of course, male.

There's a lot of tannin in the river beside my cabin, emerging as it does from a swamp. I've also visited a friend while he was, unfortunately, tanning the hide of an otter. I taste tannin in many vintages, especially American, but it's no big deal if it is slight. Wines that have never seen an oak barrel are occasionally called "oaky" but why quarrel about this? From my childhood onward up in the country I have picked wild raspberries, blackberries, blueberries, and other berries, but I must say I do not find these unique flavors in wine, though many apparently do. My perhaps naïve honesty prevents me from using these terms that would lie to my taste.

Our sensual memories are so vast, why shouldn't we use the entire reservoir when we describe our affection or dislike for a wine? Sometimes our American tasters seem to be ascetically as serious as Cotton Mather when he "barbecued" Indians. There is black and white and the multifoliate variances of grey but an alarming lack of color, reminding me of the cartoons in French publications poking fun at American wine snobs. But how often have I tasted wines in France with a fine platter of charcuterie on a table or perched on a barrel before us, with joyous badinage, laughter, with no sense that we were deciding the fate of nations.

There is a definite possibility, and I say this with my usual modesty, that what I am saying is totally wrongheaded. My notes on Corsican wines that I tasted could not be published without being Bowdlerized. Maybe a wine shouldn't be allowed to remind me of "the thighs of a rich girl depleted by lassitude," one of the tamer descriptions. Conversely we can say jug wines tend to be loutish, abrupt, faintly soiled, evoking memories of the locker room after a football game on a warm September evening. That sort of thing. Bad properly evokes bad.

I recently meditated over a mixed case of three Gigondas, a difficult assignment for a peculiar reason. I have drunk more Gigondas than any French wine except Domaine Tempier Bandol. This kind of familiarity often makes us poor critics of wives, lovers, or longtime friends. A poet friend, Ted Kooser, described the end of his first marriage beginning with the line "Neither of us would clean the aquarium."

With wine we are back in college wondering if our professor corrected our brilliant essay before or after dinner, before or after he got laid, before or after his usual fantasy about Ava Gardner in the pool house. My main objection to numerical ratings in wine is that it presumes the falsest of sciences.

That said, I thought a bottle of Château du Trignon 1999 was soft but a little weak, a boy who would never do a chin-up because he was lazy. The second bottle, however, was drunk while eating a snack, a freshly sautéed wild brown trout on a bed of sliced tomatoes from my daughter's garden. This made the Trignon quite acceptable in a not very compromised way. Fine with bold food, not alone.

With Domaine de Cayron 1999 we enter another arena. I have drunk a hundred bottles of Cayron Gigondas. It is a nostrum for blues and fatigue in Paris or anywhere. I've spent a goodly amount of time with Jeanne Moreau, the French actress, and the Cayron reminds me of Moreau at age 28, mildly irritated at you for forgetting flowers, but surpassingly agreeable when you share a bottle of Cayron. There is a nice finish and this is an appreciable wine. If you drank it before the usual obnoxious meeting you wouldn't hate anyone. Last week I drank it at my cabin with two roasted woodcock for lunch and they married pleasantly. The flavor penetrated my rib cage.

The Domaine Les Pallières 1999 threw me off a bit as I had learned to expect more from past experience. There was a sense of the androgynous rather than a decisive move in either direction, and it was rather flattish compared to the Cayron. Of course why tell a reasonably good poet that he's not Lorca or Auden, for that matter. At a dinner two of the company preferred the Pallières to the Cayron. There are no gods to direct us in this matter, but we must do our best without pretending we are Solomon, much less Moses.

ANDROGYGONDAS

By Kermit Lynch

Hey, Jim, hold on there a minute. Enjoyed reading your opinion and all that, but it is clear that your two friends at table had their palates screwed in correctly, and as publisher of this brochure and co-proprietor of one of the Gigon-

Harvest, chez *Faraud*

das domaines, I am going to recall the words of U.S. President Ronald Reagan, who said, "Wait a minute, buster, I paid for this microphone and I'm going to speak into it," or something like that.

Actually, I just tasted the three wines and I agreed with your preference, but more on preference later. First, that sense of the androgynous in the 1999 Pallières? That's a virtue, a little gift of nature. That's 1999. You will get a big dose of Pallières in its purely masculine form in the upcoming (so to speak) 2000 vintage.

The 1999 does seem androgynous, the iron fist in the velvet glove, and I treasure it. Under the fluid elegance, there's some stuff in there, man. Shapely, silky, with a penetrating, explosive . . . well, I go too far.

As to preference, in May, in Gigondas, I attended a tasting of about 15 1999 Gigondas with the wine-making crews from Trignon and Pallières. We covered the labels, trying to be objective. Pallières won. Trignon, Cayron, and a Saint-Cosme were virtually tied for second place.

Now, six months later, I compared our three imports blind again, here in Berkeley with the staff. Everyone, by the way, guessed correctly which was which. And everyone, including me, placed Cayron first and Pallières second. Am I objective or not? That Cayron, what a fabulous aroma, much more complex than six months ago, while the Pallières for the first time in its life is showing some reticence aromatically. Wines change, and glory hallelujah for that! (Although several of the wine critics like to say, "tasted five times, consistent notes." Are they storing their wines in the freezer section, or what?) Good wine has a mind of its own, and the Cayron seems to have experienced a growth spurt.

Some wineries sterilize or pasteurize their wines in order to ensure that every bottle will be identical. Once dead, always dead, I guess. But how boring. With Cayron, Pallières, and Trignon 1999, we've got a horse race, and the lead might keep changing over the next 10 to 15 years.

Just for the hell of it, after our tasting here, someone poured some of the masculine Cayron into the androgynous Pallières. The resulting blend?? Rated X.

° ° ° ° ° ° ° ° °

1998 PATRIMONIO *ROUGE* · DOMAINE LECCIA

It is Corsican. You could spend five times as much for an all-star Barolo or Châteauneuf-du-Pape and walk away with less, so why is this black beauty still available? It is waiting for you precisely because it is not wearing a famous label. That is the only reason. You won't try it because it is not familiar, and it stays a bargain because no one will try it.

I'm sorry, but my attitude is, if you can't get into this baby, get thee to a Blue Nunnery.

If you do decide to dive in, wear your goggles, because there is a lot to see but it is pretty dark in there. *Mer et montagne. Iode et maquis.* A jumble of berries black and blue. At the finish, a stoniness, and that is the *terroir* expressing itself. A chewy, powerful red with big tannins, big flavors, and a whole lot of soul.

$19.95 PER BOTTLE $215.46 PER CASE

2000 DOMAINE COLIN-DELÉGER

IN LAST MONTH'S brochure, writing about de Villaine's 2000 Aligoté, I used the term "golden zing" to describe it. Reviewing my notes from a trip to Burgundy in September 2000, I think "golden zing" seems like an appropriate description of the 2000 white Burgundies in general.

As I walked through the vineyards of Chassagne-Montrachet the day before the harvest, tasting the grapes, the style of the vintage was already discernible. The Chardonnay grapes were tiny and few, golden colored, with lots of flavor, good sugars, and a stimulating acidity that would translate later in the wines as good backbone.

If you have older Colins in your cellar, here are my reactions to some vintages tasted from my collection this winter.

1978: Still in good shape, but a bit squarish.

1979: It was my last bottle of Chassagne Les Vergers, alas, because it was perfection. A year of high yields and high quality.

1982: Sound, velvety, and unlikely to remain at such a peak for much longer.

1983: A vintage of big, rich whites with deep golden color. Opulent, still an event to taste, but they were better three or four years ago.

1989: Another ripe vintage at its peak, showing all its stuff, and should continue to peak for another four or five years.

1990: It has the gold, but lacks the zing.

1994: Reminiscent of 1982 and 1979 in its balance and style, delicious wines, but not to keep too long. I'm drinking mine with a lot of pleasure.

Ideally you would start drinking some of the 2000 Colins in a year or two, but wait on the *premiers* and *grands crus* for three, four, or five years.

THE BIRTHMARK

AT San Francisco State in the 1960s, I took an incredibly rewarding course called something like American Studies, in which we tried to find clues to the American character by reading Emerson, Melville, Paine, Thoreau, Hawthorne, and others. I was especially taken by one of Nathaniel Hawthorne's short stories, "The Birthmark," although it did not dawn on me then that it was about wine. The story stuck with me even more than *The Scarlet Letter*. It featured a beautiful babe, who could have married more wisely, and had lots of significance that is ever more significant. Have a read and see for yourself. It is only about two glasses of Bandol rosé long.

The beautiful babe is obviously a metaphor for a bottle of great wine. Her husband, Dr. Something-or-other, is a celebrated scientific genius who cannot stand that his wife is a perfect beauty except, EXCEPT (it really is too vitally important to him) for the fact that she has a birthmark, which for him is an imperfection. He experiments in his lab for years developing a serum that will erase her blemish. Convinced that he has found the "cure" (although she is perfectly healthy), he injects her with his potion and watches as the birthmark fades and disappears from (if I remember correctly) her cheek, disappears just as she exhales her last breath.

The birthmark is obviously a metaphor for a wine's deposit, or sediment.

The "cure" is filtration. However, according to "The Birthmark," perfection = death.

The moral is, accept a little sediment or you might destroy the very beauty you seek to perfect.

And so you see that my crusade against filtration is not a quibble, but a matter of life and death.

◦　◦　◦　◦　◦　◦　◦　◦

2001 BARDOLINO "LE FONTANE"
CORTE GARDONI

When this one arrived and I tasted it with my staff the other day, I asked them what we were doing wrong. "Is there a better red out there anywhere at 10 bucks?" I asked.

"No, boss," they said.

"This is as delicious as any wine at any price," I said. "We should be loading it into people's trunks by the caseload. Maybe it's my fault. Maybe I haven't gotten the message across. What should I tell people?"

"How about, 'Quaff a bottle with your date and you will surely score'?" advised Steve Waters.

"Legally, we can't make health claims in the brochure," I said.

"You can drink it with reckless abandon," Michael said.

Then Richard Kading started in about pizzas and pastas and pork roast and outdoor barbecues.

"At the price," Dixon said, "if people don't try it, they're just dumb."

"That's too blunt," said Graeme.

$9.95 PER BOTTLE　　$107.46 PER CASE

2000 BANDOL · DOMAINE TEMPIER

JEAN-MARIE Peyraud is officially retired now, although he seems to hang around the winery a lot of the time. (My god, he is only a year older than I am, and I'm not even mature yet.)

Jean-Marie's first vintage was a difficult one, 1974, the year he took over from his father, Lucien. I remember Lucien always showing up in the cellar afterwards giving advice, too, wineglass in hand. The new winemaker is Daniel Ravier, and he has had the good fortune to start with one of Tempier's best vintages ever. I went through the cellar with him just the other day, and I can still taste his 2000s.

2000 CUVÉE SPÉCIALE "LA MIGOUA"

Black color. The nose is incredibly ripe and rises like smoke with notes of cinnamon, spices, and black cherry at its blackest. Big wine.

$219.00 PER SIX BOTTLES

Jean-Marie Peyraud, Domaine Tempier

2000 CUVÉE SPÉCIALE "LA TOURTINE"

Black, black, black. Roasted coffee bean, dark fruit, luscious texture, the richest Tourtine ever, loaded with flavor. Oh, it's dark in there. Give this big, beautiful beast at least five years.

$219.00 PER SIX BOTTLES

2000 CUVÉE SPÉCIALE "CABASSAOU"

Blacker. I am not sure you have ever seen or tasted a Mourvèdre like this. It is as intense as you can imagine. In fact, even though it is dry, I am not sure it should serve as a table wine. Drink it by itself, with a friend or two, to be mind-blown. Off you go, into the wild black yonder.

$162.00 PER THREE BOTTLES

❖ ❖ ❖ ❖ ❖ ❖ ❖ ❖

2001 ABYMES · A. AND M. QUENARD

I find that in French wine circles I have a reputation as an importer capable of finding a market for little-known appellations. You should see some of the wild samples I receive for consideration. But every so often I find a treasure like this Abymes, and usually the price makes it even more attractive.

A dry white from the Savoie, Abymes is similar to Apremont (if that helps), although never have I tasted an Apremont this good. Abymes is never a flagrant wine, but this bottling is unusually ripe and expressive. Is it the old vines? It has good body with good nervosity. The flavors at first are floral and minerally, then with aeration you start to perceive honey and apricot. Instead of you tiring of it, it grows on you.

$12.95 PER BOTTLE $139.86 PER CASE

2001 SANCERRE · HIPPOLYTE REVERDY

This is my brochure and I can do what I want, right? So I am giving this new arrival (a wine that always sells out anyway) one full page in honor of the many years Reverdy has been providing us with such wonderful Sancerre, and because in 2001 he has come up with my personal favorite.

Let's call it "Old Reliable," because Reverdy's white always scores high on the impeccability scale. This one is so impeccable you notice it. I have a weakness for impeccability. I will always take an impeccable wine over one that's not, no matter the appellation.

Another attraction, and I realize that not everyone values it, is the delicacy from start to finish. The Sauvignon Blanc is rendered with such touch that it does not dominate the aroma. Here it is the combination of fruit and gunflint that defines the nose.

Subtle. Discreet. Can you dig it? And the wine unfolds on the palate with the same great style.

$16.95 PER BOTTLE $183.06 PER CASE

MY PROBLEMS WITH WHITE WINE

By Jim Harrison

(*Jim Harrison, one of America's foremost writers, is as popular in France as he is here. Author of several outstanding novels such as* Dalva *and* A Good Day to Die, *he has recently published a collection of essays,* The Raw and the Cooked, *which is available here in the shop.*)

MAY WE POLITICIZE WINE? I will if I wish. This is a free country though it is quickly becoming less so. I have noted, for instance, that the Bay Area has become fatally infected with the disease of sincerity. Last early December in San Francisco I naively looked for a bar where I might enjoy a glass of wine and a cigarette. Instead I sat in the park across from the Huntington Hotel without wine, smoking an American Spirit and welcoming the frowns of a passel of dweebs doing Tai Chi. They birdlike lifted their legs as if afflicted with farting fits. When I lived briefly in San Francisco in 1958 it was an active seaport full of jubilance, music, merriment, and heartiness. The morning I left town on my recent trip I heard of a local campaign against the evils of butter.

All of which is to say that you can't talk about wine without the context in which it exists, like life herself. Even in non-Marxian economic terms it is far more difficult to find a favorable white wine at a decent price than a red. Is it partly because the aforementioned sincere people who drink only white wine have driven the price up or because they are dumb enough to drink any swill if it doesn't own life's most vital color, the color of our blood?

We certainly don't celebrate the Eucharist with white wine. Christ couldn't have spent thirty days in the wilderness alone fueled by white blood. The great north from which I emerge demands a sanguine liquid. White snow calls out for red wine, not the white spritzers of lisping socialites, the same people who shun chicken thighs in favor of characterless breasts and ban smoking in taverns. In these woeful days it is easy indeed to become fatigued with white people, white houses, white rental cars.

This said, let's be fair. The heart still cries out for a truly drinkable white under 20 bucks. I've tried dozens and dozens. I need white wine when I eat fish and shellfish. Of late several have been acceptable if not noteworthy: Château de Lascaux, Reuilly, a Les Carrons Pouilly-Fuissé and an Ermitage du Pic Saint Loup kept me alive until I could get at my main course and a restorative red.

Whenever I have wine or food problems I consult Mario Batali in New York, or Gerard Oberle in Burgundy, France, but my most reliable trump card is Peter Lewis in Seattle, whom I consider to have the most wide-ranging and educated palate in North America. In recent correspondence Lewis said common "white wines tend to the flaccid. The 'international style' in which they're made these days emphasize the exotic: the overly floral, tropical phenolic profile coupled to heavy-handed oak treatment strip the fruit of its delicacy; whereas the truly exotic, as in Viognier from Château Grillet or Lys de Volan, combines true power with all the femininity of peach fuzz and honeysuckle (the seductive quality of the minute hairs on the back of a woman's thigh in high summer)." There!

But isn't life a struggle to gather the funds to cover one's vices? For 30 years since I first had a glass I've had an affection for Meursault, even lesser vintages than those of Henry Boillot. I've drunk Meursault when the weather was a tad chilly, say in the early spring with a simple sauté of sweetbreads, fresh morels, and a few wild leeks. To be sure my single eye flickers to the red sitting on the sideboard in readiness for the substantial main course. I wouldn't drink the Meursault alone unless it was over 90° and I was sitting with a French vixen in a shaded courtyard in Beaune and she demanded the wine. Any fool except maybe a congressman loves Chassagne-Montrachet. I could drink three bottles of Didier

Dagueneau's Sauvignon Blanc with a gross of oysters in Concale if there were an available bed three feet away for my nap. The bed would be on a pier and the great French singer Esther Lammandier would croon a medieval ditty.

I see that women and food rather than government can help me abolish my prejudices, also an extremely fat wallet. Once before giving a poetry reading I was handed a glass of cheapish California Chardonnay and I said, "This might be good on pancakes if you were in the wilderness." I actually chewed on the tip of a cigar to cleanse my mouth.

I admit I love Domaine Tempier rosé, which is about $25, and find Château La Roque rosé at $12 a more acceptable deal in this twilit world of color and flavor compromise. I drink the latter because my wife and daughters drink it so it's right there within reach, an important qualification. I just recalled that on a warmish day last year I also liked a Côtes du Rhône *blanc* from Sang des Cailloux with barbecued rabbit (a basting sauce of butter, garlic, lemon, tarragon, and dry vermouth).

White wine is Apollonian, the wine of polite and dulcet discourse, frippish gossip, banal phone calls, Aunt Ethel's quiche, a wine for those busy discussing closure, healing, the role of the caretaker, the evils of butter, the wine of the sincerity monoethic. It occasionally, of course, rises to greatness, and you may have some if you've been economically diligent or are an heir of some sort. I'm sure that even the cheaper varieties have brought thousands of soccer moms sanity-healing sex fantasies.

We drink wine with our entire beings, not just our mouths and gullets. Temperaments vary. My mother used to torture me with the question "What if everyone were like you?" I have it on good authority that both Dionysus and Beethoven drank only red wine while Bill Gates and a hundred thousand proctologists stick to the white. Peter Lewis added in a letter that we're not crazy about white wine because we don't get crazy after drinking it, because we tend not to break into song or quote García Lorca after drinking it, because white wine doesn't make us laugh loudly, because it fatigues us and doesn't promote unbridled lust, because it pairs less well with the beloved roasted game birds whose organs we love to suck and whose bones we love to gnaw.

Yes, we're fortunate that everyone isn't like me. I recall Faulkner saying, "between scotch and nothing I'll take scotch." Meursault isn't the color of blood but it's the color of sunlight, a large item in itself.

THE APÉRO FILE

By Kermit Lynch

BY ACTIONS, not words, Richard Olney taught me the virtues of the daily *apéro*, which is French slang for an apéritif. My *Webster's* defines *apéritif* as "an alcoholic beverage, especially wine, taken before meals to stimulate the appetite." Taken? Well, that's not why I "take" apéritifs.

And there is a French definition from 1750: "*qui ouvre les pores, les canaux, les vaisseau.*" Quite physical, that one, the *apéro* serving to open one's pores, blood vessels, and assorted other bodily systems. Serving to open . . . an opener, that's the apéritif. *Aperture* is from the same root. An apéritif opens the evening, the meal, the festivities, and it might as well also open up oneself.

When I used to drive up the steep, narrow driveway to Richard's place in Provence, we would embrace in the French style, then sit down under his arbor of grape vines for an apéritif. As the sun sank lower and lower, a bowl of black olives would appear, slices of *saucisson*, and iced radishes with butter and salt. The wine flowed, as did the conversation.

Often the apéritif was a cheap little dry white or rosé, always well chosen. Richard referred to them as mouth rinse. What a wonderfully unsnobby perspective! He ordered Fontsainte's Gris de Gris several cases at a time. Once in a while his mood led him to open with something a little grander, like Tempier's rosé, or a bottle of nicely aged Champagne. "The genius of Champagne seems to me best experienced at the apéritif hour," he wrote in one of his books.

Jim Harrison quotes Peter Lewis's remark that white wine "fatigues us and doesn't promote unbridled lust," but he must be referring to those kinds of whites that Jim finds syrupy enough to put on pancakes, because a good white starter should relax *and* stimulate at the same time. You want something dry and crisp, chilled and lucid, with some zing to it.

My reaction to Jim's article? Never a red without a white to precede it; never a white without a red to follow it. I am convinced that the Creator had a plan, if only in this specific instance.

But before I turn spiritual on you, consider how the arrival of the dread oenologists on the wine scene contributed to Jim's prejudice against most white wines. Once upon a time (all the way up until around 1970, in fact) wine's second fermentation, the malolactic fermentation, was not understood. It occurred spontaneously in barrel along with or after the alcoholic fermentation. Once it was understood, this gift of nature (which renders wines more interesting and swallowable) began to be blocked technologically in a lot of white and rosé wines. It is easy to block the malo. You add a good dose of sulphur dioxide (yuck) and you sterile filter (yikes).

Why would anybody want to do that? Stability. Facility. Security. Once the wine is dosed and dead, the oenologists sleep better, because dead wines don't budge. They might lack depth, smell of SO_2, and cut your palate to shreds with untransformed malic acid, but then Pleasure 1A was never a course offering at Oenology U.

Choosing openers, I seem to go through stages. For long periods Tempier's rosé can hit the spot day after day. Then I'll go on a flinty, crisp Loire jag: Epiré, Minet, Reverdy, Muscadet, and so on. This year has been a white Burgundy year, and I find myself regularly opening my evenings with a Meursault or Chablis, usually with some but not too much age. I thought it was interesting that besides reds, Harrison specified liking Meursaults, because almost all Meursaults and other white Burgundies do complete that second fermentation I was talking about. So do all reds, and so indeed does Tempier's rosé, so I'm guessing that the malolactic fermentation plays a role in Jim's wine preferences. It sure does in mine. At Chablis a lot of lazy winemakers have now, god forbid, joined the "block-that-malo" club, but I promise that you will never find one here.

Anyway, this year I have been going through my 1990 *premiers crus* from Raveneau. Also any of his 1994s. Vintages 1991, 1992, and 1994 from Jobard. Coche's 1988s. Chevillon's white Nuits-Saint-Georges makes a great opener, as does the Vézelay *blanc*. And don't forget the light little sparkler, Prosecco, which the Venetians "take."

To those readers who have braved these pages of verbal thicket, here is your reward, if you choose to see it that way, THE APÉRO SAMPLER. None of these are good on pancakes, but may your lust be unbridled.

THE APÉRO SAMPLER

		PER BOTTLE
NV	Prosecco di Valdobbiadene · Adriano Adami	$12.50
2001	Bordeaux Blanc · Château Ducasse	9.95
2001	Côtes du Rhône Blanc · Château du Trignon	12.00
2001	Muscadet sur Lie · Michel Brégeon	9.95
2001	Cheverny · Domaine du Salvard	9.95
2001	Bianco di Custoza · Corte Gardoni	9.95
2000	Bourgogne Blanc "Les Clous" · A. and P. de Villaine	22.50
2000	Chablis · Olivier Savary	17.95
2000	Coteaux du Languedoc Blanc Ermitage du Pic Saint Loup	14.95
2000	Mâcon-Farges · Henri Perrusset	14.95
1999	Savennières "Cuvée Spéciale" · Château d'Epiré	18.95
1999	Cassis · Clos Sainte Magdeleine	16.95

NORMALLY $170.55

SPECIAL SAMPLER PRICE $125.00

SOUTHERN FRANCE

2000 LIRAC *ROUGE*

DOMAINE DU JONCIER

French winemakers like to humanize and sexualize wines, which can be fun. When the staff welcomed this Lirac after hours the other evening, I noticed that Michael Butler was not spitting like we wine professionals usually do. Anyway, he offered this tasting note: "Deep, full, and spicy, reminiscent of a beloved tractor with a nude gorgeous redhead on the seat."

My own notes include the phrase "powerful yet feminine," which must correspond to Michael's redhead on a tractor? I also called it intensely Rhône, full-bodied, and tannic but harmonious, which now sounds kinda colorless.

$14.95 PER BOTTLE $161.46 PER CASE

1999 CHÂTEAUNEUF-DU-PAPE *ROUGE*
DOMAINE LES CLEFS D'OR

Claude Kolm in *The Fine Wine Review* gave this classy beast a straight A score and wrote, "Reminiscent of a blonde on a jackass." No, just kidding. Here is what he really wrote:

> This is a well-priced Châteauneuf with some elegance to it. The nose starts with the stony aromas that recall the large stones that litter the Châteauneuf vineyards. Later that turns to dark fruits, especially blueberries, and they continue on the palate in a full but elegant body. This wine has the nobility and aging capacity that ideally should set Châteauneuf apart from other Côtes-du-Rhônes. It is lovely to drink now and should be something different and even more interesting in ten to fifteen years.

$24.95 PER BOTTLE $269.46 PER CASE

2000 BANDOL *ROUGE* · DOMAINE DE LA TOUR DU BON

Dear Mr. Lynch, I've about had it with all your anti-American cuddly crap about finesse, elegance, and harmony. Harmony smarmily. What are you, sensitive or something? Don't you ever feel like drinking a red you can scrape off yer boots?
　　Sincerely yours,
　　Name Withheld

Dear Name Withheld, What remains of your pearly whites won't need flossing after rinsing your mouth with this. Guaranteed!

$24.00 PER BOTTLE $259.20 PER CASE

BARGAIN SPOTLIGHT
CHÂTEAU SAINT MARTIN
DE LA GARRIGUE

DURING BUYING trips I have seen homes and properties that make me forlorn with envy. I want to live in them! Like sightings of certain women (speaking for myself), the impossibility and desire can leave you muttering material for country songs. "Why cain't they be mine?"

The Clos Sainte Magdeleine at Cassis is one of the most incredible properties on the Mediterranean coast. And Patricia and Walter Wells's ancient farmhouse, Chanteduc, offers a view of the entire universe up above Vaison-la-Romaine,

where the sky reminded me of van Gogh's *Starry Night*. And anybody in their right mind would move right into the Villa di Geggiano where I buy Chianti. Why, even a pope slept there a few centuries ago. Another favorite is located between Pézenas (where Molière used to hang out before moving to Paris) and the Mediterranean oyster beds at Bouzigues, and it is called Château Saint Martin de la Garrigue.

There is indeed a château there, which includes a chapel from the year 847 that you should ask to see if ever you visit because the interior is so beautiful it is transporting. I felt downright spiritual in there, folks, aware of the mysterious infinity surrounding our meager yet illustrious selves. Recently a Roman canal system was unearthed, but I'll bet water was not the only thing that Romans drank at Saint Martin. And there is a lot of *garrigue* at Saint Martin de la Garrigue, grapes and *garrigue*.

In the early 1990s Umberto Guida, a man of wealth and taste, acquired Saint Martin and restored it as well as I have seen an old property restored. Happily for us winos, he hired Jean-Claude Zabaglia, a real talent, to make Saint Martin's wine. Whatever he needs in order to make great wine, the boss pays for. Isn't that something?

And the results are amazing. Here is what *The Fine Wine Review* says about Saint Martin's 2000 Bronzinelle: "The truth is, there is a lot of Côte Rôtie at four to five times the price which is no better or not even as good as this, yet in the same general style."

While on the subject of bargains, here is one of my favorite stories. In order to keep myself and my staff up to date and knowing wherewith of what we speak, I have been known to spend good money to taste wines that *we don't even sell!* Once I saw several rave reviews of a certain Cabernet (Wine of the Year, scored a kazillion points, etc.), so I bought a bottle. One hundred and fifty smackeroos, folks. We tasted it and it was good. But it reminded me of something. I grabbed the $9.95 per bottle/$107.46 per case Saint Martin Cuvée Réservée, uncorked it, and lo and behold, it was hard to choose a winner. Did my staff agree? Yer darn tootin', as my grandfather used to say.

According to my calculator, you had the choice, one bottle of the Cab or 16.75 bottles of the Saint Martin. Yet people were almost throwing around punches (not to mention big bucks) to get the Cabernet while our Saint Martin sat here developing an inferiority complex.

Now I know there are cynics out there, skeptical cynics who are saying, "Oh, sure, Lynch, instead of the leading critics we're supposed to believe you, a bloody merchant, for chrissake? What if you're just trying to trick us into buying a lousy wine?"

Well, look at it this way, pal, what if I *am* telling it like it is? Ha!

This month the Bargain Spotlight is on Saint Martin de la Garrigue.

REMEMBERING RICHARD

S OME READERS might recall that Richard Olney influenced me quite a bit at the beginning of my career. Or is that bragging? Now that he is gone, I miss him even while I work, because sometimes I used to select the wines I import with the thought in the back of my mind: would I pour this for Richard?

A native of the Midwest, Richard went to France in the 1950s and stayed. He became a respected culinary expert and wrote for France's most prestigious culinary publications. He authored several books, some of which we stock, some of which, like *Yquem* and *Romanée-Conti*, are out of print. Too bad.

He was famous for being ornery. His criticisms could be devastating. Plus, he was always right. I am never always right. If Richard was not cocksure, he would not offer an opinion. As you can imagine, it is a hell of a thing to argue with a friend who is always right.

Here is a Richard story I have wanted to tell you for a long time because of the way it reveals Richard's personality and the perils of restaurant dining in France, but I have hesitated because it seemed to catch Richard in error, of all things.

A few years ago I invited Lulu Peyraud and Richard to spend a weekend with

Lucien Peyraud and Richard Olney at Domaine Tempier

my family and me on the island of Porquerolles near Toulon. Our hotel had a Michelin-rated, one-star restaurant, and we learned that we had to pay for at least one meal a day there. Imposed meals, always a bad sign. The restaurant was a client of Domaine Tempier, so Lulu was interested in making a good impression.

The first course arrived and we all stared down at it as if some obscene violation had taken place. There on our plates was the little sea creature native to local waters called a *vioulet*. I'd better explain what a *vioulet* is because you may never encounter one. It is a *coquillage*, or shellfish, but its "shell" looks like a rock, an underwater rock often encrusted with barnacles. I wonder how a human being ever first ascertained that inside was something edible. Looks like a rock, feels like a rock, and cutting one open is knife destroying. Yet some of us consider them a rare delicacy, including all of us there at table. Normally you cut them in half, revealing the beast within, which is vividly colored: shocking neon lemon yellow, sometimes with greenish and violet tints. With your thumb you force one out of the half "shell" and you eat them raw. Most people look at a *vioulet* and refuse to try one. Of those who try, many will spit it right out because nothing they have ever eaten has such a texture. Almost rubbery. Alive and rubbery. Or they resist the incredibly potent flavor of the sea the French call *iodé*. But then there are those who have an almost religious appreciation of them.

What we saw on our plates was sacrilegious. The one-star chef had chopped the beasts into a raw hash with chunks of celery on a lettuce leaf! There was incredulous muttering from Richard, astonishment on Lulu's face. And I'm the kind of guy who thinks that even an oyster has only one valid destination: raw and chilled on the half shell. I have seen oyster terrines, oysters baked, oysters ground into paste. If you have good oysters, serve them raw; if not, don't serve them. And if that is arguably true of an oyster, it is a thousand times more true of a *vioulet*. And of a radish, by the way.

We each took a nibble. Richard dropped his fork in disgust.

After a while the maître d' (let's call him Gaston) arrived to ask if anything was wrong. Of course something's wrong, I thought. Get these plates out of sight and shut up.

Out of deference to Lulu's position as a wine supplier, Richard managed to say something innocent and uncritical, but Gaston noticed his American accent.

"Oh, that's it, you Americans are squeamish about raw food."

Uh-oh. If you knew Richard, you would know that he would not like being referred to as "you Americans." And besides, Richard is the one who introduced me to *vioulets* in the first place, with a bottle of 1974 Morey-Saint-Denis *blanc*. Richard enjoyed eating kidneys and lungs, testicles and brains. Not squeamish.

He and Gaston began to bicker and as they did so, diners at nearby tables turned to listen.

Gaston could not accept that an American knew anything about the local *vioulet* or anything about food at all. Finally Richard began to let it all hang out and told Gaston that at least he might change the menu to get the spelling of *vioulet* corrected. Gaston looked like he'd swallowed a porcupine. On the menu it was spelled *violet*. After a couple of yes-it-is and no-it-isn'ts, he told Richard that he was certain it was *violet* because it was spelled that way on his fisherman's delivery van. He saw it every morning. Richard looked down, straightened a few bread crumbs for a beat or two, then settled his eyes on Gaston. "Maybe you would be better off with a dictionary." I don't know about you, but I found that remark rather scathing.

By now, the entire restaurant watched the show, because, given the volume, it could not be ignored.

Richard explained that *vioulets* are to be served pristinely, accompanied by bread and butter and a dry white wine.

Gaston stood as tall as he could. "Monsieur (all this took place in French), you are not in some bar on the port. Don't you understand? This is a one-star restaurant and people come here for *haute cuisine*."

Richard exploded. "*Ce n'est pas de la haute cuisine, c'est de la merde!*"

The plates were removed.

Our main course followed: a filet of sole and slices of zucchini wrapped together (!) in aluminum foil and baked in the oven. How about that? A one-star TV dinner. *Haute cuisine*, indeed.

However, when I first sat down to write this story, a source in France assured me that *vioulet* is spelled *violet*. My French dictionary did not help. But Richard, wrong? It ruined the character revelation, ruined the anecdote.

Then, the other day at lunch in Burgundy with Aubert de Villaine, I told him the story. A few days later I found a fax from him, a page from *his* dictionary with the spelling *vioulet*, explaining that the word is of Provençal origin. As is the critter.

"So you see," Aubert noted, "Richard was right again after all."

◦ ◦ ◦ ◦ ◦ ◦ ◦ ◦

2000 PINOT D'ALSACE · ZIND-HUMBRECHT

If the edict stands, either this or the 2001 will be the last time that the Humbrechts can legally label this super blend *Pinot d'Alsace*. Why? The Alsatian wine police have decided that any Pinot Chardonnay (this from the great Clos Windsbuhl vineyard) is a no-no. Of all the . . . ! Here you have the highest-priced, most-sought-after Pinot d'Alsace in the known universe, and the Alsatian wine authorities won't allow it. Talk about shooting yourself in the foot! So the Humbrechts will be forced to label it *Vin de Pays* or leave out the Chardonnay. Trévallon went through a similar predicament. Ah, zose French.

We will continue to get it to you no matter what the label says.

Never tasted it? The 2000 is a dazzler, a pleasure to drink, and the great length on the palate, the way those perfumes linger and linger, is very welcome.

$24.95 PER BOTTLE $269.46 PER CASE

❧ 2003 ❧

DOMAINE DU GROS 'NORÉ · BANDOL

Ex-boxer, passionate hunter, Alain Pascal says he likes a wine to be "masculine, even a bit of a brute, with big, smooth tannins." He is a native of the region, Provençal down to the roots, but everybody has just begun talking about his wine because he only recently started bottling it. Previously he sold his grapes to Ott and Pibarnon, and they must be sad to lose them because Alain's *terroir* at La Cadière rivals La Migoua and La Tourtine for quality and classic Bandol character. Taste his 1999 and 2000 and see.

Here's Alain: He invites me to dinner with a big group, forgets to turn on the oven to roast the wild boar he shot, but heats it up and serves it anyway. It is a tooth-resistant, bloody boar and smells furry. I smile and pretend to chew while passing hunks of it under the table to his two hunting dogs, and I manage to get away with it until Alain spots my empty plate and plops another hunk onto it, thrilled that I like it so much.

But we drank well. He and his father bottled some 1993 and 1989 for home consumption, and both wines blew my mind. I have always been a fan of Tempier's 1989 Migoua, and Alain's reminded me of it. His father's name was Honoré, and everyone called him 'Noré for short. 'Noré was a mighty big fella, so Alain named the domaine after him: Gros 'Noré, Big 'Noré.

When Alice Waters visited Bandol last year, Alain handed me a bottle of that 1989 and two partridges to take home. Alice plucked the birds and roasted them with plenty of garlic and thyme. It was a tasty wine-and-food combo.

His 1999 is a beautiful, tightly structured Bandol, full of rustic breed, full of potential. It tastes great now if you decant it an hour or two before drinking it.

The 2000 Gros 'Noré is quite different, bigger and more showy, impossible to ignore or resist. It has in abundance everything we look for in a Bandol red.

Both vintages are:

$26.95 PER BOTTLE $291.06 PER CASE

BURGUNDY VINTAGE 2000

DOMAINE RAVENEAU

My first experience with great Chablis was in Chablis, the first stop on my first trip to France (for wine) in 1973. The only hotel in town had a good table and wine list, and although I was broke, I was with some pretty big spenders who ordered a bottle of Chablis Le Clos, 1929! It is hard to believe today, but back then it was not uncommon to find such oldies in restaurants. Nowadays, if you want old wine, you cellar it yourself, as I have done with Raveneau's wines over the years. Every time I uncork one, it is an event, especially when they hit 8 to 10 years of age.

DOMAINE FRANÇOIS JOBARD

Jean-Marie Raveneau shares my esteem for Jobard's great whites. Jobard's wines, too, I drink when they have some age on them. His 1979s, 1982s, and 1983s are still pristine. I would even use the word *perfection*. And to think, those vintages were filtered. Nowadays Jobard bottles unfiltered, so the longevity will be increased!

In 1988 I suggested he bottle a barrel of his 1987 Poruzots without filtration. That bottling proved that the filter was taking some flesh out of his wines. And this year, when I visited, we compared his 1986, 1987, and 1988 Poruzots. According to the charts, 1986 and 1988 were the better vintages, but the unfiltered 1987 stole the show. More fleshiness, more harmony. It has aged more successfully. The least of the three (in terms of vintage) was the best of the three.

Vintage 2000 from Jobard? Ripe, golden juice with a satisfying nervosity, beautifully vinified, deliciously flavored. I consider the 2000 Meursault En la Barre the best he's made. The Genevrières is a perfect example of this superb *terroir*, loaded with personality. I am struck by the purity of the Blagny and the Poruzots, but they are quite different, the Blagny firm and stony, the Poruzots suave, polished, and seductive.

Speaking for myself, they'll all go down into my cellar, and while they don't absolutely require age, I'll leave the cases closed until around 2010.

DOMAINE LUCIEN BOILLOT

All that white wine inspires a thirst for some red.

Those who appreciate the wines of Raveneau and Jobard will be right at home with Boillot. There is a logic to this offering. The link is the exceptional vineyard care to ensure exceptional juice, the purity of expression, the search for harmony and finesse, the willful avoidance of fruit or oak bombs, and the wines that result are true to their *terroirs*. Each year at Boillot's I am struck by the fact that no matter what the character of the vintage, there is remarkable purity to the Pinot Noir fruit and the personality of each *cru* is focused and consistent. Refined palates with an appreciation of Burgundy's diversity will cozy right up to them.

DINNER *CHEZ* CHAVE

O NCE IN A WHILE I think of writing a series about the meals I have enjoyed *chez* Chave. So many of them have been memorable occasions. Let's see, there were the sweetbreads and truffles he prepared, maybe the best meat dish of my life, served with plenty of good wines, of course, and then, from the sublime to the ridiculous, when I hit the autoroute heading off to Burgundy my car's engine expired in smoke. Tow truck. Then there's the story about the time he took me up in the hills to a back-country restaurant with a backed-up toilet. Backwater rising, repeatedly. Alice Waters was along for that stinky laugher. Or there was the time I showed up with Richard Olney and Judy Rodgers, and Chave grilled game birds (*bécasses*) for us in his 500-year-old fireplace, but that evening would fill up a chapter because of all the zany goings-on. For example, he left a case of his Hermitage reds and whites from the '30s and '40s outside the front door, bottles he had brought up from his cellar to drink with us, and did not discover again until we were leaving the next morning. Talk about a bunch of disappointed faces!

Gérard Chave is not only a great winemaker, he is also a first-rate cook.

Not too long ago, when I was in France, he called to say that Robert Parker,

Gérard and Jean-Louis Chave

the wine writer, was coming to taste and had accepted an invitation to dinner, and would I like to join them.

A few days later I heard from Boz Scaggs, the musician, that he and his wife, Dominique, would be traveling through France. I had made their acquaintance at a Domaine Tempier feast at Chez Panisse earlier that year. But, oops, it turned out that I had invited them to my place the very day I was supposed to drive up to Chave's.

When I asked Chave if I could bring along a couple of friends, I noticed a momentary hesitation. I'm not sure, but I imagined that with someone as important as Parker coming to dinner, Chave might not want to risk any distractions, so I assured him that Boz was sufficiently civilized, even a model of discretion, and that Parker might in fact enjoy meeting Boz, because Parker and I can rave on about music as much as we do about wine.

A tasting through the different cuvées and vintages at Chave's takes some time. It was late but there was still a little light left when we sat down under the huge linden tree in the courtyard for our first course: Chave's home-cured anchovies on toast.

After that, it was inside to table and a bowl of pig-knuckle salad, which tastes a lot like gramma's potato salad, but the texture is certainly different. Potatoes have more give. I must say, it was so good, I could have kept filling up with it, but then the next plate arrived, a platter piled high with *beignets d'animelles*, which means lamb's testicles dipped in batter and deep-fried. Folks, they are perfectly round

Hermitage

and slightly larger than golf ball sized. It turns out that Richard Olney's description in *Simple French Food*, "their tender delicacy," is right on the mark, although I did begin to wonder what I'd gotten Boz and Dominique into.

Next came another rare delicacy, *ombles-chevaliers*, which, Chave explained, are an ultra-deep-water lake trout, these from Lake Annecy. To preserve the species, fishermen are limited to catching one per day. Chave must have traded a number of good bottles, because I counted eight of the albino fish on the platter.

It was after midnight and I was stuffed and growing sleepy. Around the table, conversation shifted into pre-departure mode, but where was Gérard Chave? Why, there he comes out of the kitchen with a heavy iron kettle filled with veal kidneys and wild mushrooms, perfectly cooked, which is to say quite rare, and irresistibly delicious.

We also found time for an Hermitage *rouge* 1933, because, we learned, our dinner was Gérard's birthday celebration.

Driving back to my place the next day, I was still worried about my guests' digestive systems. How had they reacted, physiologically and psychologically? Between a couple of country songs on a Jerry Lee Lewis tape, I brought up the subject.

"That was quite a meal. Did it go down well?"

Boz said that he woke up at about four in the morning.

Oh no, indigestion, was my first thought. How awful.

"Yeah," he said, "I woke up and I had to laugh."

Laugh?

"Maybe you didn't know it, but I haven't touched red meat for the past 25 years."

CHANTEDUC

CHANTEDUC IS THE name of a property located in the Côtes du Rhône appellation that belongs to Patricia and Walter Wells. Patricia is the writer who has given us such notable pleasures as *A Food Lover's Guide to France* and *Bistro Cooking*, Walter is the editor of the *International Herald Tribune*, and Chanteduc is one of the most beautiful properties in France. I don't mean swank. The rustic old farmhouse is perched atop a hill above Vaison-la-Romaine, and you don't see a sign of modern civilization unless a plane passes overhead. You feel you are sitting on top of a lovely world.

Their vineyard rolls down the hillside surrounded by *garrigue* and oaks, the kind of oaks under which black truffles like to develop. If you would like to visit, Patricia does occasional cooking classes. Check out her website: www.patricia-wells.com. I have never attended one of her classes. No, when I go, Walter and I talk politics and drink white Rhônes while Patricia slaves in the kitchen. (Just kidding, folks. Or dreaming.)

Chanteduc's wine is a blend of Grenache, Syrah (30%), and Mourvèdre

(10%). Because of the vineyard site, stony soil at a higher altitude than other Côtes du Rhône vineyards, their wine really stands apart from wines down on the plain. The conditions create a more tightly structured Côtes du Rhône. Of course, the Grenache gives it plenty of fleshiness, but it has good bones underneath.

I am pleased to introduce it to you starting with the beautiful 2001 vintage, the best they've made so far. Why not start with their best?

2001 Côtes du Rhône Rouge · *Clos Chanteduc*

$12.95 PER BOTTLE $139.86 PER CASE

◦ ◦ ◦ ◦ ◦ ◦ ◦ ◦ ◦

1999 BARBARESCO · GIAMELLO

True Barbaresco perfume, fine and subtle, rises like smoke from the glass. Some have called Barbaresco "the feminine Barolo," and that description fits this one. And listen, especially those of you who tend to be macho pigs, I said feminine, not wimpy. Americans can be so weird about sex. "Feminine" is not a value judgment; wimpy is. Masculine/feminine, it is simply a way of talking about a wine's characteristics based upon certain physiological differences between men and women, that's all. And it offers us wine writers a handy vocabulary when we get tired of cherries and berries.

If you really feel like doing it up right, serve this Barbaresco with Richard Olney's Sautéed Chicken and Fennel recipe from the aforementioned *Simple French Food*. You will need two full heads of garlic. And with Giamello's Barbaresco in your glass . . . bliss consciousness!

$18.95 PER BOTTLE $204.66 PER CASE

2001 CÔTES DU RHÔNE *ROUGE*
CUVÉE SÉLECTIONNÉE PAR KERMIT LYNCH

I believe this is the best wine I have ever offered under our own label, even better than the Côtes du Rhône *rouge* from 1985, which was still drinking well four years ago. I hadn't bought that 1985 to be aged, didn't even think about it, but it just kept getting better and better.

Our 2001 is a blend of three cuvées, and two of them are actually from Côtes du Rhône-Villages appellations. Such a deal! One cuvée is from a stony Châteauneuf-like vineyard, and I fell for its black pepper, spice, and *réglisse* aroma. To it I added a cuvée that brought a lot of chewy tannin because it improved the texture, the length. Then I topped it off with one-third Syrah, a beautifully vinified cuvée that tasted more northern than southern Rhône because of its dazzling cassis and violet aroma. Sometimes you blend and the cuvées seem to cancel each other out. Here the character of each is still recognizable.

See if you don't agree that you can find in this Côtes du Rhône good, solid memories of Vieux Télégraphe (the stones, the chewiness), Clape (the cassis, the structure), Côte Rôtie (violets and finesse), and Gigondas (*réglisse*). I am not claiming it is as grand as those wines, but I am saying that those qualities jump out of the glass. They are there. And that is why I was thinking of headlining this page THE WORLD'S GREATEST RED WINE BARGAIN, but then I had a slight attack of humility and decided to sort of bury the claim here in the text.

So come and get it, tons of Rhône pleasure at an affordable price.

$9.95 PER BOTTLE $107.46 PER CASE

GRAPEVINE COOKING

I FIRST SAW it at Domaine Tempier, coals from vine cuttings used for a barbecue. During the winter all wineries prune back their vines, and the long, thin branches are usually burned on the ground in the vineyard. What a waste. Domaine Tempier always saves some for grilling, either in Lulu's kitchen fireplace or outside the door, weather permitting, on the ground. Unless they are cut into small pieces, the branches are not feasible in a Weber or other portable grill.

Vine cuttings are practical because they make perfect coals for grilling vegetables, fish, or meat. They burn down very quickly, four or five minutes will do it, yet the coals they produce burn hot and long enough, even if you are grilling thick steaks or whole fish. They do not last long enough to cook chicken, I have found.

Their smoke purportedly gives a certain flavor to the food. I say purportedly because I almost always throw branches of fresh rosemary on the coals when I grill. Rosemary smoke is delicious, but it probably obscures any flavor from the vine cuttings. Many's the time the Peyrauds have warned me to avoid cooking with pine, by the way, because they don't like the smoke's flavor.

In front of my home over there near Domaine Tempier, I have a small Mourvèdre vineyard. The grapes go into their cuvée La Migoua. I use the prunings almost daily, cooking either outdoors or in my fireplace. My national sales manager over here is Bruce Neyers, who owns Neyers Vineyards up in the Napa Valley. Bruce supplies me with vine cuttings for my fireplace cooking here.

As I said, most vine cuttings go up in smoke to no purpose. I'm not sure how friendly wineries might be to the idea of letting you collect some bundles before they burn them. It's worth a try. Vines are pruned during the period November to March.

⋄ ⋄ ⋄ ⋄ ⋄ ⋄ ⋄ ⋄

2001 AUXEY-DURESSES *BLANC* "LES HAUTES"
JEAN-MARC VINCENT

Somehow I seem to have gotten a reputation as anti–oak, but I am all for a taste of oak in red and white Burgundies and of course for the wines of Bordeaux. But no matter what the wine, I don't like too much oak, which means so much that it obliterates the taste of the wine itself.

Take this white Burgundy as an example of a deft touch of new oak. It complements the fruit and minerality, and even charges them up a bit, it seems to me. It is the kind of wine I call a jewel. It is not flagrant; it gives itself the way a diamond sparkles and glints.

$24.95 PER BOTTLE $269.46 PER CASE

2001 PODIO ALTO · DOMAINE DU POUJOL

The appellation is Coteaux du Languedoc *rouge*.

It must at times be frustrating to be a serious winemaker in the Languedoc. You do everything to make a great wine, you cut yields, you plant noble varieties, you fashion a beauty, and then it sells for nothing compared to the oaky alcoholic monsters that come out of practically every nation on earth these days. Yeah, it sticks (or they stick) in my craw. A question of swallowability. But let's be realistic. Those who appreciate fine wine can take advantage of this weird situation in the market.

$13.95 PER BOTTLE $150.66 PER CASE

INTRODUCTION BY JIM HARRISON

While Jim Harrison seems as thoroughly American as a novelist can be, strangely enough I have found that he is even better known in France. In fact, one of his biggest fans is Lulu Peyraud at Domaine Tempier.

My book, Adventures on the Wine Route, *is being republished this year in France, and the new publisher asked if Jim Harrison might agree to write a new introduction for French readers. The other day Jim sent it to me, and I would like to print it in English here, as he wrote it. Otherwise only the French would see it.*

ADVENTURES ON THE WINE ROUTE

IT IS FAR EASIER for me than most Americans to think about wine because my ethical and behavioral permissions toward myself tend to be quite liberal. As an amateur, a lover, I don't need a blindfold to be honest. I line up three bottles of wine on a table in a motel room in a remote Mormon village in the mountains of Arizona. I pull the blinds on the high noon sun to keep away the evil spirits of those who are anti-wine. I'm not entirely safe because I have forgotten my pistol back at my "casita" on the Mexican border. I have also forgotten my sacred volume of Baudelaire and I can't quite remember the poem I first loved 45 years ago but I know that I should be always drunk (*toujours ivre*) on wine or poetry or love. When I was 19 this was the voice of God telling me how to live.

Of course as a poet I am brave enough to openly drink French wine in America. I only brought three bottles on this overnight trip. I also brought along my favorite book about wine, *Adventures on the Wine Route* by Kermit Lynch. Of the three greatest pleasures in life—sex, food, and wine—I only need help on wine. I have a more than adequate palate but am modest enough to accept the fact that there is a hierarchy among palates, and that is why when I travel to France I take along Kermit Lynch's book. It is beyond information and achieves its own peculiar form. The great wine authority Hugh Johnson said, "I am bowled over by his blend of poetry and candor."

Back to the hot streets of the Mormon cow town, the drawn blinds, the three bottles of French wine, and Kermit's book upon the desk. There is a mystery in the books we love that is not revealed when we act the pathologist because the books we love are not dead. They change as perceptions change throughout our lives. During the first few of my perhaps 20 trips to France I was a lover but a neophyte in the same manner as when I read the *Adventures of Casanova* at age 14. What did I know? Not much, I assure you. Looking in the window at the girl next door fell short of a complete experience.

To discover French wine is a long voyage of discovery and I have willingly used Kermit Lynch and several friends as "captains," among them the gourmand Gerard Oberle, Guy de la Valdène, and an American, Peter Lewis. I began as an utter fool when I had my first success 25 years ago and was lucky enough to buy a collection of 50 cases, over half of them exquisite *premiers crus*. I swilled them over a few years. When I look at my daughter's scrapbook of meals for my friends and the wines we drank I break into a cold sweat. What a careless fool. "Let's see if this 1949 Latour is any good, then the 1961 Lafite, then the Richebourg, the Lynch-Bages, the 1975 Beychevelle, are all real nice with the woodcock, grouse, ducks, and venison we're eating." Once we drank more than a case while we ate an entire small deer in one day. The 1968 Château d'Yquem was good with apple pie.

I was truly an American fool! Twenty years later I have no alternative but to forgive myself. After this first wretched debacle I slowly began to educate myself. It was helpful when my income descended in the usual writer's rags to riches to rags story. One evening in Hollywood a friend, the owner of a private club with only 10 actual members, told me that he generally wouldn't sell fine wine to rock musicians because there is a limited quantity and it hurt his aesthetic sense to see them swill it like Coca-Cola. He made exceptions for Mick Jagger and Jimmy Buffet, who understand and love fine French wine.

I decided to become more worthy. I read Robert Parker, Hugh Johnson, Richard Olney, but my grand discovery was Kermit Lynch's *Adventures on the Wine Route*. I keep thinking of Kierkegaard's "purity of heart is to will one thing." Lynch is an obsessive. For years he had followed his nose and palate around France in search of the pure objects of desire, whether humble or outrageous in price.

Years ago in a café in Lyon I struck up a conversation with a cranky Frenchman who seemed to know a lot that I didn't know. At one moment he was an improbable asshole and in the next moment vastly illuminating on French wine and literature, less so on French women about whom no conclusions can fairly be drawn. I was talking about the 35 Côtes du Rhônes I had sampled through Kermit. He granted that Lynch was good for the French economy, the way he had introduced Americans to wines previously unknown to them. In Lyon they are good at food, wine, and money.

Meanwhile, in the current unpleasant political climate I do not know a single intelligent American who has stopped drinking French wine. I think a French audience will be curious and fascinated by a man who has been so curious and knowledgeable about one of their central glories. Wine is far too important to be soiled by the passing political frenzies. Read this book. It will make you more fond of yourselves.

OSTERTAG 2001 RIESLINGS

2001 RIESLING *GRAND CRU* "MUENCHBERG"

André tells me that Muenchberg is a magical site, a site of ancient pagan rituals. And that's not all. When more recent Roman Catholics built the monumental cathedral at nearby Strasbourg, they quarried at Muenchberg, seduced by the beauty of the pink sandstone rock, which André describes as "*doux et tender comme les fesses rondes des femmes.*" In addition, Mother Nature sprinkled a few volcanic stones into the Muenchberg soil.

How nice that André has mostly 60-year-old vines to produce the Riesling juice for this *grand cru*. His granddad did high-density planting, so tractors won't fit, and André must plow with a workhorse. (Hey, free fertilizer!)

The 2001 has loads of sublime, almost pagan Riesling fruit, the desirable mineral expression, and an aristocratic palate. Great wine.

$34.95 PER BOTTLE $377.46 PER CASE

2001 RIESLING "FRONHOLZ"

"With Riesling," André writes, "all the stones of the world find their unique voice." That's a good line.

The stones of Fronholz are quartz, rare in Alsace. The hill named Fronholz rises from the Alsatian plain and receives 10 minutes more sunshine per day than surrounding vineyards. Thus, the peculiarity of Fronholz is the firm core (from the quartz) and its ripe fruit exterior (from the sun).

Taste it alongside the Muenchberg and try to deny the intellectual interest of France's *goût de terroir.* You will find two intriguing personalities. It is permissible to love both, thank goodness.

The 2001 has a great combination of freshness and ripeness, with an interior both austere and complex.

$26.95 PER BOTTLE $291.06 PER CASE

KB SAMPLER

KB is short for Kuentz-Bas. When we talk amongst ourselves here at KLWM, it simplifies things. We also shorten Zind-Humbrecht to ZH. For example, we'll say, "How much of that ZH Gewurztraminer *grand cru* Rangen Clos Saint Urbain old-vines selection grain nobles Kitzelheimerkarzel-geoffenverbotengemessen is available?" instead of "How much of that Zind-Humbrecht Gewurztraminer *grand cru* Rangen . . ." Anyway, see what I mean? It saves us a lot of time. For some reason we don't shorten André Ostertag to AO, but someone the other day called him Ostie.

The *raison d'être* for this KB Sampler is to sell a bunch of wine. Oops, no way, folks. We could care less about that. There really is a good reason. I have been warning you that KB hired a new winemaker who has changed their style, and that you will be zonked by the results. His first vintage with total control from the harvest through the bottling was 2001. So this Sampler is to tempt you to try his stuff and to bear witness that he is producing wines so delicious and full of charm that you will salivatingly await our future KB releases.

The Sampler contains the quartet of great Alsatian grape varieties, three bottles each, at a special low price. The freshness and deliciousness you discover in each bottle will be especially welcome as we enter the summer months.

POUILLY-FUISSÉ
ROBERT-DENOGENT

I have a fondness for white Burgundy, and we have a stellar list starting up north with Raveneau in Chablis, then south to our great Meursault producers, Coche-Dury, Ente, Roulot, Jobard, and more. Our Pulignys and Chassagnes come from Colin-Deléger, Coche, Ente, Jobard, and Amiot.

Since working with us, some of them have changed their methods. Because of limited cellar space many growers in Burgundy are actually forced to bottle a vintage before the next harvest arrives, which pretty much imposes a filtration to clean up a wine's appearance before bottling. Also, experience tells me that 11 or 12 months is not enough time for a great white Burgundy to fully develop in barrel. Its evolution is cut short (*vinus interruptus*) by a premature bottling. In my opinion, the two together, filtration and premature bottling, serve to diminish a wine. Coche, Ente, and Jobard bottle at 18 to 20 months, unfiltered.

Roulot recently built an addition to his cellar, extending the aging time in barrel, and stopped filtering. One of Burgundy's greatest is now greater. I just wish we could get more from him for you.

Domaine Robert-Denogent is a similar story. His wines now age longer in barrel because he invested in a cellar expansion. No more *interruptus*. His 2001s are fleshy, minerally creations of great purity and unusual depth, as impressive as money can buy.

2001 Pouilly-Fuissé "Les Reisses"

$26.95 PER BOTTLE $291.06 PER CASE

2001 Pouilly-Fuissé "Cuvée Claude Denogent"

$32.50 PER BOTTLE $351.00 PER CASE

LOIRE

2002 BOURGUEIL "LES ALOUETTES"
DOMAINE DE LA CHANTELEUSERIE

The Boucard family has been making wine at their domaine since 1822. I found them in 1976. They are so kind, so agreeable, it is a pleasure to work with them.

Les Alouettes is always their prettiest cuvée, the one that delivers its charms right out of the gate. That is because the vines grow in the sandier soil close to the Loire. This year, however, after tasting through the different cuvées, I asked to try a blend of Alouettes and a little batch they called Les Tuffes. It is from chalky soil farther up the hill. I liked the depth and tannin it added to the seductiveness of the Alouettes. They very sweetly agreed to the blend, and bottled it unfiltered for us. The nose is loaded with charm, and then on the palate you have something to chew on.

$11.95 PER BOTTLE $129.06 PER CASE

2002 BOURGUEIL "TRINCH!"
CATHERINE & PIERRE BRETON

Trinch! It sounds like it might be French for *Drink!* But I can't find it in any of my French dictionaries. As it turns out, the word was coined by Rabelais. According to him, *trinch* is what a wine says if you listen to it. And it implies "the soul of truth and philosophy." Hmm. Okay. I guess I should listen more closely. But then Rabelais gets down to earth and says it right out: *trinch* means drink. As in, Drink me! I like wines that say that.

Breton is of the no-SO_2 school like Arena, Lapierre, Barral, and others, and the nose of Trinch! rushes right out to meet yours. Like the Alouettes above from Boucard, it is a Cabernet Franc/Bourgueil that will charm you, and it has a fine chassis to support it. Those who are really interested might enjoy comparing the two.

$13.95 PER BOTTLE $150.66 PER CASE

MANZANILLA · LA GUITA

Manzanilla sherry comes not from Jerez, but from the nearby seaside village San-lúcar de Barrameda. Hugh Johnson wrote, "Manzanilla finos are some of the most delicate and lovely of all, always with a faintly salty tang which is held to come from the sea."

Sanlúcar is an atmospheric little place, mostly devoted to making Manzanilla. What I fell for there is the little row of funky bars right on the shoreline, the Mediterranean wavelets daintily flopping on the sand just outside. You can stand at the bar and order a half or full bottle of La Guita or other Manzanilla and sip some while the bartender fries up some of the morning's catch *a la plancha*. It is a memorable wine-and-food combination.

Freshness is of 100% importance to both the fish and the Manzanilla, so our La Guita is shipped refrigerated from the instant it leaves the cellar. When you pull the cork, it tastes exactly as it does in those seaside bars in Sanlúcar. Shipping refrigerated from door to door is not cheap, but why drink a baked Manzanilla?

Of course, Manzanilla is most often drunk as a dry, chilled apéritif, but you might give it a try with fried fish or shellfish, too.

$5.95 PER TENTH $128.52 PER CASE
$12.00 PER FIFTH $129.60 PER CASE

2000 MONTPEYROUX
DOMAINE D'AUPILHAC

I like to cook, but nothing too time-consuming. My wife and I get together in the kitchen with a glass of white or rosé and decide how we'll prepare whatever stores we have on hand. The other night it was large portobello mushroom caps grilled in the fireplace over vine cuttings. It is easy, and they turned out smoky, garlicky, and remarkably steak-like. I went down to get a red wine for them. I browsed through some red Burgundies, then Chianti started sounding good, but I ended up at my stash of Sylvain Fadat's Domaine d'Aupilhac. Very old didn't seem right and young would have been too fresh, so I picked his 1995, and it worked.

His 2000 is a beauty that tastes good now and will age well. His 1991, 1990, and 1989, for example, are spectacular today.

$19.95 PER BOTTLE $215.46 PER CASE

AUTUMN SAMPLER

BORN AND RAISED in California, I have always been more of a summer kind of guy. Winters were something to put up with. You know, you have to wear heavier clothes, wear socks, plus it is dark when you wake up, dark when you leave work. What a drag.

Then my wine business allowed me to live in France several months per year, usually arriving back here in late November. I learned to enjoy the change of season, the vine leaves vividly changing color, a fire in the fireplace, the obligatory modification of one's dining habits as the produce changes . . . I actually began to make the best of it.

And nowadays, older than I have ever been, autumn begins to have a symbolic significance. If spring is rebirth, what is autumn? Each winter can lead one to wonder how many spring- and summertimes remain to enjoy.

Never mind. When autumn arrives I love the way my diet changes and consequently the kinds of wine I drink. Old white Burgundy with mushrooms, for example. You can't do that in July, folks. Yes, yet another mushroom feast. With friends the other night we sautéed wild mushrooms and downed a magnum of François Jobard's 1982 Meursault Genevrières. I hope the good lord put some of that one in my extraterrestrial cellar. 1982. Hmm. That's 21 years old, old enough to drink.

Old wines, however, don't work that well when the weather is hot. No, you want something bright and fresh, cool and simple. When autumn hits I start going down into my cellar more often, searching for older bottles. And I also develop an appetite for bigger, more complex wines. My Châteauneufs start making sense again. Fruit-driven wines make less sense.

Keeping in mind the autumn ambience and the kind of cuisine the season imposes, I toured our stock and came up with 12 bottles that should taste especially good over the next four or five months.

		NORMALLY
2001	Gewurztraminer "Tradition" · Kuentz-Bas	$18.95
2001	Savennières "Cuvée Spéciale" · Château d'Epiré	16.95
2001	Moulin-à-Vent · Bernard Diochon	16.95
2000	Saint-Chinian "Causse du Bousquet" · Mas Champart	17.50
2001	Côteaux du Languedoc "Mourvèdre" · Château La Roque	13.95
2000	E Prove Rouge · Domaine Maestracci	14.95
2000	Faugères · Domaine Leon Barral	16.00
2000	Bandol · Domaine de la Tour du Bon	17.50
1999	Châteauneuf-du-Pape "Les Hautes Brusquières" Domaine de la Charbonnière	32.50
2000	Lirac Rouge · Domaine du Joncier	14.95
1998	Chianti Classico · Villa di Geggiano	14.95
1998	Lussac Saint-Emilion · Château de Bellevue	19.95

SPECIAL SAMPLER PRICE $139.00

Syrah country

SAINT-JOSEPH REVISITED

Jean-Louis Chave sent us a sample of his 2001 Offerus, a Saint-Joseph *rouge* that we are currently offering pre-arrival. He sent a bottle so the staff here could taste it. I used the occasion as an excuse to revisit some older vintages from the appellation. It is my opinion that Saint-Joseph is the best value available in the growing world of Syrahs. We tasted 2001, 2000, 1999, and 1996 Offerus, 2000 Domaine J. L. Chave, 1990 Roger Blachon, and 1994, 1989, 1988, and 1983 Raymond Trollat.

We voted secret ballot, and two vintages, 2001 and 1983, tied for first choice. The youngest and oldest! Second place, almost a tie, too, went to the 1996 Offerus and the 1990 Blachon.

Everyone says that Saint-Joseph is not for aging, but as we see here, it doesn't hurt, either. That funky 1983 was still kicking around in the stall.

Amazing tasting, amazing results, *n'est-ce pas?*

◇ ◇

PROVENCE IN BERKELEY

Here I am in Provence writing about Provence Day, our annual parking lot feast. And I will arrive home just in time to take part. How cool.

Last night I went to Gros 'Noré with Tempier's winemaker, Daniel Ravier. We ate outdoors: some little fried fish to start and grilled steaks afterward with a fabulous, simple tomato dish. He roasted those elongated tomatoes (Roma is the variety in the States, I believe), grilled them over the coals until the skin was blackened here and there and the interior cooked through. Once they're on your plate, you peel them, mash them up a bit, then add the sauce, which is merely several cloves of chopped raw garlic macerated for a few hours in a good couple of cups of olive oil. A little salt and pepper . . . wow.

I took along a 1994 ZH Riesling Rangen to show them a northern wine, then we compared the 1999s, Gros 'Noré, and Tempier. Battle of the Bandols! It was so hot there, we had to put the reds in an ice bucket and pour small servings because a full glass warmed up before you could drain it. Young Bandols are really tasty served cool in hot weather. Then I poured them a *vieux* Vieux Télégraphe, 1989. We finished with a cold, fresh fruit salad bathed in Muscat de Beaumes-de-Venise.

On Provence Day in Berkeley, we re-create some of the tried and true pleasures of Provence. We close the parking lot to cars, set up tables under the olive trees, peel a ton of garlic, fire up the grill, and uncork a medley of delicious southern wines. Plus, there will be live music.

Our chef is Christopher Lee, from the Chez Panisse kitchen. The event (priced about like last year's) is presented by Café Fanny.

Come one, come all,

Live it up *à la Provençale.*

Saturday, September 20, 11 A.M. to 4 P.M.

INDEX

EDITOR Aaron Wehner

PRODUCTION MANAGER Hal Hershey

PROOFREADERS Jasmine Star & Jodie Arey

INDEXER Ken DellaPenta

At Wilsted & Taylor Publishing Services

COPY EDITOR Melody Lacina

ART DIRECTOR Christine Taylor

DESIGNER Melissa Ehn

COMPOSITOR Tag Savage

PROJECT COORDINATOR Drew Patty

Text set in Bembo with Nicolas Cochin Black display
Printed and bound in Canada by Kromar Printing Ltd.